Balanchine and Kirstein's American Enterprise

Balanchine and Kirstein's American Enterprise

JAMES STEICHEN

OXFORD
UNIVERSITY PRESS

OXFORD
UNIVERSITY PRESS

Oxford University Press is a department of the University of Oxford. It furthers
the University's objective of excellence in research, scholarship, and education
by publishing worldwide. Oxford is a registered trade mark of Oxford University
Press in the UK and certain other countries.

Published in the United States of America by Oxford University Press
198 Madison Avenue, New York, NY 10016, United States of America.

CIP data is on file at the Library of Congress
ISBN 978–0–19–060741–8

9 8 7 6 5 4 3 2

Printed by Sheridan Books, Inc., United States of America

CONTENTS

Acknowledgments   vii

Introduction   1

CHAPTER 1   1933   15

CHAPTER 2   1934   35

CHAPTER 3   1934–1935   57

CHAPTER 4   1935   81

CHAPTER 5   1935–1936   103

CHAPTER 6   1936   127

CHAPTER 7   1937   147

CHAPTER 8   1937–1938 (I)   167

CHAPTER 9   1937–1938 (II)   189

CHAPTER 10   1939–1940   211

List of Abbreviations Used in Notes   237

Notes   239

Bibliography   287

Index   295

ACKNOWLEDGMENTS

This book has taken shape over the better part of a decade, and although it would be impossible to acknowledge by name every person who contributed to its development I would like to thank several individuals and institutions for their support.

This project began during my doctoral studies in musicology at Princeton University, where I was first made aware of the work of George Balanchine in a graduate seminar led by Simon Morrison, who in turn served as an astute and attentive steward of the dissertation that it helped inspire. The encyclopedic expertise of Lynn Garafola has enriched this study in countless ways, and I thank her for sharing her deep knowledge of the dissertation's sources and subjects, especially her unmatched enthusiasm for the life and career of Lincoln Kirstein. Wendy Heller has been a generous counselor, thoughtful editor, and unstinting sounding board, and I am thankful for her support of this and my other scholarly pursuits.

Many people and institutions must be thanked for the financial support that made my research and writing possible. At Princeton I received a graduate fellowship in addition to funding from the Department of Music's Bryan Fund and the Program in American Studies. Princeton's Center for Arts and Cultural Policy Studies, led by Stanley Katz and Paul DiMaggio, provided me the Andrew W. Mellon Research Affiliate award and the opportunity to discuss and refine my early research in an interdisciplinary forum. The Howard D. Rothschild Fellowship in Dance from the Houghton Library Visiting Fellowship program at Harvard University allowed me to spend extensive time examining archival materials on site.

Funding for my final year of dissertation research and writing came from the Mellon/ACLS Dissertation Completion Fellowship from the American Council of Learned Societies, and the Virgil Thomson Fellowship from the Society for American Music afforded me the opportunity to conduct research at additional archival sites.

I also benefited from the opportunity to present my research in progress to audiences at conferences of the Society for American Music, Dance Studies Association, Society for Cinema and Media Studies, Modernist Studies Association, and the Dance Critics Association as well as during invited lectures at the University of California–Santa Barbara, the Catholic University of America, and the San Francisco Ballet. Two interdisciplinary summer programs also had a lasting impact on this project's development: the 2010 session of the Cornell School of Criticism and Theory (directed by Amanda Anderson) and the 2013 Mellon Dance Studies Seminar at Brown University (directed by Susan Manning, Janice Ross, and Rebecca Schneider). After completing my doctoral studies I was fortunate to be part of the teaching team of Immersion in the Arts: Living in Culture at Stanford University for two years, and am grateful to my colleagues Janice Ross, Kim Beil, and Nicholas Jenkins for their friendship and encouragement. I thank my students at Princeton, Stanford, and Columbia University for the opportunity to play a small part in their educational lives, as well as for sharing their perspectives and opinions on cultural objects both old and new. I am also grateful to my friends and colleagues at the San Francisco Conservatory of Music and St. Paul's Episcopal Church in Burlingame for their support during the final stages of this book's journey.

I would also like to thank Ursula Ayrout, Cecelia Beam, Jennifer Benz, Elizabeth Bergman, Karol Berger, Anna Maria Busse Berger, Philip Bohlman, Christy Bolingbroke, Daphne Brooks, Michael Burden, Scott Burnham, Daniel Callahan, Michael Carroll, Majel Connery, Alice Miller Cotter, Jeffrey Edelstein, Caryl Emerson, William Evans, Jessica Feldman, Rachel Fine, Robert Greskovic, Susan and Doug Gronberg, Barbara Heyman, Briallen Hopper, Michael Kaiser, Elizabeth Kendall, Mike Kimrey, David J. Levin, Alastair Macaulay, Susan Jane Matthews, Marie Mattson, Mary McIlhany, Kathleen Nicely, Karen and Gustavo Pellón, Michael Pratt, William Quillen, Anne Walters Robertson, Jesse Rodin, Katherine Rohrer, Jennie Scholick, Marna Seltzer, Maybeth and Ken Shockey, Martha Sprigge, David Stull, Dylan Tatz, Andrew Weaver, Edmund White, Kris Wilton, Stacy Wolf, and Amelia Worsley. Special thanks and love to the late George Pitcher, whose humanity and generosity were an inspiration to me and countless others.

Thanks also to my editor at Oxford University Press, Norm Hirschy, who has been an unflagging cheerleader and advocate for this book from its inception.

I am grateful to everyone in my family and especially my parents Ruth and Thomas Steichen for instilling in me a love of music and the arts from an early age—through piano lessons, theater trips, or impromptu sing-alongs—and for their unstinting encouragement of my professional endeavors in arts management and academia. Also on a more personal level, my partner KJ Shockey has been part of my life for all but the earliest phases of this project, providing incalculable encouragement, support, and perspective through the unpredictable twists and turns (and more than occasional tears) that accompany graduate study and humanistic research. I hope that for him and everyone else who was part of this book's journey that it will have been worth the effort.

| Introduction

IT IS WIDELY acknowledged that George Balanchine fundamentally changed the face of ballet in the twentieth century, especially in his adopted home of the United States. Balanchine has been hailed as not only the father of ballet in America but more broadly as a key link in the transmission of classical dance from its courtly origins in seventeenth-century Europe to its rebirth in Imperial Russia to its reinvention by twentieth-century modernists. "The genius of George Balanchine has enriched the lives of all Americans who love the dance," as President Ronald Reagan noted when presenting him the Presidential Medal of Freedom in February 1983, citing his signature accomplishments as "the founding of the first American classical ballet company, the great New York City Ballet, and the School of American Ballet."[1] In a subsequent condolence letter written after Balanchine's death only three months later, Reagan noted that "his is the most widely performed choreography of our time, both here and abroad," calling this a testament "to the influence of his genius."[2] Four decades after his death, Balanchine's ballets are indeed more alive and influential than ever before, assiduously preserved by a special trust and performed and viewed by more people than during his own lifetime. His choreography is regarded as "a world apart," in the words of dance historian Jennifer Homans, and his ballets stand as "the jewel in the crown of twentieth-century dance."[3] So significant and valuable is Balanchine's legacy that his own surname is protected by trademark status. In the history of dance, a notoriously transient and ephemeral art, the work of few artists has achieved such universal recognition and permanence.

Balanchine would not have achieved this status if not for his collaborative relationship with American impresario Lincoln Kirstein, who was responsible for bringing the choreographer to the United States in 1933 (and who was the recipient of the condolence letter quoted above). The early history of their efforts has been told with a set of narrative contours perhaps quite familiar to some readers of this book. In the summer of 1933 while traveling in Europe, as the story usually begins, Kirstein came upon the idea of founding a ballet company in America and invited the Russian émigré Balanchine to be its artistic leader. Balanchine accepted the invitation but insisted that a school should be the foundation of the enterprise. Initial plans called for the organization to be located in Hartford, Connecticut, under the auspices of a museum, but due to Balanchine's dislike of the provincial environs and the protests of local dance instructors, it was soon after relocated to New York City, where the first classes of the School of American Ballet were held just after New Year's Day in 1934. Six months later, students from the school presented their first public performance at an outdoor event at the family estate of Edward Warburg, Kirstein's partner in the enterprise. This performance marked the first performance of *Serenade*—Balanchine's first ballet in America— a reinvention of the classical tradition crafted to teach his inexperienced dancers how to be on the stage.

As the story continues, the early years of the school and its company, the American Ballet, were not without challenges. Although their 1935 company debut in New York was a popular success, *New York Times* dance critic John Martin—a staunch advocate of modern dance and native-born artists—relentlessly criticized the company for the European character of its repertoire and artistic leadership. Additionally, a cross-country tour planned by the company came to an inauspicious end in Scranton, Pennsylvania, after only a few weeks of performances as a result of mismanagement. Despite such setbacks, the company was unexpectedly invited to become the resident ballet company of the Metropolitan Opera, with Balanchine installed as ballet master. During their time at the opera the company mounted several notable performances, including a controversial staging of Gluck's *Orpheus and Eurydice* in 1936 and in 1937 a triple bill of works by Igor Stravinsky that included the American premiere of *Apollon Musagète*. In the end, however, Balanchine's innovative choreography for the operas was not to the liking of the conservative Metropolitan audience, and as a result the troupe was let go after its third season.

During the company's tenure at the opera, Kirstein formed a separate troupe called Ballet Caravan to provide summer employment for some members of the company. This small, chamber-sized company featured original choreography by the dancers themselves and specialized in ballets that treated explicitly American themes, from gas station attendants to the outlaw Billy the Kid. Though somewhat makeshift in character, the Caravan would continue for several seasons, achieving moderate success. Around the same time, Balanchine also took on projects for the Broadway stage and in Hollywood, in which he elevated the level of dancing typically seen in these venues and insisted on being identified as a "choreographer," an unusual request at the time. Balanchine enjoyed the extra income that these projects provided and the glamorous life they made possible for himself and his wife Vera Zorina, the star of many of these shows and films.

The story of Balanchine and Kirstein's collaboration does not end here, and it would ultimately result in the founding of the New York City Ballet (NYCB) and the establishment of the School of American Ballet (SAB) as a leading training institution. Between Balanchine's arrival in America in 1933 and the founding of NYCB in 1948, the organization envisioned by him and Kirstein underwent a remarkable set of transformations, setbacks, false starts, and new beginnings. And during this time Balanchine was by no means the canonical exponent of balletic innovation that he would eventually become. In the 1930s and for many years after, he was active in not just ballet performance but in the staging of operas and musical comedies and the creation of stage revues and film musicals at a time when the boundary between commercial and noncommercial art was more porous than it is today. On many occasions he found himself quite literally spending the morning with Stravinsky at the Metropolitan Opera and the afternoon on Broadway with Richard Rodgers (like Balanchine a member of the inaugural class of Kennedy Center Honorees in 1978). President Reagan explicitly acknowledged this dimension of Balanchine's career in his 1983 remarks, praising him for having "entertained and inspired millions with his stage and film choreography" and celebrating the fact that Balanchine "has entertained, captivated and amazed our diverse population, lifting our spirits and broadening our horizons through his talent and art."[4]

Despite this breadth of experience, Balanchine has been studied and celebrated mostly as a creator of ballet choreography, and these early years have been construed as an inauspicious if colorful prologue to the eventual and inevitable success of his collaboration with Kirstein. Accordingly, Balanchine's work in the "popular" venues of Broadway and Hollywood has been understood as marginal or at least peripheral to his official institutional undertakings. In a similar manner, the various entities that comprised this enterprise and the contexts in which both Balanchine and Kirstein were active—the School of American Ballet, the American Ballet, Ballet Caravan, and his Broadway and Hollywood projects—have been treated as separate and distinct spheres of activity with little attention paid to how they interacted with and influenced one another.

The goal of this book is to offer a new perspective that acknowledges and embraces the ungainly complexity of the early years of what I term the "Balanchine-Kirstein enterprise," from 1933 to 1940.[5] Through a careful examination of a wide range of primary source material, its ten chapters offer a new account of Balanchine and Kirstein's early collaborative efforts. Ultimately, my goal is to show both the contradictory character and unexpected convergence of their disparate efforts, which influenced one another in previously unexamined and unacknowledged ways. In short, these early years did not portend a tidy teleological culmination in the establishment of NYCB and SAB as the prominent institutions they are today, much less the emergence of Balanchine as a defining figure of twentieth-century dance. Rather, this period was the beginning of an exhilarating and haphazard journey of aesthetic and institutional experimentation, and its failures and contradictions are as instructive as its ultimate accomplishments and triumphs. In fact, this new account shows how much the tropes that have come to define this history have limited our understanding of the character and meaning of Balanchine and Kirstein's artistic undertakings, both in these early years and in the decades that followed.

The history recounted in this book is not entirely new and many of its stories have been told before in many different contexts. At the same time, these stories have yet to be put into dialog with each other or corroborated by relevant primary sources, some made available to scholars only in recent years. Writers of Balanchine's biographies and accounts of the early years of the New York City Ballet have not been as interested in his so-called popular work on Broadway and in Hollywood. Histories of musical theater and film, for their part, are not always as concerned with how their subjects affected the history of dance in the United States, much less the machinations of the Balanchine-Kirstein enterprise in particular. Accounts of Kirstein's life and career of necessity would not want to detail Balanchine's work on Broadway and in Hollywood, nor would an account of Balanchine's career want to dwell on the intricacies of Kirstein's many institutional entanglements and experiments. But these diverging histories intertwine in important ways, and all were formative influences on the totality of Balanchine and Kirstein's partnership.

It would not have been possible to undertake this new account of the Balanchine-Kirstein enterprise if not for the many perspectives that scholars of dance and music have brought to bear upon the history and meaning of the performing arts in the twentieth century in recent decades, especially research into the multiform movement known as modernism. These new accounts have offered methods not only to reconsider the breadth of Balanchine's creative output but also to situate his collaborative efforts with Kirstein in a wider cultural-historical context. In the simplest terms, modernism has been defined as founded on a desire to break with past traditions and create bold new artistic visions, whether in the spirit of Ezra Pound's dictum to "make it new" or Serge Diaghilev's imperative "Astonish me!" New approaches to the study of modernism have in large part been motivated by a desire to revisit these and other canonical figures, while at the same time expanding the terms by which its multifaceted phenomena are understood. Modernism was previously studied as a succession of "isms"—for example, cubism, Dadaism, futurism—cultivated by discrete camps of avant-garde elites in a select number of (mostly European) capital cities. Now it is construed to encompass a much wider range of practices, including not just so-called high art but also forms of mass-market entertainment, all of which were reproduced and circulated in shared networks of transnational exchange.[6]

It is now the consensus among scholars that for much of the modernist period and beyond, so-called elite and popular art forms existed in a symbiotic rather than an antagonistic relationship.[7] In similar terms, the much-maligned category of the "middlebrow," the contested field in which the elite and popular often uncomfortably mix or collide, has received increased attention from scholars of modernist art and artists as well.[8] This more expansive conception of modernism has made it possible to tell a history that encompasses individuals and practices previously considered peripheral to the "official" movements, whether the products of the new global entertainment industries or lesser-known artistic contributions by women, racial minorities, or other historically marginalized groups. Amid these realignments, scholars of dance and music have offered new perspectives on the life and work of many celebrated composers and choreographers from the period while also granting much-needed attention to lesser-known but no less significant contributors to modernist expression.[9] Particularly relevant for this present account is work by dance scholars including Mark Franko's study of the life and career of Martha Graham, Roger Copeland's research on Merce Cunningham, and Lynn Garafola's exploration of the circle surrounding Diaghilev's Ballets Russes, all of which have offered fresh perspectives on these seminal figures.[10] Others scholars have similarly broadened our understanding of the networks of lesser-known individuals from the period, including the work of Constance Valis Hill on tap-dancing performers in America, Susan Manning's account of the close relationship between modern dance and the "Negro Dance" movement, and Janet Soares's monograph on the circles around music director, composer, and pedagogue Louis Horst.[11]

In the spirit of these and many other scholars who have expanded our understanding of modernism and twentieth-century art, this book works toward the tandem goals of revisiting the narratives that have come to define Balanchine's early career in America while at the same time attending more closely to the motivations of Kirstein and other lesser-known individuals in the development of the enterprise. In the early 1930s when the story of this book begins, moreover, Balanchine's fame had in fact been some-what eclipsed by a fellow member of the Ballets Russes diaspora, Léonide Massine, who scarcely figures in most histories of the enterprise. As the star and lead choreographer of Colonel de Basil's Ballets Russes, Massine and not Balanchine was regarded as the most famous ballet artist of the day and the logical heir to the legacy of Diaghilev. As this account will show, Balanchine's career as a ballet choreographer came close to ending in the 1930s due to a variety of factors, and some thought he might devote himself more fully to Broadway and Hollywood work for the remainder of his career. In other words, Balanchine came very close to becoming precisely the kind of overlooked entertainer in need of scholarly recuperation and reincorporation into the more inclusive history of modernism being written today.

Even as the study of the performing arts in the twentieth century has undergone a radical redefinition and expansion, the early history of the Balanchine-Kirstein enterprise continues to be related with a set of familiar tropes. Though their exact origins are difficult to identify with precision, the contours of this history diverge in substantial and consequential ways from the evidence available in the wide range of contemporary sources consulted in the chapters that follow, whether diaries and correspond-ence, newspapers and periodicals, or photographs and oral histories. As a result, I suggest that most existing accounts of Balanchine and Kirstein's enterprise must now be collectively regarded as a received history, which should for the most part be read, analyzed, and cited as a primary source in and of itself.[12] This received history has been many decades in the mak-ing, the product of many instances of telling and retelling by individuals too numerous to list, not the least of whom are Balanchine and Kirstein themselves.

During the lifetimes of Balanchine (1904–83) and Kirstein (1907–96), most published accounts of the history of their ballet enterprise were what we might regard as "authorized" books—if not explicitly prepared under the auspices of the enterprise then originating from circles very close to it, most notably from the hand of Kirstein himself.[13] In 1938 Lincoln Kirstein offered his first history of the organization in his polemical monograph *Blast at Ballet*, and beginning in the 1940s and just before the founding of NYCB in 1948 the journal *Dance Index* (founded and edited by Kirstein) began the work of consolidating Balanchine's work and the predecessor organizations of their ballet enterprise in several issues of the journal.[14] Less than a decade after the 1948 founding of NYCB the first book-length history of the company was published, *The New York City Ballet*, authored by émigré dance critic Anatole Chujoy, a close friend of the enterprise and the émigré circles surrounding Balanchine.[15] Although the organization in the book's title was then barely five years old, Chujoy's monograph spanned nearly twenty years of history. The book devoted most of its chapters not to the newly founded company but to the School of American Ballet and its shorter-lived performing units, the American Ballet and Ballet Caravan. Chujoy thereby instituted a historiographical precedent by which all of these organizations are considered part of a larger trajectory and teleology leading to NYCB itself. Similarly, Lincoln Kirstein's own diary-style history of NYCB *Thirty Years*, first published twenty years after Chujoy's monograph, not only covers subjects related to the company itself but also devotes extensive coverage to the work of its predecessor organizations: the American Ballet, Ballet Caravan, and Ballet Society.[16] Though a practical solution to the tangled historiography of the Balanchine-Kirstein enterprise, these narrative trajectories have lent the events they relate a retrospective coherence that was by no means in evidence in the 1930s.

Accounts of Balanchine and Kirstein's individual lives have also helped foster a certain narrative about their collaborative efforts, in part by not fully acknowledging the extent to which their undertakings related to one another. The first and still most widely read biography of Balanchine was published by journalist Bernard Taper in 1963, based on interviews conducted over a period of six years, some of which were initially published in the *New Yorker*. Taper later published three revised and expanded versions of *Balanchine: A Biography*, the first in 1973, the second in 1984 (following the choreographer's death in 1983), and a final edition in 1996.[17] A subsequent biography by Richard Buckle and John Taras (published in 1988) hewed more closely to original sources and thus is a more reliable chronicle of the events of Balanchine's life and events in the years prior to NYCB, even though like Taper's account it is still indebted to many of the narrative tropes of the received history.[18] Two shorter biographies of Balanchine by Robert Gottlieb and Terry Teachout, published in conjunction with the one-hundredth anniversary of his birth in 2004, offer condensed accounts of the events related in the longer biographies.[19] Martin Duberman's biography *The Worlds of Lincoln Kirstein*, published in 2008, drew more directly on archival documents and other primary sources than Balanchine's biographies to build its narrative. Because its focus is Kirstein's life in all its many phases—which encompassed not just music and dance but also literature, the visual arts, and theater—Duberman's biography is not always attuned to the meaning of his activities as they related to the enterprise as a whole.[20]

Broadly speaking, this received history can be understood to serve several explicit or implicit agendas. On the one hand, it papers over inauspicious incidents in the early history of the now-firmly established NYCB and SAB, telling a story that is commensurate with their present-day stature rather than reflecting less flattering historical realities. There is more at stake than public relations, however, in revisiting the history of Balanchine's early American career. As I show, the received narratives of this period impede our understanding of the complex institutional dynamics of the origins of the Balanchine-Kirstein enterprise, which was significantly imperiled at several points in time by both internal and external pressures. What is more, they have obscured our appreciation of the character of Balanchine's choreographic style and aesthetic priorities during his first decade in America. In the 1930s Balanchine was still invested in the bold experimentation that characterized much of his initial choreographic work in the Soviet Union and his projects for Diaghilev's Ballets Russes. These dimensions of his sensibility have been marginalized if not suppressed in the received history of his career, in favor of the neoclassical profile that has come to define not just his early American career but his repertoire and reputation as a whole. The profile that Balanchine subsequently built in the course of his five-decade career in the United States was markedly different from the reputation he enjoyed when he first arrived. More simply put, the artist Balanchine became was not always the artist that he was, and the same can be said of the institutions that he and Kirstein helped create.

Toward a new history of origins of the Balanchine-Kirstein enterprise, two resources provide a firm foundation on which to build, despite their status as somewhat "authorized" publications. First is *Choreography by*

George Balanchine: A Catalogue of Works published toward the end of the choreographer's life.[21] A project of the Balanchine Trust and Balanchine Foundation, the *Choreography by George Balanchine* offers a year-by-year chronicle of all of Balanchine's work—whether for ballet companies, opera houses, the popular theater, or Hollywood—including revivals of works that resulted in significant revisions. It has been subsequently updated and expanded via a searchable online database. The *Catalogue* finds an institutional-based complement in Nancy Reynolds's *Repertory in Review*, a chronological compendium of ballets created by the New York City Ballet and its predecessor organizations, the American Ballet, Ballet Caravan, and Ballet Society.[22] Unlike the *Catalogue, Repertory in Review* includes work not only by Balanchine but also by the other choreographers associated with the enterprise, including William Dollar, Lew Christensen, Eugene Loring, and later, Jerome Robbins, through the year 1977 when it was published.

In recent decades, individual aspects of the Balanchine-Kirstein enterprise have been the subject of careful research and critique. The authors of these studies have revisited significant source materials and repositioned Balanchine's career and the history of NYCB within a larger historical and cultural context and have provided invaluable insights and models of research for this book. Most notably, Elizabeth Kendall's monograph on Balanchine's youth in Russia and the Soviet Union has now become a definitive reference on this period of his career. Kendall drew on newly examined archival sources and also endeavored to understand the way that sociopolitical forces and circumstances shaped his education and emergent choreographic sensibility.[23] Balanchine's subsequent work in the 1920s for Diaghilev's Ballets Russes has been extensively researched and analyzed by dance scholars including Lynn Garafola, Susan Jones, and Tim Scholl.[24] The contentious ballet wars that took place between the death of Diaghilev in 1929 and Balanchine's emigration to America in 1933 have received study by Kathrine Sorley Walker, Vicente García-Márquez, and Judith Chazin-Bennahum, offering important context for the period in which Balanchine and Kirstein's enterprise began.[25]

Balanchine's career after his emigration to America has similarly benefited from renewed attention by many dance scholars. Garafola's edited collection *Dance for a City* offered fresh perspectives on Balanchine and Kirstein's collaborative efforts by authors including dance scholar Sally Banes and musicologist Charles Joseph.[26] In numerous additional articles Garafola has provided important accounts of the involvement of composers George Antheil and Aaron Copland in the Balanchine-Kirstein enterprise, the genesis of Ballet Caravan and Kirstein's relations with modern dance circles, and the involvement of the Rockefeller Foundation in the subsequent history of the organization.[27] Debra Hickenlooper Sowell's monograph on the dancers of the Christensen family, drawing on archival sources and oral histories, offers important insights into the American Ballet's time at the Metropolitan Opera and the history of Ballet Caravan from the perspective of the dancers themselves.[28] Mark Franko and Gay Morris have each offered additional critical perspectives on the way both ballet and modern dance in America defined themselves in opposition to existing popular dance cultures and to one another, with particular attention to the underlying ideologies and discourses that characterized Balanchine and Kirstein's collaborative efforts.[29] Andrea Harris has offered careful analysis of the political dimensions of Kirstein's endeavors as a dance impresario and public intellectual in the 1930s and their relationship to Popular Front and left-wing movements, with particular attention given to his activities with Ballet Caravan.[30]

Many musicologists have made several notable contributions to a deeper understanding of the composers that were pivotal during this period of Balanchine and Kirstein's enterprise, in particular concerning the work of Igor Stravinsky and Aaron Copland. Charles Joseph's *Stravinsky and Balanchine: A Journey of Invention* provides a comprehensive account of this important decades-long collaborative relationship, most of which transpired after Balanchine's emigration.[31] Joseph's subsequent monograph *Stravinsky's Ballets* offers additional insights into the works the composer and choreographer created together.[32] Stephanie Jordan's *Moving Music* and *Stravinsky Dances* offer authoritative accounts of Balanchine's views on "choreomusical" relationships, including analyses of his ballets that take into account the complex interplay of music and choreography for which he is celebrated.[33] One of the central case studies of Elizabeth Bergman's *Music for the Common Man* focused on the Ballet Caravan commission *Billy the Kid*, showing how the work was imbued with leftist political sensibilities that have largely been erased by the subsequent reception history of Copland's score.[34]

Balanchine's popular career, for a long time consigned to marginal status, has also begun to receive sustained attention. The "Popular Balanchine" initiative of the George Balanchine Foundation led to the creation of special research dossiers of primary source material and oral history accounts for most of his work for film, musical comedy, and other popular venues. The scholarship of Adrienne McLean and Beth Genné has drawn more critical attention to Balanchine's work on the popular stage and screen.[35]

The research and writing of Constance Valis Hill, Sally Banes, and Brenda Dixon Gottschild have examined the ways in which Balanchine's contact with African American artists and black popular music shaped and influenced his larger style and choreographic sensibility.[36]

In the face of these and other contributions, however, the received history of the Balanchine-Kirstein enterprise still holds remarkable sway, and despite the localized interventions by the scholars noted above, the early years of Balanchine's American career as a whole have yet to be reconsidered or significantly revised. Instead it has been left to Balanchine's biographies and the other authorized histories of NYCB to fill the void, and their narrative tropes continue to be reproduced in an uncritical manner. It is thus the goal of this book to bring these scholarly interventions full circle, offering a new frame in which their arguments can be appreciated and evaluated more fully. This new history of the origins of the Balanchine-Kirstein ballet enterprise is not attuned to its triumphant teleology and culmination in NYCB and SAB but rather seeks to understand its missteps, overlooked achievements, and unsung heroes.

In other words, it is an underlying assumption of this book that even though it would be interesting and compelling to write a history of Balanchine and Kirstein's collaboration that focused on a select number of their undertakings—considering only ballet and opera, or only work on Broadway and in Hollywood—it is just as crucial to make sense of them as a collective enterprise, the way they were in fact lived out in practice. This means that in the chapters that follow, many stones will remain unturned and other paths of inquiry must be skipped in the interests of capturing the wider sweep of the enterprise's history. Indeed, many of the subjects and individual works discussed in the chapters that follow could take up entire chapters if not entire books of their own, and it is my hope that this new narrative will provide a basis on which future studies can build. At the same time, Balanchine and Kirstein's endeavors involved people and organizations who have already received substantial scholarly and critical attention in their own right, making it difficult to acknowledge the complexity of their interactions in the space afforded by this narrative. In the following pages many cultural titans are improbably relegated to the role of supporting players, among them George Antheil, Katherine Dunham, George Gershwin, Martha Graham, Samuel Goldwyn, and Richard Rodgers. But the ability of this enterprise to bring so many players into its network of activity was precisely a source of its ultimate success. The glancing attention that some of these figures will receive in these pages does not mean to diminish the significance and relevance of their own careers and cultural standing. In a similar manner, the fact that the Balanchine-Kirstein enterprise took shape during one of the more tumultuous periods of American political and economic history presents an equally daunting challenge. The somewhat attenuated treatment that such concerns will receive over the course of this narrative does not serve to imply that these issues are somehow less relevant or significant. On the contrary, work by Lynn Garafola, Mark Franko, Elizabeth Bergman, Andrea Harris, and others cited above has persuasively demonstrated that political and economic concerns were enormously influential on individual works of art produced by Balanchine and Kirstein, as well as on the structure and ideology of their individual and collective endeavors.

This account runs yet another risk by attempting to bring so many different elements together, and it is premised on what might at first seem like two contradictory assumptions. Balanchine and Kirstein's various undertakings between 1933 and 1940 were at once distinct and unique but at the same time represented a convergent whole. It would be careless to imply or presume that their activities represent a homogeneous field of cultural production solely by virtue of their continual presence in a certain period of history. Concert dance performance, opera production, ballet instruction, Broadway musical comedy and revue, and Hollywood cinema each have their own modes of production and critical histories grounded in specific and distinct material realities. Their inclusion here in one larger narrative does not serve to minimize such differences. But one reason for including these heterogeneous undertakings in one account is a common element without which truly none of them would have been possible: the continual presence of Balanchine and Kirstein, and even more crucial, the individual dancers who brought the various endeavors of Balanchine and Kirstein to life on the stage. The existence and participation of a relatively stable cadre of dancers over these years offers compelling grounds for considering these many activities as one story. Whether in ballets, or operas, or musicals, or films, their bodily labor and physical movements were the essential ingredients that tied together the work of the enterprise as a whole.

When these dancers, along with Balanchine and Kirstein, moved from one field to another they did so without regard for the disciplinary boundaries that define cultural history and academic research today. And as I hope to show, these shifts created both conscious and unconscious continuities, such that their activities ought to be considered as an entire collaborative "enterprise" with its own idiosyncratic logic, however difficult it may be to describe in a straightforward manner. In other words, everything that

Balanchine and Kirstein undertook from 1933 to 1940, both individually and together, did add up to something and ultimately helped shape their artistic sensibilities and the identities of the institutions that continue their legacies to this day. But this "something" was far from self-evident to them at the time. Their activities were and are part of one fascinating story that deserves to be understood as a complex and admittedly messy whole.

CHAPTER 1 | 1933

LINCOLN KIRSTEIN TURNED twenty-six in May 1933. Left-leaning in his politics, he was hardly unsympathetic to the challenges facing his fellow citizens in the midst of the Great Depression, but the circumstances of his birth had unquestionably inured him personally to the widespread despair that pervaded so much of the country.[1] Thanks to his mother's inherited wealth and his father's rags-to-riches success as an executive in the department store industry, Kirstein was able to cultivate wide-ranging interests in literature and the performing arts during the same years that millions of other Americans struggled with unemployment and poverty.[2] Although the Kirsteins' resources by no means ranked them among the Vanderbilts or Rockefellers, the family was firmly established among the civic elite of Boston and were prominent supporters of local and national educational and Jewish philanthropic organizations.[3]

Rose and Louis Kirstein took pleasure, perhaps with some parental resignation, in the fact that their three children were engaged in educational and cultural endeavors, whether in literature, publishing, or the performing arts. "My philosophy," as Louis explained in a letter to his brother Henry in 1934, "is that I should like to do something for them while I am alive and get some enjoyment from knowing that they are having some pleasure as a result of the work and effort I have put in."[4] Mina, the eldest, a professor of English at Smith College, was the first English-language editor of the letters of Marcel Proust and the author of a biography of Georges Bizet among other publications.[5] The youngest, George, worked in a variety of jobs and is best known for his accomplishments as the publisher of the *Nation* from 1955 to 1965.[6] But it was the middle child of the Kirstein family—named after President Lincoln, a personal hero of his father's—who would most assiduously leverage his family's literal and figurative capital as a leading advocate for modernist expression in

America, perhaps most notably as the longtime champion of choreographer George Balanchine.

Like Kirstein, Balanchine's upbringing was characterized by a certain degree of privilege but had been considerably less stable.[7] Three years older than Kirstein—and also a middle child with an older sister and younger brother—Georgi Balanchivadze was born in St. Petersburg in 1904. His father Meliton was a musician and aspiring composer who in 1889 had left his first wife and children behind in his native Georgia to pursue a career in the imperial capital. His mother, Maria Vasilieva, was a young woman of uncertain parentage (perhaps illegitimate) eager for social advancement, although it is not clear whether Meliton ever divorced his first wife or that he and Maria were ever officially married. The couple nevertheless built a respectable *haute bourgeoisie* life for themselves and their children that included music lessons, German and French tutors, and a *dacha* at a fashionable development in Finland. These luxuries were financed not by Meliton's erratic income but rather from a lottery prize of 200,000 rubles won by Maria in 1901. Thanks to bad investments on the part of Meliton, the Balanchivadzes subsequently lost their fortune, and in 1911 they were forced to abandon their cosmopolitan Petersburg existence and relocate full-time to Finland.

In 1912 Maria made a renewed effort to restore her family's social standing by unsuccessfully attempting to have their daughter accepted into the Imperial Theater School to train as a dancer. The following year Tamara auditioned again, and this time her younger brother Georgi was introduced into the audition process as well; to everyone's surprise, he was accepted even as his sister was again denied admission. After a painful period of separation anxiety, the young Georgi eventually took to his new rigorously structured existence in the dance academy, where he and his fellow students were well provided for as members of the tsar's household, and he soon acquired a new first name, Georges.

Although Georges Balanchivadze would not ultimately emerge as a major dancing star, in the course of his study he developed an interest in choreography, creating solo numbers for friends and colleagues and eventually founding an experimental company called the "Young Ballet." The Revolution in 1917 significantly disrupted the workings of the Imperial Theater system, and seeking new opportunities away from the chaotic environment of newly renamed Leningrad, in 1924 Balanchivadze and a small group of classmates made their way to Germany under the guise of a short tour. They had little incentive to return and remained in Western Europe until they were eventually recruited to join the Ballets Russes, where impresario Serge Diaghilev changed the name Balanchivadze to the more marketable "Balanchine."[8] Balanchine would serve as the last major choreographer for Diaghilev, creating among other works two ballets still performed today, *Apollon Musagète* (1928) and *The Prodigal Son* (1929). After the death of Diaghilev in August 1929 the Ballets Russes enterprise collapsed, leaving Balanchine and the company's other artists to scour the continent for professional opportunities. Over the next four years Balanchine—much like his erstwhile colleagues (and now competitors) Léonide Massine, Serge Lifar, and Bronislava Nijinska—found employment with a variety of individuals and organizations in Paris, London, Monte Carlo, and Copenhagen, working in venues ranging from the opera house to the variety stage.[9]

As family misfortune, political upheaval, the death of Diaghilev, and the financial downturn of the early 1930s—not to mention two modifications of his name—had brought a certain instability to Balanchine's early life, Kirstein's education and early career had proceeded more smoothly. By the fall of 1933 Kirstein had already established himself as an ambitious impresario, his ventures made possible by the largesse of Rose and Louis, who had financed his education at Andover, the Berskhire School, and Harvard, as well as a long string of private tutors to assist the talented but attention-challenged student along the way. While still at Harvard, in 1927 Kirstein co-founded the literary quarterly *Hound & Horn* with classmate Varian Fry and critic Richard Blackmur. Modeled on T. S. Eliot's *The Criterion*, in its seven years of publication the journal offered new work by Ezra Pound and Katherine Anne Porter, and included among its roster of critics young talents such as composers Roger Sessions and Elliott Carter and poet Louis Zukofsky.[10] A year later in 1928 Kirstein co-founded the Harvard Society for Contemporary Art, which exhibited previously unseen work by artists including Constantin Brancusi, Alexander Calder, Isamu Noguchi, and Diego Rivera.[11]

During the summer of 1933, however, Kirstein began to turn his attention away from literature and the visual arts to a new project, which like his previous ventures was made possible as much by his maniacal personal enthusiasm as the patrician laissez-faire of his parents. On Wednesday, October 11, 1933, Lincoln Kirstein wrote a breezy, newsy letter to his mother, then vacationing at the Greenbriar Hotel in West Virginia.[12] Addressed to "Mummy," the document is a telling barometer of Kirstein's diverse professional portfolio at the time, and the remove at which his family existed from the harsher realities of most Americans in the early 1930s. He reports on interviews with the Russian émigré choreographer

Michel Fokine in preparation for a forthcoming book, a recently published article in *Vogue*,[13] and also includes updates on the latest issue of *Hound & Horn*, on whose letterhead the note was typed by his secretary Doris Levine. Kirstein opens and closes this letter, however, with news of an event that would uniquely define the rest of his professional career. "My ballet people arrive on Tuesday [October 17], so you can imagine I am very excited," he wrote, adding in a similarly nonchalant tone that "I may have to go up to Hartford on Thursday to take my Russians." Such words are in retrospect a charming understatement given the challenging institutional journey on which he was about to embark with Balanchine, a collaborative enterprise that would occupy him for the rest of his life. This journey was in fact already well under way, having begun three months earlier in Paris and London.

Among the most persistent features of accounts of the Balanchine-Kirstein enterprise is the choreographer's alleged insistence that a school should be the principal priority of their new endeavor. When Kirstein swore to Balanchine that they would have a company by the time he was forty, as his biographer Bernard Taper writes, and many others have recounted before and after, he is said to have insisted: "But first a school."[14]

In fact, most evidence suggests that Balanchine's main motivation for coming to the United States was the desire to continue to create new work on the stage, with Kirstein as the true initial champion of the school. This disparity in priorities was one of many organizational uncertainties and contingencies in the early plans devised by Balanchine and Kirstein, not the least of which was the selection of Balanchine as an artistic leader.

In the summer of 1933 Kirstein found himself in Paris and London at a particularly exciting moment in the history of dance in the twentieth century. Though this was not his first trip to Europe to take in ballet performances, this year was somehow different from previous seasons with more activity than usual.[15] In both cities dance troupes led by prominent members of the Ballets Russes diaspora offered performances in overlapping engagements in an intense competition for international stature and a claim to the mantle of Diaghilev. Most established were the Ballets Russes de Monte Carlo, co-founded by René Blum and the Colonel de Basil in 1932 (hereafter the "de Basil company").[16] Although Balanchine had been this troupe's first ballet master, he parted ways with the group soon after its formation, and Léonide Massine was subsequently appointed its primary choreographer and star.[17] Two ballets created by Balanchine in 1932 remained in the company's repertory—*Cotillon* and *La Concurrence*—both of which would be performed the summer of 1933 and in subsequent seasons without his direct oversight.[18]

Competing with the de Basil troupe was a newly formed company called Les Ballets 1933, with Balanchine as its sole choreographer and organized by Boris Kochno (Diaghilev's former assistant) and Vladimir Dimitriev, the opera singer-turned-impresario who had organized the tour that had taken Balanchine and his friends to Germany in 1924.[19] The troupe was financially backed by London banker Edward James—whose wife Tilly Losch was to be a featured performer—and his support allowed them to commission new music and décor from contemporary artists true to the company's of-the-moment name. Also in the mix was the similarly short-lived company of Serge Lifar, Diaghilev's last male star, on whom Balanchine had created lead roles in *Apollon Musagète, The Prodigal Son*, as well as *La Chatte*, the latter of which would be performed by Lifar's company that summer and into the fall.

Kirstein spent most of June in Paris, after which he followed the dance companies to London in July. In both cities he sampled freely from the many offerings while the competition raged, and his ultimate collaboration with Balanchine must be understood as deeply affected and even occasioned by this unique historical confluence. From his written recollections it is clear that not only did Kirstein attend multiple performances by all three dance organizations but that over the course of the summer he took an intense personal interest in all the choreographers and companies. It was through a complex network of individuals and circumstances that his eventual selection of Balanchine took place. While all three companies held their own in Paris, by the time they arrived in London the de Basil company had established itself as the clear victor of this three-way race, in particular after its triumphant engagement at the Alhambra Theatre in early July, a watershed moment in the history of ballet.[20] The company's London engagement established the de Basil organization as the world's undisputed leading ballet troupe and Massine as an internationally celebrated choreographer.[21] Lifar's company, by contrast, would continue on for a bit longer, with a short American tour later in the year, whereupon he would return to his duties as ballet master at the Paris Opera. Les Ballets 1933 collapsed even sooner shortly after its London performances, with Edward James in a flurry of lawsuits against people involved with the company.

It is not entirely clear whether Kirstein set off for Europe in the summer of 1933 with the explicit goal of founding an American ballet company and school, though such an idea had perhaps been on his mind for some time. Kirstein's eventual partner in the enterprise, Edward Warburg, claimed they had discussed the idea of a ballet company since their college days at Harvard.[22] "We spent many hours discussing the possibilities of art patronage," Warburg recalled in his memoirs, explaining how Kirstein understood ballet as not just an artistic endeavor but an art form with unique organizational possibilities.[23] Through this collaborative art form it was possible to create an institutional structure by which artists of all types could mutually benefit not just aesthetically but financially. "Our major concern," Warburg recalled, "was figuring out how to make sure that a painter, a composer, a poet—any artist—would be able to eat regularly." As Kirstein explained to him, "the only art form that could bring the most artists together in a single production was the ballet. . . and everyone might receive a cut from the box office." Such a conception was based on a somewhat rose-colored if not entirely inaccurate understanding of the organizational model of Kirstein's hero Diaghilev, who had created a viable if idiosyncratic business model that provided varied levels of financial return to its many contributing artists.[24]

Kirstein's more immediate concern that summer was research on dancer Vaslav Nijinsky for a book he was ghostwriting on behalf of the dancer's wife Romola.[25] In the course of the summer, however, Kirstein's interests as a balletomane researcher morphed into those of a dance impresario, and his new focus became the idea of founding a ballet school and company in the United States. The runaway success of the de Basil company would take Massine out of consideration for such a project, and although Lifar had perhaps less to lose than Massine in accepting an American post, he and Kirstein did not make a strong personal connection. In the end it was Balanchine—who was both available and interested, and whose work for Les Ballets 1933 was exciting and fresh—whom Kirstein connected with most readily, thanks to both the interest of the budding impresario and the initiative of Balanchine himself.

———

In Paris Kirstein benefited from the guiding hand of American composer Virgil Thomson, who had spent significant amounts of time in the city and was an invaluable resource for visiting Americans.[26] Both Harvard graduates, the two saw each other on an almost daily basis during Kirstein's time in Paris, dining together on June 3, 1933 following his landing at Le Havre.[27] That night Thomson filled in Kirstein on "the various splits in the ballet-companies" and explained "how the great chic was not American, but German now. . . . . It will be German for a year; then American again. The ballets must anticipate styles like *modistes*."[28] This was no empty observation on Thomson's part, at least with respect to the Germans, as choreographer Kurt Jooss had one year earlier won the inaugural choreographic competition of Rolf de Maré's Archives Internationales de la Danse for his work *The Green Table*.

The following Wednesday the two attended Kirstein's first performance of the summer, the opening night of Les Ballets 1933 at the Théâtre des Champs-Elysées. Kirstein described himself as in "a fever of excitement," and he "applauded wildly at every opportunity" during the evening.[29] The program opened with *Mozartiana*, which had "dull décor but nice costumes and very lovely choreography, witty and Mozartian by Balanchine."[30] Bertolt Brecht's *Les Sept Péchés capitaux* (*The Seven Capital Sins*)[31] followed—a cause or effect of the vogue for the Teutonic—set to music by Kurt Weill that created a "wiry but intense" mood.[32] Despite his over-all enthusiasm, the program did have low points, including the Darius Milhaud–André Derain collaboration *Les Songes* ("Dreams") which Kirstein found "very dull and boring." He also had reservations about the company's dance offerings more broadly, noting that it was "too much choreography by one man for Balanchine to do perfectly" and that he was "no Fokine."[33] Two days later Kirstein would sit in on a morning rehearsal of the ballet *Errante*, in which Kirstein identified a theme that would subsequently recur in many of the choreographer's early works in the United States, the "tragic ideas of the relation between men and women, always broken up by someone jumping between."[34]

Despite being taken with Balanchine's offerings overall, Kirstein was comparably impressed by the offerings of Massine who was also debuting one of his most important new works around the time, his "symphonic ballet" *Les Présages*, set to Tchaikovsky's Fifth Symphony. Kirstein found it "a wonderful choreographic thing" but disliked its costumes and found the corps de ballet somewhat ragged.[35] Kirstein subsequently returned to the Châtelet to see the troupe again.[36] He chatted with Alexander Calder and Isamu Noguchi at the intermission, both of whom put him "in a rage": Calder for not liking the dancing despite being in discussions with the troupe about a project, and Noguchi for saying "it was all an *edition de luxe* with no point but the décor."[37] A week later at another performance by the troupe Kirstein was similarly impressed by its offerings, declaring that that he had never experienced "such extreme satisfaction" and that Massine in particular was "never so magnificent."[38] Kirstein also saw Lifar's company perform at the Opéra on June 14 in one of Nijinsky's signature works, *Le Spectre de la Rose*.[39] Though Lifar was a well-regarded performer at the time, for Kirstein the performance was a disappointing simulacrum: "A replica of the Nijinsky costume, décor, everything, except spirit. He danced well [but] absolutely unmoved me. It was no dream."[40]

Kirstein did not meet Balanchine in person until the subsequent London dance season, specifically after the opening night performance of Les Ballets 1933. Romola Nijinsky facilitated this introduction. Kirstein's diaries record that on July 8 he accompanied her to the Savoy Theatre, where the program consisted of *Mozartiana, Les Songes*, and *Errante*, and afterward Romola sent a note backstage to Balanchine.[41] She joked that Balanchine "made even the scenery dance, as he had no dancers," a dig at the chamber company's meager cadre of eight women and three men.[42] Balanchine looked tired and ill, according to Kirstein, as though he "had just had a fight on the stage," and their interaction was not very substantial.[43]

Balanchine and Kirstein had a more sustained interaction several days later following a performance by the de Basil troupe, at which Kirstein saw Balanchine's *La Concurrence* for the first time, finding it "very 1900 and sweet, pretty to look at."[44] Later on at a party at the home of Kirk and Constance Askew, he and Balanchine had a "coy and satisfactory talk," and although Kirstein remembers Balanchine as "wholly charming" in demeanor he was nevertheless full of strong opinions about his rivals.[45] Having given up a performing career, Balanchine declared that dancers "can rarely compose as they always think only of themselves, never of the others," likely a dig at dancer-choreographer Massine.[46] Balanchine said of Massine explicitly that while he created good dances he was "commercial," and his studies in Spanish dance had affected him in a negative way. He was also critical of Massine's "symphonic ballet" *Les Présages*, saying that Tchaikovsky's fifth symphony "explains itself, it never needs an accompaniment, a masterpiece."[47] Not yet thirty years old, Balanchine also declared that no dancer is good "either as a choreographer or as a performer after 40"—Massine was then nearing his late 30s—and bemoaned his present lack of financial and artistic resources. He then laid out a vision that would quickly begin to consume Kirstein:

How he wants to come to America, with 20 girls and 5 men he could do wonders. Particularly the classical style or his adaptation of it. . . . How Americans have great pointe but they are often dead from the waist up. They must be made to love the music and to love dancing. But they have spirit.[48]

Despite these lucid opinions and bold plans, Balanchine did not make a stronger physical impression than he had backstage three days earlier, seeming less well than before and breathing heavily "as if he really had T.B."[49]

If Kirstein's recollections are correct, it was thus Balanchine who successfully planted the idea in Kirstein's mind for an American ballet company and at the same time made a not-so-subtle case for himself as the only suitable leader of such an enterprise, as a nondancing choreographer comfortably below the age of forty. Whether the impressionable Kirstein was aware that he was being played is perhaps open to debate. In any case, his diary account contradicts his later recollections, in which the conversational dynamic is entirely reversed. Kirstein claims to have "made a headlong onslaught" toward Balanchine and "proposed an entire future career in half an hour," after which the choreographer said he would have to think it over.[50]

This initial conversational brainstorm subsequently became the subject of continued discussion between Balanchine and Kirstein, with Romola Nijinsky as an interlocutor. Two days after the party at the Askews, Kirstein talked over the idea of an American company with Nijinsky, and on July 16 all three convened for a lunch meeting to discuss the idea further.[51] The choreographer declared himself all but through with Les Ballets 1933, and the trio got "frightfully excited" about the potential plans.[52] Balanchine declared that working in America had long been a dream and that he "would give up everything to come."[53] He praised the talents of dancers Roman Jasinsky and Tamara Toumanova whom he wished to bring along as soloists, and he talked of plans for a "big erotic ballet." Romola for her part said that she would provide the rights to all of her late husband's ballets, and Kirstein pitched the idea of lecture-demonstrations in which the soloists provided live examples. Later in the day, however, Nijinsky privately warned Kirstein that Balanchine was consumptive and had only two years to live, a concern Kirstein dismissed with the somewhat cold calculation that "two years work will be a lot out of him[,] a real start." That evening Kirstein wrote a sixteen-page letter detailing a plan for a ballet school and company, and he was so excited at the prospect that he could hardly sleep.

———

Five years after Balanchine's arrival in the United States, Kirstein would write that although "there have been other ballet schools founded in America before us . . . few have started with such complete plans, or with such a root-grounded base of organization and instruction."[54] It is perhaps to Kirstein's credit that he believed strongly enough in the future of his still-fledgling organization that he was willing to misrepresent, or at least gloss over, the haphazard origins of the American Ballet and its school. But although the plans for the ballet enterprise would be in part scrapped and in part completely rewritten over the course of Balanchine's first two years in America, and even if Balanchine had been responsible for sparking the idea in the first place, Kirstein developed his own strong personal vision of how the organization should take shape, first summarized in letters to a friend and colleague who shared his strong enthusiasm for the visual and performing arts, A. Everett "Chick" Austin.[55]

From the same circle of Harvard-educated aesthetes as Kirstein, Austin was a logical person for Kirstein to reach out to, given his position as director of the Wadsworth Atheneum Museum in Hartford, Connecticut.[56] Since assuming his leadership role in 1927—the same time that Kirstein's own arts endeavors had begun—Austin had transformed the staid institution in the "Insurance Capital" into an unlikely showcase of modernist expression, from surrealist painting to Bauhaus architecture. Music and the performing arts had been an integral element of Austin's program, most notably with the establishment of the cheekily named "Friends and Enemies of Modern Music" series, which presented concerts of work by contemporary composers. Kirstein's efforts to bring ballet to Hartford would coincide with (and delay the execution of) one of the most significant performance initiatives of Austin's tenure, the commission of Virgil Thomson and Gertrude Stein's *Four Saints in Three Acts*, eventually premiered in Hartford in February 1934.[57] Kirstein in fact was well aware of this conflict and had no qualms about potentially preempting the opera's premiere with his ballet plans.[58]

Although Kirstein would later characterize his letter to Austin as "more enthusiastic than honest," it is remarkably clear and explicit in its goals.[59] Among the most salient themes of Kirstein's July plan is an insistence on an educational and noncommercial mission for the organization, which would be aided by being located in Hartford in affiliation with the museum.[60] Balanchine was amenable to such a plan, Kirstein assured Austin, since while he was "socially adorable," unlike artists such as Lifar "he hates the atmosphere both of society . . . and the professional Broadway Theatre."[61] Tuition would not be charged so that students could be chosen "for their perfect possibilities."[62] In exchange for their training, however, students would be required to commit to appearing exclusively in performances under the auspices of the school for a period of five years, a measure necessary to "obviate the danger of movies or Broadway snatching them up after they have been trained."[63]

If all went according to plan, within three years they could have an "American ballet," defined by Kirstein as "a trained company of young dancers—not Russians—but Americans with Russian stars to start with."[64] Kirstein and these stars would go on tour throughout the Northeast giving lecture-demonstrations to "prepare the way for the company, which will give performances *not* at the theater, but always kept on an educational level, with museums."[65] By operating in this different institutional sphere "out of the competition class," as Kirstein put it, the company would not be subject to the whims of managers and theater owners but could rather pursue its mission on its own terms. The company would still produce and perform new work, however, and Kirstein promised Austin that "by February you can have performances of four wholly new ballets in Hartford."[66] One aspect mentioned in this July plan that would not come to fruition was for the school to train a racially diverse group of dancers, with African American dancers in fact constituting half of the company. "For the first," Kirstein wrote to Austin, Balanchine would admit "4 white girls and 4 white boys, about sixteen years old and 8 of the same, *negros* [*sic*]." This idea evidently arose from the primitivist conceptions of Balanchine, who as Kirstein's letter further elaborates, "thinks the negro part would be amazingly supple. . . . They have so much abandon—and disciplined they would be *nonpareil*."[67] Not acknowledging the racist premise of this concept, Kirstein also did not consider the practical challenges that such a plan would face given de facto segregation in the North[68]

While Kirstein awaited a reply from Austin, he continued to plan with Balanchine and Romola Nijinsky in London. During a four-hour afternoon meeting on July 19, 1933, Kirstein procured a map of the United States to familiarize Balanchine with various cities.[69] Balanchine was full of ideas of his own and was evidently more focused on choreography and performance than training young dancers. He described excitedly his version of the Richard Strauss ballet *La Légende de Joseph* mounted in Copenhagen and proposed an immediate American premiere of his *Apollon Musagète*.[70] The following day Balanchine informed Kirstein that he had received an offer to teach in Paris but asked Kirstein to stay in touch since he was more interested in going to America as a long-term plan.[71] Austin subsequently gave Kirstein tentative approval via a telegram on July 26, and by early August had already raised $3,000 of the $6,000 necessary to prove to immigration officials that the foreign ballet specialists would not become public charges.[72] On August 8, Austin wired Kirstein with a more definitive green light: "Go Ahead, Iron-Clad Contract Necessary."[73] Only a day before, however, Kirstein had received a letter from his close friend Muriel Draper, who had some doubts about their choice of location. She imagined "the poor Russians in Hartford, watching Chick Austin's magic"—he was an avid amateur magician—and she was as suspicious of "the education museum chi-chi . . . as the Broadway commercial chi-chi," all of which upset Kirstein somewhat since he had to admit "it was half true."[74]

Even as his plans were being set in motion, Kirstein began to worry more about their actual execution, and he sent Austin a follow-up letter on August 11 from Paris, where he had gone to track down Balanchine, having not had word from him in several weeks. Only slightly shorter than his July correspondence from London, Kirstein in this letter delves into more practical details and rearticulates his overall vision for the enterprise.[75] Even though the necessary funds had been raised, Kirstein remained in hard sell mode to Austin, stressing the competing offers for Balanchine's talents (both in Copenhagen and Paris), touting the talents of guest artists Jasinsky and Toumanova, and perhaps most important, singing the praises of Balanchine's "friend and advisor" Vladimir Dimitriev, described as the choreographer's "regisseur" and business manager.[76] Although Dimitriev had not been party to the initial July discussions in London, Kirstein now found it necessary to add Balanchine's partner to the plan.[77] Kirstein explained to Austin that they would fulfill two different yet equally important roles in the enterprise. While Balanchine was primarily a "composer," Dimitriev would take on "the burden of teaching new pupils and making the rest practice."[78] In fact, Kirstein explained Balanchine's role in the enterprise as something novel and unique, and distinct from a traditional ballet master: "He wants to have a class for composition, that is a class for *maitre de ballets* [*sic*]—a thing never before attempted."[79] Balanchine had initially proposed the idea himself in one of their July meetings in London.[80]

Kirstein reiterates in this same letter to Austin that they should "emphasize the non-commercial aspects of the venture" and stress the educational angle, and explicitly dissociate it from commercial entertainment.[81] It was thus as a school that the initiative should begin, not as a company performing for the public, a point Kirstein repeats with notable insistence and graphological emphasis. "At first everything should be centered around the foundation of a school," he notes a third of the way through the letter.[82] He again stresses this point several pages later, in greater detail: "The School first of all to feed the troupe. . . . It is the source, training, base and pillar of the whole idea."[83] To drive home the point completely, Kirstein exhorts Austin by name, asking him to "never for a second Dear Chick, forget the school," because Balanchine will be "devoting himself to purely creative work" and "the creation of ballets demands the most intense concentration."[84] Thus if Balanchine and others would later construe this insistence on a school as his own demand, these sources suggest that this aspect of the enterprise in fact originated in large part as a priority of Kirstein. Balanchine's initial concerns centered on the creation and presentation of ballets—a division of labor that apparently met with Kirstein's approval—and if he expressed interest in pedagogy it was as a teacher of choreography and not straightforward ballet technique.

By August, matters were about to be set in motion, and the lengthy trans-Atlantic boat passages created opportunities for anxious waiting and time to plan. Austin heard from Kirstein via cable on August 12 that everything was settled, but that he did not "dare bring Balanchine until you agree."[85] Kirstein himself was set to sail that coming Saturday, August 19, on the S.S. *Degrasse* and said that Balanchine and Dimitriev could follow sometime after. Upon landing, Kirstein quickly reconnected with both Austin and his old college friend Edward Warburg, who would become the primary financial benefactor of the enterprise in its initial years. Although Kirstein and Austin by no means lacked privilege, Warburg was a league apart, with access to virtually unlimited financial resources and an unparalleled network of familial, business, and political connections that would prove crucial in the early years of the enterprise. His father Felix had been born into an already quite prosperous family from Hamburg, but through his subsequent marriage to Frieda Schiff—daughter of self-made immigrant and Wall Street titan Jacob Schiff, at the time second in wealth and influence only to J. P. Morgan—he secured a position for himself and his children at the highest levels of New York's elite.[86]

In his memoirs, Warburg suggests that his initial involvement in the enterprise was pitched as a relatively modest contribution, which if true was a canny ploy on Kirstein's part, given how deeply Warburg and his family would become invested in the enterprise in the years to come. Warburg recalls that Kirstein came out to his family's estate at White Plains upon his return from Europe, explaining how he had "talked to Balanchine and had persuaded him to come to the United States to attempt to start a ballet school here with American youngsters" with the eventual idea of founding a company.[87] All that Kirstein was asking was "the guarantee of round trip tickets from Paris to New York for Balanchine and his business associate, a Mr. Dimitriev." Kirstein had said he was covering one and asked

Warburg to cover the other. "I agreed," Warburg noted in closing, "little knowing what I was letting myself in for."

Balanchine and Dimitriev disembarked from the *Olympic* in Manhattan on October 17, 1933, after some initial confusion over their visa status, resolved expeditiously by Warburg's "magic name."[88] The possibility that they might be greeted with any attention by the press was forestalled by the arrival the very same day of a more eminent émigré, Albert Einstein, set to take up a position at the Institute for Advanced Study in Princeton.[89] After settling them on the thirty-fourth floor of the Barbizon Hotel on Central Park South, Kirstein took the new arrivals for a brief walk around midtown, after which they wasted no time in getting down to business. Over dinner at the hotel grill, Kirstein mentioned to Balanchine rumors that Balanchine already had offers for work from the Roxy Music Hall as well as Juilliard.[90] At a continuation of their discussions later on back at the hotel, Balanchine made clear his goals, saying he intended to work full time at the school but that he and Dimitriev "don't want to start small but large."[91] Creating new work was still a priority, however: "He would produce something by April or would go back to Paris," as Kirstein records.[92]

The planned school met with approving press coverage in both Hartford and New York, which provides additional corroboration that an educational and noncommercial concept initially characterized the enterprise. The day after Balanchine and Dimitriev's landing, the *Hartford Courant* announced the imminent opening of the ballet school, to be operated under the auspices of the Wadsworth Atheneum. Given its affiliation, the school "will not compete with commercial theaters" and its purpose is "to build a self subsisting ballet company" that would be able to present performances in three years' time.[93] The same day the *Courant* published an editorial praising the new dance initiative, approving of the selection of "foreign ballet experts" to lead the enterprise, since this would make possible "early performances of public interest and of sound training in classic technique."[94] At the same time, however, the editorial noted that at some point Americans would need to "add their contribution of national genius, if indeed the school is actually to achieve the high ambitions of its founders."[95] On October 19, the paper reported of the arrival in Hartford of the new artistic leadership, quoting Austin as saying that the sets and costumes for two ballets, *Les Songes* and *Mozartiana*—misspelled as *Songe* and *Mozartinia*—would be made available to the school.[96]

New York critics echoed these hopes and desires and similarly praised the noncommercial status of the enterprise. In a column for *Modern Music*, composer Marc Blitzstein (a friend of Kirstein's sister Mina) made no issue of Balanchine's nationality, declaring him "a prize" and "inevitably the right man to create a ballet out of our rich disorganized stuff."[97] Blitzstein was also optimistic about the noncommercial goals of the organization, maintaining that "there is less likelihood now than some years ago that the best pupils of the school will be speedily pumped into the machines of the commercial revues."[98] In his Sunday column of October 22, the weekend after Balanchine's arrival, *New York Times* dance critic John Martin—the nation's first full-time dance critic and the most influential dance writer in the country—lauded the project, especially the fact that no public performances would be given for the first three years, with the exception of informal exhibitions.[99] Although Martin would later criticize the organization for its lack of American leadership, he struck a conciliatory tone in this initial column, arguing that since no bona fide ballet company yet existed in America, "it is obvious that a director must be found elsewhere."[100] Martin also expressed approval of the choice of Hartford as a location, as it would lessen the temptation "to burst prematurely into performance."[101] Kirstein had in fact met with Martin several weeks earlier to brief him on the school's plans, and the critic had predicted they would be "swamped with applicants."[102]

Despite such initial optimism, in the end, the school would not be founded in Hartford, owing to an array of inauspicious circumstances related to its geographic location, problematic public relations with existing dance schools in the city, but most significantly, the Wadsworth Atheneum as a noncommercial institutional host. Several explanations for the Hartford failure have circulated in accounts of the enterprise, including Balanchine and Dimitriev's alleged displeasure with the city as a place to live and work. The two St. Petersburg–raised cosmopolitans, so the story goes, did not appreciate the more modest milieu of Connecticut's capital city, having spent most of the previous decade in Paris, London, and Monte Carlo. One example of this culture shock was Balanchine's charming request for accommodation in eighteenth-century apartments, which had of course had never existed in the city.[103] Kirstein echoes this concern in *Thirty Years*[104] and cites a second challenge mentioned in numerous accounts as well: the vocal opposition of numerous local dance teachers to the founding of a school that might compete with their organizations or poach all of their best students with the lure of free instruction by famous foreigners.[105] The same day that the *Courant* announced the arrival of Balanchine and

Dimitriev, the paper reported on a meeting of a "score" of dance instructors "to consider the possible effect of the proposed new school on the private teaching of dancing in this city."[106] In an attempt to quell these concerns, Austin took to the press himself several days later, assuring the public that the new school "will be limited to about two dozen pupils and consequently will in no way interfere with activities of local dance teachers."[107] Both of these circumstances were indeed partly to blame for the eventual failure of the plan there. "Fifty professors of Dance voiced their local regret that it would be a free school, drive them out of business," Kirstein recounted in his diary, "and that Americans were not going to be at the head of it, and that their opinion was not asked in the matter."[108] Although Dimitriev in particular was reportedly "disturbed" by this unpleasant welcome, Kirstein suggests that the controversy was not as consequential as its press coverage might indicate and was a storm that could have likely been weathered.

It was more fundamental organizational concerns that led to the relocation of the enterprise from Hartford to New York, problems that arose from the divergence of the nonprofit status and institutional goals of the museum and Balanchine and Dimitriev's ambitions. Balanchine and Dimitriev were underwhelmed by the museum's facilities, which had just been renovated at great expense. In their first tour of the buildings the two "were well satisfied with the space for the practice halls," Kirstein records, but "when we came to the theatre it was a big disappointment."[109] The newly-built Avery Memorial Theatre had little height and could not accommodate much scenery, its floor was too hard for dancing, and it could allow at maximum twenty-four dancers on stage.[110] The small dimensions of the museum's theater are in fact keenly emblematic of the misalignment in institutional priorities of the Russians and Americans. The scale had been an intentional design choice, since as a 299-seat auditorium it would not be subject to Hartford's building code requirements for commercial theaters.[111] Its inclusion in the heart of the museum was a point of great pride for Austin, but a far cry from the theaters of the European capitals in which Balanchine had worked or venues available in New York.

From the moment he had stepped off the boat and over the course of his first months in the United States, Balanchine's creative ideas had been evidently tending in a direction more suited to the larger aesthetic possibilities and entertainment infrastructure of New York than the bucolic environment of Hartford. While strolling the streets their first night in New York, Kirstein recalls that Balanchine took note of a row of mannequins dressed as movie stars in a shoe store window and "said he wanted to do a film using masks of all the stars at once: imitate their voices, etc.," and the following day mused about a "modern *Sylphides* with cellophane trees."[112] Although the degree of Balanchine's actual commitment to such passing brainstorms could be debated, accounts by Kirstein both at the time of Balanchine's arrival and in later decades confirm that the question of the organization's nonprofit versus commercial status was a decisive factor in the Hartford plan's collapse.

Writing later, Kirstein maintained that he went to Austin because although Balanchine was famous, he was "stateless and moneyless" and needed to be brought to the United States under the auspices of more than a performance-driven initiative.[113] An affiliation with an established museum such as the Wadsworth was the path of least resistance from a bureaucratic standpoint for Kirstein's purposes. In this same later recollection, Kirstein writes that Balanchine "flatly refused to have anything to do with a plan which involved non-profits."[114] America was a wealthy country, and indeed, the Hartford museum was heavily supported in part by one of its richest citizens, J. P. Morgan, and thus "was it not proper that an artist be allowed more than a mere pittance?"[115] Kirstein makes haste to point out that Balanchine was not out to enrich himself personally. Rather, his financial concerns centered on having the most expansive resources to create art, and "it was not the money that bothered him even then; it was prestige and the potential of the provinces," which could not provide the resources to realize the sort of projects that he had been contemplating since his arrival.[116]

Kirstein's diaries corroborate this later characterization of the nonprofit mission of the Wadsworth as the fundamental problem with the Hartford plan. The crux of the matter was in fact reached very quickly, on Balanchine and Dimitriev's second day in the city, when during an after-dinner conference with Austin and Kirstein the problems came to a head. In the course of the discussion a corporation was proposed, in which Balanchine and Dimitriev would be partners and own shares.[117] Kirstein does not say who first raised such an idea, but it was evidently either Balanchine or Dimitriev, since he notes emphatically that the "idea of a commercial venture being under the Morgan Memorial filled both Chick and me with utmost horror. Shares. My God! What were we getting in for."[118] Austin was particularly taken aback by the proposal, saying that "the whole idea had changed" and that the Russians had "delusions of commercial grandeur."[119]

Aside from Kirstein's recollections, this abrupt change in the institutional mission and structure of the enterprise was reported in other sources both public and private. On October 30 the *Courant* reported that

Balanchine and Dimitriev "have returned to New York, where, it is understood, they will seek to found a school along lines which did not meet with Mr. Austin's approval."[120] A report in the *Hartford Times* goes even further and characterizes the collapse of the plan as an example of Austin's principled leadership: "The flat refusal of A. Everett Austin, Jr. . . . to commercialize the proposed American ballet which was to have been established in Hartford, has resulted in a complete cancellation of the arrangements."[121]

A few days before these articles had appeared in the press, the institutional drift of the project had somehow been reported to architect Philip Johnson, who had been a $500 donor to the project. "In spite of the fact that I am paying too much," Johnson had written to Austin in late September when sending his check, "I am very glad to if it will help the ballet."[122] A month later Johnson was taken aback by the abrupt change in plans, which aside from the involvement of Balanchine contradicted almost to the letter the agenda laid out by Kirstein during the summer. "I was very happy to join a non-profit making venture to further the interests of ballet in this country," he wrote to Austin, but the new plan was "not at all what I understood on our first conversation or Lincoln's word from Europe."[123] Johnson reiterated his support for anything Austin might undertake in Hartford, but regarding the reconfigured American Ballet, he did not personally believe that in its new form "it is much more worthy of support than others which already exist in this City."[124]

In 1920s Paris, Diaghilev had been canny enough to rebrand Georges Balanchivadze as Georges Balanchine, but Kirstein and Warburg did not think it necessary to Americanize his first name or mitigate the Parisian flair of his credentials in early publicity for their school. Having not taken heed of the way that the Hartford press had mangled the exotic titles of *Les Songes* and *Mozartiana*, newspaper advertisements for the school followed Francophile convention to announce the artistic leadership of not George but "Georges Balanchine, Maitre de ballet for *Les Ballets Russes de Sergei Diaghilev, the Monte Carlo Ballet Russe, and Les Ballets 1933*," copy that aside from proper nouns and a numeral included only four words of plain English: "ballet," "for," "the," and "and."[125] Although one early ad announced that classes would begin at the start of December, the opening date was pushed back to December 11 in a second notice, a date also mentioned in a short item in the same day's paper.[126] John Martin announced the opening of the school, although not necessarily the first day of classes, as December 18.[127] Auditions were held on an ongoing basis, and although numbers were initially small, students kept "trickling in every day" and by December 28 Kirstein noted that "things look nearly ready."[128] The first day of classes, according to Kirstein's diaries, took place December 29, with twenty-two students in attendance.[129] Today the School of American Ballet perhaps understandably claims the more poetic January 2, 1934 as its first day of classes.[130]

Contrary to the decision articulated only two months before that no performances would be given for three years, notices of the opening of the school in New York did not attribute a purely pedagogical agenda to the organization. An article in the *Herald-Tribune* notes that three ballets would be presented "at a local theater" in March of the coming year,[131] and Martin's column of December 17 similarly reported that "the company when sufficiently developed will give its first program of three ballets at a Broadway theatre in March."[132] Whether by design or by grace, the New York press had not covered the collapse of the Hartford plan, with the only notable mention of the matter occurring in the same column in which Martin announced the new opening of the school. The critic delivered the potentially damaging news in the most generous and benign terms possible: "Originally planned to function from Hartford as a centre, the organization found it necessary to move to New York, where it would be more closely in touch with dance activities."[133]

While the enterprise was regrouping, the same rivals with whom Balanchine had been in competition over the summer and whom Kirstein had eagerly observed followed them across the Atlantic to New York, again with many of Balanchine's ballets in their repertoire. In November 1933, Serge Lifar made his debut performances in the United States, including *L'Après-Midi d'un Faune, Le Spectre de la Rose*, and Balanchine's *La Chatte*.[134] More consequentially, the de Basil company made its first American appearance in December 1933 in New York, after which they toured the country for four months with an extensive repertoire of ballets, including Balanchine's *Cotillon* and *La Concurrence*.[135] These outside rivals, and other internal dynamics, would put even more pressure on the nascent organization to present their own performances to the public, whether they were ready or not.

CHAPTER 2 | 1934

CONTRARY TO THEIR stated goal of creating a training institution, Balanchine and Kirstein's enterprise focused from its earliest days on not just ballet pedagogy but the rehearsal and revision of several ballets from the repertoire of Les Ballets 1933 as well as the creation of entirely new works. These projects included a collegiate satire set at the annual Harvard-Yale football game, a Hungarian fantasia danced to music of Liszt, as well as a work with special significance in Balanchine's life and career, *Serenade*, the first wholly original work begun after his emigration. In 1934 under the auspices of the newly created "Producing Company of the School of the American Ballet," the enterprise organized two performance engagements for these and other ballets: a semi-private outdoor event in June and a public engagement in Hartford in December. Official records of Balanchine's ballets and most histories of the enterprise construe these performances as previews held in advance of the company's official debut the following year in New York. But both of these engagements were significant events for internal stakeholders as well as external observers and were widely acknowledged as debuts of the organization itself and premiere performances of the individual ballets presented. Additionally, the June engagement at Woodlands, Edward Warburg's family estate in White Plains, New York, has come to loom large in the stories of *Serenade*. This ballet is universally acknowledged as Balanchine's first American ballet, and its debut performance at Woodlands has come to figure as a symbolic point of origin for the choreographer's new endeavors in the United States.

A more detailed examination of this first year of the organization's activity reveals the confusing and conflicting aesthetic and institutional priorities of the enterprise, which were reflected in a heterogeneous repertoire of new and revised ballets. Despite the best intentions of the key players, the first performance engagements by the company that would come to be known simply as the American Ballet were geared mostly toward an elite audience of Kirstein and Warburg's peers, who like them had been largely untouched by the financial downturn. Indeed, the majority of the first five ballets mounted by the company were neither obviously American nor especially calculated for mass appeal. For the most part they consisted of revivals of Balanchine's work for Les Ballets 1933, which had not even managed to capture the attention of their original audiences in Paris and London the summer before. Most striking is that during this first year, including at the much-mythologized Woodlands engagement, *Serenade* was by far one of the least significant works in the company's repertoire. This ballet received the smallest number of performances and the least amount of critical attention, and it was by no means hailed as a watershed moment in dance history as it is today. The eventual canonical status of *Serenade*, much like the future of the American Ballet and Balanchine's career as a choreographer, was anything but certain.

Balanchine wasted little time before setting some of his existing work on the students, and performance was evidently very much on his mind. Only three weeks after the school's opening, Kirstein recalled a "savage fight" between Balanchine and Dimitriev because the choreographer focused only on dancers from the Philadelphia school run by Catherine and Dorothie Littlefield, several of whom had been recruited to join the organization.[1] Balanchine was especially attentive to these experienced dancers—including rising star Holly Howard and Dorothie Littlefield herself—as he was evidently "desperate about not doing ballets this year, the first time in ten years he would be showing nothing in the spring."[2] That his and Kirstein's visions for the enterprise had been misaligned from the start was now becoming clearer, and knowing that his erstwhile colleagues and competitors were coming to his new home to perform for the public added to his frustration and urgency.[3] Balanchine began rehearsals of one of his existing works just a week after the school opened, teaching parts of *Errante*, which would not be performed by the company for well over a year, as part of its official New York debut in March 1935.[4]

Soon after, Balanchine turned to two other ballets that he had created for Les Ballets 1933, *Mozartiana* (to Tchaikovsky's Orchestral Suite No. 4) and *Les Songes* (with music by Darius Milhaud). Whether to alleviate his despair at not creating new work or to accommodate the character and talents of his new dancers, Balanchine made numerous changes and additions to these two ballets over rehearsals in the coming months. Beginning in mid-January and continuing into the middle of March, *Mozartiana* was rehearsed and modified, with Balanchine first creating new choreography for the final "Ave Verum" movement (Tchaikovsky's wordless setting of Mozart's motet). It featured the thirteen-year-old Marie-Jeanne Pelus "on her points—a living Maypole between 4 other girls who danced in bare feet"—a mirror-image of the later version of the ballet, in which four small girls frame an adult ballerina; and in the following weeks he reworked the "Gigue" movement.[5] As rehearsals progressed, Kirstein noted that Balanchine was "depressed at rehearsal that people don't show up, or get sick, or leave," a far cry from the regimented atmosphere in which he had been trained and that the idealistic organizers had first imagined for the enterprise.[6] Although the American Ballet would not tout *Mozartiana* as a premiere in its first performances, these observations suggest that if it was not remade entirely, then at the very least large sections were significantly reworked. Gisella Caccialanza, goddaughter and protégée of the legendary Italian pedagogue Enrico Cecchetti and an early soloist for the company, recalled that the ballet was "very classical, not so different from his classical steps today."[7] The Brooklyn-born Ruthanna Boris, who had received her first training at the Metropolitan Opera ballet school before joining the American Ballet, remembered it as "all very technically difficult and nice—a lovely score."[8] Boris said that parts of *Emeralds* (1967) reminded her of the now lost choreography: "lots of marvelous arms and beautiful pictures forming, a very delicate thing."[9]

While *Mozartiana* was in rehearsal, discussions began about reviving *Les Songes*—or as it would be known in its new American incarnation, *Dreams*—despite the lack of enthusiasm that had attended the work the previous summer. Although the décor and elaborate costumes for the ballet by André Derain had been brought over by Balanchine and Dimitriev, Milhaud's score was not used for the new production, according to Kirstein and others because it was not available for performance.[10] According to one account by Balanchine this was due to the fact that Milhaud could not be contacted.[11] This claim seems somewhat dubious given the composer's close working relationship with his publishers, his diligence as a correspondent, and his general eagerness to have his work performed in the United States at this time—and also, the score had been published the year of its premiere.[12] The more likely explanation for the abandonment of Milhaud's score for *Dreams* is that either Kirstein or Balanchine or both did not especially care for the music and instead simply wanted something new.

For the new score they approached Trenton native George Antheil, who had been introduced to Balanchine and Kirstein by Russian-born dancer Lisa Parnova in January 1934.[13] Antheil soon became a frequent visitor to the school—his apartment was just around the corner—and was recruited for several projects, both realized and unrealized, during the American Ballet's first two years.[14] Able to converse in French, Antheil and Balanchine developed a close personal bond, sharing a rebellious modernist sensibility and a more modest social status than Kirstein and Warburg.[15] The recruitment of Antheil in lieu of Milhaud might be seen as a way of giving the organization's repertory a modicum of American credibility. But the composer's own recollections suggest the exact opposite result. Despite the company's name, Antheil in his memoirs characterized the American Ballet's aesthetics as "pure Paris à la Russe" and that far from being eager for distinctively American music, Balanchine "was looking for an American ballet *sufficiently Parisian!*" and found what he was looking for in Antheil.[16]

While Antheil worked on the new score for *Dreams*, Balanchine in mid-March turned his attention to the first completely new work he would create in America, *Serenade*.[17] Ruthanna Boris recalled in her memoirs that Balanchine began the ballet several months after classes and rehearsals were under way and describes an atmosphere of excitement and anticipation among the dancers.[18] In an interview given later in life, dancer Annabelle Lyon, unlike Boris, does not recall the start of *Serenade* as a particularly special event: "I don't know whether *Serenade* was the first ballet he did for us or a ballet called *Reminiscence*," the latter not begun until 1935.[19] Only when reminded by her interlocutor that "legend" holds *Serenade* to be the first did Lyon admit that "it could be. It could very well be. So we started out with *Serenade*."[20] Kirstein's diary reports March 14 as the first day of rehearsal for *Serenade*, and that it was a moment of some import at least for Balanchine, who "said his head was a blank" and asked Kirstein to pray for him.[21] Similar to Kirstein's recollection of a prayer request, Boris's memories of the ballet also allude to a focused and somewhat spiritual frame of mind on the part of Balanchine, who at one point "appeared to be having a conversation with himself; his lips were moving but no sound came out."[22]

Kirstein noted at the time that Balanchine took great care in arranging the dancers for the start of the ballet, and that there was indeed something special about the opening of *Serenade* from this very first rehearsal, on a "nice sunny day," as Boris recalled. He lined up the dancers "according to their heights" beginning "slowly to compose a hymn to ward off the sun" (not "sin" as has been noted in previous accounts).[23] Boris provides greater detail on this initial process of arranging the dancers mentioned by Kirstein, noting how Balanchine brought each dancer out individually "in the manner of a cavalier," taking each woman's arm in his own as they were placed in the formation.[24] After all the dancers had been placed, they found themselves in an asymmetrical arrangement later described as an "orange grove" formation by Balanchine, evidently made necessary by the uneven number of dancers (seventeen) who were present in class when it was started. That this arrangement was wholly the result of happenstance is open to some debate. Asymmetrical arrangements of dancers had by this point become a hallmark of the "symphonic ballets" of Léonide Massine (discussed at greater length in Chapter 3), and immediately after the ballet's iconic opening, one dancer discreetly slips off stage so that the remaining sixteen dancers can arrange themselves in equally proportioned groups of four.

It is a widely held belief that *Serenade* was conceived of as a pedagogical exercise designed to teach the American Ballet's purportedly inexperienced dancers "how to be on the stage," as Balanchine himself would later relate. In fact, it was not necessarily inexperience that was the primary challenge facing the corps of the American Ballet, but rather the disparity of the styles in which its newly recruited dancers had been trained. Lyon, who had been a student of Fokine's, recalled how challenging it must have been for Balanchine in the early days of the enterprise not because of the dancers' complete lack of training, but rather because they all "came from different schools so there was a great variety of styles."[25] The functional origins of *Serenade* might thus be better understood not as a way of breaking in raw talent, as has been implied in some accounts, but rather as a means of homogenizing a disparate group of dancers, a quality for which it is indeed still prized today. Whether through the intercession of Tchaikovsky or thanks to Balanchine's practicality or both, the ballet progressed over its first week of rehearsal, and both Kirstein and even the less easily impressed Dimitriev saw the emerging choreography as something new and distinct. Kirstein saw a unique fusion of elements from earlier ballets, seeing "arms as in *Mozartiana* and groups from *Errante*" and also traces of *Cotillon*, albeit with "new uses of lines" and "new romance."[26] Dimitriev declared that the choreographer "has now hit his stride and style. For years he was doing trick stuff hoping for surprise; something no one had ever done before. Now it was pure Balanchine."[27]

While *Serenade* was in preparation, the de Basil company returned to New York from its triumphant cross-country touring, and a delegation from the American Ballet dutifully attended its performances to assess the competition. Kirstein was mostly unenthusiastic about the programs he attended, though he noted that Balanchine's *Cotillon* was a "most wonderful ballet and well received," and that Antheil was "extremely moved and inspired" by the work.[28] Even though Balanchine could exert no direct control over his ballet, after the performance he was consulted by members of the company about what might be adjusted.[29] The de Basil troupe made its own contribution to the success of its new competitor, as the experience of seeing *Cotillon* and *La Concurrence* is evidently what drew some students to the new enterprise in the first place.[30] "We were interested," Annabelle Lyon explained, when asked how she and other dancers first heard about the School of American Ballet, "because when we had gone to see the Ballets Russes, we particularly enjoyed Balanchine's ballets and were impressed with his works," which in contrast to Massine's ballets were "very creative, very fresh" and "created such an unusual atmosphere."[31]

During these initial months the dancers were not always just in class or rehearsal but were almost continually on display for visitors to the school. Guests noted in Kirstein's diary include his mother, Anne Lindbergh and her sister Constance Morrow, Nelson Rockefeller, Felix Warburg, and composer Nicholas Nabokov.[32] By the end of March with several ballets somewhat complete, there were "enormous crowds of people at rehearsal," to the displeasure of Dimitriev, who was "furious at the onrush."[33] In late April *Serenade* and *Mozartiana* "were danced before a large mob" of over fifty people, again incurring Dimitriev's ire, who declared "it would be the last open rehearsal for a long time as it wasted Balanchine's time."[34] This evidence indicates that by the end of May the dancers had in all likelihood been observed by a greater number of people in studio rehearsals than would attend their first official performance engagement in early June.

In the absence of any official artistic offerings to evaluate, debate continued in the press about the merits of the nascent enterprise, with performance figuring as a prominent aspect of its mission. Writing in the April 1934 issue of the *Dancing Times*, British ballet critic Arnold Haskell spoke approvingly of the collaboration of Kirstein and Balanchine, declaring that "no better person could have been found to harness the American point of view to the old tradition."[35] Less enthusiasm was apparent in the pages of the modern dance–oriented *Dance Observer*, whose inaugural February 1934 issue included an advertisement for the American Ballet's school.[36] This modest contribution to the journal earned the enterprise no special treatment, however, and if anything seems to have helped make the organization and Kirstein himself more of a lightning rod. The lead

FIGURE 2.1 Rehearsal at School of American Ballet, photographer and date unknown (likely 1930s) showing dancers as well as guest observers. George Balanchine Archive, MS Thr 411 (2470), Houghton Library, Harvard University.

editorial of its March issue took Kirstein to task for his critiques of modern dance and criticized his "persistence for the ballet," whose artificial and superficial practices should be discarded. "For the ballet is an inflexible set of movements," the editors explained, "which, when applied to any composition other than the rigidly formal sort, proves itself woefully, and at times ludicrously, inadequate."[37] In a subsequent editorial in May they took issue with the questionable claims of a Russian-led organization to have produced an authentically American ballet. The object of their ire was not the Kirstein-Balanchine enterprise, however, but rather the de Basil company, which had premiered Massine's much-touted American-themed *Union Pacific* in the course of its US tour.[38] The American Ballet had yet to produce anything that *Dance Observer* might critique as insufficiently American, although that would change by the end of the year.

_____

In an essay written later in life, Edward Warburg expressed bemused indifference about how the outdoor summertime performance by dancers from the School of American Ballet came to happen at Woodlands, his family's Westchester county estate near White Plains in early June 1934. "Suddenly it was decided," Warburg recalls, "that what *I* wanted more than anything else for my upcoming birthday was a performance by this company of ballet dancers."[39] The official occasion for the event aside, this engagement has come to function as a symbolic point of origin for Balanchine's American career, in particular for the "first in America" *Serenade*.[40] As noted above, *Serenade* was indeed the first entirely new ballet created by Balanchine, although the two other ballets performed at Woodlands— *Mozartiana* and *Dreams*—were to a certain degree quite new as well, having been reworked significantly in the preceding months, and with *Dreams* danced to an entirely new musical score.

Less than a month before the Woodlands engagement, it was not clear that any ballets, whether new or old, would be performed in June, and contrary to Warburg's recollections, Kirstein's diaries suggest that it was very much a decision in his partner's hands. The program for Woodlands remained in flux in the weeks prior to the event, with considerable disagreement among the four players about what should be presented. Even more troubling, Balanchine had expressed dissatisfaction with the entire repertoire and even ballet in general, declaring that "ballet, in the Diaghilev, Petipa idiom is dead" and that *Serenade, Mozartiana*, and *Dreams*, "all that with him is only commercial, of no interest," and instead he "must find new ideas."[41] In the end it was decided to present most but not all of *Dreams* and all of *Mozartiana*.[42] *Serenade* would round out the program since it could be mounted with minimal cost, though the question of its costumes would not be finalized until days before the performance.[43] John Martin characterized the event as a private engagement, clarifying that the "first public performances of the organization are planned for next season."[44]

Although the production values of the performance would be relatively simple, the larger setting of the Woodlands estate was anything but modest. Frieda and Felix Warburg's residence in White Plains sprawled over five hundred acres, at the time a relatively undeveloped area at considerable remove from the city.[45] In addition to the main house—a Tudor-style mansion with a large central tower and Gothic windows, reached by a mile-and-a-half long driveway—the estate boasted among other amenities a stable of thoroughbred horses and miles of bridle paths, a greenhouse that enclosed a tiled swimming pool with trapezes above the water, and a herd of prize-winning cows.[46] The Warburgs' city residence, a mansion at the corner of 92nd Street and Fifth Avenue that today houses the Jewish Museum, was built on a comparably spectacular scale.[47]

The day before the Saturday, June 9, 1934, performance, the weather was shaping up to be uncooperative, validating the decision to note on the invitation that in the case of rain the event would be postponed until the following evening.[48] Friday June 8 was a "good day for old clothes," according to *New York World-Telegram* reporter Helen Warden, who in response to steady downpours took the practical if unbecoming measure of donning an unflattering green poncho en route to the School of American Ballet.[49] According to Warden's column, seventy-five dancers were slated to board a bus out to Westchester the following afternoon to perform two ballets, *Serenade* and *Dreams*.[50] Kirstein's diaries provide more detail regarding the events of the weekend, reporting that by 3:00 PM on Friday the bus had already left for the evening's rehearsal at Woodlands, where rehearsals did not proceed smoothly.[51] No one greeted the delegation on their arrival at the estate, whose mansion had the "air of a castle deserted before the onslaught of invaders." Warburg was lecturing at the Westchester County Center about the Museum of Modern Art, and in the absence of any host, the house "was ransacked for overcoats, sweaters and bath-robes," in response to a cold turn in the weather. The proceedings got off to a rocky start with one of the "second-line dancers" hurting her foot and Gisella Caccialanza suffering an unexpected fall, while yet another dancer "was suspected to have female ills." The food that had been provided "was not nearly enough and very poor," and Balanchine was "furious," announcing that "afterwards he would ask Eddie to a Russian restaurant, and show him how one eats." The dancers were also displeased, "cold and peaked and hungry" such that Kirstein "feared a revolution." In the end, however, the dancers managed to get through all of the works and afterward Kirstein drove Balanchine and Dimitriev back to New York in his car, with Balanchine saying he was "pleased enough." When asked by Kirstein "who with us had talent," Dimitriev replied that his choices were (in order), Annabelle Lyon, Charles Laskey, Gisella Caccialanza, and, to Kirstein's surprise, Erick Hawkins.

The weather would not clear out in time for the Saturday show, and when everyone arrived to the estate to rehearse, a light rain had set in, costing an hour of preparation.[52] With some guests already arriving, a decision was initially made to cancel and reschedule for the next day as previously announced, but then the question arose as to what would happen if it rained on Sunday as well. The weather remained as ambivalent as the collective resolve to proceed or reschedule, with the "tarpaulin over the pianos and the stage taken off and put on three separate times." A "wholly indifferent" Balanchine left the scene entirely and "went off in his car to White

Plains to get some decent food." At one point the weather suddenly cleared and they scrambled to get things set, with Dimitriev searching "in vain" for Balanchine to rehearse *Mozartiana*, and Kirstein getting nervous and screaming at two of the boys to hurry up, for which Dimitriev upbraided him. Before a small audience with "little enthusiasm," *Mozartiana* was put on, although as soon as the stage had been reset for *Serenade*, "the rain set in in earnest" and the guests repaired to the house, and there was "great scandal of the Russians against Eddie who had not invited them in" to join the invited guests. Dinner for the performers had been set up in the garage, at which a "furious" Pierre Vladimirov, a renowned émigré dancer who had been recruited to the enterprise to augment the teaching faculty of the school, declared that "he had never yet eaten with the horses and didn't propose to now." Dimitriev similarly groused that "Eddie would learn better manners when it was here like it was now in Russia." Kirstein evidently mustered up a similar display of anger in solidarity, getting "as excited about the garage-dinner as I could for their satisfaction." It was subsequently reported in the press that guests would reconvene on Sunday "to witness the world premiere of two works," *Serenade* and *Dreams*.[53]

There was "a little sun" when Kirstein awoke Sunday morning, and despite lingering clouds the company "again completely embarked for White Plains, with an added cargo of husbands, mothers, friends." Upon arrival they rehearsed *Serenade* on a "sticky stage," and as they worked the weather continued to improve. It was decided to reorder the ballets—announced in the printed program as *Mozartiana, Serenade, Dreams*. Instead *Dreams* would be performed first, followed by *Serenade* and closing with *Mozartiana*.[54] *Dreams* was repositioned since there was consensus that it was "not yet a success," and rationalized the reshuffle to Antheil with the explanation that they wanted some of the ballet to be shown first in case rain showers again interfered. There was light drizzle throughout the performance, but they continued on, despite the fact that the piano keyboards became so wet that they were difficult to play. *Serenade* "looked very lovely," and *Mozartiana* "passed well," despite one of the dancers fainting at the end, which "spoiled the last group." Attendance was actually higher than the night before, and among those who returned were Nelson Rockefeller and Museum of Modern Art director Alfred Barr.

As a private event, the Woodlands engagement received only nominal coverage in the press and there were no official reviews of either evening. The *Times* reported briefly on the delayed "world premieres" of *Serenade* and *Dreams* as well as the reprise performance of *Mozartiana*.[55] The event merited several inches in Lucius Beebe's society column for the *New York*

Herald-Tribune, which covered the originally scheduled Saturday after-noon "safari" to the Warburg estate."[56] The fact that weather ended the show after *Mozartiana* "didn't tend to abate the smart art event," in part because for many of those gathered the highlight of the evening was as much the company as the performance itself. The "right gay gather-ing" included Gilbert Seldes, Chick Austin, Muriel Draper and her son Paul, as well "six candid camera practitioners." It was further noted that Felix Warburg, "affable and handsome in a military cloak over his din-ner clothes," regarded the proceedings with a somewhat startled look, but overall comported himself with his "accustomed *nonchaleur.*"[57] Beebe records that like his father, Edward Warburg "bore the rain and neces-sary postponement bravely," while Kirstein evidently "dripped gloom" and confirmed that the company and guests spent the rest of the evening in starkly different environs.[58] While the dancers "hung up their tights to dry in the Warburg furnace room," most of the guests "went off to the Westchester Embassy Club."[59]

Other surviving traces of the haphazard events reveal a charming infor-mality (or makeshift amateurism), such as the printed program's listing of Mozart and not Tchaikovsky as the composer of *Mozartiana*.[60] Several performance photos have survived from the rehearsals and performances, evidently the work of the some of the "practitioners" mentioned by Beebe. These photos attest to the minimalist production values of the engagement, which, according to a subsequent letter from Warburg to Jo Mielziner, did not impress the not so easily impressed elite attendees.[61] In this same let-ter, Warburg noted that the English language skills of the Russians were improving, which would hopefully lead to fewer misunderstandings, pre-sumably including any future conflicts over the ensemble's amenities.[62]

A month after Woodlands, a much graver challenge than weather or lan-guage barriers presented itself to the enterprise. In July during the school's summer break, Kirstein and Balanchine were driving to the home of cos-tume designer Aline Bernstein when suddenly Balanchine "gripped his left arm, became rigid and red" such that for a moment Kirstein "thought he was like Nijinsky, acting."[63] It soon became clear that it was not a joke but a serious medical incident, and Kirstein saw all of their efforts sud-denly coming to naught. "I thought he was dead or dying, or he would go insane," as Kirstein recalled of the violent episode, which was never conclusively diagnosed. Kirstein struggled to contain Balanchine, whose uncontrolled movements broke the car's hand brake while he was emitting "a ghastly groaning sputter."[64] With the help of onlookers Kirstein eventu-ally managed to get Balanchine to a nearby house; after a doctor arrived on the scene Balanchine suffered a second, slightly less severe attack. After this incident Kirstein recalled that Balanchine "could not speak nor know who I was. He could not see, I think. I tried to talk to him firmly thinking it was best; I couldn't believe he was really ill."[65]

Balanchine was taken to a nearby hospital and Kirstein called on him the next day. He was "sane, unparalyzed, but hiccoughing" and could not recall anything that had happened.[66] Cutting short a vacation at Lake George, Dimitriev and Vladimirov arrived the following day and speculated about various causes for the attack, including a lack of sex and mysterious injections he had purportedly received some time earlier.[67] A week later the doctors concluded that "the convulsions were largely toxemic and emotional" but that they had also found two active tuberculosis lesions, and prescribed four to eight weeks of rest.[68] Although Dimitriev assured him that they "can get on without Balanchine," Kirstein was "depressed and too bored and tired to be angry," consoling himself with the grim comfort that "a week ago tonight I thought Balanchine was dying next to me, and he is neither dead, insane nor paralyzed."[69] Kirstein's sister Mina speculated that the cause was related to Dimitriev's recent announcement to Balanchine that "there would be no ballets, just the School," news that was particularly hard on him since he "has no interest in the School, all he cares for is producing the ballets."[70] These concerns—over Balanchine's health, his opportunity to produce new work, and a possible causal relationship between the two—would loom large in the coming months and years.

The "Dance and Studio Notes" of the June–July 1934 issue of *Dance Observer* reported that the School of American Ballet was "busy hanging a veil of secrecy over its activities for next season."[71] "The only information available," the unsigned notice related, "is that it is planning for a long tour and a long New York season; that Antheil has composed the music for E. E. Cumming's [*sic*] version of *Uncle Tom's Cabin*," and with a flourish of sarcasm added that "Lincoln Kirstein is going to be a premier danseur."[72] Of these three items, only the first would come to fruition (and even then only partially), despite Kirstein's dogged but ultimately unsuccessful interest in producing the ballet *Tom*. For the time being, the school had many other issues to confront besides snarky gossip. After a summer break, it reopened on August 27, and although Balanchine seemed happy and healthy after a month of rest, the organization would immediately be plunged into intense discussions regarding its future, in particular how and when they should make a more official public performance debut.[73]

A year before, the enterprise had been focused on ensuring that its dancers would not be poached by commercial entertainment, but financial realities led them to reconsider this orthodox position. Balanchine had personally been approached with several offers of commercial work, including a new movie starring comedian Jimmy Savo (involving Antheil as well), and a new musical called *The Tricorne* by Arthur Schwartz and Howard Dietz.[74] Balanchine ultimately declined both offers and around the same time made clear to Kirstein what he was more interested in working on, that is, an ambitious original program to be performed at a house such as the Metropolitan Opera, to rival even the most ambitious undertakings of not just the de Basil troupe but the great Diaghilev himself: "Stravinsky, Hindemith, Kurt Weill; all new works; Braque, Tchelitchev, Picasso."[75] Virgil Thomson concurred with Balanchine, advising Kirstein that the school should "by no means do Broadway stuff," but should rather "start small and exclusive," and in two or three years "Broadway would catch up with it."[76] Although Balanchine continued to dream big, he and Kirstein would eventually settle on the goal of a more modest season of six ballets, most of which had already been produced or were already in preparation: *Mozartiana, Errante, Dreams, Serenade*, the new ballet *Touch Down* (eventually called *Alma Mater*), and another work to be determined.[77]

At the Woodlands performance in June, Chick Austin had extended an invitation for the troupe to perform in Hartford in advance of an appearance there by the de Basil troupe, an offer that the American Ballet accepted after several weeks of negotiations.[78] The company would appear from December 6 to December 8 and would perform two of the three ballets presented at Woodlands, *Mozartiana* and *Serenade*, while two other ballets would be entirely new, *Transcendence* and *Alma Mater*.[79] There was internal consensus that a program on this scale presented outside of New York would prepare the American Ballet for more extensive performance opportunities the following year and was preferable to the commercial offers that had come their way.[80] During negotiations with Austin, questions and concerns again rose about the small scale of the theater in Hartford, the same problems that had led the enterprise to abandon the organization as their intended home.[81]

Of the two new ballets, *Alma Mater* was longer in preparation and in its earliest conception was somewhat different in theme from its ultimate form. Over lunch in early February, Kirstein, Dimitriev, and Warburg discussed a "Rover Boy ballet in the spirit of *Barabau*."[82] An avowed fan of westerns and adventure films, Balanchine was much taken with the idea of a dance based on the popular American book series, in which a band of boys at a military academy get themselves into and out of sticky situations, and even proposed a teaser ending: "In the next book you will follow the Rover Boys on the Great Lakes."[83] Balanchine suggested Antheil for the music, and several days later Kirstein ran the concept by the composer, who "warmed up marvelously" to the idea and began improvising at the piano on "I've Been Working on the Railroad."[84] The next day Kirstein realized that he may have been too hasty in pitching the project to Antheil, and he and Balanchine paid the composer another visit, apparently to vet his music more thoroughly.

In the end, Antheil was denied the project owing to the preferences of Warburg—the author of the ballet's libretto as well as its principal patron— who thought the composer was too highbrow; Warburg decided to tap his cousin, Broadway composer Kay Swift, for the music.[85] Warburg also had an entirely different time period and concept in mind, initially wanting it to be reminiscent of the 1890s; ultimately the ballet would be set in the Roaring Twenties, more specifically in New Haven, Connecticut, on the day of the annual Harvard-Yale football game.[86] It would be two months before any of the music was ready, however, and in mid-April Kirstein, Warburg, Dimitriev, and Balanchine paid a visit to Swift's apartment to hear excerpts from the new ballet, at first called *Rah Rah*.[87] The waltz movement Swift played for them was "OK but nothing much" according to Kirstein, who was at least nominally more positive than Balanchine, who "did not care for the musical mood" and expressed misogynistic resignation at the results: "D'abords, elle est femme."[88] Balanchine offered Swift some suggestions and advice, telling her to ignore Warburg's libretto and "just write what she wanted, but not jazz; towards 1910–20, Rover Boys, college-annuals."[89]

By early May, Swift had made some progress, and Kirstein noted that the "collegiate" ballet was progressing, and by May 22 it was officially in rehearsal, with Balanchine starting on a "football-dance."[90] The second day of rehearsal found Kirstein cautiously optimistic, and even though the ballet made him "impatient," with its "football gestures, jazz, and a sweet enough entrance on a wheelless bicycle," and he again noted in a back-handed compliment that the score was better than anyone had anticipated.[91] Work on the ballet was subsequently put on hold in deference to the imminent Woodlands engagement, but rehearsals resumed immediately after on June 11, with the ballet having acquired a new working title, *Time Out*.[92] Perhaps sensing Balanchine's lack of enthusiasm for the project, Kirstein expressed his hope that the ballet "will sustain his interest until he can finish it."[93] The ballet would soon encounter more significant setbacks when

Swift's marriage to James Warburg broke down, owing to her affair with composer George Gershwin, who had initially been approached for the ballet commission and had recommended Swift instead.[94] Swift pleaded personal difficulties as the reason for her slow progress on the ballet, which had received yet another new title, *Touch Down*.[95] By October, the ballet acquired its fourth and final title, *Alma Mater*, and work continued on the music and dance until the Hartford performances.[96]

According to some sources, Balanchine's lack of enthusiasm for the score extended to the ballet as a whole, with Warburg especially disappointed that the choreographer had refused to attend an actual football game in order to understand the subject matter.[97] "The real puzzle," as Nancy Reynolds has written, was indeed "how Balanchine, recently arrived from life in Paris, Monte Carlo, Copenhagen, and Leningrad, had the vaguest idea what he was doing."[98] Ruthanna Boris recalls that if actual football had not informed the ballet, certain elements in the daily life of the school made their way into the work, at least in its opening scene. The work opened "with kids in the corps dressed in shorts, bush hats, little jackets, lying on the floor reading the funny papers," activities that Balanchine had observed in the studio.[99] Balanchine for his part later claimed that he had attended a football game, and that it wasn't so much different from the soccer he had once seen in England: "It's practically the same thing—well, that is, there's a ball and they're running."[100]

The second new ballet to be performed at Hartford was a little more than two months in preparation from initial conception to performance. While they were still negotiating the Hartford engagement, Kirstein and Balanchine discussed over lunch on September 28 the idea for a ballet to be called *Rhapsody*.[101] The day before, Balanchine had declared that he wanted to do something Austro-Hungarian on "the lives of Liszt and Paganini with a great Hungarian wedding at the end."[102] Back in April, Hungarian music had been used for the first character class given by Balanchine at the school. The "superb" exercises and Balanchine's own demonstrations had made quite an impression at the time: "So much stamping that our neighbors on the floor below came up to complain. Balanchine danced marvelously with terrific abandon; very broad; high clicks and big stamps, huge whirls."[103]

Kirstein quickly turned *Rhapsody* into a project of historically informed "period modernism,"[104] reading Sacheverell Sitwell's book on Liszt, surveying the composer's music (including the "Mephisto Waltz," which would feature prominently in the score) and even looking in vain for authentic Hungarian costumes.[105] Kirstein took Balanchine to a music store where he bought up their entire stock of Liszt piano music, and later at the school, Antheil, taking a break between film projects, explicitly invoked the precedent of Diaghilev's *Pulcinella*, saying that he wanted "to do for Liszt what Stravinsky did for Pergolesi," and would in fact end up as the arranger for the score.[106] By early October the ballet's music was in relatively good shape, and Balanchine and Kirstein had decided to approach Philadelphia artist Franklin Watkins for ideas on costumes and scenery. Photos of the Hartford engagement show that the set consisted of a somewhat abstract forest scene, while the costumes strove for a certain degree of ethnic authenticity, including elaborate headpieces for the women.[107] The score would ultimately comprise arrangements of Liszt's "Mephisto Waltz," "Ballade," and Hungarian Rhapsodies Nos. 10, 13, and 19.[108]

Balanchine began the ballet in mid-October, creating "a lovely beginning," while Kirstein was still in research mode, having found "a fine book of Hungarian folk-customs and costumes."[109] Work continued on the ballet with Balanchine arranging "semi-erotic groups" and a "spectacular and difficult adagio for [William] Dollar and Elise Reiman"; around this same time the work acquired its ultimate title, *Transcendence*.[110] In the meantime, Dimitriev provided critical feedback on Balanchine and Kirstein's efforts, pointing out the great expense of having the Liszt music completely orchestrated, complaining that there was "as yet, no dancing in it," and expressing frustration that Balanchine continued to treat the "personal, subjective" subject of love in this new ballet.[111] *Transcendence* bears a resemblance to several previous works, notably Bronislava Nijinska's *Le Bien Aimée*, created for the company of Ida Rubinstein in 1928.[112] In early 1932, Balanchine himself had choreographed a short dance for the play *Les Amours du Poète* about poet Henrich Heine's unrequited love for his cousin Amelie, inspired by and in part using the music of Robert Schumann's song cycle *Dichterliebe*.[113]

Repertoire was not the only item under negotiation around this time, as the underlying organizational structure of the enterprise was also being reconfigured. Although known today as the "School of American Ballet," the organization's initial name was the "School of the American Ballet," a small but important distinction since the school and its related performing company would operate in a close and often contentious relationship for the next five years. The official "Producing Company of the School of American Ballet," as the performers would be billed in Hartford, was first organized in October 1934.[114] All of the four key players in the enterprise were initial shareholders in this company (as they were in the school), and although the specific duties and responsibilities of each with respect to the school and company would remain somewhat fluid, generally speaking, Warburg and Balanchine would focus more on the company side, while Kirstein and Dimitriev would assume more responsibility for the school. An article written by Warburg in January 1937 for *Dance* magazine articulated the rationale for the producing company as a complementary adjunct of the school, writing that "a school can lay the grammatical foundation and physical discipline necessary for ballet production" but "only the stage can teach a dancer projection, presence and the coordination of ensemble work."[115] In other words, Warburg repositioned the performance arm of the enterprise as equally educational and important for the success of the school. Later in life, Kirstein would posit a more candid explanation for this division of labor, credited to Dimitriev's savvy. "Whatever a school cost," Kirstein wrote in *Thirty Years*, Dimitriev knew that "a company would cost more, and Eddie's father seemed a more solid resource than mine."[116]

The Hartford engagement in December was regarded as anything but unofficial and constituted a very public debut for the company, covered in the regional and national press, and the organizers were eager to tout the newness of their offerings. A press release announced the December 6 show as the "first public performance" of the American Ballet and stressed the novelty of the entire program, saying that all four ballets presented are "new to this country" and that of the four "three will be world premieres" (with no mention of the Woodlands performances).[117] Advertisements for the engagement touted the "world premiere" of "3 new ballets," and a photo of dancers Holly Howard and Charles Laskey rehearsing for the "American premiere" of *Mozartiana* appeared in the *Washington Post* and *Los Angeles Times*.[118] Warburg is quoted in one report saying that although the company had "a little try-out of some of the ballets last spring," the Hartford performances were "our first major effort."[119]

The organizers also endeavored to build up the native credentials of the organization, even though only one ballet, *Alma Mater*, had a literal American theme. *Mozartiana* is described in previews as "the only ballet on the program that has been produced before" and as the only "wholly foreign" work on the program, since all of its collaborators, from choreographer to décor, were non-Americans.[120] For the other ballets, and not just *Alma Mater*, as much as possible was made of the participation of American artists despite the European character of the repertoire as a whole. One preview touted the fact that three ballets had "native settings," a reference not to their subject matter but rather to the three American artists who had contributed sets and costumes: cartoonist John Held Jr.

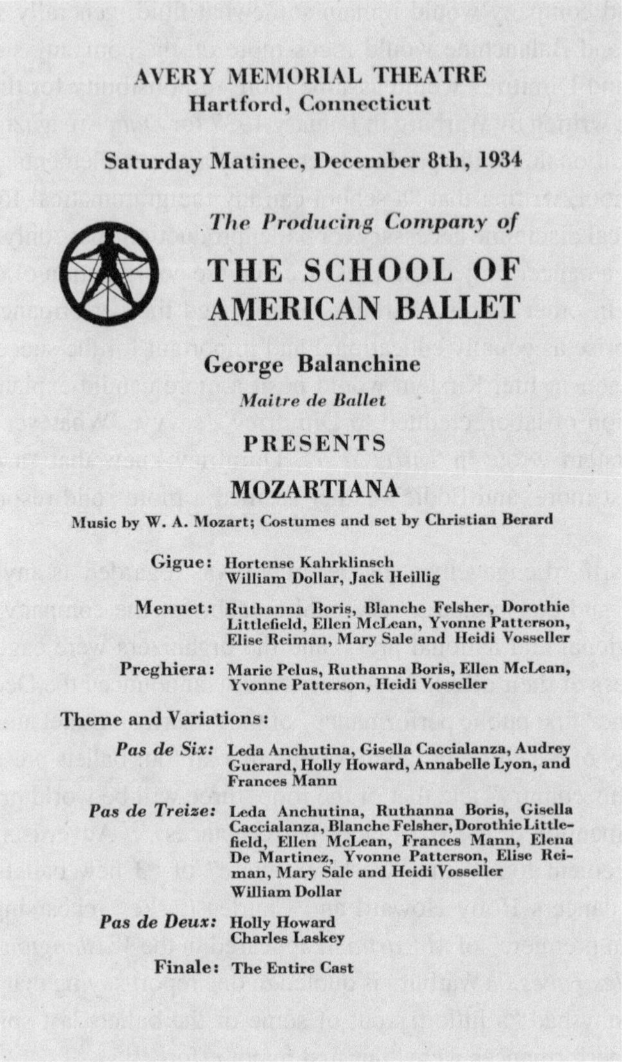

AVERY MEMORIAL THEATRE
Hartford, Connecticut

Saturday Matinee, December 8th, 1934

The Producing Company of

THE SCHOOL OF AMERICAN BALLET

George Balanchine
Maitre de Ballet

PRESENTS

MOZARTIANA

Music by W. A. Mozart; Costumes and set by Christian Berard

Gigue: Hortense Kahrklinsch, William Dollar, Jack Heillig

Menuet: Ruthanna Boris, Blanche Felsher, Dorothie Littlefield, Ellen McLean, Yvonne Patterson, Elise Reiman, Mary Sale and Heidi Vosseller

Preghiera: Marie Pelus, Ruthanna Boris, Ellen McLean, Yvonne Patterson, Heidi Vosseller

Theme and Variations:

Pas de Six: Leda Anchutina, Gisella Caccialanza, Audrey Guerard, Holly Howard, Annabelle Lyon, and Frances Mann

Pas de Treize: Leda Anchutina, Ruthanna Boris, Gisella Caccialanza, Blanche Felsher, Dorothie Littlefield, Ellen McLean, Frances Mann, Elena De Martinez, Yvonne Patterson, Elise Reiman, Mary Sale and Heidi Vosseller
William Dollar

Pas de Deux: Holly Howard, Charles Laskey

Finale: The Entire Cast

FIGURE 2.2 First page of program for December 1934 Hartford engagement of the Producing Company of the School of American Ballet. Erick Hawkins Collection, Library of Congress.

for *Alma Mater*, Franklin Watkins for *Transcendence*, and William Okie for *Serenade*.[121] Although Antheil's *Dreams* was not on the program in Hartford, the composer was still prominently in the mix, touted as having provided the arrangements for *Transcendence* and also a new setting of *Serenade* (not ultimately performed).[122] The organizers wanted to make as much of all four ballets as possible, but in their press release they placed the greatest emphasis on *Alma Mater*; it had an indisputably American score by Swift and an Ivy League setting imaginatively realized by Held, complete with 1920s fashions such as raccoon coats and flapper dresses, the number "which the young impresarios think is going to make the biggest hit," as one preview put it.[123]

The performances were also an occasion for Balanchine to make some of his earliest published comments in the press about his opinions regarding the potential of ballet in America, in particular regarding the physical aptitude of American women. Balanchine maintained that since his arrival he has been able "to analyze and define more clearly the qualities that make the American girl the ideal ballet material."[124] "The American girl," Balanchine is quoted as saying, "is '*mieux construit*,' or, as you would say, better built, than girls of other countries." This quality was due "to the freedom allowed American women and to the eager way these girls as well as their brothers enjoy athletics from childhood on." The American girl "finds greater zest in her sports and athletics because they are not so much a matter of regimentation but enjoyment and freedom," and she "enters into them with high spirits and gets a kick out of them," while at the same time she "retains her femininity—most important to a ballet dancer." To what extent Balanchine can be granted sole authorship of such remarks is debatable; considering his lack of proficiency in English at the time, there was probably a ghostwriter. However, such remarks did circulate under his name and constitute important evidence of his emergent views on American dancers.[125]

Whether by design or on its merits, *Alma Mater* was indeed the hit of the Hartford engagement. "Coming in for chief acclaim was *Alma Mater*," as the *Christian Science Monitor* put it, drawing "roars of laughter, shouts, and cheers" from the crowd.[126] Other reviews describe "laughter and cheers" from the audience and praised the "hilarious pantomime and character dancing."[127] The *Washington Post* called all three new works "fresh evocations" and proof that ballet is indeed "a completely articulated art form capable of weaving a vital and original pattern from the shuttle of contemporary America," but the "music, book, sets, costume and treatment" of *Alma Mater* were "so new as to be in the very mood of the future."[128] Impressions of the other ballets were scant but generally positive. To *Mozartiana* Balanchine had brought "an elegance, a courtliness, a simplicity and joyousness drawn not only from Mozart but from the times as well," asserted T. H. Parker in the *Hartford Courant*.[129] Although *Transcendence* was evidently created "with their limitations in mind," the dancers nevertheless "brought it precision, fluency, fine moods and fine dancing by principals and by corps."[130] But despite its appealing ethos and crowd-pleasing charm, *Alma Mater* also came in for criticism, to the chagrin of the organizers, and for some it did not necessarily pass muster as either "American" or a "ballet." "I doubt whether it can be called 'an American ballet,'" wrote Parker, "and I think it must eventually be relegated to the category known in professional circles as 'diverts.'"[131] Previews of the Hartford engagement had surmised as much and averred that ballet "cannot, even in the form Diaghilev gave it, strike roots in every national soil."[132]

The opening night show on Thursday was an especially festive occasion thanks to the attendance of "notables from the worlds of music, art and the theater, and of social eminences from all parts of the country," including George Gershwin, A. Conger Goodyear, Tod (Mrs. Nelson) Rockefeller, Kirk and Constance Askew (in whose London home Balanchine and Kirstein had first spoken the previous year), Salvador Dalí and his wife, as well as members of the Warburg and Kirstein families.[133] (Kay Swift was not among them, having gone to Reno, Nevada, to establish residency for her divorce from James Warburg.)[134] The party had begun for many of these audience members earlier in the evening at Grand Central Station, where a specially commissioned Pullman railcar whisked them directly from New York to Hartford, with both wardrobe facilities and refreshments on board and Gershwin playing host.[135] As had been the case at Woodlands six months earlier, for this audience the ballet was not necessarily the main attraction of the evening. Lucius Beebe in the *Herald-Tribune* reports that a "tidal wave of sables began engulfing the Avery Memorial Theater promptly three quarters of an hour after curtain time"; and of the two staircases leading to the theater, "the entire assembled chivalry surged down one of them—the one where the photographers were stationed."[136] During the first intermission, talk in the lobby did not center on the performance but was rather given over to the mission of securing an invitation to the party afterward.[137] Accordingly, the second intermission was "devoted to the business of securing transportation" to the party, while the hosts themselves "telephoned home to put more beer on ice and get the gardener into a waiter's suit" in anticipation of the onrush.[138]

Such ostentation did not sit well with John Martin, who in lieu of a review included an open letter to the American Ballet in his Sunday dance column of December 16. Martin's "words of welcome and of warning" enumerated three categories of error to which projects such as the American Ballet were prone, namely "glamour, snobbery, and provincialism."[139] "The accounts of your Hartford debut," he noted with concern, "dealt considerably more with the ermine and diamonds on the near side of the footlights than with the accomplishments over which you have labored devotedly for a year or more." While Martin added that "no one who has followed your organization from the beginning will believe for a moment that you are aiming merely to please a fashionable audience," the organizers were nevertheless in a position where they would need to make their true intentions clear. "The bravos of the comparatively small company of the ermine-clad are transitory," and if the enterprise truly wished to be successful in the long term it should instead seek to reach a broader and less exclusive audience.[140] Although Kirstein would subsequently cross swords with Martin, he evidently did not take issue with these particular criticisms, making note in his diary of the "excellent open letter to the American Ballet by John Martin" the day the column was published.[141] That the cultivation of a high society ethos had been driven more by Warburg is suggested by Kirstein's declaration the following day of a "campaign against Warburg" to isolate him from Balanchine and Dimitriev and thus gain more control over the future direction of the organization.[142] Kirstein's father Louis, whose money was also helping support the entire operation also concurred with the critic's observations and did not evidently take any offense. "I think it is by far the best article I have seen on the subject," he wrote to his son the day after the open letter appeared.[143]

If the organizers had done much to tout their trio of world premieres, in the end, they would present only two of the three new works. *Serenade*, scheduled for the final Saturday evening performance, was in the end scrapped in favor of another performance of *Mozartiana*.[144] It was not the readiness of the dancing but rather the sets and the suitability of the ballet to the space that occasioned the replacement. Kirstein's diary records that after the opening night performance, he took off his tailcoat and joined the team that worked until 2:30 AM "trying to put up Okie's set for *Serenade*, which had to be done if we were to rehearse tomorrow morning, the last chance we would get."[145] One preview article on the engagement described Okie's staging of the ballet as "treating the stage picture as a plastic space by the use of a large pendant sculptural shell."[146] This central feature was evidently one of the chief challenges with the set—a rendering of the design has been located in the holdings of the Museum of Modern Art—with Kirstein recalling that the "big spiral looked like hell but we finally got it into some kind of shape."[147] Despite their heroic efforts, the rehearsal the next morning produced "dubious effects" since the stage was in fact "too small for this ballet."[148] After sleeping late Saturday morning, Kirstein found that the ballet would in fact be scrapped completely, owing to the stage problems and issues with the costumes, since it "would ruin an otherwise good ballet by getting it set off on the wrong foot."[149] Thus in the end Balanchine's "first ballet in America" was not presented at any of the company's first four public performances.[150] Even without all of its premieres, the Hartford engagement helped Warburg, Kirstein, and the American Ballet make up with Chick Austin for the failed launch one year earlier. And the American Ballet would return to New York to regroup for more challenges in the coming year.

CHAPTER 3 | 1934–1935

BY THE END of 1934, the company that would come to be known as the American Ballet had premiered several new and revised ballets on two distinct occasions; however, its organizational debut is nevertheless regarded as its March 1935 engagement at the Adelphi Theater in New York City, from which the premieres of Balanchine's early American repertoire are officially dated. The Adelphi performances have also served as a focal point for evaluating the critical reception of the American Ballet's repertoire and Balanchine's choreographic style and aesthetic priorities. Three years after the fact, Lincoln Kirstein wrote in *Blast at Ballet* that the Adelphi engagement "pleased many people and disappointed others," most notably *New York Times* critic John Martin.[1] Subsequent accounts of the American Ballet's debut have focused almost exclusively on Martin's alleged bias against anything that Balanchine and his new company would undertake. Indeed, in Balanchine's biographies Martin is caricatured as either a modern dance partisan or an obstreperous heretic (or both) who would only years later undergo a Damascene conversion to the cause.[2]

A more expansive view of the American Ballet's Adelphi debut provides a different perspective on this formative moment in Balanchine and Kirstein's enterprise. While Balanchine is today regarded as one of the twentieth century's most important exponents of neoclassicism, his style in the early 1930s was widely viewed as idiosyncratic, experimental, and "personal," what we might term "modernist" in its overall character. Balanchine's early work for the American Ballet represented not a clean break with his previous activities but rather a continuation of his modernist choreographic experimentalism. This style ran against the grain of prevailing artistic trends, with composers including Sergei Prokofiev and Aaron Copland promoting their respective beliefs in "new simplicity" and "imposed simplicity" in music, and choreographers such as Martha

Graham and Doris Humphrey advocating directness and clarity of expression in modern dance.[3] At the same time, Balanchine was not regarded as the most significant exponent of innovation in ballet, with his public profile substantially eclipsed by the renown of the star and lead choreographer of de Basil's Ballet Russe, Léonide Massine. Balanchine's early American ballets—most notably *Serenade*—were keenly attuned to contemporary trends in ballet composition, in particular the genre of "symphonic ballet" recently invented by Massine.

Balanchine's puzzling aesthetic priorities were of concern not just to critics and the press; they also occasioned a prolonged period of institutional turmoil at the School of American Ballet. Among his staunchest critics was his longtime partner and friend Dimitriev, who questioned the governing aesthetics of the American Ballet's early repertoire and became increasingly frustrated with Balanchine's artistic leadership. In contrasting ways, the two ballets added to the repertoire for the Adelphi premiere—*Errante* (originally mounted by Les Ballets 1933) and *Reminiscence* (a newly conceived suite of classical-style divertissements)—exemplified the competing aesthetic visions for the company. Questions of aesthetics aside, the Adelphi engagement was also hampered by Balanchine's continued ill health and further compromised by shaky management on the part of Warburg and his team of managers.

The character and reception of the American Ballet's early repertoire were shaped not only by Balanchine's unique style but also by wider trends in ballet performance in the early 1930s. As noted previously, many ballets of Balanchine's from the late 1920s and early 1930s preceded and followed him across the Atlantic, presented by artists and organizations without his direct oversight or involvement. In the estimation of most American critics these works revealed him as an experimental modernist with a penchant for the idiosyncratic and bizarre. "The episode had a modernistic background," noted a review in *Musical America* of Serge Lifar's 1933 performances of *La Chatte*, "and the assistance of a group of young men, whose antics, clever in design and acrobatics as they were, did not shed much light on the story."[4] The *Christian Science Monitor* glossed *La Concurrence*, as performed by the de Basil troupe in December 1933, as "a farce in a street and shop window setting, amusingly realistic if conventionally satirical."[5] John Martin approvingly described this same ballet as "extraordinarily witty and ingenious," even if its story of the competition of tailors for customers had "neither line nor logic."[6] Reviewing *Cotillon*, another work in the repertoire of the Ballet Russe, Martin described the ballet as quintessentially Balanchine, insofar as it was "like Gertrude Stein's opera libretto [for *Four Saints in Three Acts*], apparently about nothing at all, yet in performance it achieves a certain mysterious meaning," and in it Balanchine has shown that "for him experimentation has no terrors."[7] A year later Martin was still very much taken with the "brilliant" *Cotillon*, calling it a "gem among modern ballets."[8]

While Balanchine was still grounded in experimental modes, in the early 1930s "pure dance" had acquired a new champion in Léonide Massine. Massine was hailed as a prodigal son returned home, having abjured the wild experiments of his youth to find "a more human and natural conception of the dance" and had "enriched the classic ballet with all that it could assimilate of rhythm, plasticity, acrobatics and the rest."[9] In other words, Massine was praised for having left behind the overtly experimental mode in which Balanchine was still active in pursuit of a purer and cleaner idiom of ballet. Other critics similarly noted that the superiority of the de Basil troupe derived not just from their more seasoned roster of dancers but from "the timely decision taken by Massine, its ballet master, to present works in which the protagonists really *dance*."[10]

Massine's renewed commitment to pure dance was most evident in a new genre called "symphonic ballet," which offered choreographic interpretations of major orchestral works by Beethoven, Brahms, and Tchaikovsky. This development was not entirely without precedent; in previous decades, Isadora Duncan, Ruth St. Denis, and Michel Fokine had each explored strategies for making dances to "absolute music" not originally composed for choreographic purposes. Today such a practice seems wholly unremarkable, so common is the adaptation of music of all sorts for choreography without regard to the original circumstances of its composition. But Massine's symphonic ballets were regarded as a distinct innovation and provocation. Skeptics argued that these canonical musical works were sufficient in and of themselves and were too intellectually complex to be visualized or otherwise embodied in choreography. The proponents of the new genre, as dance scholar Stephanie Jordan explains, held that symphonic ballet would not only help bring this significant music to new audiences but additionally that "its large-scale organicism was an important advantage for ballet, helping to unify the form of the choreography, and providing a model for structuring plotless dance over a broad time span."[11]

Massine's first symphonic ballet had premiered during the busy 1933 summer season in Paris and London, a setting of Tchaikovsky's Fifth

Symphony called *Les Présages*, or "The Fates." This ballet was hailed as the "piéce de résistance" of the de Basil troupe's offerings and helped cement Massine's status as the leading exponent of balletic innovation.[12] In an article for *Dance* magazine, critic Anatole Chujoy (an early historian and close associate of Balanchine and Kirstein's enterprise) explained how through this new genre Massine has "stood by the underlying principles of the classic tradition" and had shepherded ballet "through a period of decadence without losing the thread of its past."[13] "Up to now," as Chujoy similarly concludes at the end of his short monograph on *The Symphonic Ballet*, "the history of modern ballet was divided into two periods: pre-Fokine and Fokine. Now we have to add another period—Massine."[14] Notably, Chujoy's rhetoric in praise of Massine seems to have been lifted verbatim from accounts of ballet history that credit Balanchine alone with the reinvention of ballet in a modern idiom. And indeed, thanks to the ultimate success of both men's "symphonic ballets," which at the time merited a special label, we are today able to enjoy such works (notably *Serenade*) as simply "ballets." But if ballet history today might easily draw a direct line from Marius Petipa to Michel Fokine to Balanchine, in the 1930s credit for preserving ballet was initially bestowed almost exclusively upon Massine and his company of dancers, against whom Balanchine and Kirstein would implicitly and explicitly position their own efforts to invent a new "American" ballet.

In late 1934 and early 1935, any excitement following the Hartford performances quickly faded as the American Ballet regrouped to consider its next steps. In a postmortem talk, Warburg, Dimitriev, and Kirstein resolved that the "disorganization must cease" and the "amateurish elements in the Company must be weeded out."[15] These discussions soon evolved in the first months of 1935 into an increasingly acrimonious feud between Balanchine and his erstwhile partner Vladimir Dimitriev. On the surface the conflict appears to be a petty turf war fomented by Dimitriev—neither as famous as Balanchine nor as rich as Kirstein, much less Warburg—and was no doubt exacerbated by the amateurism that characterized the leadership of the school and company.[16] Kirstein's diaries suggest that Dimitriev's ultimate motivation in fomenting dissent was a desire for a more prominent role in the enterprise. Whatever his motive or desired endgame, Dimitriev's complaints centered on three ongoing issues with Balanchine—his artistic leadership, pedagogical disposition, and choreographic priorities—all of which resonate closely with contemporary accounts of Balanchine's work in the studio and on stage.

Dimitriev's frustrations centered first and foremost on Balanchine's artistic leadership. During the run-up to Hartford he had lamented that Balanchine "has no boss" and "no painter to jump on him, nor any Diaghilev in control."[17] Kirstein for his part held that the issue was much larger, since the company's artistic planning had been heretofore "based haphazardly on the Diaghilev formula," and they instead should formulate a more deliberate plan for their future endeavors. Balanchine only stiffened in response and said "he could not be nailed down with any definite plan" and in a nod to his more renowned competitor added that "only Massine could work like that." In response, Dimitriev dryly remarked that "for ten years [Balanchine] had always someone over him."

Also at issue was the school's pedagogical profile. A week after the Hartford engagement, Dimitriev held forth in a long conversation (not including Balanchine) about how unnecessary it was to study classical technique in order to perform Balanchine's work, and that instead they should teach only "solfeggio, music, plastic, and pantomime" in accord with the modernist estimations of Balanchine's style noted above.[18] Kirstein stressed the continued importance of the *danse d'école*, maintaining that Balanchine "had invented and developed classical style without which one could not dance *Mozartiana* or *Serenade* or *Transcendence*."[19] These debates carried over into the classroom, with several sources suggesting that Balanchine's modernist disposition did not confine itself to his work for the stage. Annabelle Lyon recalls Balanchine's classes as more unconventional than those taught by Pierre Vladimirov, the Petersburg émigré who was recruited to join the faculty of the school soon after it opened. Vladimirov's exercises "were to be expected. There was nothing unusual in them. They were beautifully put together and the movement flowed. And they felt right for the body to do."[20] By contrast, Balanchine's classes were distinct owing to their "rhythm" and "change of direction." Lyon notes that the dancers received considerably more instruction from Vladimirov, and on occasions when Balanchine did lead class, the exercises "would get a little trickier as far as the music was concerned" and he gave the dancers "more small movement; more small footwork." Lyon recalls that center work was "unusual" and "more creative in kind of tricky ways." Kirstein's diaries characterize Balanchine's classes in similar terms, describing one morning session in October 1934 as "very hard" and "tricky in time," and that he "would repeat each exercise until they had finally got it."[21] In late January, Kirstein noted a similar impression of

Balanchine's class, describing it as "too difficult musically" and "all too fanciful in the exercises."[22] It was again evident that Balanchine "doesn't like to teach" and instead "wants to compose all the time, even in class."[23]

Dimitriev also expressed concerns about Balanchine's choreography itself, seeing his new work trending unfavorably in an experimental direction or otherwise lacking vision. When *Alma Mater* had been in rehearsal in June, Dimitriev dismissed it as "too much like an old movie," which would be acceptable if it were being consciously created as such, but in fact Balanchine was merely repeating "the same tricks again and again."[24] In his memoirs, Edward Warburg recalled with bemused indifference that for this purportedly "American" work, Balanchine recycled movements from his work for Diaghilev, specifically that he "merely reshaped the standard sight gags used in ballets such as *Boutique Fantastique* [*sic*] to get a laugh."[25] As the program for Hartford was coming together with the addition of the Lisztian *Transcendence*, Dimitriev again expressed his displeasure, complaining "that there was no dancing in our repertory only *plastique* and mime and now this Hungarian thing."[26]

Although the school and company had been organized as separate corporate entities, all four players owned stock in both, despite the fact that in practice Warburg and Balanchine took a more active role in the company while Kirstein and Dimitriev oversaw the school. The entities were understood to work as complementary adjuncts of one another, and the conflict between Balanchine and Dimitriev threatened to upset this delicate balance of power, with Kirstein beginning to worry about a separation of the company and school.[27] Soon after the Hartford performance, Kirstein had a conversation with Warburg and his newly engaged business manager George "Jack" Birse about Dimitriev, during which they made it clear that they wanted to run the company on their own.[28] In fact, by late December, this institutional drift was already complete, with Kirstein noting that Warburg had no interest in the school and would much rather just "go ahead and put on Ballets Balanchine."[29] Echoing concerns already voiced by the critics—and anticipating the reception of the company's Adelphi debut—Dimitriev declared that everything presented thus far was "not the American Ballet we had dreamed of but the Ballets 1935 of George Balanchine."[30]

The discord would continue for the next two months without a definitive resolution, with Kirstein, Warburg, and the students often caught in the middle. In early January Kirstein heard a "disagreeable story" of a rehearsal of *Serenade*, during which Balanchine had "got into one of those repetitious sadistic things he sometimes can't pull himself out of," making the dancers "repeat the same step for an hour" and saying that "if they were tired they could go home," whereupon he himself abruptly walked out.[31] Echoing Lyon's recollections, dancer Charles Laskey complained to Kirstein that Balanchine's classes "were lax, had no snap, were too involved, not enough technique in them," and was told by Kirstein to report the news to Dimitriev as "more corroboration."[32] By mid-February the separation of the school and company was evidently regarded to be official enough that Kirstein informed John Martin of the new division of responsibilities at a lunch meeting, which the critic subsequently reported in a preview article on the Adelphi engagement.[33] In the end, the company's New York debut in March 1935 would bring an end to the worst of the hostilities, with everyone coming together of necessity, although many elements of the conflict would remain unresolved off- and onstage.·

Amid these discussions, preparations continued for the company's official debut engagement, which would feature a repertoire of six ballets. Four of these had already been performed at Woodlands and Hartford: *Serenade, Dreams, Alma Mater*, and *Transcendence*, and the final two were a mix of old and new. Again reaching back into the repertory of Les Ballets 1933, the company remounted *Errante* (set to Schubert's *Wanderer* Fantasy), in part owing to the presence in New York of its designer, Pavel Tchelitchev, and the availability of Tamara Geva (Balanchine's former wife) to star in the ballet. Rounding out the program was *Reminiscence*, a showpiece of classical technique newly created by Balanchine to music by Benjamin Godard that would feature the American dancer Paul Haakon as a guest artist. *Mozartiana* was not performed at the Adelphi, but remained under discussion during the planning phases and was even included in the souvenir program.[34]

Errante had been under discussion as a possible addition to the repertory during preparations for Hartford over the summer, and in the absence of Kay Swift's completed score for *Alma Mater* it received additional attention.[35] But ultimately the consensus was that the work would be both expensive to mount and difficult to dance.[36] When planning for the Adelphi season began, Balanchine was insistent on including the work, saying that it was the perfect thing to round out their programming.[37] Kirstein agreed but was concerned about the cost, but happily the next day Warburg was in a generous state of mind and said that they should move forward with *Errante* starring Geva, in lieu of *Mozartiana*.[38] The ballet did not get an official green light until two weeks later, however, when Kirstein recorded

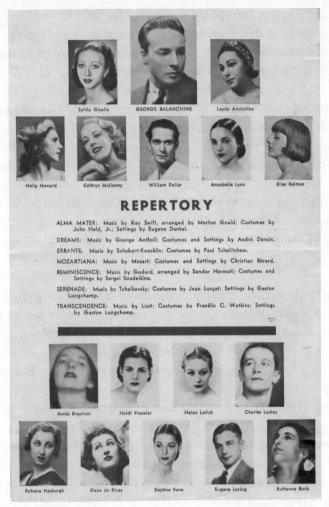

FIGURE 3.1 Company roster and repertoire list for American Ballet, from promotional flier for Adelphi Theatre engagement, 1935. Yvonne Patterson–William Dollar Papers, Jerome Robbins Dance Division, New York Public Library.

that Warburg and Balanchine over dinner "got drunk and ate hugely and as a result decided to do *Errante* which is how these things are accomplished," and the very next day Geva was officially signed on and in rehearsal.[39] Although Geva's first rehearsals boded well, Tchelitchev himself voiced doubts about the ballet, calling it a "revue fantastique pour les gens riches."[40]

The new ballet, *Reminiscence*, a showcase of Petersburg classicism, had perhaps its earliest origins on, ironically, July 4, 1934. On a walk with Kirstein at Ashfield, his family's country estate, Balanchine pitched a ballet

called *Pas Classique* to be set to music by eighteenth-century English composer William Boyce to be arranged by Constant Lambert.[41] No immediate
action was taken toward realizing the work, and in the meantime Kirstein
was occupied with several other projects, including *Tom*, a treatment of
Uncle Tom's Cabin with a libretto by e. e. cummings. Kirstein later tried
to sell Balanchine on another new ballet, *Le Bon Guerre*, "both divertissement but something without *L'Amour* as the subject-matter."[42] "L'homme
est une insecte sexuelle; everything is sex," Balanchine replied, to which
Kirstein said he "was tired of *L'amour sexuelle fantastique*."[43] Balanchine
clarified that "the act of love itself was nothing; it was the imagination
and perversity clothing it that was exciting."[44] Despite Kirstein's misgivings, this theme of a man (often an artist) in pursuit of an elusive woman
would manifest itself in many ballets created by Balanchine in the Adelphi
season and in coming years. Eventually Balanchine agreed to a more classically oriented ballet, and Kirstein hit on the compromise of using music
by Benjamin Godard.[45] Balanchine quickly had the ballet fully mapped
out, with the music selected and numbers planned for each dancer.[46]
Rehearsals began soon after, with Balanchine composing variations for
Holly Howard, whom he had been dating according to Kirstein, and
another "brilliant" dance for Dorothie Littlefield "full of Petipa tricks."[47]
By the end of January the title *Reminiscence* had been proposed, prompt-
ing a soul-searching comment that he was "upset from the Marxian angle"
about the apolitical bent of the company's ballets: "Dreams, Serenade, The
Wanderer, Transcendence, Reminiscence—but I hope it's the dancing that
counts."[48] The title was not definitively settled upon at this time however,
and some advance press on the Adelphi engagement would refer to the
ballet simply as *Variation*.[49]

In the midst of these preparations, the American Ballet had another
opportunity to try out some of their already completed work outside of
New York at performances on February 7 and 8 at Bryn Mawr, the private women's college on Philadelphia's Main Line.[50] The engagement
had been arranged by Warburg, who had briefly taught at the college,
and was part of larger festivities celebrating the institution's fiftieth
anniversary, with the proceeds from the shows benefiting a special
fund.[51] Had Warburg and his business manager done an honest assessment during their advance visit they might have canceled the engagement or at least insisted on another venue, since Goodhart Hall proved
uncongenial for ballet. Called down to assist with the performance at
the last minute, even the inexperienced Kirstein immediately grasped
that the hall was "pure gothic and couldn't have been maliciously

contrived worse for any sort of spectacle."[52] The company's program, consisting of *Serenade, Alma Mater*, and *Transcendence* was less than well executed in its first Thursday night performance.[53] According to Kirstein, who sat with Agnes de Mille in the audience, the performance was "even worse than I feared," owing to an array of challenges.[54] *Serenade* apparently fell apart owing to the last-minute withdrawal of Dorothie Littlefield from the ballet, after her mother had placed an angry phone call to Warburg insisting that her daughter not be made to dance in the corps.[55] *Alma Mater* fared better, while *Transcendence* was difficult to see because of the lack of spotlights,[56] and even the usually reliable William Dollar performed poorly. In the face of such adversity, Balanchine remained "wholly calm and without interest." The next evening's performance was not much improved, plagued by bleeding toes and unexpected falls.[57] Balanchine did not help in calming dancers' nerves, informing Heidi Vosseler shortly before the performance that she was too fat to dance in *Serenade*, which so distracted her that she could barely make it through the ballet.[58]

The troupe nevertheless received several generous notices for both performances. "Considering the short time they have been together," one review noted, "the work of the company was quite impressive" and "was indicative of promising material."[59] Like the company's Woodlands and Hartford engagements, both performances drew a "large and distinguished audience," lured by both the gala occasion and the chance to see the new ballet troupe before its New York debut."[60] Of the ballets, one review dismissed *Alma Mater* as "a rather juvenile representation of American College life easily susceptible to more subtle treatment" while another said the ballet had represented the troupe's "best, though not its most serious, efforts."[61] Opinions on *Serenade* were even more mixed, with one reviewer quite underwhelmed, calling it "an uneven composition falling frequently into mere drill figures and resembling at its best some of the weaker items of the repertoire of the Ballet Russe."[62] Another was complimentary of the choreography even though the score was not "first class," calling the ballet a truthful interpretation of the music "into three dimensional space."[63] For this same reviewer, *Transcendence* was the hit of the evening: "It had movement and variety, and although uneven as a composition reached exciting climaxes" and "introduced effective tableaux and group movements."[64] And if *Serenade* had been unfavorably compared with the repertoire of the de Basil company, *Transcendence* "achieved occasionally the sweeping force of the Monte Carlo Ballet's *Les Présages*, which it rather resembles."[65]

Similarly measured in praise was a notable audience member, the Chicago-based dancer and choreographer Ruth Page, who reported her impressions of the performance in a letter to her mother.[66] Page was unimpressed by *Alma Mater*, in part because she saw it as a knock-off of her 1926 duet *The Flapper and the Quarterback*, which had also featured costumes by John Held Jr.[67] Page was pessimistic about the work's reception in the big city despite the positive response it received at Bryn Mawr.[68] While she enjoyed the "beautiful 'modern classical' dancing" of *Serenade*, she found it lacking in "idea," and said that *Transcendence* similarly had "some marvelous moments in it but is not very clear."[69] Of the troupe as a whole she was positive but frank—"I think someday it will amount to something although it is still pretty raw now"—and noted that "Balanchine's choreography is extremely difficult to dance and I thought the dancers all did extremely well all things considered."[70]

Upon the company's return to New York, work continued on the program, with Balanchine seeming to be focused exclusively on *Reminiscence* and again plagued with health problems.[71] In addition to a role in *Dreams*, Paul Haakon was to perform a "hoop dance" in the work, a divertissement from *The Nutcracker* that Balanchine had performed at a benefit performance in Petrograd (and later included in his version of the work for the New York City Ballet).[72] Balanchine had become sick again, however, with Kirstein noting that Haakon's variation was choreographed with Balanchine "sweating in three jackets."[73] The addition of the hoop made the dance "very difficult," and Kirstein's sister Mina predicted darkly that "the sicker he gets the more difficult his choreography will be."[74] Haakon never quite mastered the hoop routine, getting caught in it in numerous performances.[75]

Balanchine had already been showing signs of illness a week before this particular incident, with Kirstein observing that he was running a temperature and feeling sick.[76] Kirstein privately noted that he would not be surprised if Balanchine had another attack, and although the fever abated the next day he stayed home in bed.[77] After a visit to the doctor the next day, however, it was determined that his tuberculosis had resurfaced and that he could probably work for two or three more weeks, but after that should take a long rest.[78] Further tests would later contradict this initial diagnosis, but the doctors still urged Balanchine to take it easy.[79] Neither Kirstein nor Warburg was particularly concerned about Balanchine's potential absence from the school, since operations would continue thanks to the presence of Vladimirov.[80] Kirstein would soon after speak with Agnes de Mille about possibly teaching at the school, to which she responded favorably, despite professing a low opinion of both Warburg and Vladimirov.[81] Balanchine's instability also led to the addition of Muriel Stuart and Erick Hawkins to the school's faculty. While Hawkins taught at the school only briefly— including providing private instruction to Kirstein for several months—the English-born Stuart, who had first danced in America on the tours of Anna Pavlova, would remain a stalwart at the school for the rest of her career.[82]

A preview article in the *Herald-Tribune* confirms that Balanchine was indeed not in the best of health in advance of the Adelphi engagement. Balanchine "appeared very frail in a huge brown velour overcoat which he wore draped about his shoulders," with "a gray suit and sweater underneath.[83] The reporter hastens to add that Balanchine was in the habit of dressing this way during classes and rehearsals, "in spite of an adequate heating arrangement for the practice room and in contrast to the young men and women of the troupe who go about in tulle and cheesecloth with great areas of their bodies exposed."[84] As a cover story for this behavior, Balanchine held forth about his long-standing aversion to being cold, owing to incidents from his youth in which he and his compatriots were forced to perform outdoors in frigid temperatures. Although Balanchine and his fellow students (along with millions of other individuals) did indeed endure a lack of heat for many years in the aftermath of the Bolshevik Revolution, Kirstein's diaries suggest that the true cause was the stress of preparations for the Adelphi engagement.[85] The general turmoil did not go unnoticed by the young dancers, who were on the receiving end of Balanchine's frustrated outbursts. During a rehearsal of *Errante* the week after he fell ill, Balanchine began disparaging his leading dancers, chastising "Elise Reiman for hypnotizing herself in the mirror" and "Holly Howard for dancing like a dog."[86] He groused that in Paris "there were only six dancers, not twelve but they were real fire, here they are dead."[87]

Later renamed the George Abbott Theater and famous as the home of the musical *On the Town*, the Adelphi Theatre on 54th Street just east of Seventh Avenue was demolished in 1970.[88] When the American Ballet performed there in March 1935 it was among the newer theaters on Broadway, touted as "one of New York's finest and most modern theatres" with an unusually large stage thirty-nine feet deep and seventy-five feet wide, a far cry from the modest scale of the venues at Woodlands and Hartford.[89] While most Broadway theaters at the time could seat about 1,000, the Adelphi had an above average capacity of 1,434, a large house that the American Ballet would not come close to filling for most of its performances there.[90] The enterprise had not rid itself of its amateurism, a failing that was evident in how indefinite the dates for the Adelphi engagement remained in the month before the performances. Kirstein records in his diary that the Adelphi was signed for on February 4, less than a month before opening night.[91] Like the dates, the repertory for the engagement remained in continual flux. On February 17 the *Herald-Tribune* reported that the company's programs were "as yet not definitively chosen" and would be selected from among *Mozartiana, Alma Mater, Transcendence, Serenade, Variation [Reminiscence], Dreams*, and *Errante*.[92] Soon after, it was reported that instead of the five shows over four days first announced, the company would present a full week of performances, with two complete programs.[93] Unconcerned about the actual dates and enthusiastic about the ever-expanding calendar of performances, Balanchine was "very happy" about finally having a New York premiere and was philosophical about the question of whether they were prematurely making a debut, remarking that, "it's all very well to wait until we are 'ready' but then in 2 or 3 years where would our troupe be."[94]

The Sunday before opening night, the American Ballet's debut received generous preview coverage, by Martin in his *Times* column and in a full-page story in the *Herald-Tribune*. Setting aside the concerns voiced in his open letter following the Hartford engagement, Martin struck an even-handed tone, recounting the many ambitious goals formulated by Kirstein, among them to "produce in consecutive seasons throughout the country ballets conceived and executed by Americans, defining perhaps for the first time on a scale worthy of its subject, what is most lyric, indigenous and essential in the American legend."[95] "It is, of course," Martin noted in a brief riposte, "too much to expect that all this has been accomplished in the company's first season, but is perhaps interesting"—in retrospect a setup for his forthcoming critique—"to approach these first performances with the ultimate intention in mind."[96] Expanding upon his previous comments about the athleticism of American girls, Balanchine in the *Herald-Tribune* preview expatiated on how this same disposition made it possible for Americans, both men and women, to begin learning ballet at a more advanced age, which was also aided by their innate rhythmic sensibility. "The reason it is possible to take American boys and girls at a greater age than nine and make dancers out of them," a practice not common in Russia, "is because of the athletic life led by Americans," Balanchine explained. "Besides that you are a musical people now and a naturally rhythmic people," as he further elaborated: "Why, I see Americans in restaurants—they seem to eat with rhythm. (Mr. Balanchine illustrated with an imaginary

FIGURE 3.2 Promotional flier for American Ballet's Adelphi Theatre engagement, 1935. Yvonne Patterson–William Dollar Papers, Jerome Robbins Dance Division, New York Public Library.

fork.) They even smoke cigarettes with rhythm (illustrating with an actual cigarette), so the learning of rhythm is nothing new for them."[97] In what appears to be a compliment to Americans' physiognomy, these comments ascribe some of Balanchine's primitivist imaginings—which in other contexts would more exclusively be ascribed to black dancers—onto American dancers as a whole.

The run up to the Adelphi performances was quite eventful. A February 25 "cocktail party rehearsal" was attended by a distinguished crowd including Russian opera star Feodor Chaliapin, designer Cecil Beaton, corporate titan A. Conger Goodyear, and composer Aaron Copland.[98] During the first orchestral rehearsal on February 27, the orchestra evidently "sounded like hell," as Kirstein recalled, not helped by the fact that conductor Sandor Harmati's dog had eaten seven pages of the *Transcendence* score.[99] Antheil's orchestration of *Serenade*—which has been lost to history—was also not proving congenial, "so full of Antheilism, it can't be used."[100] In a letter to Muriel Draper, Kirstein reported that Balanchine was in part responsible for the abandonment of the orchestration. Balanchine specifically complained about "ces affreux trompettes," one the few specific details that survive about this lost version, and Kirstein noted that Antheil was "furious" at the decision.[101] The final dress rehearsal the next day was "a shambles, half in costumes, half in pajamas or practice clothes," Tamara Geva was "furious at everyone," but William Dollar's solid dancing was a bright spot.[102]

If the American Ballet's artistic offerings would be somewhat muddled, a two-page flier and a special souvenir program produced for the occasion articulated a clear ideology for the enterprise. Although Kirstein's name is nowhere on these publications, his authorial hand is in apparent in both, despite the fact that he was not officially part of the company's management at the time. The flier features black and white photos and glowing testimonials from Stravinsky, Gershwin, and Antheil, as well as a three-paragraph introduction to the company and its repertoire.[103] Acknowledging that America has been dancing for some twenty-five years "ever since Isadora Duncan and the Russian Ballet showed the way," the copy posits the American Ballet as something new and distinct, claiming a thoroughly American identity while embracing its European heritage and leadership.[104] The flier's text concludes by promising that more overtly "American" ballets would be forthcoming and also maintaining that "alongside realistic, lyric and fantastic American scenes and subjects, there will always be, as there are in the repertory which inaugurates this institution, numbers reflecting the pure and abstract spirit of the classic dance."[105] This attempt to temper expectations of an explicitly and exclusively "American" program would ultimately prove futile, as would be the effort to construe Balanchine's modernist offerings under the new "pure dance" aesthetic newly embraced by Massine.

These talking points resonate closely with the cover of the souvenir program prepared for the Adelphi performances, a full-color and large format item comparable to the deluxe publications of the Ballets Russes and the de Basil company.[106] Drawn by artist and illustrator Louis Bouché, the cover depicts a trio of ballerinas representing the three major national centers of ballet—Italy, France, and Russia—arranged around a fourth American dancer. The cover resonates clearly with Kirstein's own numerous writings on the history of ballet.[107] "Its national origin is Italian," Kirstein wrote in an article "In Defense of the Ballet" in *Modern Music*, and "its direction soon turned towards France, and for the last twenty-five years the ballet has meant the Russian Ballet."[108] That Bouché's cover dovetails so neatly with his summaries—which are admittedly not unique among ballet histories—is no accident, since Kirstein conceived of the design himself and reports on meeting personally with the artist, who "got the idea of what I wanted at once."[109] A week later, Kirstein reviewed an initial sketch and noted that the artist had "understood perfectly" his concept, although Bouché delivered an initial draft that included a "sickle and hammer on the Russian ballerina's dress," which was subsequently removed.[110] Balanchine was further displeased by the fact that the Russian ballerina was wearing a headscarf, a correction that was not incorporated in the final version.[111]

As had been the case in Hartford, on opening night, the Adelphi welcomed "a brilliant audience which came in late, both at first and from the intermissions," as Kirstein recalled.[112] One review corroborates this observation, saying of *Serenade* that it "was unfair to criticize either the production or the dancing, since so much of it was blotted from sight by the tail-coats and ermine wraps flowing down the Adelphi aisles."[113] Kirstein had a clear enough view of the ballet to note that it was "danced well enough," but found that "the lights and the costumes were a terrible strain" and it had "no atmosphere of mystery."[114] *Alma Mater* was "OK but very tedious" and elicited "factitious applause," and on subsequent evenings, Kirstein would use the ballet as a chance to slip out and attend to other matters.[115] *Errante* fared better, and was "a powerful sexual experience," though some people laughed in the middle and "there was hissing at the end mingled with the cheers."[116] *Reminiscence* was "very good" despite its "lousy" décor and the fact that "Haakon got caught in his hoop." It was William Dollar, however, who had "danced divinely" and was the "g[rea]t success of the evening." When the final curtain came down at 11:30, Kirstein went backstage and kissed everyone he saw, and reports that Erick Hawkins was beside himself with joy, and gave credit where he believed it was due: "It's all you, Lincoln, it's all you." An "unshaved and unslept" Balanchine had been backstage all evening, praising the dancers and cursing the conductor for "taking *Serenade* so slow." Kirstein's sister Mina threw a party afterward, attended by Agnes de Mille, Virgil Thomson, and Helen and Chick Austin. Amid the festive

FIGURE 3.3 Cover of souvenir program for American Ballet's Adelphi Theatre engagement, March 1935. Illustration by Louis Bouché. Yvonne Patterson–William Dollar Papers, Jerome Robbins Dance Division, New York Public Library.

atmosphere, Kirstein privately worried about John Martin's forthcoming review.

Soon after opening night, Warburg's lack of managerial competence again came to light, when it became clear that the many individuals he had hired to assist him were enriching themselves at the company's expense. The decision to extend the run through March 17, 1935 was one of many poor choices made by Warburg at the urging of his management, who were more concerned with skimming money off the top of the enterprise. When Kirstein confronted Warburg about this situation, he replied that he had confidence in his managers and had no intention of exerting closer oversight. Kirstein "felt angry at the waste" and had another talk with Warburg, who only threw up his hands and let the unscrupulous behavior continue.[117]

The crowd for the originally planned closing night of March 7 had a "very poor house" with "300 seats given away," and the decision to extend the engagement by a week was quickly revealed as fiscal folly.[118] On the first evening of the extension the "house at the theatre was the worst yet, $300" and Kirstein was now sure that they should have closed on the original date.[119] Balanchine remained optimistic, however, predicting that "more and more will come."[120] The audiences did not materialize, and Kirstein on March 12 suspected that tickets had been given away in large amounts, commenting on "a largish (papered?) but cold audience."[121] Indeed, that same morning one of Warburg's managers had been in a panic since they had evidently taken in only $150 the night before.[122]

With one week remaining in the engagement, on Sunday March 10 Warburg summoned Balanchine, Kirstein, and his manager Birse to Woodlands for a conference about the company's future.[123] In the course of the meeting Warburg invited Kirstein to become co-director, an offer that he declined. Kirstein recalled feeling uneasy during the meeting in part owing to Dimitriev's exclusion from the proceedings and what he regarded as the unwelcome eyes and ears of Warburg's manager. Kirstein did make clear, however, that his primary concern was the security of the school, because he did not think the company would last for very long. During the drive back to the city, Kirstein and Balanchine had a discussion "about satisfaction." Balanchine said he felt satisfied "when he saw our pupils dance well" and the fact that a year ago "there was nothing and now we have had *quand meme* a success." That evening's performance, though not one of the troupe's best, did boast several notable faces in the audience, including actors Leslie Howard, Claudette Colbert, and Tallulah Bankhead.[124] Also on hand was Stravinsky, passing through New York on a busy US tour and set to return to Europe a month later.[125] Kirstein recalls him as a "strange little ratlike man" who was "sweet with Balanchine" and although he deemed the orchestration of *Errante* "dreadful," everything else he pronounced "très gentil."[126]

The final performance on March 17 was uneven and brought with it mixed emotions. Kirstein noted a "good" performance of *Transcendence* and was relieved to be seeing the *Errante* for what he surmised would be the last time.[127] In *Reminiscence*, however, "Holly Howard fell flat on her tail at the start of her variation" but "brought the house down by sticking it out," which in light of some of the critiques that were to come might be regarded as an apt metaphor for the American Ballet's Adelphi debut and subsequent trials. The final performance was also the occasion for a notable meeting of the minds, with Massine coming backstage to greet

Balanchine, an encounter that Kirstein likened to "Washington meeting Cornwallis," during which Massine declared that he "admired the corps de ballet and was glad Balanchine was starting such an important thing." Kirstein does not specify who was the victor in this meeting, nor is it clear at what point in the evening it took place. Regardless, the rapprochement of the two choreographers was not enough to allay a general feeling of melancholy. "Most of us stayed aimlessly on the stage, not wanting to leave," noted Kirstein, who apparently looked so distraught that dancer Kathryn Mullowny asked him whether he had bad news to report. Kirstein replied that he was only sad that the engagement was over, whereupon she chimed in optimistically that "it was just the beginning."

———

Despite Kirstein's worries, press on the Adelphi performances was quite positive overall. As had been the case in Hartford, *Alma Mater* was a well-received crowd-pleaser. According to one review, the ballet "more than deserved the ovation it received" with "Kay Swift's lilting music" and "boasting the colorful, comical costumes of John, Held, Jr."[128] Less obvious in its message was "something listed as *Errante*," as a reviewer for the *New York Post* described the ballet, which he hypothesized was "evidently a big symbolic number, the clue for which could perhaps be found in the words of Schubert's song," which were included in the souvenir program. If the content of the ballet was somewhat inscrutable, it was nevertheless a compelling spectacle, with Geva "garbed in a green evening gown and dragging the longest train in the history of that ornament." As best this critic could tell, Geva longed for domestic happiness, but the male or males she clung to frantically were always snatched from her by various ruthless processions of dancers.[129] Despite his own consternation, however, this reviewer notes that after *Errante*, "the curtain came down to the most frenzied applause I have heard in a theater this season."[130] Photographs taken of Geva from the front of the house attest to the dramatic scale of her gown's train and the eagerness with which she greeted her ovations.[131] Confirming the characterization of the ballet's designer, Pavel Tchelitchev, one review called the ballet the "caviar course" of the opening night program, and said that although Geva deserved her ovations, otherwise "there were incidental elements altogether too arty for any audience not composed largely of the dance elect."[132]

Serenade and *Reminiscence* prompted more outright and untroubled appreciation. The two ballets "made direct use of the classic ballet elements," and in them Balanchine "found means of bringing each of the more talented performers into focus with brief solo interludes and revealed a lively inventiveness in his arrangement of duos, trios and other groups that gave fresh aspect to traditional maneuvers."[133] The *Post* reviewer, bewildered by *Errante*, enjoyed *Reminiscence* most of all, "because I did not have to understand anything" and instead could simply enjoy "some good old-fashioned toe-dancing."[134] When all was said and done, opening night generated enough positive notices to fill a sizable "success ad," as Kirstein described the advertisement, though he admitted some "surprise" at the "excellence of its editing."[135]

More specialized voices were more pointed in their criticisms of the Adelphi programs. Writing in *Modern Music*, composer Lehman Engel was unimpressed by the company's program, finding fault with both its repertorial logic and execution in a review titled "Les Ballets Américains."[136] In *Errante*, "we writhed at the things that happened to Schubert's *Wanderer*" and "the potpourri of Godard in *Reminiscence*, Tchaikovsky's *Serenade*, and the sentimental Liszt to be found in *Transcendence* represent the kind of music that I, for one, can no longer hear with any feeling of rapport."[137] Engel was more forgiving of *Dreams*, if only because Antheil's assignment to compose music for an already created ballet "was an unfair task to assign to anyone."[138] Swift's *Alma Mater*, on the other hand, "can be dismissed after a bit of cutting as a very superior number in anyone's revue," although by virtue of the work the company had at least "proved it had been born and reared at home."[139] Overall, it still remained to be seen whether the American Ballet would live up to its name.

"The outstanding characteristic displayed by the American Ballet," a review in the *American Dancer* noted in a backhanded compliment, "was its complete kinship to the Russian ballet and to the classic ballet modes" and that in its present form "the American Ballet is a European ballet in the United States."[140] Questions of national identity aside, "for the ballets themselves no great enthusiasm can be worked up," and neither were they seen to be grounded in classicism, as Balanchine's Petersburg training and subsequent association with Diaghilev "seems to have brought about in him a cross-breed spirit."[141] A review in *Dance Observer* was even more pointed. "It was bad; all of it," wrote Henry Gilfond, "and if it was American, it was because it was certainly not Russian, nor French," a multi-pronged rebuke of the company's hybridizing claims.[142] "As a people, certainly we are not kinesthetically sentimental," he elaborated, "with serenades of a flowing pre-war sweetness, and dreams of a corrupt naïveté, knaves and princes and pages and a fairy queen."[143] The company's offerings were "a vapid gesture of no understandable significance" with "too much of the vaudevillian applause for clinical developments on the toes to warrant other than a lean and smug following for the so-called, and pretentiously so, American Ballet."[144]

In addition to his preview coverage, John Martin devoted three separate reviews to the American Ballet's programs, the first after opening night and two others later in the run to encompass all of the company's repertoire. These critiques quite astutely diagnose and summarize the underlying organizational and aesthetic issues revealed in the other contemporary evidence cited above, whether from Kirstein, Dimitriev, or other critics and observers. Martin's sometimes harsh evaluations of the American Ballet's debut were more than justified—and echoed by other critics—and were not, as has been repeatedly claimed, born of an irrational nationalism, uncritical allegiance to modern dance, or an underlying antipathy to Balanchine's work in general.

Of the four ballets from the opening program, Martin deemed only two "worthy of serious consideration as dance works while the others could be essentially written off."[145] *Errante* was "exactly the sort of thing the American Ballet must not do if it is to assume the place in the dance world to which it is entitled," despite its enthusiastic reception by the "platinum and diamond audience."[146] And while *Alma Mater* was "a thoroughly amusing little burlesque of college life as it is lived in the minds of the fiction writers," it was "really a revue sketch rather than a ballet." *Serenade* was a "serviceable rather than an inspired work," and although Martin was sympathetic that Balanchine no doubt "had his problems in devising choreography for an inexperienced company," nevertheless the ballet seemed to lack spontaneity. The closing number *Reminiscence* was the "real delight of the evening" in part because it allowed "the real abilities of the company get their first showing, and it is a decidedly impressive showing."

In his second review, Martin's opinions did not change significantly. *Dreams* was "scarcely worth the labor that has been spent on it, for it is trivial in subject matter and utterly unsuited to the style of the young dancers who make up the company."[147] *Transcendence* was slightly better and had "the quality of phantasmagoria and some of its incidents are of distinct power," but nevertheless, "whether because of its straining for choreographic novelty or because again of its complete unsuitability to the talents of the company, it remains largely incomprehensible." By the time he wrote his third review, Martin still found only *Reminiscence* worthy of explicit praise, since it offered something upon which the fledgling troupe could build.[148] Martin validated Dimitriev's concerns about Balanchine's overly modernist inclinations, observing that "it seems a colossal waste of time and energy to train dancers in the strict routine of the classic dance" when most of the company's ballets—*Dreams, Errante, Serenade*, and *Transcendence*—"belong to another style," evidence "of the decadence of the classic tradition as it is found in certain European environments," or more succinctly put, "Riviera aesthetics." "The problem resolves itself into one fundamental decision," as Martin concluded: would the company "attempt the fulfillment of its original policy of developing an American ballet, or is it to follow the direction of its present season and go on being merely 'Les Ballets Américains?'"

In the midst of these larger critiques, reviewers including Martin were quick to praise the company's dancers and seemed sympathetic about their taking on choreography that was incompatible with their talents and abilities. Engel's review noted that "the outstanding feature of this exhibition is the dancers themselves," and although all were to be praised, William Dollar had been a clear standout.[149] Another review noted, amid remarks about *Reminiscence*, that it "was gratifying to note how far these young dancers have proceeded along the traditional road of the ballet."[150] "For the essential training of the young company," Martin similarly noted, "there is nothing but praise," and that "on the whole, it is a good group of hard-working youngsters, far too good indeed to be forced, like square pegs into round holes, into choreography that does not and never will belong to them."[151]

With respect to Martin and his working relationship with Kirstein, the Adelphi engagement did mark a significant turning point. Of Martin's first review Kirstein did not record an opinion himself, but noted that Balanchine "agreed with Martin that *Errante* was silly," albeit for a different reason, insisting that "it means nothing, it is entirely simple like a dream," and he questioned why Americans "always have to see meaning in everything."[152] After Martin's second review appeared, Dimitriev and Kirstein were evidently in agreement that it was a fair assessment.[153] By the end of the Adelphi run, however, Kirstein seems to have all but written off the critic as an ally: "I now consider his interest in ballet as superficial, that he is such a chauvinist and as far as I'm concerned an enemy that I cannot make use of."[154] Soon enough Kirstein would find cause to take these private grievances public as the American Ballet lobbied to become the resident ballet company of the Metropolitan Opera over Martin's ongoing objections. Only a few years later, however, Kirstein would validate the critic's opinions on the Adelphi debut (and by extension Dimitriev's ongoing critiques and observations), writing in *Blast at Ballet* that the performances "pleased many people and disappointed others," and that "I think it was John Martin who called it *Les Ballets 1935*, and with some reason."[155]

One final set of impressions from the Adelphi engagement merits mention to close this chapter of the American Ballet's history. Notably not just *Alma Mater*—and, however unintentional, *Errante*—elicited laughter from the audience at the Adelphi opening night performance. According to several accounts, one of the most famous moments in the first movement of *Serenade* struck an unexpected chord, understood by the opening night audience as a comic event and accordingly greeted with "fragile laughter."[156] This moment was when Balanchine "permitted one of his dancers, after steps of unerring grace, to lose her place in the ballet and dash about to regain it. Hearty applause greeted her success."[157] Another critic similarly detected in *Serenade* an intentionally humorous agenda, noting

FIGURE 3.4 Posed photograph of *Serenade*, likely taken mid-1930s, depicting the ballet's original costumes, photographer unknown. George Balanchine Archive, MS Thr 411 (2471), Houghton Library, Harvard University. Choreography by George Balanchine © The George Balanchine Trust.

that "certain details were well calculated to stir the risibilities of observant spectators."[158]

It is striking how incongruous such observations are today given the enormous symbolic authority invested in *Serenade* as an emblem of Balanchine's commitment to classicism at the start of his American career.[159] As this discussion has shown, however, Balanchine did not leave his modernism behind when he crossed the Atlantic, and his interest in the bizarre and experimental did not cease with his work for Les Ballets 1933. Balanchine's now iconic "first ballet in America" did not mark an especially dramatic turn in his style but was rather very much of a piece with its reportorial siblings. Like the other debut offerings of the American Ballet, *Serenade* elicited mostly lukewarm responses that must be acknowledged, however sacrilegious it might seem with respect to the present form and reputation of the ballet. These now strange and remote qualities of *Serenade* serve to remind us of what was novel and surprising about Balanchine's choreography more generally, and how much his style had yet to develop. Had his career as a serious ballet choreographer ended in the 1930s—due to organizational duress or his own ongoing health problems—Balanchine would likely be regarded along the same lines as Massine, one of many distinguished but ultimately short-lived participants in the tumultuous aftermath of the era of Diaghilev. And *Serenade* might be no more beloved or known than *Les Présages*, one of many curious experiments in the now obsolete idiom of symphonic ballet.

CHAPTER 4 | 1935

THE PERIOD BETWEEN the March 1935 debut of the American Ballet at the Adelphi and the beginning of its duties as resident dance ensemble at the Metropolitan Opera in December that same year has received relatively little attention in accounts of the Balanchine-Kirstein enterprise. Most narratives draw a direct line from the Adelphi to the Metropolitan, with the decision by the opera to take on the American Ballet construed as an unexpected and providential offer that directly resulted from the company's debut.[1] "The invitation was so unsuspected," Lincoln Kirstein wrote in *Blast at Ballet*, "the opportunity so wonderful, there was scarcely a thought of refusal."[2] A wide range of evidence suggests that in fact the American Ballet's road to the opera was not paved by the company's artistic achievement or youthful allure, but came about owing to larger institutional turmoil at the opera, an organization over which the family of Edward Warburg suddenly found themselves with considerable leverage in early 1935. The discourse that surrounded the announcement of the American Ballet's new post, moreover, reveals just how unexpected their engagement was, with many critics, most notably John Martin, expecting the opera to appoint an American ballet master or an artist with ties to modern dance.

While the American Ballet was negotiating to join the Met, the company appeared before the public in several engagements, including a nationwide tour launched in October that was abruptly canceled after only two weeks. These performances provide invaluable insights into the character of Balanchine's choreography in these early years and how American audiences outside New York City reacted to his work. These engagements offer further evidence of Kirstein's and Warburg's different visions for the future of the enterprise and how each thought the organization should best compete with its biggest competitor, de Basil's Ballet Russe de Monte

Carlo. In the end, the uneven quality of the American Ballet's public performances and the mismanagement that resulted in the collapse of the tour would call into question the company's readiness to assume the role at the Met that they had lobbied so hard to secure.

In early 1935 the Metropolitan Opera was in the midst of an intense period of transition due to the impending end of the directorship of Giulio Gatti-Casazza.[3] The impresario's twenty-five-year tenure had witnessed over five thousand performances of nearly two hundred operas, among them many featuring conductor Arturo Toscanini and tenor Enrico Caruso. Gatti-Casazza's final years had been less auspicious, however, with the organization profoundly unsettled by financial woes brought on by the country's economic downturn. Departing along with Gatti-Casazza was his wife Rosina Galli, a dancer trained at La Scala who had first come to the Metropolitan as a soloist in 1914 and remained the company's star ballerina until her retirement from the stage in 1930.[4] In 1919 Galli had assumed the role of ballet mistress and carried on the Italian ballet tradition that had been established at the company and its affiliated school from its earliest years.[5]

The already fateful question of who would succeed Gatti-Casazza was made even more complicated owing to the involvement of another organization in the affairs of the opera: the Juilliard Music Foundation, which had been helping to keep the Met financially solvent in the early 1930s. In its inception, the Juilliard Foundation—created on the death of textile merchant Augustus D. Juilliard in April 1919—was not founded with the express purpose of supporting the performing arts academy that today bears its benefactor's name. Juilliard's will instead stipulated, in quite vague terms, that his funds should support a range of musical endeavors: the instruction and education of promising students, the presentation of concerts and recitals, and the operations of the Metropolitan Opera.[6] The uncertainty surrounding Juilliard's true philanthropic intentions led to many decades of wrangling over the proper use of his estate.[7]

When the Met began experiencing financial difficulties, a lawyer representing several singers began a campaign to secure Juilliard funding for the opera, arguing that the general public should not be asked to prop up the house with a $300,000 fundraising drive when foundation funds could be allocated instead.[8] Juilliard president John Erskine eventually agreed and authorized grants of $50,000 in 1933 and $40,000 in 1934. Even this decision sparked controversy from some quarters, as opera fundraising organizers argued that such largesse would undermine their efforts to raise smaller sums from the public.[9] These grants came with additional requirements, moreover, with Erskine stipulating that the Foundation's support should be used to produce nonstandard repertoire, including operas by American composers.[10] This served to advance the interests of Juilliard students as well as Erskine himself, a polymath scholar who was an advocate of new and experimental work.[11]

The initial Juilliard bailouts were not enough to set the opera's finances completely in order, and by early 1935 the organization was once again near bankruptcy. In the meantime, the issue of identifying a successor to Gatti-Casazza had become an equally pressing concern. Juilliard again came to the rescue with an even more substantial grant of $150,000, and this more significant sum had additional strings attached.[12] The opera was required to raise subscription prices and operate with a balanced budget as well as to offer a new spring season of English-language opera at "popular prices," that is, comparable to the rates at Broadway theaters.[13] To ensure proper oversight of these plans, three Juilliard trustees would be appointed to the Metropolitan board, and it was also understood that the Foundation's preferred candidate, Herbert Witherspoon (a singer and former faculty member at Juilliard), would be appointed as Gatti-Casazza's successor.[14]

This resolution of the opera's latest financial crisis as well as the appointment of Witherspoon were announced on March 7, 1935—in the midst of the American Ballet's Adelphi engagement—and met with general approval in the press, especially his new public outreach measures. The *Herald-Tribune* praised his plans to revitalize the artistic offerings of the house, in particular through the new spring season of performances at accessible "popular prices," with an article in the *Chicago Tribune* carrying this headline: "[The Met] Will Seek Audiences in Telephone Book Rather than Social Register."[15] Outreach would be the explicit goal of the spring season, which would also offer an opportunity to showcase lesser-known works and also up-and-coming singers, including promising students from Juilliard.[16]

Responsibility for managing the new spring season fell to Witherspoon's primary rival for the director position, another singer-turned-impresario, Edward Johnson. Born in Guelph, Ontario, Johnson had gone to Italy to begin his career, singing for five seasons at La Scala—under the stage name Eduardo di Giovanni—and marrying the daughter of a Portuguese nobleman.[17] To the Metropolitan's management he would bring not only this cosmopolitan biography but also good looks and a knack for navigating the byzantine social networks that underpinned the organization.[18] These skills quickly proved useful for more than Johnson's spring season duties, when only two months after these realignments Herbert Witherspoon died of a heart attack in his office.[19] Although various other candidates were again considered, within a week the opera board opted for the expedient solution of promoting Johnson to the director role, and he would hold the position until 1950.[20]

Edward Warburg had hardly proved himself an exemplary manager of the budding ballet enterprise of Balanchine and Kirstein, as incidents associated with the Adelphi debut made clear. What he lacked in managerial prowess, however, Warburg would make up for in not just financial resources but also social and institutional clout, including significant access at the Met. The Warburg family had a long-standing relationship to the Metropolitan through their affiliation with the financial firm of Kuhn, Loeb, of which the previous opera chairman, Otto Kahn, had been a partner.[21] When Juilliard began to take an active role in the management of the Metropolitan in the 1930s, their access was further enhanced, since the Warburgs had deep ties to the Juilliard Music Foundation as well. Edward Warburg's great-uncle James Loeb had been the founding benefactor of the original Institute of Musical Art created by Frank Damrosch in 1905, which after considerable negotiation merged with the troubled Juilliard Music Foundation in 1925, creating the Juilliard organization that is still in operation today.[22] Warburg's uncle Paul and father Felix had served on the board of the Institute and were subsequently named trustees of the new organization.[23] When Juilliard bailed out the Metropolitan in March 1935, it had requested three seats on the opera board, and a few days before Witherspoon's death in May it was announced that the Foundation would in fact receive four seats, with the newly acquired seat to be filled by Felix Warburg.[24] As a result Edward Warburg would have direct access to the highest levels of decision making at the opera in the months to come. Although lacking the entrée of Warburg, Kirstein did his best to keep abreast of developments at the Met through his own channels about who was in the running for the ballet master post—including Alexandre Gavrilov, a Ballets Russes alumnus and student of Fokine and Vienna State opera ballet master Margarete Wallman.[25] Ever ambitious and eager, Kirstein resolved that the company should try to book some performances at the Met to make sure they were in the public eye.[26]

When the American Ballet's debut engagement at the Adelphi began, Witherspoon was only a week away from being officially installed in his new position, and Johnson similarly was slated to assume his second-in-command role in charge of the popular price spring season. If the opera's larger leadership was close to being settled, the question of a new ballet master was still officially open; however, evidence suggests that Witherspoon had already made a tentative offer to hire dancer and choreographer Ruth Page. In addition to her work in opera ballet in her native Chicago—where Witherspoon had both performed and worked in administrative roles at the opera[27]—Page had several years earlier made a well-received choreographic debut at the Metropolitan with dances for a 1927 production of Smetana's *The Bartered Bride* and had performed solo numbers in *Mignon* and *Aida* in 1927 and 1928, in addition to her notable career as a soloist and choreographer elsewhere.[28]

Correspondence between Page and her mother suggests that she and her husband Tom Fisher had been in discussions with the Metropolitan in general and Witherspoon in particular about the position. In February 1935 Page wrote that she and her husband would be staying with "Mr. Cravath" while in New York, likely referring to Paul Cravath, chairman of the Metropolitan board.[29] By early April, Page indicates that some official meetings had already taken place in New York and that she had been in contact with Witherspoon; although nothing had been officially settled, some verbal understanding was in place, and she made it clear that she was waiting to hear something definitive.[30]

Several days into the Adelphi performances, Tom Fisher made contact with Kirstein to strategize about the Metropolitan situation. When introduced a year earlier, Fisher and Kirstein had immediately bonded over their similar interests and demeanors.[31] Reconnecting with Kirstein in March 1935, Fisher pitched to him the idea of installing Page as ballet master, who would in turn invite Balanchine, Martha Graham, Doris Humphrey, and Charles Weidman as additional contributing artists.[32] Such native talents were among those being touted around the same time by John Martin, who was lobbying strongly for an American to assume the post—among others Humphrey and Agnes de Mille—on the principle that it was time for America not to be dependent on foreign expertise to produce its art.[33] Martin had voiced public disapproval of rumors that Balanchine and another foreign artists were front runners for the position.[34]

Around the same time that Witherspoon was in discussions with Page and Fisher, Edward Johnson made contact with Kirstein and paid a visit to the School of American Ballet. Still a month away from receiving his sudden and unexpected promotion, Johnson came to observe classes and also spoke with Warburg about the spring season; he possibly also discussed the engagement of the company as resident ensemble at the Met, saying that he would keep them apprised of discussions on the ballet.[35] Johnson told them that much depended on the opinion of John Erskine, suggesting that decision making at the Metropolitan was strongly influenced by the organization's Juilliard benefactors.

The sudden death of Witherspoon and promotion of Johnson in early May considerably altered the ballet situation at the Metropolitan. Less than a week after Johnson had assumed his new post, Kirstein and Warburg were angling for a meeting with him to ask for additional performance opportunities at the Met.[36] Tom Fisher for his part was lobbying anew for a collaborative plan of action and claimed to Kirstein that not only had Page been promised the job before Witherspoon's death but was also still the leading candidate. He proposed that Page and Balanchine jointly run the company, a plan of action that Kirstein approved of.[37] Kirstein attempted to get word to Warburg "as to what he should say tomorrow morning about cooperating with Ruth Page and our Ballet Co," thinking that Fisher's plan was the best strategy for the American Ballet.[38]

If Warburg had more often than not demonstrated a general incompetence regarding the American Ballet's management, in this instance he would redeem his past managerial misdeeds. Whether by instinct or due to insider information or both, he correctly surmised that Fisher's proposal would not help Balanchine or the American Ballet but was rather a play to salvage the candidacy of Page, whose chances for the post of ballet master had died along with Witherspoon. Before their meeting with Johnson, Warburg assured Kirstein that "Tom Fisher protests too much" and that he didn't think they had "to play with Ruth Page at all."[39] Warburg turned out to be correct, as Johnson made clear during their meeting, saying that he was not an advocate of Page and would prefer Agnes de Mille for the post.[40] Johnson asked if they could "manage the opera ballets" and also Sunday night performances devoted solely to ballet, but despite this enthusiasm, Kirstein still had doubts as to their chances, again not realizing that Warburg had the connections to win over these influential men to their side.[41]

Although the job was now evidently the company's to lose, the deliberations continued well into the summer, in part because it was unclear how the American Ballet could fulfill obligations to the Metropolitan and pursue its own performance engagements elsewhere, including a planned three-month cross-country tour to begin in the fall. Over breakfast with Warburg, Kirstein discussed the opera deal and Johnson's suggestion to recruit Agnes de Mille to be an assistant choreographer, something

Balanchine opposed since he didn't want de Mille herself to dance.[42] But it was not until August 6, nearly five months after the Adelphi debut season had concluded, that all was settled, and Kirstein for once had to give Warburg his due. "Warburg says it is all very well for me to make fun of his Harvard connections and capitalist entrée," he wrote in his diary, "but that's what pulled it off."[43] "I hope we can make use of what we've got as long as we can," he added with his habitual worry, but for the time being he "was too relieved to want to do anything but flatter the hell out of Eddie."[44]

In his remarks on August 7 announcing the engagement of the American Ballet, Edward Johnson hailed Balanchine's previous experience under Diaghilev in Paris and at the opera in Monte Carlo as his chief credentials, in addition to "the keen interest awakened by the then newly organized American Ballet's first public program in New York last season."[45] The *Dancing Times* reported approvingly that Balanchine's selection "will reinstate the dance as a feature of [the Met's] season's productions this winter for the first time in almost a decade" and "constitutes one of the most exciting plans yet revealed for augmenting the Opera's audiences and popularity."[46] Less enthusiastic was the editorial board of *Dance Observer*, who termed the decision merely a "logical choice for the new management" of the opera.[47] Although they allowed that American Ballet was "somewhat of an improvement on the old Galli troupe which was long overdue," their opinion was one of bemused resignation, noting that Balanchine's choreography could "scarcely detract from the much-dated opera" and "will probably be sufficient."[48] They saw a silver lining in the failure of a modern dancer to secure the post, arguing that it is better for such a candidate "to steer his course through the 1930s, his art the product and the understanding of his contemporaries, time and temper," rather than being constrained by the rearguard sensibility of the opera.[49]

Not content to offer sarcastic resignation, critic John Martin provided a strong rebuttal opinion on the appointment, opening his weekly column with criticism of the Metropolitan for passing over American candidates for "a high artistic post for which at least half a dozen of them are eminently fitted" and lamenting that "the old tradition has not yet been eradicated that we are a crude pioneer people and must import our culture from the European fountainhead."[50] Martin's disapproval of the American Ballet's appointment to the Metropolitan (like his critiques following the Adelphi season) has been typically cited as further evidence of his strident nationalism, stubborn allegiance to modern dance, and irrational antipathy to Balanchine.[51] Martin's actual concerns were more nuanced, however, and centered first on the readiness of the young and inexperienced company to assume such a prominent post. Most important, he regarded the American Ballet's alliance with a large and conservative performing arts organization as a poor strategic move for the company itself, seeing the merger as an implicit disavowal of the company's goals of establishing an innovative new tradition of American ballet.

Earlier in the summer, Martin had written about the different standards to which American and foreign artists were held in the New York dance scene. Whereas "European importations" drew acclaim "rather through the charm of the exotic than purely on merit," American dancers "devoid of this marketable quality must make their way on other grounds."[52] Martin did not claim that such empty allure was the sole criterion for Balanchine's selection by the Met, and acknowledged him as "a gifted artist beyond the shadow of a doubt, and not merely the latest Russian to arrive."[53] Moreover, he praised Balanchine's experimental sensibility, noting that he is "unusually inventive in his choreography, and all his work is stamped with the highly personal mark of a creative individual."[54] About the American Ballet itself, however, Martin was less complimentary, and based on their recently completed performances he argued that "it was difficult to picture them as representatives of what has sometimes been termed the world's leading lyric theatre" since the young organization was "still an apprentice group rather than a company of artists."[55]

Martin went further, however, to claim that the American Ballet's alliance with the Metropolitan was an implicit abandonment of the previously articulated mission of the enterprise, namely, "the creation of a type of theatrical dance that should develop the full flavor of American life and culture, starting with the technical tradition of the academic ballet as nothing more than a framework."[56] Echoing the concerns of his December 1934 and March 1935 columns, he lamented that the company had missed an opportunity to cultivate a new audience and a new kind of ballet, and had instead repurposed Balanchine's earlier work for the same elite audiences to whom the choreographer had been beholden in Europe. Martin pessimistically predicted that "any hope of recovering the original purpose of the enterprise appears to have been extinguished."[57]

Prior to the Adelphi performances Kirstein had greeted Martin's critiques as justified and constructive, but by this point he had had enough, and a letter to the editor from Kirstein appeared a week later in the Sunday August 25 newspaper.[58] Dated August 20, 1935, Kirstein's letter in fact represented a collective response hashed out during a lengthy meeting on the evening of August 19 at the Russian Tea Room that had included Balanchine and Warburg.[59] Although management of the school and company had indeed undergone a gradual separation over the last year, Kirstein articulated a unified leadership front for the two organizations, maintaining that he, Warburg, Balanchine, and Dimitriev all still served as the four directors of both entities.[60] Having thus corrected these more superficial "errors of fact," Kirstein went on to take issue with what he regarded as Martin's "chauvinistic construction" of the word "American" and how it might apply to ballet.[61] In his response, Kirstein went so far as to impute dubious views to Martin, associating the critic with the increasingly controversial figure of choreographer Mary Wigman, who had become the subject of an acrimonious debate about her collaboration with the Nazi regime, a controversy that also embroiled Hanya Holm, the head of the New York branch of her school.[62] Although Martin was not a central player in this particular debate, he had been a longtime advocate of Wigman's work, and Kirstein thus eagerly seized the opportunity to impute questionable politics to the critic in defense of his own enterprise.

Other news outlets in New York were less critical, instead merely reporting the news and the American Ballet's plans. According to Johnson's statement at the announcement, Balanchine intended to retain from the existing Metropolitan troupe "the best-looking ones, the best dancers and those with the best extremities."[63] The *Dancing Times* also noted that looks would play a role in the selection process for the new troupe: "It is expected that the best qualified (and best looking) members of the Metropolitan's ensemble will be combined with the American Ballet."[64] "We have done here in a short time, a year and a half, more than could be done in a much longer time in Europe," Balanchine maintained, in part because American dancers were "very quick to learn, very musical," and their "physique and build he found well suited for dancing."[65] Regarding his dances for the operas, he announced his agenda as follows:

> I am anxious that our dances should be of the same epoch and of the same style as the opera and the music. A modernistic dance would be out of place in *Carmen* or *Rigoletto*. In the regular operas the dances are to remain much the same as before, at least in costumes and general plan, although, naturally, there will be different movements or steps, so that as far as the actual dancing is concerned, these dances will be new productions.[66]

Such comments are typically glossed as evidence of Balanchine's principled aesthetic independence, or desire to shake up the staid conventions of dancing at the house, and he would rearticulate them later in defense of his sometimes controversial (and unpopular) work at the Metropolitan. Balanchine had not invented such impulses out of whole cloth, however, since a kind of imaginary historical realism had been one of the founding principles of the "new ballet" of Michel Fokine, thought it would remain to be seen how much actual research would go into Balanchine's allegedly historicist interventions.[67]

Outside of New York, the opera's announcement was met with generally positive coverage and benefited from the additional synergy of the upcoming cross-country tour of the American Ballet slated to begin in October. Reports in Chicago and Baltimore drew from an identical set of talking points (perhaps from a wire service or press releases) that read as a rebuttal to Martin's critiques, expounding on Balanchine's ideas and plans for ballet at the Metropolitan and in America more generally. If the tone and quality of writing suggests that these statements were for the most part ghostwritten (perhaps by Kirstein), the underlying ideas appear to have their origins in Balanchine's experiences and sensibility. Balanchine declares in these reports that dance in America "is regaining the glamorous estate attained by history making ballets of the past" and "because of the definite similarities in aesthetic pursuits which prevail in Russia and this country, the dance will flourish here."[68] If American companies were not yet in a position to mount the "captivating spectacles" of 250 plus dancers then possible in Leningrad and Moscow, "in a few years productions exceeding such programs will be realities."[69] This would be possible in part because of the "definite similarities in aesthetic pursuits which prevail in Russia and this country," as well as the fact that America has a "love of bigness that is so important in the ballet" and its "skyscrapers, vast fields, gigantic machines—all make for thrilling spectacles."[70] "Every phase of the national character here," he elaborated, "its vastness, imagination, resources and curiosity, plus a healthy interest in the arts, makes me hopeful that we can equal and perhaps surpass the creations and technical skill of the great companies of the past."[71]

To this end, American themes and influences would be central to the company's aesthetic program, and Balanchine declared that such subjects "occupy a prominent part of our repertoire and have tempered our technique so that already there are distinctly American variations of the classic form."[72] At the same time, Balanchine maintains a commitment to a certain level of abstraction, disavowing implicitly if not explicitly the aesthetics of Massine's more programmatic "symphonic ballets." Although "modern influences have striven to make the dance a medium solely for the expression of ideas," Balanchine instead "insists that the ballet is purely a spectacle":

> It is pictorial, but it is more than that, he asserts. It expresses movement, it appeals to the eye and to the ear, it is a synthesis of color, movement and music. "No other art form accomplishes this as purely and as simply as the ballet," he declares. "If ideas emanate from the dance, they are implications only. The primary appeal is to the senses," he added. "In my opinion that is all the dance should strive for."[73]

Two weeks after the announcement, open auditions were announced for the opera ensemble, with applicants invited not to the opera but rather to the School of American Ballet's studios on Madison Avenue.[74] The results of these sessions were not particularly fruitful, however, with only three students invited to return for follow-up consultations.[75] Existing members of the Metropolitan's ballet ensemble had not fared much better, having had to audition to remain in the group. According to an interview in early September, Balanchine had retained only five girls and two boys in his auditions thus far. Although the tryouts were ongoing, he made no promises about how many dancers would be kept and suggested that the existing troupe had considerable dead weight: "It is very sad, but I have no place for the old spear carriers. It cannot be helped."[76]

On the heels of the official announcement on Wednesday, August 7, of their engagement by the Metropolitan, the American Ballet had several opportunities to show the public what they would be bringing to the house, with two large-scale public engagements in New York and Philadelphia. They in fact took advantage of an expansion of summertime dance activities, at least in the view of John Martin, who in his weekly column in early July noted that "never before has there been such an extensive program for the vacation period as that which has already begun to get under way this summer."[77] Foremost among the summer offerings were the seasons of two major outdoor venues, the Lewisohn Stadium in upper Manhattan, and the Robin Hood Dell in Philadelphia's Fairmount Park, both of which would host the American Ballet for performances in August.[78]

Named in honor of its benefactor, Adolph Lewisohn (uncle of dance philanthropists Audrey and Irene), the sizable pseudo-Grecian amphitheater originally located on the campus of City College in upper Manhattan could accommodate upward of fifteen to twenty thousand spectators.[79]

Operatic offerings of the Stadium's 1935 summer season included *La Traviata* and *Tosca* while the classical repertoire ran the gamut from Beethoven's "Emperor" piano concerto and "Eroica" symphony to a new work by Spanish composer José Iturbi.[80] Monday and Tuesday were set aside for dance performances, and Michel Fokine's company filled these slots for the month of July, with programs that included his evergreen *Schéhérazade* as well as new ballets set to Mendelssohn and Paul Dukas's *The Sorcerer's Apprentice*.[81]

The American Ballet drew a sizable but by no means standing-room-only crowd of five thousand for its first performance on August 12, and the strong turnout was attributed by one reporter to "the glamour surrounding the American Ballet . . . now being the official corps de ballet of the Metropolitan."[82] John Martin chalked up the relatively small audience to the company's presenting ballets that had all been previously seen in March.[83] Although the troupe did in fact present no premieres—the three ballets (*Serenade*, *Alma Mater*, and *Reminiscence*) had all been part of the Adelphi programs—the loyalty of returning spectators would have been by many reports sufficiently rewarded. One critic went so far as to say that the three ballets gave the impression of having been "almost re-made" in light of the troupe's more advanced training.[84] Another reviewer noted that although it was still a "young organization" the American Ballet had not disappointed, and if there was "no furore last evening," as yet another described the Monday night reception, there was at least "good, healthy appreciation."[85] Since the Adelphi debut, Balanchine had been able to "mold them into the finished article," and the company's "earnest and serious study . . . is all beginning to show with a vengeance."[86] A review of the performances in the *Dancing Times*, on the contrary, concurred with Martin's opinion that the company was still somewhat green. Although its March debut in New York had shown "that the company had youth and spirit on its side and a technical groundwork that was excellent," it was the general opinion of New York dance critics that "they were exposed to public view too soon."[87] Given his experience with Diaghilev, the column continued, Balanchine must surely be aware "that ballerinas cannot be created in a twelve-month and that coryphées must go through a stern and lengthy apprenticeship before being revealed."[88]

A summer thunderstorm rained out the next evening's performance and also a rescheduled Wednesday night show.[89] However inauspicious, this delay could be credited with the much larger crowd of ten thousand that turned out for the rescheduled performance the following Monday, August 19, perhaps drawn by the positive press coverage following the first performance.[90] It is impossible to know exactly how many had previously seen the company in March, but the fifteen thousand spectators who saw the company at the Lewisohn Stadium was likely equal to if not greater than the gross audience for the entire run of the Adelphi performances.

Reviews of the Stadium performances reveal a broad range of viewpoints about the American Ballet's repertoire. One review praised *Serenade* as "beautifully carried out, with distinct dramatic outlines and logical dance design, and a most effective ensemble."[91] Another critic went even further to describe the ballet as evincing "continuity, style, smoothness and precision" and that "sincerity was written all over it."[92] Yet another had a more mixed opinion, finding "some arresting choreography in the first two episodes," and deeming the final "Elegy" "somewhat too sentimental for modern taste."[93] It was not *Serenade* but rather *Reminiscence* that allowed the troupe "to prove they could do something in the classic spirit."[94] Another critic also saw the two ballets as contrasting works, with *Serenade* posited as "a modernized version of the classic ballet" while *Reminiscence* represented "the classic ballet itself."[95] Similarly, the *Dancing Times* reported that while *Reminiscence* gave the company "a chance to show what it can do with classic ballet routine," the choreography for *Serenade* was "one of M. Balanchine's most interesting patterns that employs the entire ensemble picturesquely."[96] As had been the case in previous engagements, *Alma Mater* did its service of providing a contemporary and crowd-pleasing spectacle, although its reception would continue to be mixed. A music critic for the *Daily Mirror* declared it the most interesting of the three ballets, and another critic reported that the audience "went hook, line and sinker—as the saying goes—for *Alma Mater*, which, if nothing else, proves that despite intellectual trends audiences still laugh at slapstick comedy."[97] For another, the music and décor were the chief highlights, while yet another said the ballet "seemed slightly less entertaining than on first viewing."[98] All agreed, however, that the ballet's undisputed highlight was William Dollar's reprise of his role as the villain.[99]

Kirstein's diaries attest to the attendance of numerous VIPs at the first Stadium performance and also to the apparent generosity of the press in praising the company's technical improvements. Edward Warburg was content owing to the presence of Edward Johnson and also several younger members of the Roosevelt family, in addition to his mother and father.[100] Michel Fokine and Carl Van Vechten were also on hand, the latter declaring to Kirstein that Wiliam Dollar "was in his opinion a great dancer, or finally that he was crazy if he didn't get better."[101] "Lousy stage but the kids looked sweet" was Kirstein's only personal observation, and of the individual dancers he singled out only Kathryn Mullowny for explicit praise.[102] Kirstein's close friend Muriel Draper, recently returned from an extended trip to the Soviet Union, was also in attendance and was "sweet and sympathetic" about the company's offerings.[103] The week before he had brought Draper to see a rehearsal of *Reminiscence*, and though she had been "very sweet with Balanchine," Kirstein admitted to being "acutely self-conscious of the way the kids danced, how badly in comparison to the Russians she'd been telling me about."[104] Draper had been forthright in response, saying that "perhaps this first crop would be sacrificed and would have to be plowed under" since "the Slavonic material still is the best dancing stock," as Massine had said to her.[105] Such observations suggest that Martin and other critics were not entirely off base in their critiques of the apparent inexperience of the troupe.

Between the two Monday performances at Lewisohn Stadium, the company went down to Philadelphia for performances at the Robin Hood Dell in Fairmount Park, touted as the "young and brilliant organization which made its Philadelphia debut at Bryn Mawr last winter."[106] The weather system that had rained out their Tuesday and Wednesday performances in New York also occasioned delays for their Thursday and Friday night appearances in Philadelphia.[107] The skies eventually cleared, however, allowing the company to put on two performances and a "goodly crowd was on hand to welcome this intensely interesting troupe, lately appointed to take over the ballet section of the haughty Metropolitan Opera."[108] The music critic of the *Daily News* declared the group much improved since their Bryn Mawr performances six months earlier and said the company "has taken on a glittering charm that makes it praiseworthy."[109] He deemed the girls "well trained and capable" and described them as "the prettiest dancers that these eyes have ever seen."[110] Of the ballets, *Serenade* was "an avalanche of lovely settings and choreography" while *Reminiscence* was an "opportunity for the individual members to display their talents."[111] *Alma Mater* was not only "just as funny on being seen and heard for the second time" but was furthermore "the most entertaining ballet production in ten years."[112] Although Kirstein did not make the trip with the troupe he recorded in his diary that they "had a great success in Philadelphia" despite the unfortunate incident of dancer Helen Leitch taking a spill "into the cymbals."[113]

If these summer engagements saw the company reaching out to wider audiences, they were still put to use for an ermine-clad clientele. In late September the company took to the stage for a performance at the

Westchester County Center in White Plains.[114] The Saturday September 28 benefit performance was presented by the Westchester County Girl Scouts to raise funds for Rock Hill Camp (efforts that met with some success since the camp is still in operation today).[115] Edward Warburg's participation was evidently limited to providing the evening's entertainment, but both his father Felix and brother Frederick are listed among the box holders for the benefit.[116] Over 2,500 were expected to attend the performance, for which Mrs. V. Everit Macy Jr. was chair of the box-holder committee and Mrs. Giles Whiting the head of the "patronesses committee."[117] The generously programmed evening included three ballets—*Mozartiana, Alma Mater*, and *Reminiscence*—as well as the overture to *Die Fledermaus*, Gershwin's *Rhapsody in Blue*, and an orchestrated version of Debussy's *Golliwogg's Cake Walk*.[118] Kirstein's involvement at the time continued to center on the school and not the company, perhaps explaining why his diary is silent as to the planning of the event, but he did make the trip up to White Plains to see the performance, which was for him a distressing experience.[119] *Mozartiana*, which had not been performed publicly since Hartford, was "simply dreadful. Over rehearsed. Lights went wrong."[120] Annabelle Lyon apparently hurt her foot during the "Ave Verum," Holly Howard was "awful" in the pas de deux, and during *Reminiscence* Gisella Caccialanza's shoelaces came undone.[121] Balanchine as was his wont was "imperturbable," while Kirstein regarded the proceedings as "all too grisly" and after the performance "said nothing but left at once feeling dreadful."[122] Two days later he discussed the "lousy" performance with Warburg, who was as usual more sanguine, saying he disagreed and according to Kirstein "was very nice about my panic and hysteria."[123] Even if Kirstein's concerns were perhaps a bit overblown, there was no question that the stakes for the company were about to become higher.

Before its duties at the Metropolitan began in December, the American Ballet had a nationwide tour to attend to, set to run from mid-October 1935 to January 1936. To accommodate the tour and obligations at the opera, it would be necessary to split the dancers into two units, one going on the road and the other remaining in New York to perform at the opera (termed the American Ballet Ensemble). Balanchine intended to remain involved with both troupes, however, telling one reporter that "I will fly from one to the other," with a headline announcing that he would "Direct Both by Phone during Season."[124] After the tour concluded in January the ensembles would once again be combined for a total of some sixty dancers. Such a strategy was similar to a trick from the playbook of the de Basil company, which in early 1934 contrived dual-company strategies to take advantage of touring opportunities.[125]

The tour began auspiciously enough with a warm and festive send-off from Rockefeller Plaza on Tuesday, October 15, documented in news reports and small snapshot photos in the collections of William Dollar and Yvonne Patterson.[126] "What with the gay, young American dancers in their gay young American clothes," the *Herald-Tribune* reported, "the party suggested a theatrical school treat starting for a big afternoon of pink lemonade and buns somewhere up the Hudson."[127] Although Kirstein did not go on the road with the troupe—remaining behind to manage the school and also prepare the proofs and plates for his forthcoming book *Dance: A Short History of Theatrical Dancing*—he did go to see the dancers off and recorded in his diary a scene of photos and goodbye kisses, and also his request to Eugene Loring to report back to him from the road.[128]

Balanchine was evidently still taking extreme precautions about his health, as one report of the send-off says he "was muffled up sufficiently to have stood a cruise to Vladivostok," although "on his face among the wrappings a broad grin was visible."[129] Balanchine was evidently in good spirits about the upcoming journey and charmed one reporter by playing the role of bemused and mystified foreigner: "I am much interested in our little experiment. . . . . We are presenting ballet in many places which have never seen ballet, and in some quite small cities, too. St. Louis, I think is the littlest," a comment calculated to elicit a "faint cry" of protest from St. Louis-born Dollar.[130] He also jokingly anticipated local reception of *Alma Mater* at their upcoming Ivy League venues: "You know in Princeton, I think there will be scandal, and at New Haven perhaps tomatoes will be thrown. In our *Alma Mater* we have a place where a Yale father has a Princeton son. I am told that is very shocking."[131]

All joking aside, this nationwide tour was the young troupe's chance to prove itself the institutional equal of the de Basil troupe. Warburg posited the tour as the arrival of the American Ballet as a legitimate dance institution, and if he otherwise took little interest in the school, he was happy to use it and the two companies—the touring group and the American Ballet Ensemble at the Metropolitan—as evidence of the organization's arrival, and even more broadly that "classical dancing is on a sound basis in this country for the first time."[132]

Their first day of touring took the specially chartered "American Ballet" buses a short thirty-mile drive to Greenwich, Connecticut, where they gave an evening performance of *Serenade, Alma Mater*, and *Reminiscence* in the

FIGURE 4.1 American Ballet tour sendoff at Rockefeller Plaza, October 15, 1935, photographer unknown. Lincoln Kirstein depicted in center. Yvonne Patterson–William Dollar Papers, Jerome Robbins Dance Division, New York Public Library.

high school auditorium, presented by the Wednesday Singing Club.[133] The next day took them another thirty miles to Bridgeport, where they danced *Mozartiana, Alma Mater*, and *Reminiscence* at the Central High School Auditorium, presented by the local Musical Research Club.[134] The program here was augmented by several musical selections of a non-native character, opening with the overture to *The Marriage of Figaro* and with Emanuel Chabrier's *España* and Gabriel Pierné's *Pavane et Saltarello* between the ballets. Thursday, October 17, brought the troupe to a more official theatrical venue, New Haven's Shubert Theatre, where they reprised the program from Bridgeport.[135] A review of the performance noted that the troupe's efforts "to ground Diaghilev's art in the United States" met with a somewhat mixed but positive reception, "awed" by the classicism of *Mozartiana* and *Reminiscence*, and giving *Alma Mater* "the most prolonged laudations of the evening."[136] Just how many people were at the Shubert is unclear, however, and Kirstein's diary records the second-hand news that the New Haven audience was not large, but happily with no mention of tomatoes having been thrown.[137]

From New Haven the company headed two hundred miles south to Allentown, Pennsylvania, for a performance at the Lyric Theatre, with the overture to Glinka's *Ruslan and Lyudmila* and *Serenade* replacing the *Figaro* overture and *Mozartiana*.[138] A review praised the choice of "widely divergent" ballets for the tour's programs, from *Serenade*, "poignantly effective in its tragic, poetic pantomime," to the "hilariously satirical" *Alma Mater* to *Reminiscence*, "in the traditional classic form in which each dancer is given opportunity to display all the skill at his or her disposal."[139] The description of the energetic response of the audience reads like a moment from Kirstein's happiest daydreams, and "the dance audience of the future was evident in the enthusiasm of gallery and balcony, where young students of the dance were plentiful among the spectators, and theatre patrons were completely won to appreciation."[140]

From Allentown they went east to Princeton's McCarter Theatre, where the program consisted of *Mozartiana, Alma Mater*, and *Reminiscence*, with the *Figaro* overture as opener.[141] Kirstein would later find out that in Princeton Balanchine had renewed his manipulative emotional games with the women of the company. Holly Howard's mother Lois reported that Balanchine "had been dreadful to Holly" following the show because she wanted to go out with some of the college boys.[142] On returning from her night out, Howard was informed by Balanchine that Elise Reiman, his erstwhile seatmate on the bus, danced better than she did.[143]

They then traveled to Harrisburg, Pennsylvania, presenting the full orchestral and dance program given in Allentown.[144] According to a review, the company "received a tremendous ovation at the Majestic Theater last night when it interpreted the art of Terpsichore in all its phases and color."[145] The setting and costumes of *Serenade* were described as "modernistic in somber colors of gray, black, white and blue," in accord with the "somber mood" of Tchaikovsky's score.[146] The ballet was "excellently performed" by a company "beautifully trained in precision and in adaptation to the moods of music."[147] *Alma Mater* provided a "gay" mood in contrast, with its "hilarious farce of a college football game," while the

FIGURE 4.2 George Balanchine and Yvonne Patterson in front of American Ballet tour bus, 1935, photographer unknown. Yvonne Patterson–William Dollar Papers, Jerome Robbins Dance Division, New York Public Library. BALANCHINE is a Trademark of The George Balanchine Trust.

setting for the classical *Reminiscence* was described as "a majestic Roman court," in which solo numbers "followed each other in rapid succession and many types and variations of the dance were displayed."[148]

Scranton, Pennsylvania, was the next and, as it would happen, the last stop on the American Ballet's tour. Kirstein wrote later in *Thirty Years* of the cross-country journey simply that "the tour collapsed in Scranton, Pennsylvania," as if of its own accord.[149] Although this and other accounts of the tour imply a poetic ignominy to this geographic circumstance, it should be noted that Scranton was a routine one-night-stand for touring dance companies, and in previous decades it had hosted performances by Diaghilev's Ballets Russes, Rolf de Maré's Ballets Suédois, and more recently the de Basil company. The question of location aside, the underlying cause of the tour's demise will always remain somewhat obscure. It is likely that Edward Warburg's poor oversight of his company manager, Alexander Merovitch, was ultimately responsible. These problems finally came home to roost and were exacerbated by (or the cause of) an apparent psychological breakdown on the part of Merovitch, whose mental troubles were already manifest several days before the company arrived in Scranton. On October 17, Kirstein received a midnight phone call from Warburg, who reported from New Haven that Merovitch "had been behaving outrageously, calling everyone names, screaming at the kids."[150] Warburg was apparently rattled enough to return to New York the following day, with the troupe continuing on to Allentown without him.

Kirstein was not troubled enough to forgo his usual weekend retreat in the country with his sister, but on returning to New York he immediately regrouped with Warburg to assess the situation. The troupe was "now as yet unpaid in Scranton," and Balanchine was "terribly tired and worried," but Kirstein felt "it will nevertheless go on."[151] The following day, Kirstein and Warburg met with their lawyers at the Harvard Club to discuss how to proceed now that it was apparent that Merovitch's company had apparently gone out of business, with a "Sign on door telling of closure till further notice" and Sol Hurok already declaring the venture "a flop."[152] The question now was what to do with the stranded dancers and musicians and whether to try to salvage the rest of the tour. In the end, the decision was made to cancel the rest of the tour, and Kirstein accompanied Warburg and his lawyer Dave Somers to Hoboken, where they caught a train to Scranton.[153] On arrival they discovered that the performance had taken place as scheduled, but they returned with the company to New York the following day.[154] With everyone back in town Kirstein learned more details of Merovitch's paranoid and delusional "madness," which, if an act, had been a very convincing one.[155] The dancers had been so shaken by the incidents that they could "scarcely dance."[156] Kirstein also learned that in Scranton Balanchine thought he might be getting sick again also.[157]

As the tour had been touted in advance so widely, news of its collapse, including the bizarre behavior of Merovitch, inevitably found its way into the press, which offered contradictory accounts of the incidents. The *New York Times* offered the most judicious coverage, relaying statements from Warburg's attorneys to the effect that the company "had contracted with the Musical Art Management, Inc., for the latter organization to manage the itinerary" of the tour.[158] At the seventh stop on the tour, in Scranton, "it was understood, the musicians refused to continue unless they were paid in full. The tour came to a halt when payment was not completed."[159] Other news outlets eagerly played up this intriguing angle, based on observations of Merovitch's behavior after his return to New York. "Mystery veiling the sudden collapse of the American Ballet's 28-week tour," reported the *Daily Mirror*, "was dispelled when its manager was discovered in the Park Central Hotel announcing that he hopes to 'end all war.'"[160] Another article reported on Merovitch's erratic behavior during a return visit to his Rockefeller Plaza offices, where he angrily confronted his staff and blamed his deputy Jack Birse—also apparently suffering from mental woes—for the collapse of the tour, all within earshot of a witness.[161] The article goes on to relate a statement from Warburg included in this same press release, which is apologetic to the company's audiences and diplomatic toward Merovitch. "I regret that the many people who had counted on seeing the ballet company in the next weeks will be disappointed," he explained, adding that the ballet hoped to return for performances at a future date.[162]

The full scope of the planned tour gives a sense of how great the disappointment and embarrassment at its collapse must have been for all concerned.[163] The next city after Scranton was to have been Ithaca, New York, and from there they were to have made several stops—including Binghamton, Buffalo, and Cleveland—en route to Chicago.[164] The Chicago performances at the Civic Opera House November 8–10 (including Saturday and Sunday matinees) are touted in a surviving flier, hailing the company as a "Leading Dance Troupe of the Day."[165] They were to have left their tour buses behind in Chicago to take to the rails, heading to the West Coast for week-long engagements in Los Angeles and San Francisco as well as performances in Portland, Seattle, and as far north as Vancouver.[166] On their way back to the East Coast they were to make stops in several cities including Omaha, Tulsa, Dallas, and, as already mentioned by Balanchine, St. Louis.[167] As many as sixty total stops were planned for the ninety-eight-day tour, which would indeed have rivaled the coast-to-coast journeys of the de Basil troupe had it been completed.[168] An article in the *Dancing Times* suggests that the tour might even have extended beyond continental North America to include engagements in Cuba and Bermuda after the company returned to New York at the end of January.[169]

Fallout from the debacle was relatively modest, and while Warburg departed for a month-long escape to Mexico, Kirstein again fixated on the possibility of Balanchine's suffering another breakdown.[170] A week later

FIGURE 4.3 Promotional flier for unrealized Chicago performances of the American Ballet in fall 1935. George Balanchine Archive, MS Thr 411 (2765, folder 59), Houghton Library, Harvard University.

Kirstein wrote to his father that the deal with the opera had not in fact been endangered and the dancers were in good spirits despite the chaos.[171] Two weeks later, order had been further restored, and rehearsals for the opera were set to begin shortly, which would give the company a real chance to redeem itself.[172]

CHAPTER 5 | 1935–1936

THE THREE YEARS that the American Ballet was affiliated with the Metropolitan Opera as its resident dance ensemble have been construed as an unfortunate detour at best or a Babylonian captivity at worst, an outcome all the more ironic given how hard Warburg and others had lobbied to secure the post. But the company's first year at the opera did not represent a complete loss for the enterprise, even though its official duties, providing incidental dances for opera productions, would prove the least satisfying element of their activity during the 1935–36 season. Balanchine's choreographic contributions to the opera attracted attention mostly when they invited critical comment or controversy and were otherwise greeted with indifference. Less than ideal working conditions for the company and Balanchine's unorthodox artistic tendencies in many opera ballets quickly made it clear that the American Ballet's new post was not the best fit on either an institutional or artistic level. Balanchine's dances for operas including *Aida* and *Lakmé* emerged as particular flashpoints for criticism, containing movement deemed too lascivious and out of keeping with the opera's restrained aesthetics.

The American Ballet fared better when performing their own repertoire, including two new ballets, *Concerto* and *The Bat*, along with works from their existing repertoire. These ballets were offered either as prologues or afterpieces on shorter opera programs or as part of special "opera concerts" featuring a variety of arias and excerpted scenes. Even more consequential, in April the American Ballet was a key participant in a new institutional initiative launched by the Met: a "popular price" spring season of performances intended to expand the opera's calendar of production and reach out to wider audiences. For this initiative Balanchine contributed dances for a new production of *The Bartered Bride*, and the American Ballet produced an experimental dance-intensive production of Gluck's

Orpheus and Eurydice. While *The Bartered Bride* came in for criticism similar to Balanchine's other opera work, the *Orpheus* production occasioned a critical bloodbath and was widely and roundly criticized for its arcane dramaturgical interventions.

A brighter spot during this time was Balanchine's independent projects on the already popular price Broadway stage, work that would prove more popular than anything yet offered to the public by the American Ballet. He first signed on as a collaborator for the 1936 edition of the *Ziegfeld Follies*, overseeing dances for Josephine Baker, tap dancers Duke McHale and the Nicholas Brothers, and popular ballet star Harriet Hoctor; he also created the surrealist ballet *Words without Music*, his first collaboration with émigré composer Vladimir Dukelsky, better known by his stage name Vernon Duke. A month before the Met's spring season began, Balanchine premiered his first work for Richard Rodgers and Lorenz Hart in the musical comedy *On Your Toes*, the first of several shows on which the three would collaborate. With a backstage plot that brought together the worlds of Broadway and the Ballets Russes, the crossover ethos of *On Your Toes* was exemplified by its title number, which featured twin dance choruses of tap and ballet dancers. In addition to this show-stopping sequence, there were two other big moments for dance: the Act 1 *Princess Zenobia* ballet, which emulated and made light of the orientalist fantasy *Schéhérazade*, and the musical's concluding *Slaughter on Tenth Avenue*, a dramatic narrative ballet in which a "hoofer" falls in love with a nightclub dancer. Balanchine's work on the musical, and in particular the creation of *Slaughter on Tenth Avenue*, would prove a watershed moment in his career and in Broadway dance more broadly. Praised as widely as *Orpheus* would be panned, *Slaughter* was hailed as an exemplar of what a new and innovative American ballet might look like. Thus two and a half years in, the Balanchine-Kirstein enterprise would finally give rise to a work that fulfilled the goals it had articulated, albeit outside the official institutional orbit of the American Ballet's school and company.

Far from merely eclipsing the efforts of the American Ballet, *On Your Toes* had at least one tangible impact on the artistic priorities of the official enterprise itself, inspiring a short-lived project conceived of by Kirstein. On the heels of the musical's premiere, Kirstein planned and proposed a new work for the American Ballet that would blend ballet and tap dancing, a project that for a short time was slated for inclusion in the company's contributions to the Met's spring season. Inspired by Balanchine's *On Your Toes* choreography, it was planned to showcase innovative tap performer Paul Draper as a soloist with the American Ballet dancing to music by

J. S. Bach. This short-lived "Bach ballet" represents not only an early trace of Balanchine's subsequent masterpiece *Concerto Barocco*, but more important, shows that Balanchine's Broadway work had the potential to influence the core activities of the American Ballet in unforeseen ways.

The Metropolitan Opera's 1935 season opened on December 10 with a standing-room-only performance of *La Traviata* during which the American Ballet made its first appearance as the opera's new dance ensemble. "It was not until the end of the third act that the audience had an opportunity to see the American Ballet in its Metropolitan debut," as one report explained, with the credit that the dancing was "arranged by George Balanchine" the only additional detail provided.[1] To this meager picture, a review by Olin Downes added only that the ensemble had displayed "more youth and enthusiasm than technical finish."[2] The modest size of the American Ballet's contributions to this performance and the glancing attention they received in reviews is a pattern that would be replicated often during their tenure at the opera. A review subsequently noted of the company's dances for *Faust* only that the ensemble's "choreographic forces were considerably livelier" than in previous productions of the opera.[3]

Following the collapse of the American Ballet's tour in October, Warburg had been advised by Met director Edward Johnson to keep a low profile, and rehearsals for the new season began in mid-November with little fanfare.[4] Observing preparations for *Carmen*, Kirstein noted how Balanchine was working "swiftly and brilliantly," and that he was handling the volume of work at hand "marvelously."[5] But it was clear to Kirstein that the abandonment of the dual company scheme had been for the best, since it was far from clear what would have been possible if any significant number of their dancers had been on the road.[6] If the "Gypsy dance" Balanchine created for the company's *Traviata* debut had lacked a certain polish it was not owing entirely to the youth and insecurity of the ensemble's dancers. The American Ballet had been given the chance to rehearse on the opera house stage for the first time only two days prior to opening night, a three-hour rehearsal in which they had to prepare for not only *Traviata* but the other two operas scheduled for the first week of the season, *Aida* and *Faust*.[7] Before the year was out the company would debut dances for four other operas—*Lakmé, Tannhäuser, Carmen*, and *Rigoletto*—a total of seven in less than a month. Given the volume of new work they had to create in such a short period of time and the relative institutional neglect of the opera toward them, the company acquitted themselves fairly well, and Balanchine's previous work on the opera stage in Monte Carlo and elsewhere meant that he had ample experience to draw from.

The company more eagerly anticipated the opportunity to perform their existing repertoire on the opera stage, the primary payoff of their new alliance with the Met. The American Ballet was given its first such chance during the second week of the opera season, when *Reminiscence* was performed following a performance of *Hansel and Gretel*. This was the first time in almost a decade that a stand-alone work of ballet—that is, not an excerpt from an opera ballet—was being presented by the Met, news given prominent coverage by John Martin.[8] For the occasion, the ballet had been reworked slightly, with a mazurka and a "large classical waltz" replacing the sections that had been danced by guest artist Paul Haakon at its Adelphi premiere. The American Ballet was subsequently given the opportunity to offer many of its ballets in conjunction with shorter opera programs or on special "gala concert" programs of opera arias and scenes. In February, *Serenade* was performed on several occasions—including as an interlude between the one-act operas *Cavalleria Rusticana* and *Gianni Schicchi*—for which it was lit with white lights and costumed with "patches and red wigs for the boys," according to Kirstein's recollections.[9] *Mozartiana* was the centerpiece of a heterogeneous concert program including music by Verdi, Meyerbeer, and Massenet, while *Errante* was offered as the second half of a double bill with *Cavalleria*.[10]

As the season progressed, Balanchine's operatic work began to garner more attention in a way that confirmed his reputation for bizarre and experimental tendencies. "If the dances are not worse than those of previous years," a review noted of his dances for *Lakmé*, "they cannot be considered much better," and it appeared that Balanchine was "striving too eagerly to be striking."[11] In the opera's "Persane" or Persian dance, Holly Howard and Charles Laskey had performed their steps "with gruesome effectiveness," even though the choreography was decidedly not in the best of taste and seemingly "painful in its contortions."[12] Balanchine's dances for *Aida* subsequently made even bigger headlines for similar reasons. "Instead of the usual petticoated gentle flutterings," as *Variety* reported, "the Balanchine troupe did snaky wiggling."[13] In quotes to the press Balanchine attacked not only critics' ability to evaluate his dances— "They do not know one dance from another"—but defended the authenticity of his innovative "Egyptian" dances, claiming that what the critics saw as anachronistic was in fact "the way Ethiopians danced in those days"—not "on the toes, in nightgowns, but with the hips!"[14] Aside from Balanchine's flights of fancy, the youth of the American Ballet emerged as a potential problem rather than a virtue. A review of *Carmen* noted that the "youthfulness" of the dancers was "very noticeable next to the mature types threaded through the singing ensemble," a contrast that heightened the ongoing aesthetic clash between music and dance.[15]

In the midst of the opera season, Balanchine debuted new work in an entirely different institutional context, a new edition of the *Ziegfeld Follies* that premiered at the end of January. Balanchine's engagement for this new project was reported several weeks prior to the start of the opera season, and initial announcements suggested that the show would include members of the American Ballet.[16] John Martin reported that although this project did not represent "a new field for Mr. Balanchine," as he had previously staged work for variety stages in London, the added responsibility "would seem to indicate a busy period" for the artist.[17] In the end, dancers from the American Ballet would not appear in the show, which included Fannie Brice and Bob Hope among its impressive roster of performers and collaborators.[18] Balanchine's innovative tendencies evidently found a more comfortable home in the context of the *Follies*, adding "effective and stirring studies in somber and macabre movement" to many parts of the revue.[19] For popular ballet star Harriet Hoctor he devised a "Night Flight" number that had the dancer "hovering like a released and almost transparent soul over an airplane's grim shadow," choreography that represented an "intensification and clarification" of the dancer's unique style.[20] Hoctor was also featured in *Words without Music*, a "surrealist ballet," described as a work of "fascinating weirdness" in which "the imaginative whim-wham of the ineffable [Salvador] Dalí takes form in action."[21] The ballet featured three men portraying "Figures in Green" and another group of "Figures in Black," four men who "lie on the floor and move about as if they were the others' shadows," cast by a single "Figure with the Light."[22] In the course of the ballet, the Figures in Black arise from the floor to spirit Hoctor away from the Figures in Green, to the accompaniment of music by Vernon Duke and amid sets designed by Vincente Minnelli that included a "ramp of apple green, background of lavender," and "porticos . . . of pale violet."[23]

Balanchine also helped arrange two numbers for another featured performer, Josephine Baker, recently returned from Europe for the production. Baker's appearance had been "awaited with much curiosity" but by some accounts her performance did not live up to the high expectations.[24] Both numbers traded on the dancer's self-exoticizing aesthetics and featured interpretive movement rather than structured choreography. In a "West Indies" number, Baker danced an "incendiary" conga, while in the "artistically staged" number "5 A.M." the performer worked herself "into quite a state of something with the African gods."[25] In the course of production, Balanchine had the opportunity to make the acquaintance of other notable performers featured elsewhere in the show, tap dancers Duke McHale and the Nicholas Brothers, the latter appearing in one of Baker's numbers as tuxedo-clad page boys.[26]

While the *Follies* continued its run and in the final weeks of the opera season, Balanchine contributed to two other projects in a more classical vein, one back in Hartford and another at the Met. For a special February gala event at the Avery Memorial arranged by Chick Austin, Balanchine produced a small *piece d'occasion* called *Serenata*, set to an unidentified score by Mozart.[27] A more substantial work premiered on the final opera concert of the season on March 22, a setting of Chopin's F-minor piano concerto eponymously titled *Concerto*, a collaboration between Balanchine and William Dollar. Dollar was responsible for the first and third movements, while the second movement comprised an adagio that had been created earlier by Balanchine and was included at Dollar's request.[28] Reviewing the ballet in a subsequent season, critic Edwin Denby called it "swift, pleasant, interesting, and very well danced" and said that the ballet proved that "the American Ballet has grown up to be the first class institution it was meant to be."[29] The ballet further demonstrated that Balanchine "has done more than anyone could have expected in so short a time,"[30] in his ability to foster "a personal quality in his dancers."[31] *Concerto* did not similarly impress *Dance Observer*, which continued to view Balanchine's methods as disturbingly alien. Despite improvements to the company's skills evident in the ballet, Balanchine's fundamental problem "lies in the choice of movement and concept"—that is, classical ballet—"so foreign to the American idiom."[32]

———

Around the same time that Balanchine signed on for the *Follies* he was recruited to join the team of a new musical by Richard Rodgers and Lorenz Hart, *On Your Toes*, the first of several hit shows on which the three would work jointly. The success of these musicals has been credited to an innovative creative formula devised by the composer-lyricist team: not having a formula.[33] "As Rodgers and Hart see it," as a cover story in *Time* later explained, "what was killing musicomedy [*sic*] was its sameness, its tameness, its eternal rhyming of June with moon," and the duo accordingly explored strikingly different subjects for each show.[34] Its no-formula formula show *On Your Toes* capitalized on two different trends: the Depression-era boom in classical music appreciation and the ballet fever sweeping the country in the 1930s, more specifically the popularity of Russian ballet companies.[35] Much more than a lighthearted backstage musical that happened to be about art, *On Your Toes* was thus enmeshed in the same debates in which Balanchine and Kirstein's enterprise was engaged over the proper way to Americanize art forms such as classical music and ballet. The high-art angle of *On Your Toes* also owed much to the tastes of its producer, Dwight Deere Wiman, an independently wealthy balletomane interested in elevating the quality of Broadway entertainment and a subsequent producer of several other Rodgers and Hart musicals that involved Balanchine.[36]

When *On Your Toes* opened in 1936, the role of dance in the show was discussed as a sophisticated and classy feature, and the musical in general was viewed as a luxe item for which its producer had evidently spared no expense. Wiman had "equipped *On Your Toes* with musical comedy's richest appurtenances," and foremost among these features was the presence of a modern version of ballet created by a bona fide contemporary choreographer, who would ensure the stylishness and authenticity of the show's dancing.[37] Aside from Balanchine's personal relationship to the ballet establishment satirized in the show, the setting and characters of *On Your Toes* are a virtual roman à clef of the Diaghilev diaspora, beginning with the "Cosmopolitan Opera House" in New York City, where the bulk of its scenes take place. The art-imitating-life dimension of *On Your Toes* was made even more apparent during the musical's opening weeks in New York, as the de Basil company found itself performing at the very same time at the Metropolitan Opera. The Ballet Russe troupe evidently took the musical's humor in stride and went so far as to boast in advertisements for their Met engagement that "only the great deserve the darts of satire."[38]

The lead character of *On Your Toes* is not a Russian dancer but rather the all-American Phil "Junior" Dolan III, a third-generation vaudevillian who has left behind his career on the stage to work as a music professor. Among Junior's students are the aspiring songwriter Frankie Frayne and composer Sidney Cohn, who discover their teacher's hidden talents and persuade him to reconnect with his dancing roots. Junior agrees, but not content merely to return to vaudeville he instead declares his intention to aspire to something higher and join a Russian ballet company. This aspiration is good not just for Junior's ambitions but also the goals of Sidney, who hopes the company can be persuaded to mount an innovative "jazz ballet" he is composing. The plot thickens when Junior, immersed in the new and exotic world of the ballet company, finds himself torn between the all-American Frankie and the company's prima ballerina. Much of the succeeding action—including the character of the show's dances—is occasioned by the collision of these disparate worlds.

Aside from romantic entanglements, the plot of *On Your Toes* is precipitated by another art-imitating-life dimension: the financial instability of the ballet company that Junior is attempting to join. Headed up by the impresario Sergei Alexandrovitch, its stars are the self-obsessed Vera Barnova and her equally egotistical partner Konstantine Morrosine—thinly veiled caricatures of Serge Diaghilev, Irina Baronova, and Léonide Massine, respectively—the latter two locked in a battle of affections and egos both on- and offstage. To set the company's finances in order Sergei has turned to wealthy American benefactor Peggy Porterfield for financial support. When the audience first encounters all of these characters, the company is at another fiscal dead end, and this time the straight-talking Porterfield decides she is not content to sign yet another blank check, deciding instead to use her clout to change the artistic direction of the company, in a more colloquial echo of the goals of Balanchine and Kirstein's enterprise. "Your public is tired of *Schéhérazade, Le Spectre de la Rose*—they've seen all those Russian turkeys," she explains to Sergei, who is also her not-so-secret lover.[39] As something fresh and novel she pitches the new American "jazz ballet" of Junior's friend Sidney. This proposed project is initially rejected out of hand by Sergei, who cites the noble tradition that he is bound to uphold (another nod to Diaghilev, who had no interest in jazz or popular music), but in the end, Porterfield gets her way by threatening to withhold her line of credit—and perhaps other personal resources—unless the company puts on the jazz ballet, *Slaughter on Tenth Avenue*, performed as the concluding scene of *On Your Toes*.

Slaughter is premised on a love triangle of its own, in which a woman nightclub dancer is caught between her controlling and violent manager and an eager hoofer. In the course of the action, the dancer is shot and killed, and it reaches an even more dramatic conclusion in the context of the musical. At the end of the ballet Junior realizes that to save his own life he must continue dancing until the police apprehend the hit men (contracted by the jealous Morrosine) who have arrived to shoot him under the cover of the audience's applause. Tamara Geva, who originated the role of Vera, maintained that the original version of *Slaughter* "was quite serious" in its tone and effect.[40] Reviews of the musical confirm that *Slaughter* was indeed received as a weighty moment as well as being a crowd-pleaser, and the *New York Post* explained "real tension as well as genuine comedy abounds in the *Slaughter on Tenth Avenue* ballet which concludes the program."[41] Geva recalls the opening of the ballet as a "Gypsy Rose Lee" striptease in which she ended up in only nude body tights and three small American flags strategically placed for the sake of modesty.[42] After a thirty-second costume change, however, it was then a tour de force to the end, and not to be taken lightly. "All I can tell you—I can't explain the steps," as Geva explained, "but it was a dramatic performance, something that made people sit there and never laugh."[43] Ray Bolger, the original Junior, similarly recalled the genuine desperation that his dancing was meant to convey, and how his physical exhaustion and endurance was a great part of the drama of the scene: "You've got to do a step. You've got to jump up. You've got to keep dancing. You've been on for fifteen minutes. . . . And if I stop dancing they're gonna shoot!"[44]

In Broadway history and Balanchine's biographies, *Slaughter* has been retrospectively hailed as one of the earliest examples of an "integrated" dance number, in which a ballet is used to further the plot rather than merely provide entertainment. At the time of its premiere, however, *Slaughter* was not discussed as a plot-furthering innovation but was viewed as evidence

FIGURE 5.1 Photograph of *Slaughter on Tenth Avenue* from *On Your Toes*, photographer and exact date unknown, likely 1936. Collection of Robert Greskovic. Choreography by George Balanchine © The George Balanchine Trust.

that American ballet was coming into its own.[45] Numerous critics saw *Slaughter* as a thoroughly authentic and quite successful "modern ballet"[46] in an American idiom. The *Hollywood Reporter* called it "one of the finest musical and choreographic numbers ever presented" and was thus surely being scouted for the silver screen.[47] The ballet was an "impressive theatrical miracle," in the estimation of *Time* magazine, which "would probably evoke an ovation from modernists anywhere outside *On Your Toes*."[48] In a bit of double-edged praise, the *Brooklyn Eagle* even claimed that the musical represented a temporary step "up" for Balanchine, insofar as it took him briefly away from what the writer termed "his activities with the amateurs of his American ballet."[49] The fact that only an American dancer such as Bolger could have pulled off such an accomplishment was articulated in the book itself as well as being noted by critics. In the plot, Junior is recruited to play the lead in the ballet only after it becomes evident that Morrosine is unable to figure out the unexpected rhythms of the music. In stark contrast to the uneven offerings of the American Ballet, *Slaughter* proved that Americans—in this case the "jazz Nijinsky" Bolger—were capable of matching and even surpassing their more serious ballet rivals.[50] It was thus a bittersweet achievement that *Slaughter*, produced on Broadway by a fictional Russian ballet company and staged in the fictional Cosmopolitan Opera House, received the unequivocal praise denied the real-life American Ballet at the actual Metropolitan Opera.

On Your Toes featured two other substantial dance sequences, both of which were comparable to *Slaughter* in scale, length, and the critical praise they received, and both helped further the musical's plot in their own ways as well. The first of these was the somewhat serious parody of *Schéhérazade*, *La Princesse Zenobia*, which was the culminating event of the musical's first act. The *Dancing Times* summarized the number as "a nightmare hodgepodge of *Schéhérazade*, *Tamar* and all other Franco-Oriental ballets"—in other words, one of the so-called Russian turkeys that Peggy hoped Sergei would abandon in favor of *Slaughter*.[51] The ethos of *Zenobia* was less than subtly indebted to *Schéhérazade*, hinging upon the title character's choice of a suitor and taking place in her fantastically appointed "presentation room" in the palace, loosely inspired by Léon Bakst's original sets. The princess is attended by handmaidens clad in harem pants and veils, whose dance at the opening of the scene is soon interrupted by a fanfare that heralds the arrival of the three rich but not so physically desirable suitors vying for her hand. Of course, the princess has fallen in love instead with the penniless and more comely slave Abu. In order for her impoverished lover to keep up with his aristocratic rivals, who each offer extravagant gifts in exchange for her hand, she provides a dowry to Abu in the form of five "Nubian slaves."

These slaves, portrayed by five of the Russian dancers in blackface makeup, occasion the humorous unraveling of this at first quite serious ballet number. Junior Dolan, recruited to fill in for one of the dancers at the last minute, is not able to master the routine in such a short time, and also makes the rookie mistake of putting makeup on only his face instead of his full body. As one review quipped, Junior is "a Nubian slave who didn't Nube below his collar bone and who, when they snatched off his cloak, disclosed his horribly pale skin surmounted by a puss of darkest lampblack." A stage direction in the script highlights the importance of the visual gag, instructing clearly, "We must manage in placing the ranks and formations that the white body continually kills the effect."

In the face of such antics many reviews glossed the ballet as straight-forward comedy—while making no mention of its racist conceit—noting that *Zenobia* would "make it impossible for anyone to ever meet *Schéhérazade* again with a straight face."[52] In *Zenobia*, "the ballet is on its toes, executing—in the sinister meaning of the word—*Schéhérazade*," and was danced well enough that even "a professional pirouetter in the audience found it ever so amusing."[53] Despite some of its obviously

FIGURE 5.2 Photograph of *La Princesse Zenobia* ballet from *On Your Toes*, photographer and exact date unknown, likely 1936. Collection of Robert Greskovic. Choreography by George Balanchine © The George Balanchine Trust.

comedic elements, however, the original Princess Zenobia maintained that the ballet began in a quite serious and straightforward tone, and that the scene succeeded because of its real balletic virtuosity. Geva described the duet between the princess and Abu as a "very difficult adagio," which "started out seriously and gradually . . . became a satire on the ballet."[54] Reviews explicitly praised this aspect of the ballet and noted the divergent responses of different segments of the audience, corroborating Geva's claim that "the balcony recognized that it was supposed to be funny much earlier than the orchestra."[55] The ballet was danced "with such intense gravity and determination that it was several minutes before the audience grasped the fact that the *Princess Zenobia* ballet was reaching heights of satirical brilliance."[56] In other words, *Zenobia* was not a complete joke, and owed its success to Geva's real talents and Balanchine's familiarity with the style and conventions of such ballets, in which he had danced himself for many years. By some accounts the ballet ran a certain risk by trying to have it both ways at a time when *Schéhérazade* was still one of the most popular (and un-ironic) offerings of the real-life Russian Ballet. The *Dancing Times* noted this potential for confusion, explaining that the ballet provided "genuine amusement in exaggerated comparisons for the real balletomanes and confusion for the uninitiated."[57] Regardless of who may or may not have been in on the joke onstage or off, the *Zenobia* ballet might better be regarded as not merely a comedic incidental dance but quite "integrated" with not just the plot of *On Your Toes* but with Balanchine's larger creative interests and talents as well.

Unlike *Zenobia* and *Slaughter*, the third major dance sequence of *On Your Toes*, its title number, does not boast a fully realized libretto in surviving scripts, although many details have been preserved in descriptions from reviews and dancers' memories. Generally speaking, the number's dancing, lyrics, and music, and the way all these elements are framed by the plot, reveal the number as an *ars poetica* for the musical, appropriate enough for a title song. The song and succeeding dance, in which dual choruses of tap and ballet dancers shared the stage, enact the aesthetic synthesis of Old World and New ultimately realized later in the jazz ballet *Slaughter on Tenth Avenue*. Much like *Zenobia*, moreover, the "On Your Toes" number stands as more than incidental with respect to Balanchine's creative output. From a logistical perspective, it involved arguably the largest ensemble of dancers that he had ever worked with in his career. On a conceptual level, the number was a serendipitous outlet for ideas that he had been pondering for several years on his own about mixing popular and classical dance forms, and more crucially, the combination of African American and white dancers in contrasting styles.[58]

Along with *Zenobia* and *Slaughter*, reviews singled out "On Your Toes" as one of the show's most memorable scenes and praised its innovative musical and choreographic qualities. Audiences "will remember for a long time the imaginative and intriguing presentation of the title song, with the composer of the American ballet explaining how he would orchestrate the number" and the "choreographic accompaniment to this tune brings out the show's full force of ballet and tap dancers in a breathlessly exciting routine."[59] The *Dancing Times* described how the number effected a creative blending of the contrasting styles of ballet and tap, while using a uniform musical tempo, with one group "hopping and 'shagging' in syncopation, while a whirl of pirouettes, toe dancing and elevations represent the other."[60]

Balanchine did not come up with such effects entirely on his own, however, and for *On Your Toes* as a whole he benefited from the assistance of African American tap dancer Herbert Harper, credited as an "assistant to Mr. Balanchine," whereas the "choreography" was credited to Balanchine

FIGURE 5.3 Photograph of "On Your Toes" number from *On Your Toes*, photographer and exact date unknown, likely 1936. Collection of Robert Greskovic. Choreography by George Balanchine © The George Balanchine Trust.

alone.[61] Balanchine also benefited from the assistance of William Dollar—then a principal dancer for the American Ballet—for the musical's ballet choreography, with Dollar accorded an "assistant" credit identical to Harper's.[62] There is some disagreement about the terms of the creative relationship between Balanchine and Harper. Fred Danieli maintained that "Balanchine always liked tap" and that he and Harper "collaborated" to devise the 'On Your Toes' number, further describing Harper as a "very good tap teacher."[63] Dancer Grace Houston Case recalled differently that Harper was recruited to assist Balanchine after rehearsals had already begun, in response to the choreographer's lack of both expertise and interest in tap dancing.[64]

What is not disputed is that Balanchine treated his tap dancers with a gentility and respect that they were not accustomed to. In contrast to the militaristic way in which Case was used to being ordered around during her time as a Rockette, Balanchine treated her and her fellow female hoofers like his own dancers from the American Ballet. "I had never had a choreographer take me by the hand and lead me by the fingertips into a group and then into another group," she remembered, noting how Balanchine led each dancer by the hand, "instead of shouting 'give me line-ups, get the lead out, let's go' over that PA system they shouted through. . . . Balanchine came in as though he were in Swan Lake."[65] Aside from establishing a more refined atmosphere in rehearsal, Balanchine combined ballet and tap in more literal ways in the "On Your Toes" number. Case recalled "arm waving and a kind of ballet turn" in one of her combinations, and that even though they were tap dancing, a style grounded mostly in the feet, "there was a lot of arm work." Case also recalls the complexity and swiftness of the number in general, how its forty dancers "worked in groups of two, three, and four" and Balanchine "would take a group of four across the stage; then a group of six would appear; then four, very quickly on and then off the stage; that's how he kept it moving."[66]

Although On Your Toes had an all-white cast and was not explicitly engaged in questions of race—the offensive blackface humor of Princess Zenobia notwithstanding—other contemporary evidence from Balanchine's early years in the United States suggests that above and beyond Harper's direct involvement, black dancing and dancers were manifest in the "On Your Toes" number in more diffuse ways. Many statements attributed to Balanchine during his early years in the United States reveal how his interests had been trending in the direction of crossover dance numbers on the model of "On Your Toes" long before his work on the musical, often with black dancers, in particular black women, foremost in his mind. In addition to Balanchine's initial interest in recruiting a racially diverse group of students for the School of American Ballet, black dancers continued to occupy his creative imagination in both theory and practice following his arrival in the United States. Only weeks after arriving in America Balanchine declared to Kirstein in another primitivist brainstorm that "it would be fine to do a classical ballet with negresses in tutus of gold and silver pailletes and white bodices."[67] In a January 1934 interview with critic Arnold Haskell, Balanchine articulated his interest in mixing black and white dancers in contrasting styles, describing "the effect that would be produced by six Negresses dancing on their pointes and six white girls doing a frenzied jazz!"[68] These statements suggest that Balanchine had independently arrived at the central conceit of the "On Your Toes" number several years before Rodgers and Hart's musical, with an explicitly racial dimension ascribed to the encounter of ballet and popular dancing. And of course, just as *On Your Toes* was beginning production, Balanchine had just completed his first work for the *Ziegfeld Follies* which featured Josephine Baker, the Nicholas Brothers, and Duke McHale.[69] All of which suggests that the despite its all-white cast and lack of any literal engagement with questions of race and regardless of Balanchine's authorial control of the ultimate form and content of "On Your Toes," the number shows that his popular projects had the potential to be more than merely work for hire, but an actual outlet, however serendipitous, for his own creative imaginings.

———

With *On Your Toes* up and running, in May 1936 at the end of their first season at the Metropolitan Opera, Balanchine and the American Ballet presented two performances of the first and last opera production over which they would have complete artistic purview, a dance-intensive staging of Gluck's *Orpheus and Eurydice*.[70] Conceived of in collaboration with artist Pavel Tchelitchev, the opera was performed with the singers and chorus in the orchestra pit and the dancers on stage portraying the characters. In accounts of Balanchine and Kirstein's enterprise this production has been mostly regarded as a minor *succès de scandale* that offended the rearguard sensibilities of the opera's affluent patrons. But the Balanchine-Tchelitchev *Orpheus* was in fact presented not to the Metropolitan's usual audience but for the more economically diverse clientele of the Met's experimental "spring season," which offered performances at "popular prices" comparable to Broadway fare—that is, for audiences with few if any pearls to clutch—an initiative that responded to a wider mandate in Depression-era

America to broaden access to cultural resources. Such efforts were especially strong in New York City thanks to progressive Republican mayor Fiorello LaGuardia, a fan of classical music and opera who saw the arts as a source of civic pride and spiritual uplift for working-class citizens.[71] Ironically, the American Ballet's marquee contribution to this popular initiative proved remarkably unpopular with virtually everyone who saw it.

Besides the ambitious *Orpheus* production, the Met's spring season featured two other new productions involving the American Ballet. Adding to the American Ballet's own repertoire, Balanchine created a new one-act work called *The Bat* set to selections from *Die Fledermaus*. The up-beat and imaginative *Bat* was a sleeper hit, a crowd-pleaser consisting musically of a "generous assortment of tunes from" the popular Johann Strauss operetta.[72] The ballet benefited from considerable visual appeal, featuring "bright-hued raiment against a luminous blue-green background," and most spectacularly, an ingenious costume conceit for the title character, who was "portrayed by two dancers . . . each in spangled black and each armed with one huge bat-wing," played by Holly Howard and Lew Christensen in the original production.[73] As described in a later account, the ballet was "an evocation of the spirit and environment of old Vienna," with a vague plot about an artist in search of a muse.[74] The title character came across as more endearing than scary: "If he, or they, filled the cast with terror, the audience, for its part, had nothing but pleasure of the whole show, which it received with unstinted enthusiasm."[75] *The Bat* was premiered two days before *Orpheus*, on a double bill in which it followed *Lucia di Lammermoor*, and was reckoned "a likeable and well contrasted epilogue for the evening's entertainment."[76] It was performed a total of six times during the spring season alongside other operas and was subsequently kept in regular rotation during the company's remaining tenure at the Met.[77]

The other big premiere of the spring season in which the American Ballet participated was a new production of *The Bartered Bride*. *Musical America* declared it an undisputed hit of the spring season, and the *Herald-Tribune* reported that the opera "was generally regarded as an unusual and significant success."[78] Although its sets were not totally new they "had the look of having just been made," and the peasant costumes "possessed a singular freshness and gaiety of color."[79] The opera's dances, by contrast, would be reckoned as one of the production's low points.[80] Reviews criticized the "jarring" qualities of the choreography by Balanchine, who had "not only disregarded the Czech dance idioms which are indispensable to any valid realization of Smetana's indications, but violated the character of the music itself."[81] The reviewer vowed that in the future he would watch the production with closed eyes to avoid "the clash between the music and the dancing."[82]

But the main endeavor of the American Ballet for the spring season, and indeed the biggest production the company would ever attempt, was *Orpheus*. Kirstein would later describe the project as "a reckless manifesto designed, rehearsed, and produced within three weeks' time," a slight exaggeration as far as "designed" is concerned.[83] For most of March and April the spring season in its entirety had been in limbo, and as a result the opera did not go into production in earnest until early May, only three weeks prior to its premiere on May 22.[84] The planning and conceptualizing of the opera had begun several months before production began, but its three weeks of rehearsals would be grossly insufficient given the scale of the creative vision for *Orpheus*. The production called for intensive production elements underpinned by an elaborate conceptual apparatus, as revealed by a variety of written and visual traces as well as recollections from its original performers and audience members.

The first scene "At the Tomb of Eurydice" depicted "a moon-cratered valley of lifeless dust" in which Orpheus and his companions have memorialized the fallen Eurydice with "a monument made of her portrait, her drapes, and the broken household utensils which remained from her domestic life."[85] Performance photos reveal that this makeshift effigy of Eurydice was the dominant visual feature of the scene, and sketches show a ladder, broom, pitchfork, and draped fabric as its main components. According to Tchelitchev's biographer Parker Tyler, the placement of this cloth was part of the action: "they *climb up* to put her face on a huge easel, and drape it . . . so . . . just so . . ."[86] The second scene, labeled in the program as the "Entrance to Hades," featured the opera's memorable "Dance of the Furies." One reviewer described "a giant cage contraption which housed furies and scarlet demons," a structure also depicted in surviving sketches. The stage showed "the red glow of hell, a sliced hornet's nest filled with flames in which the souls of the damned were steamed and lashed by flying furies,"[87] more specifically, "white ghastly whips of the military Furies."[88]

The third scene in the Elysian Fields might be regarded as the heart of the production, exemplifying Tchelitchev's interest in the fusion of human performers and scenic elements, in particular through the use of translucent fabrics and lighting, all of which had been hallmarks of the American Ballet's previous project with the artist, *Errante*. "In that production I remember one scene with what looked like actual trees with roots hanging down," Elliott Carter recalled of the mise-en-scène.[89] "The underworld was a whole forest of roots and trees," and the audience "could see the trunks of the trees halfway up the stage. It was extraordinary."[90] Tyler's biography maintains that Tchelitchev had "insisted whole leafless trees be brought down from Connecticut" and surviving sketches and photos show how these various elements—sets, props, and dancers—combined to form a striking spectacle.[91] Several photos of the performance show the women of the corps with hands joined together weaving one of Balanchine's signature spiral formations, likely a moment from the most iconic number of the scene, if not the whole opera, the "Dance of the Blessed Spirits," danced in stylized Grecian tunics that would hardly have been out of place in an Isadora Duncan performance.[92] The final scene in the "Gardens of the Temple of Love" employed a quite literal interpretation of its deus ex machina that reunites the happy lovers in the "Paris" version of the opera that was used. Kirstein later recalled the *coup de théâtre* by which Amor reunited the lovers by whisking Eurydice "up to a sky sprayed with constellations and milky way," and the fact that Tchelitchev insisted that the wires be "painted a proud white, to state the mechanism as blatantly as possible."[93] Dancer Annabelle Lyon remembered this scene because of the troubles it caused, recalling how William Dollar "was supposed to touch earth in an arabesque position and his foot didn't quite touch and he kept groping with his toe."[94]

If this partially reconstructed storyboard seems seductive, other descriptions of the production's décor and costumes show how its elaborate apparatus had the potential to overwhelm. Lyon recalls that Tchelitchev was the real creative force behind the production, that it "was more his ballet than anybody's," and that the costumes were a quite salient feature: "I remember that we, in the group, wore a lot of costumes made out of cellophane. . . . A lot of cellophane."[95] "All of the characters, with the exception of the principals, were covered in grey greasepaint and translucent costumes to appear as mere shadows of life," another account explained.[96] Kirstein and others recall with special fondness the crystal lyre carried by Orpheus, which almost became a character itself. Made of cellulose, the custom-made prop had been a special bone of contention for Warburg, who had complained about its forty-five dollar price tag, although when the lyre was put into action it "looked like a million dollars," according to Kirstein.[97] Tyler writes of how the lyre contrasted starkly with the dark costume of Orpheus, and others explain how it served as a "visual manifestation of his poetic gift, which attracted and absorbed whatever light might be in the places he entered," whether the red glow of Hades or the milder haze of the Elysian Fields.[98]

Recollections by dancers and others suggest that the choreography of *Orpheus* was rather diffuse in character, a decision driven as much by design, given the complex nature of the scenery and décor, as by necessity, given the limited preparation time. Ruby Asquith recalled the choreography as grounded less in actual steps than a more idealized stage presence.[99] She remembers that Christensen "walked"—not danced—"with such beauty and such dignity and carried himself with such poise that it was just arresting to watch."[100] According to Christensen's own recollections, the first section of the opera was apparently not completed in time, and as a result Balanchine had to coach him through the scene via whispered cues from the prompter's box.[101] Lyon recalled the dancing as "very vague and ambivalent" and remembers mostly "not knowing much about what we were doing."[102] In contrast to the highly technical choreography of *Chaconne* (created by Balanchine in 1976 to excerpts from the opera), the choreography was "more interpretive" and was danced in soft shoes.[103] Ruthanna Boris similarly remembers the dancing as "an organic movement growing out of what was happening" with "slow walking, bending."[104] Tyler's biography describes several choreographic details that similarly suggest a freer movement style but also qualities that recall Balanchine's penchant for the acrobatic. Eurydice's anger at Orpheus for not looking back at her was visceral and physical in its depiction: "Eurydice running at Orphée from the back to make him look at her, jumping on him, hitting him with her knee. *Plonk!* like that. Sensational—but elegant."[105] Tyler also marvels at how Dollar as Amor was able to actually dance with very large wings on his back: "And such wings: at least life-size. No one expected it—dancing *with those wings on. Such things* George thought up."[106]

The "things" that Balanchine and Tchelitchev had devised did not sit well with the majority of critics, who held that the production had undermined the sanctity of the "true" meaning of the opera itself.[107] This failure was notably not attributed to the relative prominence of dance in and of itself, but rather the incongruity of the production as a whole with the perceived nobility and dignity of the work, a common critique of unconventional opera production to this day.[108] Upon this original sin, the production had piled on many other transgressions, and critics found *Orpheus* by turns comical, sentimental, and commercial. Of course, the irony is that the vehemence of these critiques translated into quite vivid descriptions, and they thus provide an additional lens through which to reimagine the short-lived production.

Time declared the opera "the most inept production that present-day opera-goers have witnessed on the Metropolitan stage," which added insult to injury owing to the fact that the "long-neglected masterpiece" had not been performed for over twenty years.[109] "There were settings like nothing ever seen anywhere," according to the *Baltimore Sun*, "with trapezes or something of the sort, dangling from the wings, and most of the miming and posing obscured rather than exemplified the beauty of Gluck's heavenly music, also the hellish portions."[110] The *Herald-Tribune* lamented that instead of "classic simplicity in both choreography and settings one gazed upon groupings as inane as those offered earlier this season by the Hollywood Ballet in its version of *Prometheus*"[111] and dismissed the entrance to Hades setting as "a giant cage contraption which housed furies and scarlet demons who proved no more terrifying than Punch & Judy puppets."[112] The Furies danced in a manner "that would not have frightened an infant in arms,"[113] and "lost souls swarmed up the trapezes after the manner of a kitten up the parlor portieres.[114] The ethereal stage effects of the Elysian Fields were derided as "white leafless trees, their roots completely exposed, dangling in mid-air . . . which further boasted huge, frosted cones, presumably of sugar, perhaps intended as pabulum for the happy shades."[115]

Even if the dance-intensive conceit was not regarded as the root problem of the production, the choreography itself did not redeem the endeavor, with the dancing dismissed as "a study in diligent ineptitude."[116] One critic noted that most reviews had "spared the dancers, who had merely followed their instructions" and instead focused their critiques on "Balanchine and his bogus conceptions."[117] "The choreography was thoroughly poor and the dance-miming of Lew Christensen as Orpheus and William Dollar as Amor so uncertain, ill-defined and lacking distinction as to make one squirm," as the *Dancing Times* reported, adding that "Daphne Vane as Eurydice was by far the best performer, which is not saying a great deal."[118] The under-rehearsed motions of Christensen did not go unnoticed, as one review described sarcastically how he "expressed his sorrow by thrusting his fists into the air, swaying before a funereal mound."[119] But critics saved their most virtuosic turns of phrase and unflattering metaphors for the opera's final tableau. According to one source, this final scene elicited laughter rather than shock from the audience, while the *Dancing Times* compared Dollar's final exit heavenward to "Little Eva going to Heaven in a road show of *Uncle Tom's Cabin*. . . . [I]t was all too, too bad."[120]

If virtually all of the critics had been displeased, the production was an important personal milestone and formative experience for Kirstein. He described the experience of the premiere on May 22 as "one of the most exciting and happy days of my life," a notable instance of unqualified joy in a diary otherwise crowded with anxiety and second-guessing.[121] Despite a rocky dress rehearsal, in the end Kirstein thought the show came off well, despite a few unsteady aspects and a palpably chilly reception from the audience.[122] The overwhelmingly negative critical reception caught some but not all of the production team by surprise, and notably was not the reason that the Met offered only two performances of the production.[123] According to the minutes of a spring season board meeting conducted soon after the *Orpheus* premiere, the opera was only ever scheduled for two performances, and thus its relatively brief run cannot be construed as an instance of the Met pulling the plug in response to the critical back-lash.[124] Balanchine claimed to have expected the response, telling Kirstein that "he knew that either the critics would be marvelous or lousy."[125] The dancers were somewhat "dashed" by the reactions, while Tchelitchev was "delighted" at the minor scandal, boasting that "he'd never got so much space."[126]

Kirstein did not respond to the critics himself, although his friend Glenway Wescott permitted him to see the initial draft of the letter subse-quently published in *Time*, in which he defended the boldness of the pro-duction and chastised critics for having "taken sides with the powerful old guard" against a "potent young generation."[127] Such sentiments posited the Met audience as stuffy bluebloods, even though the "popular price" crowd would have been likely more diverse than the opera's usual audience. And *Orpheus* was evidently unpopular with more progressive and educated audience members as well. Kirstein recalls the attendance of poet Muriel Rukeyser, critic B. H. Haggin, and Carl Van Vechten, all of whose "hostil-ity" he sensed on opening night.[128] Muriel Draper, while more positive in her assessment, was not shy about expressing her disapproval of Dollar's "final flight."[129]

In early May 1936, the *Hartford Courant* reported that "the canonization of tap dancing will come at the Metropolitan Opera Monday when Paul Draper will do a routine to strains of Bach. This apotheosis will be part of a ballet by George Balanchine."[130] A report in *Variety* around the same time noted the obvious affinity between this planned ballet and one of Balanchine's other projects at the time, the title number of the recently opened *On Your Toes*: "Stepping will be to Bach with Draper centered on a dais, and the artier terpers cavorting around him."[131] In the end this so-called "Bach ballet" would not see the stage in 1936 with Draper as a featured performer, but it nevertheless stands as an intriguing and previously unexplored connection between the American Ballet's activities and Balanchine's work on Broadway.

Notably, the project was not the result of Balanchine's experimental flights of fancy but was rather conceived of by Kirstein after his experiences as a spectator at *On Your Toes* and solo performances by Draper. Kirstein saw *On Your Toes* twice in the space of two weeks, first in its Boston tryouts and again on April 14 in New York a few days after opening night. Aside from these two performances, Kirstein had attended several rehearsals for the musical in the foregoing months and had otherwise been kept apprised of Balanchine's involvement with the show.[132] After one rehearsal he made note of the "nice nos [sic] mixing ballet and tap," likely a reference the "On Your Toes" number.[133] On April 16, two days after his second viewing of *On Your Toes*, Kirstein went to the Rainbow Room at Rockefeller Center where he saw a performance by Draper, who had begun to gain modest fame for dancing to classical music and blending tap technique with elements of ballet, innovations that had been in part facilitated by study at the School of American Ballet.[134] Draper was otherwise well connected with Balanchine and Kirstein's enterprise through his mother Muriel, who had been a close friend and personal confidante of Kirstein's since his move to the city in the early 1930s.

After Draper's Rainbow Room performance Kirstein resolved that he must get Balanchine "to do a show for him" and quickly devoted his full energy and attention to the project, which had the potential to complicate the realization of the *Orpheus* production.[135] Kirstein nevertheless made the ballet a short-term priority, speaking with Draper's mother about having her son appear in a "ballet piece" and subsequently meeting with Draper himself.[136] On April 29 Draper came to the Met for a preliminary rehearsal of the Bach ballet, attended by all of the company's dancers who were proficient in tap, suggesting that he would not be the only tap dancer on stage.[137] Draper hit it off with the dancers, who seemed to like him despite his somewhat haughty demeanor, while Balanchine evidently "doubted the possibility of anything coming from it."[138] A few days later Kirstein came to the realization that it would be "impossible" to "rush the Bach through before *Orpheus* got started."[139]

The Bach ballet was more than a passing fancy for Kirstein and also perhaps Balanchine, as shown by its reappearance as a possible project in subsequent months and years. Several weeks after the spring season ended and Kirstein was in a new burst of activity organizing the chamber-sized summer touring company Ballet Caravan, he mentioned the Bach ballet in a list of potential new projects, and a year later in May 1937, a similar ballet featuring Draper was included in a prospectus prepared by Kirstein for a series of "collaborative evenings" involving the Caravan.[140] For an evening titled "The Classic Dance and Tap Combined," in which Draper would perform alongside members of the Caravan, the program was to conclude with Draper dancing to the Bach Double Violin Concerto with choreography by Balanchine.[141] At least one published source from this period references the same project, noting that Kirstein's series was slated to include a performance featuring "outstanding tapper Paul Draper, supported by the [Ballet] Caravan ensemble in Bach's Double Violin Concerto, choreographed by Balanchine."[142] Taken together these sources suggest that the Draper project was perhaps an early inspiration for Balanchine's neoclassical masterpiece *Concerto Barocco*, not ultimately created and staged until 1941.[143] But even if it had to wait over five years to see the light, *Concerto Barocco* thus reveals itself as not just diffusely bearing the traces of tap dancing and other American popular dance, as dancers and scholars alike have long observed and surmised.[144] Rather, its journey to the stage arguably began with the aesthetic collision of tap and ballet in *On Your Toes*.[145]

CHAPTER 6 | 1936

ANOTHER INSTITUTIONAL PREDECESSOR of the New York City Ballet, the chamber-sized touring organization called Ballet Caravan, was the second significant performing entity to emerge from the Balanchine-Kirstein enterprise.[1] The Caravan has been mostly understood as an independent organization operating separately alongside the American Ballet and School of American Ballet in the later 1930s. The company has earned this status, on the one hand, due to the special leadership role that Kirstein played in its formation and management and, on the other hand, owing to the more overtly American and politically progressive agenda of many of its works.[2] Kirstein himself stressed his central role in the Caravan's organization in his pamphlet *Blast at Ballet* and later in *Thirty Years*, his diary-style history of NYCB.[3] "Early in 1936 it had come to me that, all else failing, I had best attempt to form some sort of company by myself," he recalls, and he accordingly "decided to organize a small troupe on my own and call it Ballet Caravan."[4] The company was planned to be "self-sufficient, using a dozen of our best dancers, who would also serve as stage managers and stagehands," who would "travel by bus and truck with our own lighting equipment, portable switchboard, drapes, and bits of scenery."[5] In fact, Ballet Caravan was not initially conceived of in such independent and determinative terms and was hardly an American-focused, much less a politically leftist, endeavor in its inception. Neither a dancer-driven initiative nor a carefully conceived attempt by Kirstein to pursue an American artistic agenda, the Caravan was a hastily organized affair conceived of barely six weeks prior to its first performances in July 1936 and was for the most part a strategic response to an array of institutional crises facing the wider ballet enterprise, including Balanchine's ongoing health problems and Edward Warburg's increasing disillusionment with the company.

Most accounts of the Caravan have focused on its later repertoire, with particular attention granted to the troupe's two most successful ballets, both premiered in 1938 and the only two works to have outlived the company's five-year life span: *Filling Station* and *Billy the Kid* (discussed in Chapter 9).[6] These and other ballets of the Caravan's later seasons, including *Yankee Clipper* and *City Portrait*, evince an explicit commitment to native and vernacular themes, inspired by and in turn contributing to regionalist and politically activist trends in the visual and performing arts in Depression-era America.[7] But these themes were for the most part absent from the Caravan's first season. Notably, the Caravan's 1936 season saw the debut of the earliest choreographic efforts of Erick Hawkins, but far from pointing to a softening of Kirstein's adamant opposition to modern dance, this work provides further evidence of the young impresario's continued commitment to ballet modernism.

During Ballet Caravan's first year it was not the boldly experimental and politically engaged troupe that it would subsequently become, and far from a carefree and democratic collective, the Caravan was closely controlled and supervised by Kirstein in almost every respect. Its activities in 1936 accordingly seemed to repeat some of the earlier missteps of the American Ballet by offering ballets in an art-for-art's sake and Diaghilevian idiom that were novel mostly for the more modest scale of their execution and the unconventional venues in which they were performed. In the eyes of many critics, however, these innovations were reason enough to praise the Caravan as a more successful version of the American Ballet, even as it replicated many elements of the aesthetic program of its parent organization. In short, the American Ballet and Ballet Caravan reveal themselves, at least in the Caravan's first season of the summer and fall of 1936, as more contiguous than distinct, sharing personnel, aesthetic values, choreographic styles, and the involvement of Balanchine himself. Although the success of the troupe's first year allowed Kirstein to strike out more definitively on his own to pursue the explicitly American agenda for which it is mostly celebrated today, during this early phase, Ballet Caravan was for all intents and purposes the American Ballet's Caravan.

———————

Although Ballet Caravan and its activities have been discussed and studied in a range of critical and scholarly contexts, the precise reasons for its creation in 1936 and its relationship to the wider ballet enterprise of Balanchine and Kirstein have remained obscure. According to existing accounts, Kirstein's creation of the troupe was motivated by a range of concerns: discontent with the lackadaisical commitment of Edward Warburg to the American Ballet, concerns over Balanchine's ill-health and his new prospects on Broadway, and a desire to pursue a new artistic agenda focused more exclusively on original work by American choreographers.[8] Despite their differences, all accounts maintain that Ballet Caravan was conceived of to complement or supplement the activities of the American Ballet in some respect.

Early press accounts and promotional materials suggest that there was indeed a close relationship between the two entities, and Kirstein evidently took great pains to maintain the group as an official affiliate of the American Ballet, not as a distinct organization, and the Caravan's association with the company (and by extension the Metropolitan Opera) was an important selling point for the troupe. An early promotional brochure created for the first season describes the Caravan membership as "twelve accomplished dancers, all members of The American Ballet Ensemble which has recently completed its first season with the Metropolitan Opera in New York."[9] Press coverage of the Caravan's first summer season identified the troupe as composed of dancers from the American Ballet and made frequent references to their affiliation with the Metropolitan Opera.[10] Similar talking points referring to the American Ballet and the Met appear in press releases for the Caravan's other summer performances, while other notices mention only their opera affiliation, describing them as "young dancers from the Metropolitan Opera," leaving out the American Ballet entirely.[11]

The company's roster speaks to the almost indistinguishable boundaries between the Caravan and the American Ballet. Twelve dancers, seven women and five men, formed the core of the group: Ruby Asquith, Ruthanna Boris, Gisella Caccialanza, Harold Christensen, Lew Christensen, Rabana Hasburgh, Erick Hawkins, Albia Kavan, Charles Laskey, Eugene Loring, Annabelle Lyon, and Hannah Moore.[12] All had been affiliated with the School of American Ballet and its company since its opening two years earlier in 1934, though many had acquired extensive training and performing experience elsewhere. The leaders of the group were two of Kirstein's protégés: dancer and choreographer Douglas Coudy, also his lover at the time,[13] who was the company manager, and Lew Christensen, the group's ballet master.[14] In addition, William Dollar, one of the principal male dancers of the American Ballet, choreographed a ballet for the company's first season, as well as appearing with Kirstein in a lecture-demonstration in the fall.[15] Despite this close relationship, Dollar is not named among the company members and is explicitly identified in the press as "not a member of the present company, but of the American Ballet, of which the Ballet Caravan is an offshoot."[16] The core dancers, however, felt no need to distinguish between their affiliation with the Caravan and their affiliation with the American Ballet, and they continued to take class at the School of American Ballet, where the Caravan's initial rehearsals also occurred. Annabelle Lyon recalled virtually no distinction in her work for the Caravan and her work for the American Ballet. When asked whether early rehearsals were "preparation for a new company with a new name," Lyon pointedly clarified to her interviewer that the Caravan was not thought of as something they were doing "instead of the American Ballet" but was rather something just for the summer "to give us work when the company was not functioning."[17] These contradictory views on the Caravan's institutional independence could be explained by the troupe's being a distinct latecomer to the 1936 summer season. Despite his claim in *Thirty Years* that he developed the plan for the Caravan in "early 1936," Kirstein's diaries and press coverage of the company attest to a more compressed time frame for the group's formation.[18] Kirstein first mentions the very concept of a summer touring group in a diary entry dated May 28 and again on May 31, when he uses the "caravan" label.

Ballet Caravan gave its first performances at Bennington College's summer dance institute, the spiritual home of American modern dance in the 1930s, and this engagement has been understood as symbolic of the troupe's indebtedness to both the aesthetics and institutional structures of modern dance.[19] Such observers include Kirstein himself—an erstwhile critic of what he regarded as modern dance's less structured and more idiosyncratic movement vocabularies—who stated years later, "Modern Dance may be said to have launched Ballet Caravan."[20] Kirstein approached Bennington founder and director Martha Hill directly to request a slot for the Caravan on the festival's program, which was ultimately granted over the objections of Hill's associate Mary Jo Shelly.[21] Sources suggest that the Caravan's performances on July 17 and 18 were somewhat hastily arranged, like the formation of the company itself only six weeks earlier.[22] The Caravan's engagement was evidently intended to provide ideological balance and new perspective to the Bennington Festival's offerings. Hill justified the inclusion of the troupe based not only on her latent affinity for ballet but also on the grounds that "Kirstein's new effort might ferret out choreography that championed a healthier American spirit and perhaps serve as a counterbalance to the angst and browbeating of the leftist voices."[23] The Caravan's performances were ultimately presented separately from the official festival programs, perhaps in a conciliatory gesture to Shelly and other more partisan stakeholders.[24] This distinct status was made plain in press accounts, which describe the Caravan's performances as "unscheduled," "unexpected," and "outside the regular festival series."[25] All of this indicates that the Caravan was initially included in Bennington's activities owing to its balletic credentials as an affiliate of the American Ballet. In other words, the troupe's affinity with modern dance circles might be better understood as a result, not necessarily a cause, of their Bennington debut.[26]

Despite this outsider status, the company received a much warmer welcome than they had anticipated for their performances, which evidently "added to the eclectic mix of dance offerings without much commotion."[27] According to Kirstein's diaries, the dancers were worried enough about their reception that they had mentally prepared themselves for "even heckling," but in the end the festival was more than generous and accommodating to the Caravan.[28] The group even earned special praise from Martha Graham, with whom Kirstein had begun to cultivate a close and mutually admiring relationship.[29] "Miss Graham was charming and demonstrative," according to Kirstein, and "said she realized we were in different worlds but she firmly believed in our destiny and in the vitality of the classic form."[30]

Although its Bennington debut positioned the Caravan among the leading and most influential exponents of modern dance, the company's subsequent performances would embrace its culture in a different way, that is, by patching together a summer season through a heterogeneous itinerary of colleges, civic auditoriums, movie theaters, and other popular and private venues. Although the barnstorming journeys of Anna Pavlova had followed similar circuits (to much larger audiences), the more immediate model for the Caravan was closer to the touring enterprises of Ted Shawn, Doris Humphrey, and Martha Graham.[31] This was perhaps no surprise since the woman responsible for the Caravan's management, Frances Hawkins, had made her name booking talent for such artists, most notably as a manager for Graham, and enjoyed direct entrée to the inner circles of modern dance.[32] Kirstein was well aware of Hawkins's unique portfolio, including her vaudevillian pedigree, and saw it as an asset for the Caravan's efforts.[33]

According to Kirstein's diaries, he first met with Hawkins on June 5 to discuss the possibility of her managing the Caravan, only a week after he had first mentioned the idea of the troupe, and on June 16 she was officially contracted to manage the tour. "The mechanics of traveling seem far easier than I thought," Kirstein noted in late July, "due mostly to the efficiency of our manager Francis [*sic*] Hawkins a very nice person indeed."[34] Although Hawkins did not remain with the group for the entirety of the tour, she was "on hand at all important junctions and very helpful."[35] In contrast to the recollections of Lew Christensen and others that the Caravan was a dancer-led initiative, Kirstein's diaries suggest that this story was in fact a cunning public relations gambit of Hawkins's invention. In part to contravene the perception that the Caravan represented an institutional schism with the American Ballet, Hawkins advised Kirstein to downplay his involvement and instead pretend that the concept for the troupe had originated with the dancers themselves.[36] Thus, despite Kirstein's perceived ownership of the Caravan, the success of the troupe's first summer season—launched at the seat of modern dance and continued in a series of popular venues—might be credited more to Hawkins's unique professional network and expertise than to any distinct strategy on his part.

If it is sometimes unclear where, what, and for whom the Caravan performed on each stop of its first summer tour, the overall complement of dances presented is well documented. Many of the dances in this repertoire outlasted the summer, moreover, and appeared in several engagements in the fall of 1936 and in subsequent seasons. Initially the Caravan's repertoire included four one-act ballets, two of which were typically presented at any given performance. Lew Christensen's plotless *Encounter*, set to Mozart's *Haffner Serenade* is described by turns as a "classic ballet" or a "neo-classic ballet," and featured costumes inspired by drawings of German sculptor J. G. Von Schadow.[37] Eugene Loring contributed the more narrative "ballet pantomime" *Harlequin for President*—initially called *Harlequin's Election*—a commedia dell'arte–inspired "satire on contemporary politics" with music by Scarlatti and costumes by Keith Martin.[38] The choreography for the "character ballet" *Pocahontas* has been generally credited to Christensen—one account claims it was "composed by the group jointly"—with an original score by Elliott Carter and costumes inspired by historical engravings of Theodor de Bry.[39] William Dollar's *Promenade* used Ravel's *Valses nobles et sentimentales* and featured costumes modeled on work by French painter Horace Vernet; it was said to be based "on the modes and manners of the ascendant middle class of France in the period just after the revolution."[40]

In *Blast at Ballet*, Kirstein maintained that the decision to include work by a variety of choreographers was an intentional strategy on his part: "Realizing the danger Diaghilev risked by never having more than two choreographers at his disposal at one time, and only five in his entire career, I started off by mounting four works by four different dancers."[41] There was a darker side to this strategy having to do with Balanchine's poor health, but Kirstein's decision was also likely born of necessity given the haste with which the company was organized and the inexperience of his young choreographers. What is clear is that Kirstein had primary artistic purview over the Caravan's repertoire, and most of the season's ballets were based on concepts that originated with him. In early June at Ashfield (his family's estate in western Massachusetts) Kirstein met personally with Elliott Carter to discuss the commission of *Pocahontas* and coached Christensen through its conception and creation.[42] The music, décor, and libretto for William Dollar's *Promenade* similarly originated with Kirstein, who consulted Vernet's *Incroyables et Merveilleuses* engravings at the Metropolitan Museum in his research on the ballet's costume designs.[43] Christensen's *Encounter* and Loring's *Harlequin* were the two exceptions, although both were clearly pursued with Kirstein's approval and ongoing consultation.[44]

These four ballets were to be rounded out by a complement of shorter divertissements, comprised of "national dances and solos to music of Glinka, Prokofiev, Brahms, Corelli, and many other composers."[45] An early promotional brochure describes them as the concluding part of each program, calling them "a series of divertissements demonstrating in national dances and ballet solos the virtuosity of the company."[46] Nine such dances were created and as many as seven were to be included on a program.[47] Although none of these short pieces is credited to a specific choreographer, Kirstein's diaries indicate that company manager Douglas Coudy was responsible for at least some of them.[48] Interestingly, this embrace of the crowd-pleasing divertissements as a rousing closing act shows an affinity with the practices of performers such as Pavlova and La Argentina, against whom Kirstein in other contexts would position his own institutional efforts.[49] The Caravan's divertissements were apparently more bewildering than engaging, however, perhaps providing context for Marjorie Church's remark in a *Dance Observer* review of the Bennington performances that the Caravan's dancers "seem a bit lost in ecelcticism, at present, both of style and of technique."[50] As a reminder, this extensive musical repertoire was all performed with only piano accompaniment.[51]

The Caravan's debut programs at Bennington became the basic template for its eclectic approach to programming during its first year. The first performance paired the classic *Encounter* with the more narrative *Harlequin*, while the second included *Promenade* and *Pocahontas*, the latter performed despite being incomplete.[52] The first program was rounded out by a series of seven divertissements, but for the second night, the shorter pieces were scrapped entirely, owing to their uneven quality, and it is not clear to what extent they were included in subsequent engagements.[53] Variety continued to be a goal for the Caravan, however, with the narrative ballets complementing more abstract fare on its programs and the combinations of ballets remaining flexible.

The Caravan's fifth ballet, added to the repertoire partway through the summer tour, was *The Soldier and the Gypsy*, a "character ballet in seven scenes" with music by Manuel de Falla choreographed by Douglas Coudy.[54] The ballet was a condensed retelling of *Carmen*, albeit with a different score, and featured Spanish-inspired costumes by Charles Rain.[55] Edwin Denby praised the narrative quality of the ballet, reporting that it was "an interesting attempt to combine dancing with *parlando* movement."[56] Like *Pocahontas* and *Promenade*, the concept, score, and décor (and in this case even the casting) for this ballet originated with Kirstein, who in mid-July mentions the idea of "a Spanish ballet on *Carmen* for Ruthanna Boris" to be created by Coudy.[57] Although the Caravan has been characterized as a democratically run organization in which there were no stars and decisions were made collectively, the addition of this fifth ballet at the insistence of Kirstein provides evidence to the contrary.[58] According to Kirstein's diaries, there was grumbling in the ranks about this particular decision, as several of the dancers thought the troupe's funds might have been better spent to augment their salaries.[59] Thus despite his own Popular Front politics, magnanimous labor relations toward the troupe's dancers did not always override Kirstein's own artistic vision and priorities.

In addition to these five ballets, early press accounts mention a sixth work called *Rondo*, a "ballet in classic style" choreographed by Erick Hawkins to music by Carl Maria von Weber, which would occasion one of the more tumultuous episodes in the Caravan's early history.[60] This ballet was in fact abandoned in rehearsal after the dancers revolted against its confusing and overcomplicated choreography, with the situation becoming so dire that Hawkins was briefly voted out of the Caravan by his fellow dancers, to be reinstated later after careful politicking by Kirstein.[61] Unlike the dancers, Kirstein remained committed to Hawkins's ballet despite seeing its faults as it was under development, at first describing it as "too full of difficulty but may be OK when cleaned up" but later recognizing that the ballet was "impossibly difficult and complex and the kids hate to do it."[62] Kirstein felt a keen sense of loyalty to Hawkins, since the dancer had been the first consulted about the idea of the Caravan, and Kirstein cites this early enthusiasm, as well as his talent, as a reason for keeping him on.[63]

Rondo is mentioned in two previews of the Caravan's summer activities and in an August report in the *Dancing Times*, perhaps written and filed before the ballet was definitively scrapped.[64] In addition to references in the press, *Rondo* is listed alongside *Encounter, Pocahontas*, and *Harlequin* in an early Caravan promotional brochure; however, none of the ballets are attributed to specific choreographers, suggesting Kirstein may have been hedging his bets.[65] Its contentious backstory aside, *Rondo* is notable as a choreographic credit for Hawkins one year earlier than what is generally regarded as his first ballet, the 1937 *Show Piece* (also created for the Caravan, and discussed in Chapter 9). Kirstein's advocacy for *Rondo* also demonstrates his early belief in the talent of Hawkins, who would ultimately achieve his greatest success not in ballet but in modern dance as the partner of Martha Graham, who first became personally and artistically involved with the dancer in part thanks to the Caravan's appearances at Bennington.[66]

After Bennington, the Caravan stayed in the immediate vicinity for several performances in Vermont, performing on July 20 in Burlington, presented by the University of Vermont's Summer Session,[67] and the following day before a capacity audience in the gymnasium at Middlebury College, at the invitation of Professor André Morize's summer French program.[68] The Caravan would return to northern New England in mid-August, performing in Keene and Claremont, New Hampshire; in Dorset, Manchester, and Woodstock, Vermont; and then after a considerable journey up the coast, in Skowhegan, Maine.[69] John Martin reported that several of these engagements were part of a larger arrangement with a chain of movie theaters.[70] Kirstein's diary mentions this theater owner by name and reports a generous gesture on his part after a lightly attended performance at a movie theater in Keene: "Mr. Latchi the Greek proprietor of a string of 14 movie houses refused his percentage (some $10) because we'd made no complaints."[71] Demetrius Latchis was in fact the name of the theater owner, a Greek immigrant whose name still adorns a theater complex in Brattleboro, and whose Claremont, New Hampshire, venue, where the Caravan performed in August, was called the Latchis Theatre.[72]

If the Caravan was practical enough to accept gigs dancing in movie theaters—and the dancers well-behaved enough to endear themselves to the owners—the group also made itself available to more exclusive clients. On two occasions it scheduled what amounted to command performances in summer enclaves of the East Coast elite. Such engagements demonstrate that the Caravan was both willing and able to operate in multiple spheres during its first experimental season, benefiting not just from Hawkins's knowledge and expertise but also from the same kind of connections that had made possible the American Ballet's first performances at the Warburg estate in White Plains and the company's engagement at the Metropolitan Opera. The above-mentioned performance in Manchester, Vermont, on August 18 was one such engagement, evidently not arranged by anyone as recently arrived to America as Mr. Latchis. The Caravan was instead the evening entertainment for a gala dinner in Manchester, recorded only in a society column, which, true to convention, is devoted almost wholly to reporting the names of couples slated to attend the event and mentioning only in passing the "ballet caravan" that was to perform.[73]

The Caravan received more extensive, albeit similarly nominal coverage for a semi-private engagement in East Hampton, Long Island, on August 9. Mrs. Lorenzo E. Woodhouse was the hostess of the benefit performance, which was held in the gardens of the "playhouse" on her estate. No fewer than two additional social events were held in advance of the Caravan's appearance, beginning with a reception and tea "for the Southampton and East Hampton patrons' invitation committee for the Ballet Caravan" and a luncheon for "several Southampton members of the junior commit-tee who will act as ushers at the performance of the Ballet Caravan."[74] The Caravan's upcoming performance held a prominent enough place on the summer social calendar that it was mentioned even in the byzantine accounts of the comings-and-goings of people with no involvement in planning the event itself.[75] Although Kirstein's diary does not explain how the engagement came about, it does capture its uninspiring atmos-phere, describing Mrs. Woodhouse as "a dreary white woman who was dashed because I wouldn't let her play her Wurlitzer in the intermission" and the assembled audience as "cold and Republican."[76] Among the few details reported of the engagement in the press was the frosty reception that greeted *Harlequin for President*, which according to *Variety* prompted some of the "starchy guests"—many sporting the sunflower emblem of FDR's Republican rival Alf Landon—to depart from the "swanky garden party" before it concluded.[77]

The Caravan's adaptability was also demonstrated by the first of its two extended engagements of the summer, an appearance in a weeklong pro-duction of Molière's *The Would-Be Gentleman* at the Country Playhouse in Westport, Connecticut, beginning on August 3.[78] This English-language production was produced by Theatre Guild co-founder Lawrence Langer and starred vaudeville star Jimmy Savo. (Both Langer and Savo would cross paths with Kirstein and Balanchine later: Langer as a co-founder of the short-lived American Shakespeare Festival with Kirstein, and Savo as a lead actor in Rodgers and Hart's 1938 *The Boys from Syracuse*, discussed in Chapter 8.) The Caravan was credited by name in advertisements for the play, a high-low admixture—Louis XIV meets vaudeville—that served the Caravan's mission of providing choreographic experience for its dancers, and the troupe was responsible for four original incidental dance numbers. For music they turned to Lully's original *comédie-ballet* score, with Eugene Loring creating the *Dance of the Tailors* and the *Ballet of the Cooks*, while Christensen was responsible for a ceremonial dance in the play's Turkish scene, in addition to adapting *Encounter* as an interpolated number.[79] The fourth new number, the *Ballet of the Peacock among the Roosters*, is attributed to Erick Hawkins—like the above-mentioned *Rondo* a choreographic credit one year earlier than his 1937 *Show Piece*. In the end, some of their efforts would be for naught. According to Kirstein's diary, Loring's ballets "looked neat" and were presumably given in their entirely, while only half of Hawkins's *Peacock* ballet made the cut, and only the last movement of Christensen's *Encounter* was ultimately included.[80]

The troupe's second extended engagement of the summer was also its last, a week-long "dance festival" at the summer stock theater owned and operated by Walter Hartwig in Ogunquit, Maine, beginning August 31 and closing on Labor Day, September 7.[81] Unlike their weeklong appearance in Westport, this series of performances included all five works of its core repertoire in three different programs.[82] According to one account, it was "believed to be the first time in this country that a ballet company is playing a week's series from its own repertoire in the summer season."[83] Of their offerings at Ogunquit, *Harlequin for President* was evidently better received than it had been in the Hamptons, and it even elicited vocal acclaim from the otherwise quiet theatergoers. "The highlight of the evening was the end of the ballet called *Harlequin for President*," it was reported, "which a few weeks ago aroused the indignation of certain conservatives in the audience on Long Island."[84] Despite a comparably conservative clientele, in Ogunquit "the interpretation of the satire seemed a bit different, and there were shouts of 'Bravo' from the front rows—the first time this season that the patrons had ever raised their voices during a production."[85] Kirstein's diaries describe the audiences as "sparse but enthusiastic," and that the weather was "cool and damp."[86] Kirstein also maintains that it was the Ogunquit performances that had occasioned the addition of *The Soldier and the Gypsy* to the company's ballets, since without a repertoire of five ballets they would not have been able to secure the engagement, a successful and satisfying end to what only two months earlier had appeared to be an uncertain summer of touring.[87]

Buoyed by its summertime success, the Caravan carried on into the fall, with several performances in New York City and surrounding areas. While the Caravan was still performing in Maine, John Martin's column announced the troupe's most significant booking to date: the opening performances of the Young Men's Hebrew Association (YMHA) dance series, opening a season including Martha Graham, Doris Humphrey, and Anna Sokolow and performing all five core works from their summer tour.[88] Prior to this New York debut, on October 13 Kirstein and members of the Caravan presented a lecture-demonstration on "the development of the ballet" at the New School, the third event in a series termed "The Dance in the Social Scene."[89] These two engagements at key institutional homes of modern dance point to Kirstein's larger ambitions for the group's permanence and aesthetic independence. The Caravan also went back on the road to New England, performing in Montpelier, Vermont, at the invitation of the town's Theatre Guild, and two days later at Amherst College at the invitation of the campus group, the Amherst Masquers;[90] the Caravan also appeared at Smith College[91] and in Hartford and Danbury, Connecticut.[92]

Kirstein's decision to continue the troupe's activities into the fall did not lend much credence to the claim that it was merely a summer adjunct of the American Ballet. And indeed, despite the insistence on the Caravan's collaborative relationship with the American Ballet, there had been rumors of schism from the start, made all the more plausible given how quick Kirstein had been to insist upon the cordial relations between the two entities. Martin's initial report on the Caravan quoted the organizers as maintaining that the group is "neither a secession from nor a part of the American Ballet, but a collective arrangement of its members, and enjoying the good wishes of the directors of the American Ballet itself."[93] Economic necessity was also cited as a practical rationale for the existence of the group, promoted via the innocent cover story concocted by Frances Hawkins: "Its personnel consists of twelve young members of the American Ballet," as Martin reported, "who were anxious to keep at work and earn a livelihood during the long interval when the parent organization was inactive."[94] And in fact, the majority of the fall performances of the Caravan did not interfere with the American Ballet's duties at the Metropolitan Opera, whose 1936 season did not begin until December 21.[95] The Ballet's opera duties thus resumed at the start of December, meaning that Kirstein had to secure a special dispensation for only one of the Caravan's performances, on December 1 in Hartford, the troupe's final performance of 1936.[96]

If the Caravan's schedule initially avoided conflicts with the American Ballet's obligations at the Met, the organization did begin to assert a more independent status in the course of its summer tour and into the fall. A brochure prepared for the company later in this first season maintains explicitly that the Caravan, despite drawing its membership from the American Ballet, "is a separate entity and its entire repertory is newly composed by its own dancers."[97] *Musical America* in a November report termed them "a group of thirteen dancers from the American Ballet, but independent from the parent organization," even as the headline of this same notice calls them a "unit" of the American Ballet.[98] Most notably, Edwin Denby's review of their October performance at the YMHA refers to them as the "American Ballet Caravan," a name that would not be used by the troupe itself until 1939.[99] This inadvertent amalgamation shows that the two branches of the organization remained more or less institutionally contiguous during this first year, two interdependent units of the larger Balanchine-Kirstein enterprise.

Kirstein's *Blast at Ballet* ascribes both nonchalance and intentionality to the formation of the Caravan and parrots Frances Hawkins's talking points to emphasize the interest of the dancers themselves in pursuing a new kind of ballet: "So I organized a small troupe of dancers from our own school, which had been incidentally very successful, and from among those of the American Ballet proper who were dominantly interested in classic ballet choreography applied to native themes."[100] Kirstein even posited larger ambitions for the group, calling it "in microcosm a permanent laboratory for classic dancing by, with and for Americans."[101] Kirstein's private reflections, by contrast, reveal that the decision to form the Caravan did not in fact arise purely from his own interests or those of the dancers. The Caravan was a venture thrust upon him by necessity, a response to a constellation of circumstances suddenly facing the American Ballet.

These challenges centered first and foremost on Balanchine's ongoing health problems, which continued to be a source of consternation, not the least during the period leading up to the American Ballet's official company debut in March 1935 at the Adelphi Theater. In the months prior to the formation of the Caravan, Balanchine's condition took another turn for the worse. On May 25, 1936, Kirstein recorded that Balanchine was home sick for several days and that William Dollar had to oversee the ballet's rehearsals at the Met.[102] Balanchine's health episode was severe enough, especially in light of previous incidents, that it sent Kirstein scrambling to make contingency plans with him even contemplating "what to do if Balanchine died."[103]

At the same time that Kirstein saw Balanchine's life in danger, the American Ballet's summer performance schedule was also looking bleak. Following its Adelphi debut in 1935, the company had been relatively active during the summer months, with performances at the Lewisohn Stadium in upper Manhattan and the Robin Hood Dell in Philadelphia. Heading into the summer of 1936, things initially looked just as promising, as the troupe had been tentatively slated to appear not just again at Lewisohn Stadium but also at Jones Beach for several weeks of performances. In late May, however, just as Balanchine was falling sick, this engagement fell through because the Lewisohn management insisted that the group not reprise their existing repertoire but rather present new work, which the company was not in a position to do.[104] In the end, both engagements fell through, leaving the company without major performance opportunities for the summer.

This loss of work would not have been so devastating in and of itself had it not been for the related challenge of Edward Warburg's decreasing interest in the American Ballet. "The kids w[oul]d go and come back," Kirstein noted after the summer engagements fell through, "but I hate to let them go for the whole summer as I fear Warburg w[oul]d lose interest."[105] Warburg for his part was not just losing interest in the American Ballet but was also resistant to the idea of the Caravan, perhaps correctly understanding it as a covert power grab by Kirstein. Warburg even cited trumped up legal concerns to delay the signing of Frances Hawkins's contract, which only made Kirstein's resolve stronger.[106] Kirstein soon after managed to get Warburg to admit that he wanted out, that his involvement amounted to "being screwed without pleasure," and that he continued to remain involved only out of a sense of guilt.[107] Despite his ambivalence, Warburg remained with the company for the summer and into the following year, and only deepened his financial investment, acquiescing in August 1936 to Balanchine's request for a $5,000 Stravinsky commission for *The Card Party*, eventually premiered the following spring by the company during a special festival devoted to the composer's music.[108]

Even as Kirstein became increasingly frustrated with Warburg and wanted to keep the Caravan to himself, the troupe did not represent a definitive break with Balanchine. And even though Balanchine's bad health had been one of the precipitating events that had led to the creation of the Caravan, he was healthy enough to be consulted regularly about the Caravan's activities over the course of the summer. Only a week after Kirstein had been contemplating the choreographer's imminent death, Balanchine was again on the mend.[109] Soon after, he was back in the studio for the Caravan's initial rehearsals and, notably, advised Erick Hawkins not to use Debussy but rather the sonatas of Weber for his new ballet.[110] Balanchine decamped the following day to Westport, Connecticut, to convalesce but he would remain involved in the planning of the Caravan's season.[111] In mid-June, Kirstein, Coudy, and Dollar made a special trip to Westport to update him on the progress of the Caravan, during which Balanchine expressed his reservations about the troupe, specifically about whether "the boys can do choreography," although he held back in expressing this opinion.[112] At the end of June, Balanchine returned to the city to observe the progress of the Caravan's first three ballets. He apparently concurred with the growing concerns about Hawkins's *Rondo*, deeming it "too confused," but like Kirstein he saw greater potential and declared that "in four years he [Hawkins] would be an excellent choreographer."[113] Christensen's *Encounter*, by contrast, "had taste and brilliance and was complete," and while he was not taken by Loring's *Harlequin* ballet, he thought it would be a crowd pleaser.[114]

When the Caravan came to Westport for their appearance in *The Would-Be Gentleman*, Balanchine was again back in the mix but still not fully recovered. On the one hand, he was "full of necessity to have Stravinsky and Gershwin ballets and two months of rehearsals," but on the other hand, he declared himself too weak to sign a first edition of Noverre he had purchased as a gift for Kirstein.[115] Kirstein and Balanchine met on August 1 in Westport to discuss the future of the Ballet, and both were evidently at peace with Warburg's potential defection, in part because they surmised that "as soon as [he] has no responsibility [he] will give twice as much cash."[116] As he had done earlier in the summer, Balanchine came to rehearsal and provided a good deal of feedback about the incidental dances for the play and "was very nice with the kids."[117] Kirstein still had concerns about his health, however: "Doesn't seem terribly well. He coughs and is not a dry atmosphere here."[118]

Balanchine's involvement, however sporadic, gives lie to the status of the Caravan as operating entirely apart from the American Ballet, and while the troupe's dances were still in preparation, Kirstein readily noted the influence of the choreographer: "Choreography will continue straight through from George Balanchine but it must have this chance."[119] This influence was obvious not just to Kirstein but to outside critics, showing how also with respect to its initial choreographic style the Caravan remained closely aligned with its parent organization. A review of the Caravan's Hartford performances captures the Balanchine ethos that pervaded the repertoire, noting that "no one is going to deny that it shows the impress of the troupe's real maitre, George Balanchine."[120] The company's dances have "much of his free style, in which the classic restraint is rather unlaced, but in which the classic manner and form is always there" as well as his "penchant for continual movement," his "sense of build-up and climax," and his "partiality for the athletic."[121] Not only had the dancers internalized their master's technique, but they had also gleaned the better qualities of his style, eschewing his more experimental inclinations. The same observer noted, approvingly, that the Caravan's work "happily does not employ the grotesqueries to which Balanchine has been too often drawn."[122]

Ballet Caravan has often been posited as the most explicitly American of the several antecedent companies of the New York City Ballet. "At first our ideas were disjointed and vague," as Caravan dancer Ruthanna Boris recalled, "but gradually they connected themselves and emerged as a beautiful, possible dream—a dream of American ballet dancers dancing America!"[123] and in reviews of their debut season Edwin Denby called the troupe "pleasantly un-Russian."[124] Such enthusiasm aside, it is evident that there was very little that was explicitly American about Caravan's first season. This should not be regarded as a failure of the organization, for Kirstein's belief in an American ballet company was rooted in the eminent adaptability of the *danse d'école* in new contexts. And to be sure, the makeshift quality and hodgepodge venues of the Caravan's first tour certainly distinguished it from its more established European forebears and Russian competitors.

Nevertheless, it is remarkable to what extent the repertory of the Caravan's first season remained within the aesthetic comfort zone of the Franco-Russian tradition consolidated and cultivated by Diaghilev and the Ballets Russes diaspora. Even as Kirstein's Caravan sought to shed the pejorative "ballets américains" label that had dogged the American Ballet, they were for all intents and purposes still heavily indebted to the Europhile aesthetics for which the Caravan was supposed to be the antidote. Their ballets featured classical music by Scarlatti, Mozart, Ravel, and de Falla—with Elliott Carter as sole native-born exception—and were based on material from the French Revolution to *Carmen*. Despite

Kirstein's claim of pursuing stripped-down production values, each of the Caravan's ballets included an explicit credit for costumes, whether for the actual designer or the artist who had inspired them, in keeping with Diaghilevian practice, and all works were in the one-act format long codified by the Ballets Russes. The earliest days of the Caravan confirm in a very direct way Nancy Reynolds's observation that Kirstein quite consciously modeled his aesthetics and career as an impresario on the great Diaghilev.[125] In another respect, Kirstein's mentor-like (and sometimes erotic) relationships with the Caravan's young and exclusively male choreographers should similarly be understood as an implicit if not explicit emulation of Diaghilev.

More broadly, the Caravan's repertoire in its first year was not substantially different from the initial offerings of the American Ballet, and certainly not much more American, except in being choreographed, danced, and designed by Americans. Following the American Ballet's example, the Caravan presented only one work with an explicitly American subject and a newly commissioned score by an American composer, Christensen and Carter's *Pocahontas*, the same way that the collegiate satire *Alma Mater* had been the American Ballet's only native calling card. Loring's *Harlequin*, with its American political subject matter—and anti-Republican ethos, evident at least in its Hamptons performance—still only partially passes muster on this account, given its commedia dell'arte aesthetic and score by Scarlatti. It might seem odd that the Caravan reproduced the very aesthetic that they were trying to break free from, but in light of the internal politics discussed above, in which the Caravan was not an independently conceived organization but rather an insurance policy designed to keep the American Ballet from collapsing, this convergence of style is perhaps less surprising.

Even as the Caravan's repertoire represented an aesthetic alignment with the American Ballet, in other respects the troupe was understood by some as a more successful foil to its parent organization, especially in the modest scale of its production values. Margaret Lloyd of the *Christian Science Monitor* explicitly praised the Caravan as a more satisfying kind of American ballet than had been attempted by the first seasons of the American Ballet. Although both organizations excelled in the youthful exuberance of their performers, it was the Caravan that had leveraged its talents and acknowledged its limitations appropriately, living up more fully to the name of its parent organization. The American ballet had been "rushed to a task they were not ready for" and "pushed too far ahead of its capacities," with only the dancers' "youth and vivacity" to fall back on.[126]

The Ballet Caravan, by contrast, had given its young dancers "a chance to compose for themselves and an opportunity to work together in that cooperative spirit" with the goal of "developing a truly American ballet."[127] Denby similarly praised the naïve and genuinely American ethos of the Caravan, whose charm and commitment compensated for any apparent faults in technique or execution. "There is an American freshness and an American modesty that is charming" about the troupe, and even though there was evidence of "the usual faults of beginners," what was more important is that "the enterprise as a whole is lively and real and part of us."[128]

Kirstein in *Blast at Ballet* downplayed the successes of the Caravan's first summer tour, calling it "more of a hard vacation than work, a feeling-out of our future" and saying that it was "of not much interest except to the dancers and myself."[129] But somewhat ironically, the Caravan in fact represented the best and most consistently successful offerings of the Balanchine-Kirstein enterprise as a whole. By not attempting to emulate the large-scale, high-budget cross-country touring of the de Basil company—as the American Ballet had unsuccessfully tried the previous fall—the Caravan became something of a sleeper hit. The American Ballet had made its debut in a Broadway theater and subsequently aligned itself with the Metropolitan Opera, one of America's most establishment performing arts organizations, and one in which dance was treated as subordinate. The Caravan, by contrast, had improvised an organizational model out of a variety of institutional resources, in a structure that, if somewhat makeshift and fragile, placed dance, more specifically original choreography, in the foreground. John Martin saw the Caravan's innovations as something distinctive and hailed the company's summer season as an example that others should emulate to fill the otherwise fallow months of the summer. "Starting out the middle of July with very little advance preparation," he noted, "the company has managed to play twenty-five performances in seven weeks," which must "constitute a record of sorts, for available statistics reveal no other instance of a Summer tour of anything like so extended a character by any company of dancers hereabouts." [130]

With his experiment thus deemed a success, Kirstein was eager to keep the Caravan going. Even before the 1936 summer tour had concluded, he was busy brainstorming ideas and setting his own goals for the group's 1937 season. During the Maine engagement, he wrote in his diary that he saw the first season as the "foundation for 8 weeks of solid work next summer and 2 months in the fall."[131] The coastal atmosphere of Ogunquit inspired him to begin planning one of the Caravan's ballets for the coming season, *Yankee Clipper*.[132] And if the American Ballet and Metropolitan Opera still remained part of Kirstein's overall strategy, by the end of 1936 he was beginning to regard the Caravan as his primary professional affiliation. In correspondence from Kirstein to his father, letters sent through October appear on letterhead for the School of American Ballet, on which he was listed with the catch-all title of "Treasurer-Secretary." Beginning with a letter dated November 4, Kirstein's preferred writing stock would be letterhead for Ballet Caravan, of which he was the "Director."[133] Although it had begun as a practical and perhaps short-term response to long-term challenges facing the American Ballet, the would-be summer Caravan was here to stay.

CHAPTER 7 | 1937

"IMAGINE YOUR BILLS are paid," suggests the opening line of a song from Rodgers and Hart's 1937 musical *Babes in Arms*, a message that no doubt appealed to Depression-era audiences. "Imagine you made the grade," the lyrics continue, "With no dishes in the sink / All you do is drink / Claret lemonade." During the first half of 1937 everything looked upbeat indeed for both Balanchine and Kirstein, in part thanks to the success of endeavors including Balanchine's second major Broadway project, *Babes in Arms*. On the heels of the well-received first season of Ballet Caravan, their enterprise witnessed a string of virtually unqualified successes. In April 1937 the American Ballet presented a critically acclaimed Stravinsky Festival at the Metropolitan Opera, featuring three ballets: the American premiere of Balanchine's *Apollon Musagète*; the world premiere of the newly commissioned *The Card Party*, and a new version of *Le Baiser de la Fée* (*The Fairy's Kiss*). The festival gave the American Ballet much-needed positive coverage in the press and helped renew the creative relationship between Balanchine and one of the world's most esteemed living composers. Around the same time, Balanchine would follow up his successful dances for *On Your Toes* with choreography for *Babes in Arms*, his second hit musical with Rodgers and Hart in as many years, working alongside artists such as the renowned tap-dancing duo the Nicholas Brothers. Balanchine's Broadway success in turn led to a contract from Samuel Goldwyn to stage the dances for his upcoming film extravaganza *The Goldwyn Follies*, which began filming in the summertime months that followed. In the midst of all this, the American Ballet's duties as the resident ensemble continued at the opera. During this same period, Kirstein refocused his energies on Ballet Caravan, with plans to transform the company from a modest summer adjunct of the American Ballet to a full-time enterprise with transcontinental ambitions and a more nationalist aesthetic agenda.

While all these successes add up to a mostly positive picture in aggregate, they were ironically a portent of an imminent rupture in Balanchine and Kirstein's collaborative relationship. That is to say that these projects were all pursued mostly as separate endeavors rather than as a coordinated effort, and a certain ambiguity regarding the individual and collective priorities of Balanchine, Kirstein, and the American Ballet had become a matter of open discussion in both private and public. In March, John Martin noted "two announcements of widely different characters" from the American Ballet: on the one hand, the final plans for the Stravinsky Festival; and on the other, the recruitment of Balanchine and the company for *The Goldwyn Follies*.[1] Later in May, Martin noted that Balanchine was being discussed as a potential new collaborator for the newly organized Ballet Russe, adding that the choreographer "has been consistently active in other fields since the beginning of his association with the American Ballet," and thus this kind of association would be "in no wise contrary to precedent."[2] In a related vein, Balanchine's success on Broadway was increasingly difficult to square with his work for the American Ballet at the Metropolitan, not because the variety of his endeavors seemed incongruous but because of the uneven quality of his work as a whole. "The case of Mr. Balanchine is a puzzling one," one critic wrote in the wake of the premiere of *Babes*, since his Broadway work is "almost invariably clever" while the work of the American Ballet had been "generally dismal and often downright inept."[3] And despite the positive reception of the American Ballet's own work at special performances at the opera, their contributions to productions continued to be ignored at best and criticized at worst.

Thus while the American Ballet remained in a holding pattern at the opera, Balanchine and Kirstein were each increasingly imagining and making into reality a bright future for themselves on their own terms. Their Broadway and Ballet Caravan endeavors were more and more focused on projects outside the institutional orbit of the American Ballet company and school, even as they both continued to draw dancers from that organization's ranks and use it as a home base of operations. Their de facto abandonment of the American Ballet as a focus of their artistic priorities would eventually lead to the company's dissolution in early 1938. But for a brief moment in the spring of 1937, everything seemed to be working at full speed: the American Ballet finally found its artistic and institutional footing with the Stravinsky Festival, Balanchine was cementing his status as a

Broadway player, and Ballet Caravan was set for bigger ventures built on its previous success. But far from cementing the collaborative relationship of Balanchine and Kirstein, these high points instead marked a moment when their paths would begin to diverge, perhaps for good.

For the 1936–37 opera season, American Ballet's duties were similar to those of their first year, with the ensemble contributing regularly to both new productions and revivals. The company also continued to have the opportunity to showcase their own work in special mixed-bill performances or as the prologue to shorter operas, which were well attended by the public and mostly well received by critics. The youth and charm of the dancers continued to gain them favorable attention, but for the most part the company was regarded as a peripheral supporting unit of the opera rather than an artistic leader. The season thus offered further confirmation of John Martin's admonishment and prediction regarding the American Ballet's decision to join the Met, with the company losing as much in institutional identity and vitality as it gained from the bigger audiences and larger platform afforded by the affiliation.

The new productions to which the American Ballet contributed included a world premiere and an obscure revival, both of which were positively received, perhaps because audiences and critics had little with which to compare them. For the world premiere of the new opera *Caponsacchi* by American composer Richard Hageman, the ensemble supplied "pleasing dances" that "made no attempt to do anything" beyond "traditional things," and the "youth and charm and enthusiasm of the dancers gave manifest pleasure."[4] For *La Gioconda* the dancers provided a "gay furlana" in the first act and "evoked a thunderous reception" for their "Dance of the Hours."[5] Although many of their contributions to the Metropolitan Opera were not remarked on, the American Ballet did have the opportunity to show itself off in a variety of other contexts. Several of the company's ballets, including *The Bat, Concerto*, and *Serenade*, were used as the opening for shorter operas or other mixed bills.

Because much of the opera's repertoire remained the same from the previous year, Balanchine did not need to create as much new work, although he did make certain changes to existing ballets, including to his much-discussed dances for *Aida*. A review of New Year's Eve performances of the opera noted changes in the ballet, "notably the recruiting of a group of young boys and girls in their early teens, some perhaps younger" for dances at the court of Amneris.[6] The young dancers moved "vigorously" and inadvertently added some comic relief to the scene when upon exiting the stage they "barged into a wall instead of the wing" to laughter from the audience.[7] The youthful cast remained on call for subsequent performances of *Aida*, perhaps evidence of a new strategy for Balanchine to avoid controversy and allow his older dancers an evening off.[8] Interestingly, the decision to showcase youthful talent resonated with Balanchine's concurrent work on *Babes in Arms*, for which he had been contracted in the fall, and which also included an extended number inspired by *Aida*.[9]

In keeping with Rodgers and Hart's "no formula" formula, *Babes in Arms* offered something different from their previous show, and the most significant element of contrast was its young and mostly unknown cast. Set in the fictional town of Seaport, Long Island, the musical writes adults out of the picture almost completely, focused on what transpires when the children of struggling vaudevillians are left behind after their parents are enlisted to join a WPA-sponsored tour. When faced with the prospect of having to move to a New Deal "work farm," the youngsters decide to prove that they can fend for themselves by, of course, putting on a show. Through several plot twists involving their performance efforts and the deus ex machina emergency crash landing of a famous French aviator, the "babes" are in the end allowed to stay at home. Today *Babes in Arms* is mostly celebrated for the many iconic songs that it contributed to the American songbook, among them "The Lady Is a Tramp," "My Funny Valentine," and "I Wish I Were in Love Again." While the subsequent film adaptation starring Judy Garland and Mickey Rooney preserved only the barest contours of the musical's plot and only a few of its songs, in its original form the musical represented something more weighty in tone. It was praised by some as achieving the elusive high-low synthesis longed for by the aspiring composer Sidney Cohn of *On Your Toes*, "halfway between Debussy and the modern American idiom."[10] As scholar Andrea Most has noted, the stage version was far from a feel-good vehicle for hit tunes or musical sophistication but stands as a rich document of the left-wing political ethos of the 1930s, with its youthful characters engaging in quite adult debates about political topics.[11] At many turns the plot hinges on the question of where certain characters stand on the issue of racial segregation and the regional conflicts between northerners and southerners.

For Balanchine, *Babes in Arms* confirmed the status he had earned through his work for *On Your Toes* as a successful choreographer for the Broadway stage and even beyond. The backstage ethos of the musical afforded numerous opportunities for inventive spectacle, many of which foregrounded dance, and like the numbers in *On Your Toes*, these were closely integrated into the musical's plot, including what many consider the first "dream ballet" in a Broadway musical. These dances brought Balanchine even more exposure to American dancers, in particular tap dancers Duke McHale and the Nicholas Brothers, whom he had previously encountered through his work on the *Ziegfeld Follies*.

Youthful talent was a key selling point of the show, and it was noted that its genteel producer Dwight Deere Wiman had evidently "robbed every talented cradle in the land" to assemble his cast.[12] But although the cast had "the charm and buoyancy of youth," there was nevertheless "nothing amateurish about them," in part thanks to the guidance of "oldsters who know their business."[13] Writing in *Theatre Arts Monthly*, Edith Isaacs praised the youthful cast for their work on the show, giving special notice to their "fresh and fluent skill" and "power of projection" that was "distinctly disarming, not to say impressive."[14] *Babes* was successful insofar as it harnessed the youthful talent of his cast into a coherent whole, a dynamic that aptly describes the way in which its dances were created. While Balanchine was again accorded the credit of "choreographer," both reviews and recollections of dancers suggest that his role was closer to that of a conventional Broadway dance director, and that the individual performers contributed their own expertise and experience to the creation of most if not all of the musical's dance numbers. Balanchine's role was focused more on shaping and managing the various contributions of the individual dancers and the ballet and tap ensembles, rather than the more specialized choreographic creations he had devised for *On Your Toes*.

Thus the question of collaboration and credit, as well as the specter of cultural appropriation, arguably looms even larger over the dances of *Babes in Arms* than was true with *On Your Toes*. As noted previously, the historical record is frustratingly silent about Herbert Harper's perspectives on Balanchine's collaborative process for *On Your Toes*. In the case of *Babes*, Balanchine was working with a racially diverse cast of young tap stars, who all brought their talent and expertise to bear upon dances ultimately credited to him alone. While overseeing the larger scope and scale of the production, moreover, he again had the help of an assistant, Johnny Pierce, for the tap routines. One dancer in the show, Marjorie Jane, maintains that Balanchine did not work directly with the tap ensemble, leaving those routines to Pierce entirely. Although she also recalls that there was more tap dancing than ballet in the show overall, she notes that Balanchine and Pierce choreographed and staged many scenes jointly.[15]

Fayard Nicholas similarly recalls that Pierce arranged the tap numbers but that he and his brother Harold choreographed much of their individual dancing themselves, albeit in consultation with Balanchine.[16] Although Balanchine did receive official credit for the dances in the musical, reviews consistently singled out McHale and the Nicholas Brothers for explicit praise and credit, showing that they achieved at the very least the kind of authorship of their dances that many tap dancers asserted over their creations through the charisma of their performances, as elucidated by recent research into choreographic copyright by Anthea Kraut.[17]

Even if Balanchine found himself in a more conventional role, there was quite a bit to manage and his calm and at times detached demeanor evidently allowed him to be successful in his supervisory capacity. The show employed an abundance of production elements, including "manifold scenery, much costumery, a wilderness of props," as one preview explained, "and a three-layer orchestra with two twitching pianists, a brass section that whinnies, whines, yelps, and brays."[18] A preview article from Boston recounted the "perfect bedlam" on stage in the weeks prior to the tryout openings, with "fifty-two children, from eight to twenty, swirling in ballet costumes and concealing their faces behind pasteboard masks, a blond pianist thumping through the score; innumerable electricians and mechanics bearing innumerable gadgets across the stage; assistants this and assistants that."[19] This same reporter described two of the key principals as untroubled by all this activity, with Balanchine "crouched on the footlights, waving a vague hand" and Richard Rodgers "sitting very placidly in the third row puffing a cigarette."[20]

In keeping with the do-it-yourself ethos of the show, the two main dance numbers were an occasion for whimsical theatrical effects and experimentation. The first main dance number, the *Johnny One-Note Ballet* was the concluding act of the "Follies" mounted by the children, their ultimately unsuccessful attempt to prove that they could stay at home unsupervised. The eponymous song that sets up the ballet tells of how the egotistical opera singer Johnny is punished for his selfish behavior by being cursed with being able to sing only one note. The ballet in fact takes place during an imagined performance of *Aida*, in which the restraint of the Egyptians devolves into frenzied dancing, perhaps a nod to the recent controversy over Balanchine's dances for the opera at the Met. The number's costumes and props were made of everyday objects and materials. Termed a "novelty number" by some critics, its success was attributed in part to the "gay and amusing Egyptian effects out of dish cloths, mops, and towels" designed by Helen Pons.[21] Another account similarly described the

Follies cast as "hilariously costumed in Turkish towels, coat-hangers, and mops" noting that they conducted themselves with a "mock seriousness" that heightened the comedic effect, and a photo published in *Theatre Arts Monthly* shows these elements in action.[22] Balanchine's "choreographic conceptions" were deemed "rhythmic and sometimes startling" by another reviewer, who especially praised the "astonishing—and funny" effects created through the humble elements of "guest towels, Dutch Cleanser cans, torn pages of stage magazine, and clothes hooks."[23] Although few details about its choreography have survived, dancer Marjorie Jane recalls that it employed both tap and ballet dancers in separate groups.[24]

The Egyptian fantasy was the context for one of the most virtuosic moments of the entire show, performed by the Nicholas Brothers, and an example of the complex dynamics of collaboration at work in the show's dances. This is one of several short moments from the musical's dance numbers that has been preserved thanks to home movies recorded backstage by the Nicholas family's chauffeur.[25] In this routine, Fayard and Harold Nicholas took turns jumping over and sliding through the legs of a line of chorus girls. "One by one, girls were added until there was a line of eight girls," as a summary by dance scholar Constance Valis Hill explains, "pressed together and bent over with legs straddled." To heighten the thrill at the end, Fayard timed his jumping such that he joined the end of the line of the girls, and thus his brother Harold slid through his legs as well. According to the brothers' recollections, the idea for this moment originated with Balanchine, who suspected they would be up to the challenge. But as Fayard Nicholas explained, "Balanchine didn't show us how to do it, he just told us to do it" and "didn't show us any steps," leaving it to them to work out the mechanics of the routine.[26] Their expertise was acknowledged by many reviews, which explicitly praised the brothers' "unabashed expertness," noting that they could "carry a show by themselves," which in fact they evidently helped to do.[27]

At the same time, many reviews did not attribute the brothers' accomplishments to any supervision from Balanchine or Pierce, much less to the rigorous professionalism they had cultivated since their youth, encouraged and carefully managed by their parents.[28] Instead, many identified the source of their talent in racist essentialism, an ideology that was the subject of a song embedded in the show itself—"All Dark People Is Light on Their Feet"—which purported to celebrate the innate rhythm and musicality of black performers. The brothers performed this number despite their distaste for its content, with Fayard noting drily in an interview that of "all those wonderful songs" in the show, this was one that "got nowhere," and was cut from later versions of the show.[29] The way critics discussed the brothers' performance in *Babes* reveals that the song's sentiments were by no means out of the mainstream, even in a cosmopolitan north-ern city such as New York. Brooks Atkinson's review for the *New York Times* praised the brothers' dancing using exactly the same the racist ide-ologies expressed by the song's lyrics, neither of which need be dignified by repetition here.[30] In some performances the brothers managed to voice a protest by pointedly singing "are" rather than "is" when the title's lyrics recurred, as they found the incorrect grammar as offensive as the song's content, a correction for which they were reprimanded and which they were unable to repeat at most performances.

The second big dance number of the show, *Peter's Journey*, was even more ambitious and featured the talents of tap dancer Duke McHale as its eponymous protagonist. The ballet uses the song "Imagine" as its point of departure, taking the protagonist on a fantastical journey around the world, which is possible for Peter thanks to a sizable cash prize he has won at a raffle. At least one reviewer dryly noted the contradiction between the left-wing tendencies of the musical's book and the premise of the ballet. "Peter, a Communist when it suits him," the reporter grouses, "wins $500 at a bank night in a motion picture theater," but instead of sharing this windfall with his peers uses it to travel to Paris, Rome, and London.[31] The trip began in New York, with Peter encountering "a man on stilts, look-ing like a caricature of John D. Rockefeller, giving him a dime" and his subsequent voyage across the ocean was depicted "by the simple means of a cardboard ship and strips of waving silk."[32] In the end, Peter is ship-wrecked on a desert island, where he ultimately awakes from his dream, but not before having "ample opportunity of studying the jungle fauna" in addition to catching a glimpse of "comely maidens garbed in transparent seaweed."[33] *Variety* noted the humble theatrical means of what it regarded as the show's standout number, which was "delightfully dressed by a pro-longed series of changing locales of a dream, marked only by a flock of set-pieces."[34]

Like *Johnny One-Note* and the musical as a whole, much of the charm of *Peter's Journey* lay in the homespun quality of this fantasy journey, which featured "cardboard skyscrapers, swirling seas of blue-cloth ocean, and the tropical enchantment of paper palm trees and cellophantasy mermaids."[35] More important, *Peter's Journey* managed to strike a balance between this youthful charm and artistic seriousness, declared "a Wonderland fantasy of the highest order" and "an artful but not seriously arty ballet," in which the talent of Duke McHale "abets the superb Balanchine choreography, enters lithely into fantasy without making it Fantasy, into whimsy without making it Whimsy."[36] McHale's performance was widely praised, with one review noting how he skillfully "prances through a ballet-fantasy of subtle artistry."[37] But evidently McHale did not use his considerable experience as a tap dancer in this particular number. Recollections by some original dancers note that the number used only ballet technique and other interpretive movement. The tap dance chorus donned ballet slippers to augment its visual effects, including its underwater scenes. "Peter, during his journey, had to swim in the water," Marjorie Jane recalled, and "we had these waves, and we had to wave them up and down" wearing "little chiffon sort of costumes."[38] These imaginative uses of dancers and inventive stage materials not only recall the short-lived *Orpheus and Eurydice* production of the previous year, but its maritime journey to fantastical ports of call resonates with a work soon to be premiered by Ballet Caravan, *Yankee Clipper*.

Either because *Babes in Arms* lacked the more explicit ballet angle of *On Your Toes*, or because Kirstein was too busy planning the next season of Ballet Caravan, the new Broadway production did not engage him as intently as Balanchine's previous Broadway project. *Babes* is mentioned in passing in Kirstein's diaries in late February, and Balanchine later invited him to one of the tryout performances in Boston, which Kirstein enjoyed "in spite of longuers in the book."[39] Always scouting talent, he added that McHale was "very sympathetic," and more important, Kirstein was relieved that Balanchine "looks better in spite of his heavy schedule and seems to have found a formula whereby he does not exhaust himself with his commercial jobs."[40]

Like *On Your Toes*, the opening of *Babes in Arms* was a social event of some distinction and evidently attracted a good portion of the well-heeled audience that made up the core constituency of the American Ballet, another reminder that a small set of Americans had no need to imagine what a better life might feel like. Among the attendees at a dinner following the show were Paul Whiteman, Paul Draper, Condé Nast, Lee Shubert, George Abbott, and Mrs. William Randolph Hearst.[41] At this gathering, society columnist Lucius Beebe drolly noted that "the social pressure became so great that a bottle of champagne exploded gratuitously in its bucket," drenching author John O'Hara "with a deluge of '28 Roederer, an as yet intractable and untamed vintage." At intermission and after the show the scene was equally rambunctious, such that "you couldn't fight your way into Sardi's at the intermission" and "the encroached tables on the postage stamp floor at Morocco afterward reduced dancing to an absolute minimum." Beebe also noted of the festivities that "such a congress of Miss Jessica opera veils and Valentina cloaks" would not be assembled again until "Eddie Warburg's Stravinsky festival later this month at the Met."

The two-day Stravinsky Festival mounted by the American Ballet on April 27–28, 1937, was the high point of the company's three-year tenure at the Metropolitan Opera, if not its entire existence as an organization. Whether intentionally or not, the event was virtually critic-proof in its conception and execution, offering three ballets by Stravinsky, one of the world's most renowned living composers, whose presence on the podium as conductor lent the evening extra cachet. The opening ballet, *Apollon Musagète*, was billed as the "first New York performance" of the work, having been originally choreographed by Balanchine for Diaghilev's Ballets Russes in 1928. In fact, the festival represented the American premiere of Balanchine's version of the ballet, which was commissioned and first performed at the Library of Congress in Washington, DC, choreographed by and starring Adolph Bolm (six weeks prior to the premiere of Balanchine's version for the Ballets Russes). *Apollon* was followed by the world premiere of a new ballet, *The Card Party*—Stravinsky's first new ballet composition in many years—and concluded with another quasi-premiere, *Le Baiser de la Fée* ("The Fairy's Kiss"). Drawn from the same period in which Balanchine had first staged *Apollon*, the work had been originally commissioned in Paris in 1928 by performer and impresario Ida Rubinstein and was first choreographed by Bronislava Nijinska.

The Stravinsky Festival has been discussed extensively by music and dance scholars, most notably Charles Joseph and Stephanie Jordan, who have offered detailed accounts and analysis of the event and its three works.[42] As they and other scholars have noted, the festival is regarded as historically significant today for reasons having nothing to do with its own artistic merits or the life of the American Ballet. Rather, the event is notable as a moment that helped revive Stravinsky's interest in dance composition and even more crucially, an endeavor that renewed the creative relationship between the composer and Balanchine, a collaboration that would later produce notable works including *Orpheus* (1948) and *Agon* (1957). In the context of Balanchine and Kirstein's wider enterprise, the festival is significant for the way it reflected debates about the merits of Balanchine's work and the conflicting ways in which the American Ballet's repertoire continued to be received. Despite the festival's overall success, it mostly reaffirmed the doubts that many still harbored about

Balanchine's overly experimental tendencies and the "Riviera aesthetics" of the American Ballet. And it seems that more than any effort on the part of Balanchine or the dancers, the star power of Stravinsky helped to carry the day. One reporter pointedly asked, in response to the rapturous ovations of the audience, "How much of this enthusiasm was for Stravinsky rather than for the dancers?"[43]

Although the American Ballet earned great praise for the festival—the group "covered itself in honor," in the words of John Martin—they did so not by reinventing but rather by refining the aesthetic frameworks in which they had been operating in the previous years. Like the company's earlier programs, and much like the first season of Ballet Caravan, the program was Diaghilevian both literally and figuratively, consisting of a series of one-act ballets of a contrasting character, with two of them drawn directly from the Parisian milieu of the final years of the Ballets Russes. Comprising an artistic allegory drawn from Greek mythology, a fantasy on the theme of poker playing, and a Tchaikovskian fairy tale adapted from Hans Christian Andersen, the three ballets invited the same complaints as the previous work of the company, which favored "instances of transplanted themes," as a review in *Dance Observer* put it, that "do not easily flourish in American soil."[44] In a perhaps symbolic gesture that slightly mitigated the program's European bent, *The Card Party* was identified in the program and publicity materials using an English title (rather than its French title, by which the score is mostly known today, *Jeu de Cartes*).

In the wake of the *Orpheus* debacle, the Metropolitan Opera had declined to support any new independent productions by the American Ballet, and it was left to the company to mount the festival with their own financing. In practice this meant that Warburg would foot the bill for most of the expenses, including the commission of *The Card Party*. On Balanchine's part the project had been under discussion as early as August 1935, and Stravinsky's correspondence and compositional sketches suggest that he began work on the score well before the theme of the ballet and the terms of his commission were settled.[45] Kirstein's diaries record that *The Card Party* commission was settled in early August 1936, when Balanchine prevailed upon Warburg to agree to Stravinsky's fee of $5,000.[46] Kirstein wrote in *Blast* that he was unenthusiastic about the concept of the festival, holding that it was too backward-looking in character, an attitude that Martin Duberman ascribes in part to Kirstein's being sidelined from the planning of the event, which was mostly a Warburg and Balanchine affair.[47] Kirstein's diaries suggest that he nevertheless followed and was involved in the planning and execution of the performances quite closely, and among other duties he helped recruit artist Stewart Chaney to design new sets for *Apollon*.

Today the festival's American premiere of *Apollon Musagète* is cited prominently in program notes and other accounts as an important milestone in the work's performance lineage, with its star Lew Christensen the first of many notable American dancers to embody the title role. The work holds a special place in Balanchine's career as one of his earliest works to have remained in continuous performance and as the work that he regarded as a turning point in his development as a choreographer—and its first performances in America were indeed a notable event.[48] Although Balanchine made significant revisions and cuts over the years to the work, which is now known simply as *Apollo*, the version performed in 1937 recreated the original one staged for the Ballets Russes, including the dramatic "Birth of Apollo" that opens the ballet.[49]

In sharp contrast to its celebrated status today, in 1937 *Apollon Musagète* was the least notable work on the festival program. Especially in its longer original form, the ballet seemed to offer further evidence that Balanchine was too invested in the bizarre and experimental. And even for those more enthusiastic about these dimensions of Balanchine's style, *Apollon* lacked a certain polish and was not regarded as especially effective on a musical or choreographic level. *Dance Observer* praised the company overall for improvements in their skill, but found that *Apollon* specifically suffered from "insecure dancing," noting archly that the ballet "has a certain sophisticated precocity which gives it novelty, or did so when it was new."[50] The more mainstream *Musical America* paid the ballet a different kind of backhanded compliment explaining how its music and choreography were well suited to each other. "The pantomime is attractive in line, if of an arty simplicity that is first cousin to the affectation in Stravinsky's adroit score," and while the score was "beautiful in the rich and tender sound of its divided strings" it was also "replete with melodic clichés of the most cloyingly sentimental order."[51] Critic Jerome Bohm maintained that on a musical level *Apollon* still displayed the same "intrinsic weaknesses" that were in evidence at its Washington premiere a decade earlier, but that the music was at the very least "infinitely superior" to the other scores performed the same evening.[52]

Other writers for both general and specialist publications voiced their lack of enthusiasm with viewpoints ranging from indifferent to antagonistic. "*Apollo* has always impressed this reviewer as one of the most tiresome of all Stravinsky's scores," as one explained, "and the dancing of Lew Christensen, as its central figure, was not of the sort to redeem it."[53]

One laconic summary explained how the "husky" Apollo "wrestled with three girls through some extremely ridiculous dance patterns, to music which hardly enhances Stravinsky's reputation."[54] The *American Dancer* was even more blunt and direct, and while ultimately complimentary of the work, its description resonates closely with previous criticism of Balanchine's tendencies:

> The choreography is bizarre, and it is in this rather affected form that Balanchine excels, giving rein to his imagination. Its flights frequently border on the line of insanity, achieving fascinating and exotic distortions; but—alas—they occasionally go completely over the border, resulting in sheer madnesses [*sic*]. However, these are at least usually diverting if nothing else. . . . I find his originality stimulating, though the audience obviously did not.[55]

Apollon also had "something to tempt the risibles," in particular, "the sight of one of the muses sitting down momentarily on the recumbent Apollo's knee, her back to the audience, and then flitting away again."[56]

Apollon also had a small and notable cadre of admirers. Comparing the 1937 ballet to its Ballet Russes original, Elliott Carter rated the newer performances "less static" and held that the work "had greatly gained in feeling since its Parisian performance," with the "jerks from one statuesque pose to another" replaced by "a very beautiful plasticity having both nobility and repose."[57] And where other critics still found only idiosyncrasy, Carter perceived an emerging continuity with some of Balanchine's other works, noting that in *Apollon*, "as in his *Serenade*, there was a constant line of movement which bound all the steps together and never ceased until the curtain fell." There was something "magical and stirring about this drawing of the invisible lines in the air" and the individual variations showed "a highly creative imagination at work in every small detail."[58] Erick Hawkins was observed by Kirstein backstage during a rehearsal of the ballet with a wet handkerchief "weeping tears of beauty," and on opening night Kirstein presented Lew Christensen with a gold watched he had purchased and engraved with "Apollo 1937" to mark the occasion.[59]

By contrast, *The Card Party* was rated as well executed if somewhat superficial in its conceit and ethos, and its appeal was no doubt significantly enhanced by its world premiere status and the seventy members of the New York Philharmonic playing the score under the supervision of the composer himself. The ballet consisted of three "deals" of a game of poker, in which "the situation is complicated by the endless tricks of the perfidious Joker," portrayed by William Dollar.[60] Of the four suits portrayed by the dancers, the major suits of Hearts and Spades were best represented at ten and eight cards each, with the minor suits of Clubs and Diamonds assigned only an Ace, King, Queen, and Jack. The first deal results in a draw, with each hand holding a straight and the Joker unable to upset the balance, but in the second deal, four Aces beat four Queens, with an assist by the Joker. In the final deal the conflict comes down to a battle among four flushes, including a Royal Flush, which the Joker is powerless to contravene. Although the ballet's plot did proceed according to the real rules of poker, the distributions of the individual hands in each deal, much less their occurrence in succeeding rounds, defy any rules of probability.

For many *The Card Party* came across as somewhat uninspired and conceptually thin. *Dance Observer* found the ballet "by far the most novel and ably danced" of the works on the program, but despite its charming visual effects, it was conceptually "a little like Marie Antoinette's cake."[61] Carter found the premise of the ballet to be one of its fundamental problems, as "a pack of cards is a pack of cards and gives little chance for contrast"; he noted that the choreography "had to be followed carefully to be appreciated, as all its effects were microscopic."[62] *Musical America* politely voiced doubts that the score would join the ranks of the composer's *Petrushka* and *Firebird*, and while praising its momentum and "agreeable blitheness," the review characterized the soundscape as "purely surface music, with no emotional quality whatever."[63] This superficiality was not necessarily a bad thing since it was entirely consistent with the conceit of the ballet, whose "cards remain just cards. They are not personifications."[64] John Martin echoed such sentiments and suggested that given Balanchine's "knack for revue," a nod to his growing status on Broadway, the ballet could have been more effective with "more experienced dancers" and free of the "incubus" of Stravinsky's score.[65] Carter praised the jazz references in the choreography, "which is certainly a good way of revivifying ballet technique and skillfully added to the general grotesquerie and cuteness of the ballet."[66] If the music and dance of *The Card Party* did not especially delight, the visual elements compensated handsomely, and the scenery and costumes by Irene Sharaff, whose concept was playful verisimilitude, were almost universally praised. "The onlooker seemed to be looking down from above on a huge green table which had for background a crimson carpet; part of the table occupying the backdrop, part the stage, in defiance of all laws of perspective."[67] Against the red backdrop and the green of the card table in front, the "crisp whites of the costumes" created a "stunning picture."[68]

The final offering of the festival, a new setting of *Le Baiser de la Fée*, has received the least amount of attention in accounts of Balanchine and Kirstein's enterprise despite its being the most warmly received of the three ballets. An homage to the Silver Age classicism of Tchaikovsky, the ballet consists of a whimsical marriage plot complicated by the magical kisses bestowed upon a youth by a fairy. It was deemed "the best of the lot," by one observer, in part because it offered "many opportunities for real dancing."[69] Others found the work bogged down by "by adherence to the lengthy score," and despite its simple theme, the production was "rather foggy in outline."[70] According to *American Dancer*, the work showed both the ensemble and soloists at their best: Kathryn Mullowny "sustained the drama of her role" as the Fairy, William Dollar "danced the Youth with expert technical flourish," and Gisella Caccialanza "was graceful and light with a sympathetic appeal."[71] Carter saw similar shine in *Baiser*, which included "some of the finest soli and pas de deux since the days of the Imperial Ballet," in particular the dances of Dollar and Caccialanza in the third scene, which were "remarkable for their tenderness, brilliance, compactness and variety."[72] The dancing "was often the best that the American Ballet has given us and the music served its purposes exceedingly well."[73] These efforts were contrasted favorably to the American Ballet's participation in Met productions, with one reviewer noting that the "snowflakes, mountaineers and peasants were distinctly better than similar ensembles in the opera ballets of the last two seasons."[74] Martin was effusive in his praise of the ballet, which contained "more choreographic body and fuller phrases" than any of Balanchine's previous work, and "puts him far more in his mettle as a choreographer instead of a deviser of tricks."[75] He added that there had by no means been a complete "transformation" of Balanchine's style, however, since the ostensibly classical work included "passages which come crashing through the style like a herd of wild anachronisms," such as the shock of seeing "the unearthly fairy wrap one leg around her young protégé's torso."[76]

Kirstein's private recollections suggest that the festival went off fairly smoothly and was successful enough to counter his typical pessimism and worry. At the final dress rehearsal he found that *The Card Party* was "insufferable," and "even *Apollon* was tedious."[77] And at several points Stravinsky chastised the assembled audience for interrupting the proceedings with applause, led in part by the cast of *Babes in Arms* in attendance on their Monday off.[78] But in the end, opening night saw "a very brilliant house and a superb performance" and even the usually dour Kirstein had to admit that "success was everywhere in the air."[79] Afterward Stravinsky noted how pleased he was to be working with "a young organization which was coming up instead of a famous one in disintegration."[80] The second night went off even better, in part thanks to calmer nerves among the dancers. Daphne Vane, whose Calliope variation in *Apollon* had received no applause the night before, remarked before going on stage the second evening that she was determined to "make the bastards clap," and evidently she succeeded."[81]

In the early summer of 1937, Kirstein and Balanchine made a somewhat official decision to part ways. At its core, the transaction was fairly straightforward: Kirstein ended his affiliation with the American Ballet (leaving it entirely to Balanchine and Warburg to manage), and Balanchine formally ended his relationship with the school (leaving it to Kirstein and Dimitriev). Ballet Caravan would now be a completely separate entity managed by Kirstein, and Balanchine would carry on with the American Ballet's duties at the Met as well as his Broadway work. According to Kirstein's correspondence with his father, all of this was settled by the middle of June. "I have absolutely no future with the Metropolitan Opera or with the American Ballet," Kirstein wrote, adding that "the American Ballet is a one-man company which I feel is much too limited in its scope, since it banks entirely on Balanchine, who, while he is a very great man, is nevertheless only one man."[82] He hastened to add that he and Balanchine have maintained a "most friendly relationship."

This institutional realignment coincided with the start of significant new projects for both Balanchine and Kirstein. Balanchine was about to begin work for Samuel Goldwyn's movie *The Goldwyn Follies* and headed to the West Coast around this time along with two dozen dancers from the American Ballet. Kirstein was busy launching the second season of Ballet Caravan, which would begin touring in July and perform through the end of the year. In *Blast*, Kirstein wrote that he was "neither disillusioned, disappointed, alienated, or sad" at Balanchine's decision to take dancers from the company to Hollywood, a string of modifiers that suggests he might protest too much.[83] As in his letter to his father, Kirstein insists that everything was happening for the best, implying that the American Ballet had outlived its usefulness as an outlet for realizing his goal of creating a company to rival the de Basil company. "I knew that my service to this American Ballet was over," he wrote, because the company was not going to offer the dancers "any opportunity to perform in the kind of dances which I wished them to create."[84] He officially absolves himself of any obligations to Balanchine, noting that the choreographer now "had Hollywood and his enormous popular success."

Reading between the lines, one might be tempted to infer a causal relationship between Balanchine's "defection" to popular culture and Kirstein's decision to focus on the more high-minded Ballet Caravan. A September 1936 article authored by Kirstein for *New Theatre* suggests as much, reading like a preemptive critique of Balanchine's Hollywood venture. "What has already been done with the dance in films has been, all things considered, very little," adding that "it is difficult to see why a dancer of intelligence" would expect much real opportunity in Hollywood.[85] In later press accounts, Kirstein was unambiguous in his critiques of the institutions he had left behind. In an Associated Press feature on Ballet Caravan he clearly voices his disappointment with his previous efforts with Balanchine and Warburg, noting how they had "turned out to be good, but not American."[86] Kirstein also laments that when the American Ballet was taken over by the Met it lost its identity, and he "had not fought, bled and spent his family's good money for that."[87]

But Kirstein's own actions over the previous months contributed to this parting of the ways as much as any interest in Hollywood on Balanchine's part, especially with respect to his ambitions for Ballet Caravan. During the six months the Caravan had been dormant it was never far from Kirstein's mind as a means by which he could chart his own independent course. As early as December 1936 Kirstein had been hard at work planning the company's next moves, designing a new brochure and corresponding with Frances Hawkins about how much work they might secure and speaking explicitly about a separation from the American Ballet.[88] Beginning in February, moreover, planning for the Caravan took a back seat to an even bigger independent endeavor of Kirstein's, a series of "Collaborative Evenings" to be presented at a New York City theater.[89] Ultimately unrealized, this ambitious plan would have included Ballet Caravan as performers with Balanchine was one of several contributors, including Martha Graham, Paul Draper—in the tap-dancing "Bach ballet"—and even British choreographer Frederick Ashton. Kirstein's ultimate ambition was the establishment of a permanent "lyric theater" in New York, and toward this goal he solicited the support of A. Conger Goodyear (then chairman of the Museum of Modern Art), Nelson Rockefeller and Rockefeller Center architect Wallace Harrison, and the William C. Whitney Trust.[90] A surviving prospectus for the series shows the breadth of Kirstein's vision for the series, which sought to juxtapose dance with other art forms in programs such as "Lyric Drama and the Dance" and "The Dance as Choral

Movement."[91] In an interview with *Dance*, Kirstein described the project as a "dance repertory theater," which would present shows over fifteen consecutive weeks beginning in December, including not just dance but also performances of chamber operas by Copland and Milhaud and a fifteen-piece orchestra.[92] This proposed project differed in substantial ways from what Kirstein would pursue with the Caravan in both scale and scope: it was to be based at a single theater in New York (rather than be a touring organization), be multidisciplinary in nature (rather than focused on dance alone), and would draw on established composers and performers (rather than nurturing young and mostly unknown talent). Ultimately the Caravan—which Kirstein often characterized as "experimental" in character—gave him the opportunity to explore these same ideas on a smaller and more manageable scale and it might be understood as a wholly independent and mobile "lyric theater" with ballet as its focus.

As the paths of Kirstein and Balanchine diverged, the fact that the Caravan was an increasingly independent operation no longer had to be finessed through carefully worded public relations strategies, as had been the case during its first year. Announcements about its new season did not suggest that it was going to be modest in its goals, nor that Kirstein was at all concerned about accommodating dancers' commitments related to the American Ballet at the Met. John Martin reported at the end of May in his weekly column that the "little offshoot" of the American Ballet "is planning not only a second summer tour but also independent activities for the following fall season."[93] In a letter to his father written around this same time, Kirstein similarly reported that arrangements for fall touring were already in process.[94] Although Martin's column hastens to add that there was as yet "no sign of an official division," the writing seemed to already be on the wall, as several dancers in the Caravan "are reported to have decided finally not to return to the parent group" when the Metropolitan Opera season resumed.[95] Individual recollections by dancers confirm that it was indeed a time for "difficult decisions" about which company they would elect to remain with.[96]

Aside from a burst of positive public relations, the American Ballet did not gain much from the Stravinsky Festival over the long term. Echoing Kirstein's private disclosures to his father, outside observers were also beginning to regard the American Ballet as an experiment that had run its course and to note that Balanchine's interest in the company as well as its school had waned considerably. "The whole enterprise has not grown; it has been arbitrarily put together," was the conclusion of a survey of American ballet in the *Manchester Guardian*, which noted that the American Ballet had enjoyed "a rather chequered career in its three years of existence."[97] One of its principal challenges was that it is "too much dependent upon one already famous man whose permanency is questionable and whose interests are not enough tied up with the company's training school."[98] And indeed, one year after the Stravinsky Festival, the American Ballet would cease to exist as an organization, leaving it to Kirstein and Ballet Caravan and Balanchine's Broadway and Hollywood endeavors to continue the work of their enterprise through other means.

CHAPTER 8 | 1937–1938 (I)

IN JANUARY 1939 the Associated Press released a photo of two happy newlyweds identified as George Balanchine, the "former ballet master of the Metropolitan Opera" and the creator of "numbers for the movies and Broadway hits," and Vera Zorina, a movie actress as well as the "dancing star" of several musicals. Balanchine's capsule biography, focused as it was on his "popular" endeavors and the American Ballet's uninspiring tenure at the opera, might strike many as incongruous considering his present reputation as the one of the foremost exponents of ballet in the twentieth century. At the time of its publication, however, this caption was a quite accurate characterization of Balanchine's professional status, as a survey of his activities during the preceding year and a half makes clear. From the summer of 1937 through the end of 1938, Balanchine immersed himself increasingly and almost exclusively in projects on Broadway and in Hollywood. Soon after the close of the Stravinsky Festival he and dancers from the American Ballet went west to rehearse and film ballets for *The Goldwyn Follies*, released in early 1938. Before the movie had even wrapped, Balanchine was already engaged for his third Rodgers and Hart project, *I Married An Angel*, and soon after a fourth, *The Boys from Syracuse*, which would end up running simultaneously on Broadway in 1938 alongside a third, shorter-lived show, *Great Lady*. In between and sometimes concurrent with these projects he was still responsible for the American Ballet's duties at the Metropolitan Opera, although this particular position would come to a dramatic if entirely foreseeable end—along with the American Ballet itself—in April 1938.

Existing accounts of the "popular" years of Balanchine's life and career tend to regard this time as a troubling caesura that must be explained away or otherwise rationalized. Many authors implicitly or explicitly construe this work as peripheral to the wider Balanchine-Kirstein enterprise that

FIGURE 8.1 George Balanchine and Vera Zorina. Original caption: "They'll step it off as a married duo, they announced in New York on January 15, 1939, making known they wed the day before Christmas. He's former ballet master of the Metropolitan Opera and has staged dance numbers for the movies and Broadway hits. She's the dancing star of *I Married an Angel*, Broadway musicomedy [sic], and has been in the movies." Associated Press. BALANCHINE is a Trademark of The George Balanchine Trust.

would ultimately result in the founding of the New York City Ballet. Balanchine's time in Hollywood is an especially significant flashpoint in this regard, but his work on Broadway is often equally implicated, especially owing to the prominent involvement of Zorina in both spheres. Balanchine's popular period, so the story goes, was an inconsequential idyll during which he had nothing better to do than spend his generous salary on the finest wine, food, and cars, and this unwilling seduction into the world of popular celebrity was consummated by his marriage to the glamorous siren Zorina. Even as Balanchine's work from this time is often regarded as less serious at best and trivial at worst, many accounts simultaneously overcorrect in the opposite direction, offering excessively elevated rationalizations for his decisions and motivations to work in these popular media. Balanchine is praised for his insistence on identifying himself as a "choreographer" and for his principled attempts to create ballets of a more serious character. These negative and positive tropes are of course two sides of the same coin, allowing his work to have some meaning while not according it undue significance in contrast to his "real" work as a ballet choreographer.

A more measured view of this period reveals more continuity than rupture and little explicit evidence that Balanchine worried about the changing character of his professional life in the later 1930s. If anything, Balanchine's pursuits in commercial entertainment grew quite organically from his prior engagements and do not appear to have been pursued out of desperation or failure, having begun well before the collapse of the American Ballet. This new phase was also profoundly affected by, and arguably premised upon, his fruitful and by most accounts quite congenial relationship with Zorina, with whom he formed a partnership that seamlessly intertwined the personal and professional. If anything, much like Kirstein's continued efforts with Ballet Caravan, Balanchine's Broadway and film projects offered an opportunity to continue the work of the American Ballet through other institutional means and in the process provided some of the company's dancers well-paid and stable work, even more welcome in the wake of the company's dissolution. Balanchine found in Zorina a glamorous muse, and his entrée into the entertainment industry through her meant that his work reached a much greater audience than either the American Ballet or Ballet Caravan could dream of. Zorina found in Balanchine a doting husband and creative partner uniquely capable of crafting work suited to her talents and abilities. Thus even as Balanchine raged against the conservative leadership of the Met after his firing, he had in fact already successfully made the transition from ballet choreographer to popular dance man, with thoughtful and ambitious ideas about how to bring ballet to wider audiences on both stage and screen.

———————

Several months before the premiere of *Babes in Arms* it was announced that Balanchine and the American Ballet had been engaged by Samuel Goldwyn to provide dances for the movie extravaganza *The Goldwyn Follies*.[1] Whether prospectively predicting this outcome, commemorating the event after the fact, or being a mere coincidence, this news was embedded in the lyrics of "Imagine," whose bridge declares, "You're such a handsome kid / Folks tell of what you did / No wonder Mr. Goldwyn made a bid." The New York–based trade publication *Film Daily* announced Balanchine's engagement in late February 1937, reporting that Goldwyn "plans to develop an entirely new departure in dancing from anything else that has appeared on the screen."[2] *The Goldwyn Follies* had far greater ambitions than showcasing new techniques for dance on screen, however, aiming to make quality entertainment with mass appeal, an elusive goal that had come to consume many Hollywood producers at the time.[3] Goldwyn was in a unique position to contribute to this cause, having been shut out of the big studios through a complex series of corporate realignments and personal feuds. While the big studios thrived by producing a steady stream of content, with new movies arriving every two weeks in the theater chains that they themselves controlled, Goldwyn worked somewhat independently and produced one film at a time. This method resulted in well-crafted films such as *Stella Dallas* and *Arrowsmith*, and his reputation for high artistic standards was mythologized as the "Goldwyn touch."

The Goldwyn Follies was conceived of as the ultimate embodiment of its producer's ethos, planned to be the first in a series of annual films and an explicit ploy to place Goldwyn in the company of legendary entertainer Florenz Ziegfeld.[4] The movie is a thinly veiled allegory of its own creation, telling the story of producer Oliver Merlin's efforts to create a film thoroughly imbued with a "sense of humanity" and thus perfectly engineered to balance quality and mass appeal. Its plot hinges on the importation to Hollywood of the young ingénue Hazel Dawes—nicknamed "Miss Humanity"—who serves as a single-person focus group, rendering judgment on every aspect of the movie to ensure that it will have a true human touch. The thin plot thickens only slightly when Merlin (of course) becomes romantically interested in Hazel, whom he has kept in seclusion to shield her from corruption by Hollywood, but who (of course) meets and falls in love with hamburger-slinger-and-aspiring-crooner Danny Beecher. On the corners of this love triangle are hung the other ancillary "acts" of the *Follies*, some of which come to bear upon the plot itself, including ventriloquist Edgar Bergen and his wooden sidekick Charlie McCarthy, the slapstick comedy trio the Ritz Brothers, as well as Metropolitan Opera stars Helen Jepson and Charles Kullman performing excerpts from *La Traviata*. Such an ambitious endeavor did not come cheap, and Goldwyn's extravagant $2 million budget for the movie placed it atop a list of seven-figure productions in the works.[5] But despite its ambitions and lavish production values—including the novelty of being shot entirely in Technicolor—the endeavor ended up as Goldwyn's first and last *Follies*, losing close to $700,000 and widely derided as "Goldwyn's Folly."

Today *The Goldwyn Follies* is regarded as historically significant mostly because of the involvement of two notable artistic teams in its creation. The first is Zorina and Balanchine, whose relationship began during the film's production. Zorina's memoirs explain that she made his participation an explicit condition of her own appearance in the movie, and she signed on to the film a few weeks after his contract was settled, via a "Transatlantic phone" from London, where she was starring as Vera in a second production of *On Your Toes*.[6] For the other notable team, George and Ira Gershwin, the project was an unexpected swan song. During the early phases of production George Gershwin began experiencing crippling headaches that would be diagnosed as a fatal brain tumor.[7] Following Gershwin's unexpected death Vernon Duke was brought in to complete the movie's music, but not before the brothers had written most of the film's songs, including two masterpieces of the American songbook, "Love Walked In" and "Love Is Here To Stay."[8]

While it is not clear that the participation of the Gershwins was an explicit inducement for Balanchine to sign on to the film, their collective presence on the project represented a potential realization of long-held plans of the wider Balanchine-Kirstein enterprise. Balanchine and Warburg had both expressed interest in an American Ballet commission from George Gershwin as early as 1935, and the composer had been associated with the company as early as 1934 in part through his relationship with Kay Swift.[9] Goldwyn initially asked the composer to write a single ballet for the *Follies*, tentatively titled *Swing Symphony*, and according to biographer Howard Pollack it was Gershwin's intention to repurpose this score as an orchestral work or a project for the American Ballet.[10] With this score not even begun before George Gershwin's death, Goldwyn opted instead for two shorter dance numbers.

As one of the new shorter numbers, Balanchine and Ira Gershwin collaborated to produce *Exposition*, set to *An American in Paris*, a narrative ballet in which a man pursues a woman through the various attractions of a world's fair. According to a surviving three-page draft scenario, the ballet was conceived to feature Paul Draper as the male protagonist alongside Zorina.[11] The ballet was not ultimately included in the film after Goldwyn balked at the elaborate cinematography proposed by Balanchine. Instead of filming the number like a performance on a traditional proscenium stage, Balanchine had devised a concept that would take advantage of the medium of film and spent three weeks planning the various shots.[12] When he attempted to walk Goldwyn through his conception—a process that required crouching on the ground and clambering over various pieces of equipment—the producer became flustered and subsequently scrapped the ballet, in part because he was confident that the "miners in Harrisburg" would not understand its complexity. Balanchine expressed his disdain for such concerns—perhaps not remembering that the American Ballet had received positive reviews for the work they presented in Harrisburg in October 1935—and came close to walking away from the movie over the debacle.

But by most accounts, the time that Balanchine and the American Ballet spent in Hollywood proceeded fairly smoothly and represented a continuation of their life as a company. The dancers arrived in Hollywood in mid-July, a time coinciding with the annual summer holiday of the School of American Ballet, and they returned to New York in mid-October in time to prepare for the coming season at the Met.[13] "Each day classes and rehearsals take up the customary five or six hours," the *Dancing Times* reported, "so that this 'vacation' from the New York studio and performances at the Metropolitan Opera House has only the novelty of a 'studio lot' to differentiate it from regular routine."[14] According to some reports the dancers were kept in a kind of seclusion similar to the heroine of *The Goldwyn Follies*, working assiduously on a "remote corner of the United Artists lot" specially built for the company.[15] They were so shut out from the world that "they know nothing of Hollywood," even though evidently Hollywood came to them, with a steady stream of visitors passing through the studio to observe them at work, and their attire of "full-length black wool tights" drawing attention for its relative modesty by studio standards.[16] Their monastic existence was reported to have been constrained even further by a rule imposed by Balanchine, who allowed each dancer only one date a week, with the other six nights meant to be spent at home resting.[17]

The movie's two ballets both featured newly composed music by Vernon Duke and each resonated closely with themes from Balanchine's previous work on the ballet and Broadway stage. Notably, they represent the earliest choreography by Balanchine to be preserved in any original and definitive form that is still available to view to this day. The first was an adaptation of *Romeo and Juliet* in which tap-dancing Montagues go to battle with ballet-dancing Capulets. The conceit of the ballet repurposed the premise of the "On Your Toes" number, which had juxtaposed contrasting dancing choruses, and showcased well-drilled dancing on the part of the American Ballet corps as well as a striking pas de deux by William Dollar and Zorina. The second, *Water Nymph* ballet, was an even more elaborate affair and embodied some of the innovative cinematic goals that Balanchine had intended to include in *Exposition*.

In a variety of published comments during and after the production of the *Follies*, Balanchine articulated a thoughtful and serious ideology for his work on screen, characterizing his efforts as having the potential to

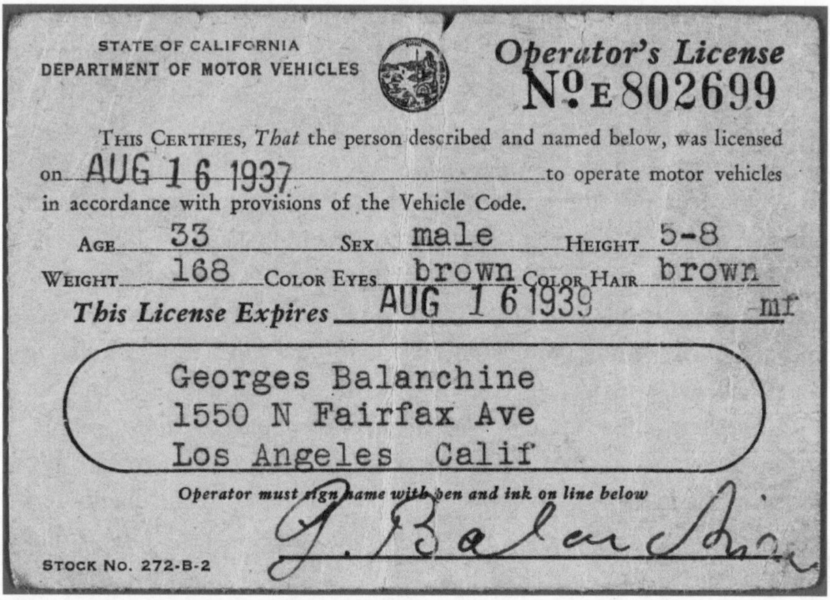

STATE OF CALIFORNIA
DEPARTMENT OF MOTOR VEHICLES
Operator's License
№ E 802699
THIS CERTIFIES, *That* the person described and named below, was licensed on AUG 16 1937 to operate motor vehicles in accordance with provisions of the Vehicle Code.
AGE 33 SEX male HEIGHT 5-8
WEIGHT 168 COLOR EYES brown COLOR HAIR brown
This License Expires AUG 16 1939 mf
Georges Balanchine
1550 N Fairfax Ave
Los Angeles Calif
Operator must sign name with pen and ink on line below
G. Balanchine
STOCK NO. 272-B-2

FIGURE 8.2 George Balanchine's California driver's license, August 1937. George Balanchine Archive, MS Thr 411 (2811), Houghton Library, Harvard University. BALANCHINE is a Trademark of The George Balanchine Trust.

bring ballet to a broader audience and create entirely new aesthetic experiences.[18] Film could overcome the constraints of traditional theaters, in which sight lines could be compromised for a variety of reasons and continuity could be achieved only through carefully timed exits and entrances aided by lighting and set changes. Balanchine saw the movies as "an ideal field for fantastic and imaginative creations" that were by no means alien to the art form but rather the "proper domain of the ballet."[19] Balanchine also thought that ballet had something special to contribute to Hollywood in its own right. "Much as I have heard about the glamour of Hollywood," he noted in an interview around the time that the American Ballet began work on the *Follies*, he and his dancers had "something very definite to add to it."[20] Glamour was "one of the prime elements of ballet," he added, and this special quality "can be best expressed on the screen, as the ballet is essentially pictorial."[21] All of these qualities were manifest in his *Follies* ballets, whether in the quick cuts and dramatic close-ups of the *Romeo and Juliet* ballet or the even more striking special effects of the *Water Nymph* ballet, at the beginning of which Zorina rises from a pool of water and then instantly begins dancing on its surface.

Understanding implicitly the special power of the work of art in the age of its technological reproducibility, Balanchine held that artists working in film should aspire to even higher artistic standards than those working on the stage, since they are "addressing not a selected group of people, not only a city public, but large masses of people all over the world."[22] "It is absurd to regard movies as only a relaxation and pastime," he added, noting that artists "should have the same attitude toward motion pictures as one has toward any other form of theatrical art."[23] Accordingly, Balanchine opposed any effort to water down his product to make it palatable to new audiences. "The public wants new things," he maintained, "even if it does not know what they are."[24] Of course, these sentiments are directly opposed to the central premise of *The Goldwyn Follies*, in which the producer endeavors to give the public what it wants at all costs, and were directly contravened by Goldwyn's abandonment of *Exposition*.

Initial reviews of the film were positive, and its early release drew large crowds to theaters, with many critics impressed by the quality of its dances.[25] *Film Daily* praised the "absorbing, tuneful, tastefully wrought musical" as "entertainment of patent power," in part thanks to the "brilliance of the ballet numbers" with the *Water Nymph* ballet singled out for special distinction.[26] The *Hollywood Spectator* hailed the overall good taste and "admirable restraint" of the film, noting how the ballet scenes featured "only a score or so of dancers" in contrast to the masses of bodies featured in other films.[27] *Dancing Times* film critic John Newnham called the movie's dance sequences, and the *Water Nymph* ballet in particular, "easily the best Ballet yet seen in any American picture" and lauded Balanchine's "perfect screen technique."[28] "This is Ballet as it should be in pictures," Newnham concluded, since it takes "every advantage of the screen's superiority over the stage" and although some "trick-work is used, there is none of that bewildering mechanical juggling seen in so many films."[29]

But despite Balanchine's high hopes for bringing serious and innovative dance to the screen, reports from many theaters in which *The Goldwyn Follies* was shown suggest that the ballet and opera were an uncomfortable fit in a film aspiring for true mass appeal. An assessment in the trade publication *Film Bulletin* warned exhibitors about the perils of the "pretty boring musical show," which was overlong and in need of editing, and advised them to promote the appearances of Charlie McCarthy and the Ritz Brothers, who "rescue it from complete failure."[30] "Zorina is a splendid ballet dancer and a surprisingly good actress," the report added, but along with the rest of the movie as a whole "her Water Sprite Ballet could use a pair of shears."[31] Subsequent reports filed by local exhibitors in small towns and rural areas related that the opera and ballet in the *Follies* met with mixed reactions. A report from the Chief Theatre in Marcelline, Missouri, summarized attendance for the movie as "fair" adding that it had "too much opera and ballet for this town."[32] In Paynesville, Minnesota, there was a stark divide between older patrons who approved of the film, and younger viewers who found it "a little overdone."[33] "A little too much opera and dancing," the manager added, and further explained that, "we'll have to do a little cutting on some of these exceptionally long shows if the studios won't."[34] Small town audiences were not the only ones unenthusiastic about the movie, with one theater in Detroit noting that the movie was "too high brow for our neighborhood patronage" and "the ballet dancing and opera singing were not appreciated."[35]

The movie met with some enthusiasm in these same venues, reported to be a "fine show, liked by all" at screenings in Old Town, Maine.[36] Audiences in Saguache, Colorado, were more enthusiastic, to the surprise of the manager there. "This one really had me worried as our folks don't go for quite so much class in their singing and dancing," but in the end those who attended a Sunday screening "went away so well pleased" that their word of mouth recommendations resulted in double the usual attendance for Monday and Tuesday shows.[37] Ultimately he declared the film a "real class production that will please 95 percent if you can get them in."[38] Most viewers had a stark love or hate reaction to the movie. "Too long, way too long" was the verdict in Charleston, West Virginia, while in Newport, Washington, the film was declared "one grand show."[39] In Penacook, New Hampshire, the movie reportedly garnered "fifty percent satisfaction" from audiences, and while Charlie McCarthy drew most viewers in, "the ballet and operatic numbers drove them out."[40]

———

During the months between the American Ballet's time in Hollywood and the release of *The Goldwyn Follies* in early 1938 the character of Balanchine's life and career continued to evolve. Although he and Zorina were not yet married they were virtually inseparable, and his Broadway and Hollywood work became, if not his sole focus, an even more significant part of his professional portfolio. Balanchine returned to New York in early November 1937, a month before opening night of the opera season and a few weeks after the dancers' own departure from California; Zorina remained behind to film her dramatic scenes, returning from the coast just before the Christmas holiday.[41] With the *Follies* still in production, Balanchine was already in negotiations for a new Broadway project in which Zorina would also have a featured role, the Rodgers and Hart musical *I Married an Angel*. By late November it was being reported that both Balanchine and Zorina had signed on officially for the show, which would premiere in May 1938.[42] Back on the West Coast, Balanchine's name was being floated as the possible head of new special dance project that would build on the work begun in his dances for the *Follies*. The proposed unit was to work for six months to "practice the filming of ballet and nothing else," shooting individual dancers and ensembles and "studying what 'shots' from what angles give the best results, studying speeds and grouping and the possibilities of trick photography."[43]

When the Metropolitan Opera season resumed in December 1937, the morale of its resident choreographer and dance company was quite low, and the success of the Stravinsky Festival had not improved the internal status of either Balanchine or the American Ballet. Scattered observations about the company's dancing during the 1937–38 opera season suggest that Balanchine had become resigned to a more conservative and restrained aesthetic. No special scandal occurred at performances of *Aida* in early December, with the ballet performing "creditably" and "marking no new artistic milestone in its career."[44] For *Samson et Dalila* the ensemble "danced a fitting and graceful dance" in the first act and "received approval" for the third act Bacchanale, which featured Daphne Vane as a soloist.[45] Balanchine found himself responsible for another set of dances starring Montagues and Capulets, for a new production of Gounod's *Roméo et Juliette*. Although this version did not include any tap dancers, some element of genre mixing was evidently introduced, with one reviewer raising an eyebrow at a curious " 'Virginia Reel' figure incorporated into the terpsichoreanism of the opening scene."[46]

The American Ballet continued to showcase their own works on mixed bill opera evenings and Sunday evening concerts. In early February they danced *Mozartiana* in addition to the Venusberg ballet from *Tannhäuser*.[47] Having been readied for the stage for the Stravinsky Festival, *Apollon* was presented in conjunction with shorter operas as part of the regular season. The ballet preceded a performance of *Salome* in February 1938, where it did not make a more favorable impression than it had a year before. Olin Downes lamented the "dreary emptiness and banality" of the music, and that it could not be said that the performance "relieved the character of the score."[48] Another critic noted that while the ballet "seemed well done at the time," it was "totally eclipsed by the performance of *Salome* which followed," an apt metaphor for the American Ballet's ongoing struggle to maintain a meaningful artistic profile at the opera.[49]

The American Ballet's tenure at the Met came to a dramatic and very public end in mid-April, when it was announced—while *Angel* was in previews in New Haven—that the company and Balanchine would not be returning for the following season. According to Anatole Chujoy, the development was precipitated by ill-advised actions on the part of Balanchine, who at the urging of Dimitriev pushed the issue of the company's renewal to Edward Johnson at a meeting in mid-March. Although what transpired at this meeting is unclear, the American Ballet was soon after advised in writing that its contract would not be renewed, with some speculating that they might have been kept on had Balanchine not forced the issue.[50] Having been fired did not prevent Balanchine from arranging a press event three weeks later to announce that he and the American Ballet were in fact quitting their Met post owing to artistic differences with the opera. "The tradition of the ballet at the Metropolitan is bad ballet," Balanchine declared, adding that the opera was "a good place for those who don't want to do anything."[51] He held that he had been given "no chance to create" and likened his working conditions to "being in prison for life" and "putting a bird of flight in a cage."[52] Edward Johnson explained more diplomatically that following three years of institutional reorganization the opera was now better equipped to develop a new ballet program of its own and thus no longer needed the services of the somewhat independent organization.[53]

The opera's decision was greeted with approval in some quarters while others rose to the defense of the company and Balanchine. John Martin reported in restrained terms that the development "brings to an end an alliance that has been something less than ideally satisfactory to either side from the very beginning" and that very few tears would be shed over the news.[54] He concurred with Balanchine's assessment of the state of ballet at the Met, averring that the artist's talents lay "in entirely different directions" and that he should not be blamed for "refusing to submerge himself and his choreography meekly in the tradition of ballet" at the opera.[55] Like Martin, *Dance Observer* had greeted the American Ballet's hiring unenthusiastically three years earlier and continued to lament the lack of American leadership at the opera. Nevertheless its editorial board voiced its support for Balanchine, since regardless of their opinions on his work, his treatment offered further evidence that the Met was at best "a grudging host to the dance."[56] Other publications greeted the decision as an overdue comeuppance. The editorial board of *Musical America* maintained that the root problem with the relationship had been Balanchine's failure "to think of opera in terms of opera," and as a result there had been a "persistent clash of styles" between his dances and the productions in which they appeared.[57] Within his dances themselves, moreover, there had been significant problems, with frequent "frank disagreement between the dancing and the music" resulting in effects that were often "disillusioning if not actually distressing," and those who went to the opera "for opera's sake, not ballet's sake, were right in expecting the ballet to conform."[58]

While the American Ballet's dramatic departure and Balanchine's bold public statements made for good headlines, in retrospect it is clear that not only had the relationship between the company and the Met run its course, but that it had in fact been an unwise merger from the start. For the better part of a year, moreover, the wider enterprise of which the American Ballet was the public face grappled with an increasingly challenging set of pressures that contributed to the ensemble's instability as much as any hostility or neglect on the part of the opera. After the formal parting of Kirstein and Balanchine earlier in the summer, Kirstein had turned his focus more exclusively on Ballet Caravan while Balanchine was busy lining up his Broadway projects, both having realized that the opera was an aesthetic and institutional dead end. In other words, the decline of the American Ballet was not solely caused by the Met's poor treatment of the company and the hostility of conservative "dowager" patrons, as has been emphasized in many accounts. When it became clear that the opera was taking them nowhere, the principal players turned their attention elsewhere and in effect left the original ensemble to wither on the vine. In other words, Balanchine's and Kirstein's decisions to pursue other projects in the face of the unhappy situation at the Met were at once causes and effects of the American Ballet's increasingly precarious position.

In addition to the organizational drift that accompanied both men's new endeavors and priorities, an unforeseen development in the life of Edward Warburg helped hasten the decline of the American Ballet and left the company in an even more unstable position financially and managerially. In September 1937, Warburg's father Felix passed away, and management of the family's considerable wealth and philanthropic endeavors suddenly fell to Edward. In light of this new commitment, he decided to step down as the leader of the American Ballet, leaving management in the hands of Balanchine and Dimitriev. This decision has been construed by many as a convenient alibi for Warburg, who from the start had never been as committed to the endeavor as Kirstein; and given his uneven record as a manager, the change in leadership had the potential to offer the American Ballet a fresh start. Writing to his father from the road in Pennsylvania with Ballet Caravan in mid-November, Kirstein reported that Warburg had formally ended his association with the company, and he believed that as a result "the whole future of the school will go along a great deal better from now on" especially since Dimitriev would be taking over the management of the school and the company's obligations at the opera. "It's too bad that it was such a long way around to home," Kirstein mused, "but I guess these things have to be learned through experience."[59]

Instead of providing a new beginning, however, Warburg's departure created a leadership and financial vacuum from which the American Ballet would not recover. In the meantime, shifting organizational alliances in the wider ballet marketplace did not play to the advantage of the American Ballet. Around the time that the company was working in Hollywood, Léonide Massine had begun exploring the possibility of forming a new ballet company independent of the domineering Colonel de Basil, to be financed by American investors and perhaps to include Balanchine as a potential collaborator. Massine eventually found a new institutional home when impresario René Blum, who had founded a rival Ballet Russe company based in Monte Carlo several years earlier, arranged to sell his company to impresario Serge Denham. Soon after Massine had assumed his new role in early 1938, there arose talk of merging the de Basil and Denham-Massine organizations to create one massive enterprise, an ultimately unsuccessful gambit in which impresario Sol Hurok was involved.

In their efforts to chart a new course, Balanchine and Dimitriev embroiled the company in these complex realignments without any meaningful results. The possible reorganization of the American Ballet as part of a larger Ballet Russe-style touring company was hampered not only by the already intense competition for investors and audiences but also the unwise invitation to involve lawyer and de Basil associate Jacques Lidji in their planning and negotiations. Lidji proved to be an unhelpful advocate for the American Ballet, more interested in maximizing potential financial return than realizing the company's artistic vision or ensuring a stable livelihood for its dancers. "One cannot list all the wonderful schemes" devised by the mysterious operator Lidji, as Anatole Chujoy explains: "There were so many of them," and all of them came to naught.[60] By the time of the Met firing, the American Ballet had run out of time and money (with no more contributions from Warburg forthcoming), and the company was left to quietly fade away. The school remained mostly unfazed and even offered a novel six-week summer course in Bermuda during its usual vacation period.[61] But for the foreseeable future, Ballet Caravan and Balanchine's Broadway and film projects now constituted the only official performance outlets of the increasingly splintered enterprise. And in the immediate future, Balanchine and Zorina were poised to make a new start on Broadway in *Angel*.

I Married An Angel is not the brightest star in the Rodgers and Hart firmament, having never received a full revival on Broadway and with comparatively few of its songs in the core repertory of the American songbook. And the reputation of the show was perhaps permanently damaged by its 1942 film adaptation, notable today mostly as the inauspicious end of the film musical juggernaut of Nelson Eddy and Jeannette MacDonald. When it premiered on Broadway in May 1938, however, *Angel* was a major theatrical event and would run longer than any Rodgers and Hart show since 1927. Among its fans was First Lady Eleanor Roosevelt, who noted how pleased she was to have seen a play "written on the question of actually telling the truth."[62] Her son John and his fiancée Anne Clark had attended the show as well, and at their wedding several weeks later—a major national news event—the musical's title song was played for their first dance.[63]

Adapted from a Hungarian play, *I Married An Angel* relies on a clever if deeply misogynistic conceit, recounting the romantic woes of the Budapest-based Count Palafi, whose desire for a perfect wife is fulfilled when an angel literally descends from heaven. The Count soon learns to his dismay that his Angel makes a less than an ideal spouse. She is unable to lie and thus repeatedly offends her husband and many others with her blunt honesty. The Angel's upstanding morals are not her only singular quality, with her otherworldliness further enhanced in the context of the musical by her ability to dance. A dancing female lead was one of the most important "no formula" qualities of the musical, and the role of the Angel was explicitly built to showcase the talents and personality of its star Zorina.

"Novel" and "novelty" recur frequently in many reviews of the show, notably a report in *Variety*, which offers a concise summary of its innovative technological and choreographic resources. The curtain rose on "a Venetian-blind effect and a couple of acrobats in full-dress" who "do hand-to-hand stands in the middle of a Hungarian waltz."[64] This quality was especially evident in its dance numbers, which included "a team of sled-pulling wolfhounds," a "ski dance," and "some surrealist Terpsichore, in which a sea god stands on a rock in the middle of the ocean, suspending a bicycle over his head."[65] Like the musical itself, these innovative and intriguing dances do not feature prominently in Broadway history (compared to the attention accorded to *On Your Toes* and *Babes in Arms*), and only about a minute of video footage of them survives.[66] But through written and visual traces it is possible to get a sense of their character and meaning and their place in Balanchine's emerging body of work both on and off Broadway.

The main dance event of the first half of the show was a multi-scene "Honeymoon Ballet," during which Count Palafi and his angelic bride travel the world. Most striking about this number was its quick changes of scene, made possible by a combination of traditional and technologically intensive means. On the one hand, the ensemble of dancers literally used their bodies to arrange themselves in various formations, while a pair of treadmills moved sets, props, actors, and dancers on- and offstage in a simulation of the quick cuts of the cinema. In the Honeymoon Ballet, Balanchine thus had a second chance to reimagine some of his recent innovations in dance cinematography in a theatrical context, once again showcasing his glamorous muse. *Variety* explicitly acknowledged this innovation of the show, calling the Honeymoon ballet "the first attempt at blending the kaleidoscopic camera sweep in filmusicals [*sic*] with the exigencies and limitations of legit presentations."[67]

As recounted in a written scenario, the honeymoon journey begins at Le Bourget airport, where the lights came up to reveal five girls dressed in white silk tights and silver wings, who enter and do a brief "airplane dance," alongside male dancers portraying mechanics.[68] When the newlyweds enter, dressed in aviation attire, the dancers arrange themselves in the form of an airplane—the girls forming the wings and the boys the cockpit—with a set of silver steps brought on to enable the honeymooners to climb aboard. The lights then come down for a "night flight," during which the Angel and the lead male dancer, Charles Laskey of the American Ballet, performed a pas de deux downstage, as scenery scrolled behind them on the upstage treadmill and the moon rose on a backdrop. The Angel and her partner finish their duet downstage in two, allowing for the back panels to open up to reveal the first stop on their trip, a visit to the Geneva Zoo, where the couple examines the birds of various nations, each of which does a brief national dance. The final stop of the Honeymoon was Norway, a nod to the national heritage of Zorina, and in this final "snow ballet" a larger ensemble of dancers joins the Angel and the male dancer in a dizzying whirl of entrances and exits, "snow" effects, and changes in lighting all enhanced by the motion of the treadmills. The snow ballet ends with the Count arriving in a sled pulled by a team of real Norwegian huskies. He helps his new bride aboard after wrapping her in a white fur coat.

Brooks Atkinson was likely praising this ballet when he noted how "one long sequence is done entirely in ballet and pantomime" with "settings that capture perfectly the enchantment of the story."[69] *Variety* marveled at the technological means that made all this possible, noting that the musical was literally one of the heaviest productions in recent memory, with a second stage superimposed on the existing boards to accommodate the treadmill mechanism.[70] This machinery caused a few mishaps, with either scenery and props or actors transported on stage too early or removed too late. Nevertheless, the generous investments by producer Dwight Deere Wiman in this elaborate innovation evidently paid off, and it is possible to see something of an early "megamusical" aesthetic at work in its elaborate production apparatus. Zorina in her memoirs noted that the role of the Angel was one in which she could practically do no wrong, that from her first entrance on a dark stage as she came floating down with immense shimmering wings, the audience "invariably broke into applause."

The crowd pleasing did not stop with the Honeymoon sequence. Even more carefully engineered to draw in audiences was the big dance number of the second act, a show within a show that satirized Radio City Music Hall. Unlike the Honeymoon Ballet, this even lengthier sequence was framed by a song that recounts the experience of attending a show "At the Roxy Music Hall," where "an usher puts his heart in what he ushes," a "fountain changes color when it gushes," and the seats "caress your carcass with their plushes." After this prologue, the number proceeded to offer a send-up of a typical Radio City review. According to a surviving script, the revue was originally planned to begin with a ventriloquist routine featuring *Goldwyn Follies* co-stars Edgar Bergen and Charlie McCarthy continuing with a minimalist parody of the famous Rockettes, in the form of a kick line with only two dancers. After a beer-themed number featuring the Count, there was a two-for-one parody number called "Ted Fawn," presumably a send up of Ted Shawn and *Afternoon of a Faun*. Reviews allude to the minimalist Rockettes bit but a slightly different lineup for the rest of the ballet, including a "hippy" modern dance parody and a humorous riff on Walt Disney's *Snow White*.

The heart of the Roxy City number, however, was its finale, a large-scale surrealist ballet created by Balanchine starring Zorina, one of the biggest moments of the entire musical. The ballet was somewhat tangential to the plot, satirizing the surrealism of Salvador Dalí and accordingly pulling out all the bizarre stops that it could. Reviewers and apparently also audiences ate the number up, calling it "one of the best satires ever offered behind the footlights."[71] Zorina rose "from the waves against an oyster shell, leered at by a man encircled with a snake gnawing at his heart, and holding a bicycle aloft," while a "headless man" stood by observing the proceedings.[72] It would take another entire chapter to recount the full blow-by-blow of this ballet as preserved in the script, and even then it is unclear how obvious its intentions would become. Balanchine claimed to know exactly what the ballet was about, saying that it was based on the story of Othello. Director Joshua Logan voiced the opinion of many audience members when he noted how this explanation only increased his confusion about the ballet's content.[73] Logan reports asking Balanchine about the identity of the man who carries his own head around: was this supposed to be Othello or Iago? Balanchine's playful response was that he was both, and perhaps the lack of actual meaning was his ultimate rebuke of Dalí's surrealism. This ambiguity is commemorated in the final chorus of the number, with a slanted rhyme sung at the conclusion of the song that explains "the ballet that you saw is called Othello / Though it might as well have been some other fellow." If the premise was something of a joke, at least the dancing was serious business and something that was achievable only by the classically trained Zorina and Laskey.

The two dance numbers of *Angel* worked at cross purposes where formal integration is concerned. The Honeymoon ballet clearly helped advance the plot, using dance as a medium for storytelling and the characters portrayed as their "real" selves. The Roxy Music Hall number, by contrast, was more of a dance for the sake of a good number, with the surrealist mood adding an additional arbitrary dimension. Rodgers and Hart and Balanchine saw no problem with this lack of generic coherence, and Hart addressed Logan's misgivings by telling him to think about it as an operatic divertissement. Logan later admitted that his colleagues had been right in their instinct not to worry about explaining the number or giving it a stronger pretext—if you want to give the audience something good just for fun, you should do it with no apologies. The mostly positive reviews of the ballet confirm that audiences and critics took no issue with its lack of integration, and several favorably compared the ballet to Balanchine's more obviously integrated dance numbers in previous shows. If the exact content of the surrealist ballet will always be a little murky, its basic contours suggest a love triangle involving an elusive female muse and two male suitors, a plot that by this point Balanchine had made the premise of a half dozen ballets. Notably, in the context of a whimsical Broadway show, in contrast to the ballet stage, it was a resounding success.

With *Angel* continuing its successful Broadway run, Balanchine signed on for two other musical projects set to premiere at the end of 1938: *The Boys from Syracuse*, his fourth collaboration with Rodgers and Hart, and *Great*

Lady, a short-lived musical that marked the inauspicious Broadway debut of composer Frederick Loewe. Vastly different in terms of their content, dramaturgy, and success, the two shows demonstrate that Balanchine's new identity as a Broadway choreographer was hardly homogeneous, and these different projects reflected distinctive artistic and institutional priorities. His dances for *Boys* were simultaneously a recapitulation and reinvention of his previous Broadway work, blending ballet and tap and incorporating dramatic conventions used in his previous musicals and *The Goldwyn Follies*. Through this show Balanchine even more conclusively established himself as a Broadway player; he was branded as doing "an ace job on the terp angle" by *Variety*, and his work on the show was declared "a high spot in his illustrious career" by Walter Winchell.[74] In a different vein, *Great Lady* drew more exclusively on ballet and marked the Broadway debut of not just Loewe but also dancers Alicia Alonso and Jerome Robbins as well as featuring Ballet Russe star André Eglevsky. By many accounts, Balanchine saw the show as an attempt to keep some of the dancers of the American Ballet working as an ensemble following the company's collapse earlier in the year.

For Rodgers and Hart, *The Boys from Syracuse* was further proof that the duo was an almost unstoppable force on Broadway. In retrospect, the musical marked the beginning of the end of their partnership, with Hart's substance abuse making him increasingly unreliable in the course of production. But for the time being the two could seemingly do no wrong, and a two-part profile in the *New Yorker* and a cover story in *Time* magazine provided an auspicious summertime prologue to the premiere of their next hit. The jaunty adaptation of Shakespeare's *Comedy of Errors*, whose plot turns on the separation and reunification of two sets of twins, successfully gambled that it was possible to reinvent the Elizabethan drama in a contemporary idiom. In addition to Balanchine's talents, the show benefited from the guiding hand of director George Abbott and the generous funding of Wiman as producer. Shakespearean reinvention was already in the mix in the New York theater scene at the time, with Orson Welles directing an innovative staging of *Julius Caesar* under the auspices of the Federal Theater Project. In contrast to Welles's more serious director's theater-style intervention, which "committed mayhem on the bleeding body of the Swan of Avon," Abbott's adaptation showed that he was "a genial murderer who commits his crimes for entertainment rather than ego."[75] One inspiration for the show was the coincidence that star comedian Jimmy Savo (alongside whom the Ballet Caravan had performed two summers prior in Westport) bore a striking resemblance to Larry Hart's brother Teddy. The new take on Shakespeare retained only two lines of the original play's text, and was decidedly adult in its humor, with songs abounding in racy double entendre such as "Sing for Your Supper," leavened by more straightforward romantic numbers like "This Can't Be Love."

In contrast to Balanchine's previous Rodgers and Hart shows that featured multiple extended dance numbers, the dances of *Boys* were woven more intricately into various songs and moments in the plot, with only one proper "ballet" number occurring in the second act. The least regarded of the show's dances, this number was an amalgamation of conventions from his previous Broadway work: a satirical surrealist dream ballet. Described by turns as an "extraordinary burlesque ballet" and a "dream ballet that is a surrealist wonder-work," it featured Jimmy Savo in "a savage parody of the classic *Afternoon of a Faun*."[76] But critical consensus was lukewarm at best, with one observer finding it "beautifully done" but at the same time "somewhat out of key" with the first half of the show.[77] Although it got off to a good start, the ballet evidently quickly became "top heavy by dragging in too much stuff," and it was suggested that the number "would register better with slicing."[78]

By contrast, the majority of the show's other dances—in particular, several moments in the first act—differed markedly from the status of either a diegetic dance number or formally integrated dream ballet. Instead these dances worked in tandem with the book and music in a more diffuse manner. While the *New Yorker* offered a "minority report" that criticized this aspect of the show, contending that it contained "too much ballet," most critics disagreed and praised the use of choreographic effects to enhance the book and music in an abstract and nonrepresentational manner. Brooks Atkinson marveled at how Balanchine "found a way of turning the dancing into the theme of the comedy and orchestrating it into the composition of the scene."[79] These dances also managed to offer a pleasing blend of styles, showing how Balanchine could combine "his better ballet training with tap dancing interludes that have a true Broadway swing."[80] *Variety* noted explicitly that Balanchine had "done well in transplanting his talents from the American Ballet" to the medium of the musical, and that in this context his "art is displayed to a vastly larger audience than that which follows the straight ballet programs."[81]

Balanchine's role in creating such effects was comparable to his process in *Babes in Arms*, with his assuming responsibility for the larger structure and character of the dances but leaving many decisions and individual steps up to the dancers themselves. Like *Babes, Boys* featured several dancers with unique backgrounds who contributed their expertise and talents to the show's choreography but who were not officially credited for their work. Particularly consequential in this regard were the show's three principal dancers: Heidi Vosseler, a stalwart of the American Ballet since the company's early years; George Church, a bodybuilder turned ballet and tap dancer who had performed in the 1936 *Ziegfeld Follies* and *On Your Toes*; and Betty Bruce, a versatile performer who had trained and danced at the Metropolitan Opera before branching out into Broadway. All three were singled out for individual praise in reviews, with Bruce and Vosseler hailed as "extraordinarily skillful" in their ability to "translate the revelry of a musical rumpus into dainty beauty."[82] Walter Winchell praised Vosseler for her "graceful toe work," while the "magical toes" of Church produced tap dancing that was "something out of the clouds."[83] Among the three, however, Bruce was a clear audience favorite, with her "exquisite" dancing garnering major ovations that often threatened to bring the show to a halt.[84]

Among the most evocative and remarkable choreographic moments was a trio that was "danced as a refrain" for "The Shortest Day of the Year," sung in the first act. The dance that accompanied this number was by turns deemed "one of the most novel creations" in the show and "as fetching a thing as anything that has been exhibited among the musical shows."[85] In its creation and execution this trio was a complex collaboration; Balanchine came up with the concept while developing the choreography in close association with the dancers, similar to the genesis of the leg-sliding number by the Nicholas Brothers in *Babes*. In the trio, the man (Church) was torn between the two women, with Vosseler dancing ballet while Bruce performed tap, the result described as a "modified adagio" and an "odd combo of ballet, tap and adagio."[86] "Working in the middle, I would perform both ballet with Heidi and tap with Betty," as Church explained, with the three dancers "intertwining from time to time" in "dream-ups" devised by Balanchine.[87] This trio marked a combination of several recurring tropes from Balanchine's dances over the last five years, layering the tap and ballet competition of *On Your Toes* and *The Goldwyn Follies* with the elusive muse plots of *Errante* and *The Bat*. Achieving similar effects was a solo danced by Bruce in the first act, which "chronically enlivens the proceedings" with its "happy marriage of tap and ballet."[88] It is unclear which song Bruce's solo was attached to, but this "artistically blended tap-and-ballet number" was one of the moments that helped her bring the house down.[89]

While both *Angel* and *Boys* were still running, Balanchine took on a third Broadway project in 1938, the short-lived musical *Great Lady*, which would close after less than a month of performances.[90] The show was based on the life of Eliza Jumel, a woman who pulled herself out of poverty by marrying into a French wine fortune and later became the wife of Vice President Aaron Burr.[91] However ballet was to be integrated into the plot, Balanchine regarded the show was a means to provide for his dancers and keep the company together following their firing from the Met.[92] Owing to an unknown conflict between Balanchine and one of the show's producers, the dances were credited to William Dollar, who assisted with the choreography and danced in the show, alongside American Ballet dancers Holly Howard and Yvonne Patterson, among others.[93] *Great Lady* holds the further distinction of marking the Broadway debut of Jerome Robbins as well as its composer, Frederick Loewe.

Although the producers spared no expense by engaging a premiere roster of dancers, including Ballet Russe star André Eglevsky as well as Annabelle Lyon and Leda Anchutina as principals, critical consensus was that the show was too long and that the heavy emphasis on dance felt forced, even if the individual numbers themselves had pleasing effects.[94] A first act ballet set in a dressmaking shop featured Eglevsky as the "floorwalker," Lyon as the shop's forewoman, and Anchutina as the shop's assistant.[95] Displaying the hand of its actual creator, this "gay exaggerated divertissement" was described as evincing a keen eye for "pantomime and the eccentric" and a pas de trois with "commendable" pointe work.[96] The other major dance moment was a dream sequence associated with the song "There Had to Be the Waltz," "a neatly devised fantastic ballet" inspired by "the waltz of Napoleonic times."[97] A high point of the show for some, the number was praised for being "lavishly set and dressed" with "good ensemble work as well as some expert leaping and twirling by the principal dancers."[98] Lyon recalled that the number as "just typical ballet" and thus somewhat "surprising" in the context of a musical.[99] Another notable dancer who made her Broadway debut in the show, Alicia Alonso, recalled the number with fondness and remembers it as the "blue waltz" owing to its long blue costumes, which were "something like a classical tutu."[100]

In the end, the musical's use of ballet was deemed to be somewhat contrived and along with the show's lengthy book helped doom Balanchine's attempt to reconstitute his company on the Broadway stage in the way Samuel Goldwyn had underwritten the American Ballet's Hollywood sojourn. One critic held that "even a patron of the art of the dance" could not enjoy prolonged dance elements when they were "jammed into the middle of a play" for "purely commercial reasons."[101] In contrast to the more organic way in which dance was woven into *Boys*, in *Great Lady* "the interspersing of ballet and musical numbers at times weakens the continuity of a tale which is good enough to carry on by itself."[102] The failure of *Great Lady* did not dampen Balanchine's wider Broadway success, and both *Boys* and *Angel* continued to run for many months after. And any disappointment over *Great Lady* was likely swept away when only a few days after its close Zorina finally acceded to Balanchine's entreaties to marry him. The couple was wed in an impromptu ceremony in Staten Island on Christmas Eve, arranged to avoid excessive publicity. As headlines and photos subsequently proclaimed, Balanchine had literally married the Angel, news made all the sweeter by the fact that Zorina had been widely rumored to be close to tying the knot with Hollywood royalty Douglas Fairbanks instead. The New Year would bring the newlyweds more opportunities to work together bringing ballet to American audiences in New York and beyond, while Kirstein and Ballet Caravan attempted the same.

CHAPTER 9 | 1937–1938 (II)

"WHATEVER THE BIRTH pangs of our Caravan's first season," Lincoln Kirstein wrote nonchalantly in *Thirty Years*, "a second season seemed justified," a laconic rationale for the continuation of the erstwhile summer adjunct of the American Ballet.[1] As noted previously, Ballet Caravan was a quickly assembled strategic response to challenges facing Balanchine and Kirstein's nascent enterprise in the summer of 1936. Similarly, when the Caravan reconvened in 1937 there was nothing casual about its agenda or mission, although the decision to reconvene the group was somewhat more deliberate. In fact, the organization's second year would see it move in an increasingly independent direction in both artistic and organizational terms following Balanchine and Kirstein's formal parting of the ways in mid-1937. Although the Caravan did not cut ties completely with the American Ballet or its school, the 1937 summer season and the months following saw the troupe and Kirstein mostly charting their own course, with the American Ballet allowed to slowly fade away before it would be officially dissolved in spring 1938. In fact, the decline of the American Ballet and the success of the Caravan—as well as Balanchine's increased involvement in Broadway and Hollywood—existed in an inverse proportional relationship: as the Caravan and Balanchine's popular career took off, the American Ballet slowly faded away.

The Caravan's increased success beginning in 1937 and continuing through 1938 can in retrospect be seen as a complete reboot of the performing arm of the ballet enterprise. Under Kirstein's leadership, the young dancers and choreographers of Ballet Caravan created a repertoire that offered audiences everything that the American Ballet had yet to deliver; in fact, it almost seemed to reverse engineer the missteps of the early years of the enterprise. Unlike the American Ballet's offerings, Ballet Caravan's new works focused increasingly on American topics and themes, were set to newly composed music by leading American musical talents, and were presented with fresh and inventive décor and costumes that neither overwhelmed the choreography nor alienated audiences. And unlike the American Ballet, the Caravan mostly performed outside of New York City, building its reputation more slowly in modest venues.

In contrast to Balanchine's commercially oriented endeavors around this same time, Kirstein's efforts to build the profile of the Caravan might seem like a move in a different direction. And indeed, Kirstein's curatorial hand aimed for a quite high level of artistic accomplishment. He recruited serious American composers and visual artists and employed his own scholarly research as the basis for many of the troupe's works. The Caravan would continue to be subsidized by the Kirstein family's personal wealth to a significant degree, and although it managed to achieve financial self-sufficiency, it was in essence a break even, or in today's parlance a nonprofit endeavor.

But Kirstein's ultimate goal for the Caravan was not entirely different from Balanchine's ventures in popular culture. In the end, Kirstein wanted the Caravan to have mass appeal and be commercially viable, and his ultimate goal was for it to displace the Ballet Russe companies as the leading dance company in the United States. In Kirstein's private and public writings he continually fumed over the success of these companies, and their ambitious presenter Sol Hurok, as well as the monopolistic hold on national theater circuits enjoyed by CBS and NBC (discussed later in the chapter). But far from disavowing such commercial opportunities, Kirstein sought ways to break into these circles by building up the Caravan's artistic profile one performance at a time and in some cases leveraging his father's corporate connections for assistance. In other words, Kirstein was by no means trying to disavow or work outside the corporate entertainment system in which Balanchine was increasingly ensconced. In fact, he was quite eager to break into this realm, viewing it as the most viable path toward sustaining a new American ballet troupe and building a broader national audience for the art form.

Although Kirstein's efforts to breach the entertainment monopolies were ultimately unsuccessful, the Caravan's ambitious schedule of touring accomplished on a shoestring budget what the more generously funded American Ballet had not been able to do in several years of efforts. Initially remaining relatively close to home, the troupe in the summer of 1937 retraced the steps of their debut season, touring New England along with presenting performances in New York State and the mid-Atlantic. Beginning in January 1938 they ventured even farther afield, making their way down the coast from Washington, DC, to Georgia and from there to Havana. In October 1938 they set out from Michigan to traverse the upper Midwest all the way to the West Coast, headed south from Seattle through Oregon and California and returned to New York via the Southwest and central Midwest in December. Along the way they would encounter audiences and critics of all sorts and make sometimes favorable and sometimes mixed impressions. In the end, the Caravan's year and half on the road from 1937 to 1938 was a high-water mark for the wider enterprise insofar as it had made good on its initial goals in the most direct way: offering ballet in an American idiom in virtually every corner of the country, and even a few places beyond.

Despite its broader ambitions, a modesty and do-it-yourself quality continued to shape the ethos and repertoire of the Caravan in its new season. The troupe "has no camels in spite of the implication of their name," as one reporter explained to potentially puzzled readers, noting that the company is designed with versatility in mind, equally prepared to perform in theaters or high school gyms.[2] Traveling by bus (and for parts of its journey in a special rail car), the group brought along "their own lighting equipment and stage effects in order to assure a complete theatrical performance."[3] Much like the Caravan's 1936 debut season, its second tour saw it intersecting with a variety of cultural spheres, from elite social circles to modern dance venues, a testament to the ingenuity of its manager Frances Hawkins, the ambition and connections of Kirstein, and the dancers' adaptability and versatility. The Caravan's July engagement at the Modern Theater in Manchester, Vermont, was announced amid society notices, their performances presented as a benefit for a local nursing association.[4] Later in the summer, its August performances in Bar Harbor, Maine, were timed to coincide with "the resort season rapidly approaching its peak," during which there was a special emphasis on "concerts and recitals as well as group performances from metropolitan areas."[5] Having been warmly received the previous year in Bennington, the Caravan also returned to the spiritual home of American modern dance, albeit in performances that were again explicitly billed as separate from the official offerings of the School of Dance. In January 1938 they would make their second appearance as part of the prestigious dance series of the YMHA in New York.

Early reports about the Caravan's next steps did not paint a portrait of stability or careful planning. It was initially reported that five new ballets

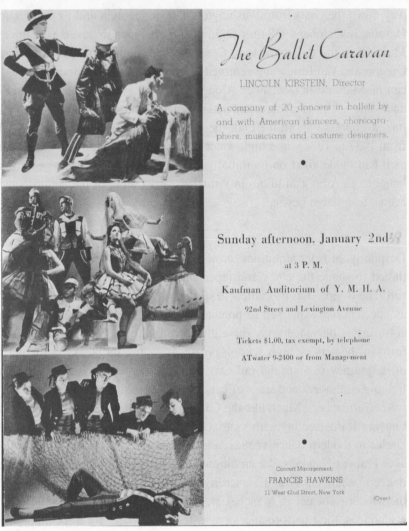

The Ballet Caravan

LINCOLN KIRSTEIN, Director

A company of 20 dancers in ballets by
and with American dancers, choreographers, musicians and costume designers.

•

Sunday afternoon, January 2nd

at 3 P. M.

Kaufman Auditorium of Y. M. H. A.

92nd Street and Lexington Avenue

Tickets $1.00, tax exempt, by telephone

ATwater 9-2400 or from Management

•

Concert Management:
FRANCES HAWKINS
11 West 42nd Street, New York

(Over)

FIGURE 9.1 Flier for 1938 performance by Ballet Caravan. Erick Hawkins Collection, Library of Congress.

would be part of the Caravan's summer season, two of which would ulti-mately not be produced: *Bombs in the Icebox* (with choreography by William Dollar and music by Elliott Carter) and *The Ballroom Guide* for whom no choreographer or composer was announced.[6] True to Kirstein's characteristic eagerness, both of these unrealized works were included in early publicity materials.[7] At the same time, the Caravan had not yet estab-lished a completely independent profile, with press accounts continuing to refer to the troupe as part of the Metropolitan Opera ballet or an "offshoot" of the American Ballet.[8] And despite Kirstein's distancing of himself from the wider enterprise, the Madison Avenue home of the School of American Ballet served as the Caravan's home office, which consisted of two rooms and an overstuffed closet, with the sounds of students thumping away at their exercises above providing a continuous soundtrack.[9]

For its new season of touring, the company retained three ballets from its existing repertoire, *Promenade*, *Encounter*, and *Harlequin for President*. If in the Caravan's first season Kirstein mostly replicated the Diaghilevian aesthetics of the American Ballet, for the new ballets added in 1937 the watch-cry seems to have been variety with a slightly more American bent. All three new ballets—*Folk Dance*, *Show Piece*, and *Yankee Clipper*—consisted of collections of short dances linked by a theme or narrative conceit, and the Caravan continued to showcase choreography by multiple choreographers drawn from the male ranks of the company. In *Blast at Ballet*, Kirstein maintained that these new ballets were meant to resonate with and "seem familiar" to their intended audiences and accordingly should contain "no Spanish, Russian or Italian manual pantomime or character-dancing."[10] While these three new ballets did move the Caravan's repertoire in a more American direction than its previous efforts, they were still quite heterogeneous in character, with some works in the Caravan's repertoire "less consciously national" than others.[11]

Despite what one might infer from its title, Douglas Coudy's *Folk Dance* was the least American in character of the new ballets. Set to music of French composer Emmanuel Chabrier, it drew on "national dances springing from a common Latin inheritance."[12] The work in fact explicitly celebrated the long-standing tradition of character dancing in ballet, especially Spanish dancing, and its intention was to "synthesize the gaiety, tragic style, and sense of fun" inherent in these dances.[13] The erudite description in a promotional brochure of the various dance forms incorporated into the ballet—including the Catalan *Sardana*, the Basque *Karrika Dantza*, and the Spanish *Asturiana*—suggests the guiding hand of Kirstein.[14] A Philadelphia critic noted that *Folk Dance* "gave evidence of much scholarly research," and that "it was a pleasure to see the more authentic note" in the ballet."[15] The least critically acclaimed of the new ballets, it remained in steady rotation on the Caravan's programs for around six months.

The ballet *Show Piece* by Erick Hawkins is regarded as the dancer's first official choreographic credit although, as noted earlier, the first season of the Caravan had already given him several opportunities to make dances on the company. While not a conclusive hit, *Show Piece* proved a reliable crowd pleaser and prompted thoughtful commentary from critics.

As implied by its title, the ballet was designed to "illustrate the virtuosity and style of its individual dancers."[16] It unfolded within a circus setting with "the numbers all designed to show the technical virtuosity of individual members of the company and the whole affording an eye-filling picture of youthful vivacity."[17] It was praised as an "interesting contribution of ballet form and in a way a departure,"[18] with its "circus ring" imaginatively configured with "a half dozen chromium chairs stretched with red."[19] "One after another," as one reviewer explained, "in groups, duos and solos, the dancers appeared to disport themselves in all manner of terpsichorean beauties, burlesque, grotesqueries or absurdities, to vivid music which constantly changed its tempo and its rhythm."[20] Music critic Irving Kolodin was quite taken by the work, noting its "fine gaiety and excellently sustained pace" and the fact that it avoided "taking recourse in the conventional repertory pieces of classic ballet."[21] Although the ballet had "only the continuity of the dancers' humorous efforts to excel each other" as a means of uniting its thirteen individual numbers, "on this slender base Erick Hawkins has built choreography of charming lightness and unremitting fantasy."[22] Elliott Carter praised the straightforward conceit of the ballet and its lack of "fuss and pretention."[23] The work made "no attempt to build up an elaborate atmosphere" and its choreography showed ingenuity and imagination while working within the classic vocabulary.[24]

For other observers, *Show Piece* had a somewhat incoherent profile despite achieving its stated goal. A review in *Dance Observer* offered qualified praise of the ballet as "adequately interesting" and that it "approached the vaudeville in quality."[25] According to another critic the ballet's problems lay in the score by Robert McBride, which was "broken up and jerky, albeit jazzily amusing in spots," and as a result, "the sophisticated style of choreography is disjointed . . . rather like a shattered mirror with a few of the bits still big enough to glitter brightly."[26] Carter similarly found "a certain formlessness and lack of emphasis in the music" which "somewhat clouded the brilliance of the dancing."[27] Nevertheless, among the standout moments it provided to its dancers were a "sparkling pizzicato" by the "piquant ballerina" Albia Kavan, a grand adagio by Marie-Jeanne and Fred Danieli with an "enchanting finish," and the "many striking combinations" in a solo by Lew Christensen.[28] But in the end, "*Show Piece* was more like a *play* piece," as one critic summed up, "since the mood often verged on clowning, with not enough pure dancing."[29] And while the "colorful costumes" by artist Keith Martin were supposedly inspired by real-life American garments, "it didn't work out quite that way, as the effect was (but pleasingly so) rather Mardi Gras."[30]

The standout addition to and critical darling of the Caravan's 1937 repertoire was Eugene Loring's *Yankee Clipper*, set to a score by Paul Bowles and with costumes by Charles Rain. Like *Folk Dance*, the ballet was something of a potpourri of styles, albeit with a stronger narrative structure than the other new works. "A young famer goes on a trip around the world," as one reviewer explained, "and in every port he receives a gift which is accompanied by a dance in the particular style of the country from which it comes," including Argentina, the South Pacific, Indonesia, and West Africa.[31]

The ballet was hailed as the highlight of their performance in Bennington, where before "an audience composed mainly of modern dance students, the Caravan commenced the evening with a ballet in pure classical style."[32] Loring was praised for dancing "with perfect control and remarkable humor," the costumes by Charles Rain were rated "outstanding," and the score by Paul Bowles merited "special comment for it fitted perfectly the main action and covered large imaginative stretches."[33] The performances by three male leads in the ballet were praised as "astonishing in their virility, yet coupled with a fluidity of motion generally associated with things feminine."[34] "There was nothing feminine, however, in the bullying of a new deck hand by sailors, in the Nantucket sailor interpretation and in the friendship dance between Eugene Loring, farm boy turned sailor, and Lew Christensen, ballet master and one of the organizers of the Caravan."[35] Others were more critical of the work, noting that it was hard to discern whether the ballet was meant to be satire. It was also found to be somewhat lacking in fidelity to original sources, with the West African dance called "very poor Harlem" and other episodes in the ballet lacking in taste and polish.[36] But the ballet was singled out for a special distinction from John Martin in an end-of-season overview, in which he declared Loring "the most promising new personality in the field" based on the strength of the piece.[37] Carter similarly hailed the ballet as the Caravan's "most deeply felt work," with its music and dance striking a satisfying balance between boldness and tenderness and in general evincing a "touching and evocative charm."[38]

During this initial summer tour, the Caravan made good on its goal of building its profile and gaining new fans for ballet in far-flung locales, as well as impressing more professional and discerning metropolitan audiences. A Syracuse critic praised the Caravan's program as having been "presented with a finished grace worthy of the best traditions of Europe."[39] At a performance at Clark University in Worcester, Massachusetts, "a sympathetic audience found much to enjoy in it and applauded generously the skillful dancing."[40] An engagement in Lowell proved the troupe "an expert ensemble, capturing the evident good will of an audience of 3,500, virtually a capacity house, and holding its interest until the final curtain."[41]

Several critics made note of the growth of the company since its previous season, and commended especially the "general good taste that pervades the entire enterprise" thanks to "Lincoln Kirstein's intelligent guiding hand."[42] "The girls of the company are lovely, the boys well-built," this same critic noted following their Philadelphia performances, "the choreography clever, the music good and the costumes artistic; but what predominates is the dance."[43] Equally effusive praise greeted performances at the Brooklyn Academy of Music, in which a "youthful spirit, an athletic charm and a sense of humor combined favorably with the lyric grace and technical aspect of the classic dance to make their work noteworthy."[44] And similar to the previous season, the Caravan was posited as a fresh and vital iteration of the American Ballet, having "picked up the threads" of their parent organization to create "something different and substantial."[45] Even the pages of *Dance Observer*, while offering lukewarm assessments of the troupe's performances, averred that given more time and opportunity to work together the company could eventually prove itself an "interesting and adventuresome troupe."[46]

Two special engagements in New York brought the Caravan's initial round of touring to an end and helped consolidate the group's growing stature. On December 12 they were the opening act for an evening of ballet as part of the "Dance International" festival, a sprawling event that showcased a range of dance styles from around the world, performing *Show Piece* as the opening work of an evening dedicated to ballet. In a different realm, a special exhibition of "Ballet Caravan Collaborators" organized by the Julien Levy Gallery showcased the four visual artists working for the troupe, including Paul Cadmus, whose provocative designs for *Filling Station* would see the stage in the New Year.[47] On the heels of these successes, Kirstein was confident enough to assert in a January article in *Dance Observer* that ballet in America was in quite good shape, and that the Caravan seemed to have what the public wanted. "Americans can dance well, are dancing better than they have before, will dance much better," and most important, "there is a great public awaiting their results eagerly."[48] Whether such a sentiment was only wishful thinking on Kirstein's part, the Caravan's even more ambitious calendar of touring in 1938 would show that the impresario was determined to make it a reality.

Having stayed close to home in December, the Caravan was back on the road in January 1938 and set to premiere an especially significant new work: *Filling Station*, with a score by Virgil Thomson, scenery and costumes by Paul Cadmus, and starring its choreographer Lew Christensen. *Filling Station* was the Caravan's first decisive hit, and along with Balanchine's well-received work on Broadway was arguably the best example of a vibrant and authentically American ballet to emerge from the first five years of Balanchine and Kirstein's enterprise. The ballet proved popular with both savvy insiders and ballet novices, and it remained a part of the Caravan's repertoire for the rest of the company's existence. Most important, it provided a template for the Caravan's even bigger premiere later in the year, *Billy the Kid*. Along with *Billy the Kid*, *Filling Station* would be one of only two ballets to outlive the company, revived by the San Francisco Ballet in 1951 (under the direction of Christensen) and most recently in 2008 as part of the company's Seventy-fifth Anniversary festivities.

The place and context in which *Filling Station* premiered was the "Friends and Enemies of Modern Music" series organized by Chick Austin at the Wadsworth Atheneum in Hartford. The Hartford premiere was significant for both Thomson, whose opera *Four Saints in Three Acts* was premiered there four years earlier, and of course equally so for the wider enterprise, since Hartford had been the first brief port of call for the American Ballet in the fall of 1933. Like the American Ballet's 1934 appearances in Hartford, this appearance by Ballet Caravan was an event that drew many notable attendees from New York, including an entourage headed by Whitney Museum director Juliana Force.[49] "At the close of *Filling Station*, riotous applause, cries of bravo and prolonged clapping brought the dancers and the composer back again and again," a Hartford reporter recounted, and the ballet may "well become as popular as the Stein opera."[50]

In publicity materials prepared for the 1938 tour of the Caravan, *Filling Station* is termed a "Ballet-Document in One Act"; these materials state the premise and rationale of the work as portraying the everyday experience at a real-life gas station through the idiom of ballet. By interpreting a modern and mundane scene through classical dance, the work achieved a "heightening [awareness] of our immediate lives around us," rather than merely offering "a continual revival of past epochs or styles."[51] The ballet purported to find drama in an unexceptional setting, "in the routine of a mechanic's life, a violent and exciting day, but no more unreal than those experienced by millions of other motorists or mechanics."[52] Mac the station attendant was the protagonist of the action, and in the course of the ballet he interacts with a family of

FIGURE 9.2 Ballet Caravan Brochure. Erick Hawkins Collection, Library of Congress.

motorists, a pair of spoiled rich children, and also a gangster and state trooper.

The question of its political efficacy aside, the clarity and relevance of *Filling Station* was singled out for praise by many critics, and Virgil Thomson's previous premiere in Hartford served as an explicit point of comparison. As a *Newsweek* article explained, the new work was "intelligible to anyone who has traveled in an automobile" and "enacted the commonplace incidents" of the road.[53] If this legibility disappointed those who had come to Hartford expecting a reprise of Thomson's *Four Saints in Three Acts*, "simpler folks thought it more fun to know what the show was all about."[54] Elliott Carter identified a cinematic quality in the ballet's setting and musical accompaniment. "As if in a movie the characters are all brought together at a gas station," he noted, likening Thomson's score to "old-time, pre-sound, film piano-playing" which rather than closely imitating the action on stage, instead created "a running background that catches the simplicity of character and situation amusingly."[55] In a *Musical America* review of the premiere, critic T. H. Parker lauded the aesthetic synthesis achieved by this "fable in chromium and scarlet neon" and its episodes of "banditry and knights-errant of the State Police" and "co-ed princes and princesses," starring Mac the station attendant as a "new style Prince Charming."[56] Parker likened the aesthetic of the ballet to another American medium, the comic strip, noting how "the same buffoonery alternated with the same high seriousness."

Its new ballet deemed a success, the Caravan moved on from Hartford to make stops elsewhere in New England and the New York City region. During January performances in Boston, Kirstein delivered a lecture-demonstration on ballet that was ranked as a premiere social engagement, attended by a large number of local luminaries, many of whom were observed "standing on their chairs rather than miss any of the fascinating examples" in his discussion.[57] Following the Boston engagement were stops at Vassar College, Newark's YMHA, and the Women's Club of Orange, New Jersey, before the troupe returned to New York to take part in a special series of performances at the Federal Music Theater commemorating Washington's Day. Although the show was not the company's first appearance before New York audiences, it did represent an official Broadway debut for the dancers and was rated "a distinctly agreeable evening" by John Martin, who wrote that the performance "revealed a first-rate little ballet company in the making."[58]

But for many it was still unclear just what the Caravan amounted to. For some observers, the troupe still had much room to grow, and one of its best assets, its youthful charm, was also rated a weakness. "As charming as naïvete can be, it can also lapse into childishness," as Margaret Lloyd observed of the Caravan's Boston performances, saying that the company offered "more cake than raisins."[59] The company's reinvention of ballet felt forced at times and "comes to light as a process of grafting new material on old technique rather than a natural growth and merging of material."[60] She nevertheless praised the high production values of the Caravan's sets and costumes, arguing that they often outshone the choreography in quality, and she also suggested that a small orchestra instead of piano accompaniment "would further enhance the manifold pleasures the company has now, and potentially in greater measure, to give."[61] Despite his enthusiasm, Martin noted that the Caravan "has both the faults and the compensatory virtues of youthfulness," but he added that "its approach is fresh and unpretentious and it possesses several distinctly talented young artists."[62]

The next ballet added to the Caravan's repertoire, William Dollar's *Air and Variations* (set to selections from J. S. Bach's *Goldberg Variations*) represented something of a retreat from the vernacular character of *Filling Station*. Dollar was coached through the ballet not by Kirstein but rather the Caravan's talented émigré accompanist, Trude Rittman, who evidently vetoed choreographic choices when she deemed them not in keeping with the music.[63] Dollar used different combinations of dancers for each variation, "sometimes permitting a single male or female figure to convey his intentions, at others combining dancers of both sexes, or using combinations of female dancers exclusively."[64] As playing time for the full set of variations is over an hour in length, the piece was cut to around fifteen variations to fit in the Caravan's mixed bill programming, and these were subsequently orchestrated by Nicholas Nabokov.[65] In language that recalls the rhetoric of symphonic ballet, one critic said that Dollar had "managed to effect upon the stage the same thing that goes on in the musicians' pit" and "created an orchestration among the dancers which matches the fluid quality of the Bach variations."[66] Pitts Sanborn was struck by not only the performance of the "well drilled ensemble" but also the "excellence of the color scheme, the terra cotta or gray of the costumes against a black background."[67] A Norfolk, Virginia, critic declared the ballet "a thoroughly delightful bit of imaginative grace," and that dancers Gisella Caccialanza and Lew Christensen "led an ensemble of beautiful women and well-knit men through ingenious patterns with consummate skill."[68]

Air and Variations was premiered during the Caravan's second round of touring in 1937, a southern leg that took them down the eastern seaboard with a final stop in Havana. In Charleston their performance at the Dock Street Theater "pleased a large audience" and "established the American group's significance and entertainment value."[69] The "richly contrasting series of dances" by the Caravan "presented a vital picture of the dance . . . freed of any hampering tradition or convention, woven against the sturdy and telling background of the American theme in scene and in music."[70] Exemplifying this was the troupe's performance of *Filling Station*, "in which all of the dancers are immediately recognizable American types; in which the costumes are beautifully drawn caricatures, colorful and attractive."[71] Lew Christensen's performance was "marked by effortlessness, form, and beauty, and achieved for him the difficult task of creating the personality and character of the usual, upright young station attendants" and the "striking brunette appearance and fine dancing" of Marie-Jeanne as the Rich Girl "asserted itself whenever she appeared."[72] Kirstein's own impressions of Charleston, and the South in general, were less enthusiastic. He felt a "general apathy as if the whole south were a convalescent ward," and "the magnificence of Charleston houses and gardens" only made the rest of the environs seem more depressing.[73] "Not only has time stood still here, it's moved backwards," and although he couldn't speak to all of the South, he said that "the Carolinas and Georgia aren't even ripe for the Declaration of Independence."[74]

The Caravan was just as positively received in the Cuban capital, where they were the season-ending engagement of the Sociedad Pro-Arte Musical.[75] In the audience was sixteen-year-old Alicia Alonso, whose mother-in-law was president of the distinguished performance series.[76] Over two evenings the dancers presented six of their works, through which Kirstein and his troupe offered "a choreographic spectacle of exceeding novelty" that "had managed to clearly demonstrate that ballet has no boundaries."[77] "Modern and humorous ballet is Ballet Caravan's strength," noted another review, and for this reason while *Air and Variations* represented a "good effort" on the group's part it produced the weakest effect. *Yankee Clipper* was rated the standout work; its score was praised as "more suggestive than descriptive, and animated with decisive rhythm."[78] The ballet as a whole "glides along happily and easily"—"se desliza alegre y fácil"—and Loring distinguished himself as a "dancer of the first order."[79] *Estación de Servicio*, as *Filling Station* was translated, was rated "humorous but less aesthetically distinguished" and the score by Virgil Thomson "was of no importance at all." The critic did single out the "notable efforts" of Lew Christensen in the work, as well as the "clownish" charm of the other dancers.

In 1938 the Caravan was not on the road during the summer months for the first time in two years, taking a break from performance to prepare for their first transcontinental tour. This journey would kick off in Detroit in early October, followed by performances in Chicago, Fort Wayne, and

Milwaukee and Ripon, Wisconsin, before the group set off for the West Coast.[80] For this stretch of their tour the Caravan premiered a work that would have the longest staying power of any of the company's projects, Eugene Loring's *Billy the Kid*, to a new score commissioned from Aaron Copland and with costumes by Jared French. The ballet was the product of a long gestation period and collaborative process between Loring and Copland, facilitated by Kirstein's helpful coaching along the way, and the result was a work that offers a complex and somewhat contradictory representation of the legendary outlaw. The ballet was an important milestone in the creative careers of both Loring and Copland, and the substance of the ballet and its score have been discussed extensively by scholars including Howard Pollack, Lynn Garafola, Elizabeth Bergman, Beth Levy, and Andrea Harris.

Regarding the life of Ballet Caravan, *Billy* was significant as their most successful effort yet to tell an American story through ballet, even more so than *Filling Station*. Kirstein held up *Billy* as an exemplar of the Caravan's aesthetic innovation, which avoided turning the story into a "picturesque cowboy legend" or "the tragedy of an individualistic, romantic desperado"—as he alleges the Russian ballet companies would have been tempted to do—and instead explores the outlaw's life "as only a fragmentary, if symbolic incident in the expansion of our vast frontier."[81] Billy was a representation of "the basic anarchy inherent in individualism in its most rampant form," as Kirstein elaborated in an article for *Dance Observer*.[82] Instead of serving as a "pastiche of the Wild West," the ballet is as "bare and as haunting" as the ballads quoted by Copland's score.[83] The *New Republic* declared it "the most native and wonderful story ever danced," praising the "sweep and motion by which it is realized on the stage."[84] The orchestral suite that Copland subsequently adapted from the ballet's score in 1939 has given the work an even larger reach.

Aside from published reviews and other accounts of the Caravan's touring, Kirstein's private musings offer rich perspectives on this time in the company's life, in particular a series of lengthy letters written to his friend and confidant Muriel Draper. These confessional writings offer insights into how audiences received the Caravan, the difficulties the troupe encountered in the course of their touring, and the variety of places in which Kirstein and the dancers found themselves. Among the most vivid are a series of observations captured as the company was "passing at a snail's pace through the Dakota Badlands" en route to the Pacific Northwest from Wisconsin.[85]

To pass the time the "less serious" among the group played bridge and slept in "cramped abandon," while the "more serious members" were "practicing entrechat six on the berth heads" even as the porters were trying to make up their beds for the night. He reports that Marie-Jeanne was reading the novel *Trilby* in French, while Erick Hawkins busied himself with Freud, "penciling it heavily." Adding to the atmosphere, at one point he recalled how "a nun and what I take to be her captive or hypnotee, a blank young girl with glasses, keeps passing back and forth through our car," and guessed that "they are fascinated by our profligate physicality." At one point Eugene Loring put on one of the girl's hats and did his "famous imitation of a half-man, half-woman being both swish and butch, hip and bicep, hip and bicep" while Harold Christensen more chastely observed that the group would "soon be in the land of delicious, baked, crispy, giant Idaho potatoes."

Kirstein describes dozens of other anecdotal encounters with Americans of various backgrounds, enough to fill a whole chapter in and of themselves. The company's travels in the desert Southwest and Midwest provided some of the most vivid incidents. "The culture out here is very strong like onions on a chickiburger sandwich," he wrote from Kansas City, adding that "chicken fried steak is good and so is grapefruit, date, American cheese, and olive salad with old mayonnaise," a sarcastic observation made clear by his subsequent statement that "all I want is the Ritz Bar *forever*."[86] He found Austin a "creepy crawly place full of longhorn legislators" and noted that the "cattle ranchers sure doan [*sic*] like Roosevelt. Or niggers. Or I regret to say Jews."[87] Noting wryly that America "sure does ripen a lot of fine young fellows," he recalled his encounter with a friendly fraternity brother majoring in "culture," and who was reading one of Kirstein's books as an elective assignment.[88]

In San Angelo, Texas, the company was entertained at the home of a rancher and amateur taxidermist who had "2 horned stuffed Jack Rabbits" which caused a "great sensation," and prompted their host to tell Kirstein that "hell, boy, if you stay in this hyah countreh [sic] you'll sprout horns too."[89] He described Kansas City as full of "street walkers, Turkish baths with lady wrestlers in attendance who will relieve a gland for 50 cents extra my taxi driver told us fellows, gambling joints of transparent dishonesty, a big tomb of an art museum with some nice things." In Texas, Eugene Loring was introduced to a man described as "an insane ancient full of whiskey, old age and disease" who had known Billy the Kid personally.[90]

Colorful encounters aside, the company's touring schedule was quite brutal and took a toll on everyone, Kirstein included. In his account of this time period in *Thirty Years*, Kirstein focuses mostly on the thoughtful intellectual and artistic journeys that led to the creation of such works as *Filling Station* and *Billy the Kid*. But such stimulation was the exception rather than the rule, and the bulk of Kirstein's duties were quite mundane. An Associated Press feature characterized Kirstein as "director, owner, manager, stagehand, and stooge" of the troupe, which was run "on what a commercial manager would consider a shoestring."[91] "The trip is instructive but not a lot of fun," he wrote to Muriel Draper from South Carolina, adding that it's all "grim, hard work, lots of driving, incalculable mechanical difficulties with shiftless stage hands, managers, ticket people."[92] From Los Angeles he wrote that 90 percent of his job was concerned with "managerial quarrels" while only one-tenth focused on dancing per se, an observation included in letter dated "Wednesday night, too fucking late."[93] The economics of the Caravan left the troupe in a continual bind, since if they reduced their schedule they lacked enough money to break even, and squeezing in additional performances sometimes meant punishing turn-around times. To cite one example, en route to the West Coast the company made a stop to perform in the town of Cheney, Washington, near the Idaho border. Having traveled by train for forty-eight hours, they arrived at 6:10, danced at 7:30, and by 10:00 PM were back on an overnight train bound for Seattle, where they would perform the following evening.[94] "We have travelled too much to be hapo," he confided in Draper on another occasion, his jovial slang masking or reinforcing their real fatigue, "and instead are nervo and misero."[95]

For all these efforts and hardships, the Caravan was often met with mixed reviews, or at least some of its audiences were left lukewarm at best and bewildered at worst. Of their performances in Ripon, Wisconsin (80 miles south of Green Bay), Kirstein overheard "a fellow ask a fellow if he had liked the ballet," with the answer that "it was nice but rather artistic."[96] "I didn't care for Emporia, Kansas much," he admitted later, hastening to add "and if the truth were known Emporia didn't much like us."[97] Indeed, Kirstein's private observations differ markedly from the glowing praise heaped on the troupe in published reviews and echo the mixed reception that greeted Balanchine's ballets for *The Goldwyn Follies*. At the very least, they show how creating mass appeal for serious American ballet was as difficult for Kirstein as it had been for Samuel Goldwyn, with audiences similarly confused about whether they considered serious ballet to be truly enjoyable. "The audiences are a little more than apathetic," he wrote to Draper from Los Angeles, lamenting that the "middle class people whom we sell our middle-class entertainment to" are "lazy," while the "educated" people were "naturally the worst."[98] Notably, he observes elsewhere that the Caravan was usually better received when sponsored by a college or club, and less so when offered as an "attraction" like the movies, again offering evidence of why the opera and ballet of *The Goldwyn Follies* had been an uneasy fit.[99] "Everybody likes us OK," he wrote of the response from southern audiences, for whom their work seemed unfamiliar and new, and many viewers were "not sure it's 'entertainment.'"[100]

In the midst of Ballet Caravan's 1938 touring, Lincoln Kirstein released his self-published *Blast at Ballet*, a "corrective for the American audience" and a bold attempt to diagnose and propose remedies for the ills affecting ballet in America. With this publication Kirstein hoped to solidify his position as what we might today call a thought leader regarding dance in America, and it served as a compendium for ideas that he had articulated over many years in lectures and publications. *Blast* stands as an important document in the history of Kirstein and Balanchine's enterprise, and it has frequently been cited (including in these pages) as a significant contemporary account of its early history. Less attention has been paid to its discussions of the economics and institutional structures that determined how and when dance performance circulated in the United States in the 1930s. Today these parts of *Blast* seem far removed from our present-day experience of dance or perhaps irrelevant in light of Balanchine and Kirstein's ultimate success in founding the New York City Ballet. But Kirstein's criticisms of the American entertainment industry and the way it shaped the character of ballet in America are in fact essential to understanding the underlying goals, ambitions, and indeed the very name and identity of Ballet Caravan. Most crucially, they help explain why it was so important that the company remained above all a touring ensemble, and why Kirstein was so determined that it reach audiences from coast to coast. If the Caravan began its existence as a somewhat hastily assembled experiment, by 1938 it had evolved into something much more consequential, no less than a vehicle by which Kirstein hoped to reshape the landscape of American ballet.

In *Blast* Kirstein lays out the contours of what he calls the "Great Conspiracy," the monopolistic control of theatrical venues throughout the United States exerted by the two major broadcasting conglomerates, CBS and NBC. These corporate interests, Kirstein contends, were responsible for stunting the growth of the arts in America by not allowing local arts leaders choice regarding the attractions that they presented, whether dance, classical music, or theater. The way this worked in practice was quite simple. A local Women's Club, for instance, undertakes to present a season of attractions in their hometown and contacts the corporate managers about what is available. The managers accordingly offer them, as Kirstein put it, "a soprano, a lecturer on world affairs, a symphony orchestra, a virtuoso instrumentalist, a travel lecture, and a single dance attraction," all of which happen to be scheduled for national tours arranged by the home office.[101]

Although Kirstein acknowledges that this system makes it possible for audiences in far-flung locations to secure appearances by prestigious foreign talent that they might not otherwise have access to, it also exacts a heavy price as far as autonomy is concerned, with local presenters "hardly ever permitted to choose what they prefer to hear or see from their own native attractions."[102] In other words, programs were typically offered as an all-or-nothing package deal and left little room for customization in accordance with local taste or interest. The negative influence of these practices on dance was more specific, insofar as dance was often equated with ballet, and ballet was understood to be Russian ballet. As Kirstein explained, "In order to sell the Russian ballet, it has been ordained that all ballet on this continent should be Russian, or else it isn't really ballet at all."[103] Combined with the inflexible programming model imposed on local presenters by the monopolies, this narrow definition of ballet made it extremely difficult for American artists, such as Ballet Caravan, to get a break.

Kirstein and the Caravan were not entirely without recourse in the face of these monopolistic forces. In an effort to gain entrée into this system, Kirstein secured meetings with several executives and managers at NBC, hoping that once the problems were explained they would help take action on behalf of American artists such as his choreographers and dancers. In *Blast* he writes of one such meeting with "the general director of the greatest of these monopolies," characterized as a casual encounter made possible "because he happened to be a close friend of a friend of mine."[104] In the course of their conversation, Kirstein forcefully outlined the problems with the booking system but was met with indifference on the part of his interlocutor. The executive explained politely that the dance and music division brought in a negligible amount of money and was kept going mostly to enhance the company's civic profile.[105] Kirstein writes that he left the meeting "frightened and vengeful" and appalled by the "grotes-query of the situation."[106]

Kirstein's inability to effect change in this system was perhaps all the more galling to him given the circumstances by which this meeting came to pass and the identity of the two unnamed people referenced in *Blast*. Surviving correspondence makes it clear that the "close friend" was no less than NBC senior executive David Sarnoff, and the second "friend" (who facilitated the meeting) was Kirstein's own father Louis. Sarnoff is mentioned in their correspondence beginning late December 1937, when Louis suggested his son seek a meeting with him, to which Lincoln was receptive but skeptical as to the results.[107] "David, of course, could do a great deal," Lincoln wrote, "but I don't see why he should," since the Caravan would not provide any "quick returns."[108] Louis counseled him against going into the meeting with preconceived notions, writing that Sarnoff "certainly does not lack imagination" and Lincoln "should make every effort to convince him" that an investment in the Caravan would be wise.[109] Several days later Lincoln reported back to his father about the meeting, noting that while Sarnoff treated him very nicely, he showed "absolutely no interest either in his musical or in his dance attractions," since they brought in only eight to ten million dollars a year and were mostly a break-even proposition.[110] Contrary to his version of events in *Blast*, Kirstein was evidently not so exasperated by his meeting as to write off Sarnoff completely as an ally. One month later Kirstein asked his father to intervene personally with Sarnoff, hoping that a word from him could help the Caravan secure dates at NBC venues.[111]

As the Caravan continued to tour, Kirstein redoubled his attempts to make inroads into CBS and NBC, although his interactions would prove frustrating and produce few concrete results. In January 1938 he met with a manager at CBS, who expressed interest in the Caravan and even offered them the possibility of performing with an orchestra, with the stipulation that Paul Haakon, a star with more name recognition, be added to head-line the troupe.[112] Although Kirstein was amenable to such a plan, and the manager was evidently enthusiastic, the opportunity did not ultimately materialize. Having already made a run at Sarnoff at NBC, over lunch in July Kirstein probed his friend Nelson Rockefeller about connections to CBS chief William Paley.[113] On the road in California later in the year, he confided in Draper of "feeling horrid" following "a week of bickering and vicious bastardy with these fucking managers," and lamented that he "was not *rich* enough that's all."[114] That someone with Kirstein's stature and access was so stymied by these systems suggests that his seemingly hyperbolic portrait in *Blast* was not quite as overblown as it might appear.

Such interactions reveal the lengths to which Kirstein was willing and able to go on behalf of his ballet enterprise, not to mention the continued role that Louis Kirstein played in guiding his son's efforts.[115] Interestingly, they show the multiple sides of Lincoln: on the one hand, a committed leftist with sympathies to Popular Front politics—as was increasingly manifest in the Caravan's repertoire; but on the other hand, equally at ease working personal connections with corporate titans such as Sarnoff, Paley, Rockefeller, and of course his own father. If Kirstein saw no contradiction in these parallel lives, his father at least called him out when he seemed to move too far in one direction, or, put another way, when the political leftist seemed to bite the corporate hand that was feeding him. After the publication of *Blast* Louis specifically called out his son regarding a vivid metaphor included in the "Great Conspiracy" section, in which he claimed that the competition between the CBS and NBC monopolies was "on the same pattern as the Standard Oil Company of New Jersey's earnest competition with its arch-enemy the Standard Oil Company of New York."[116] Louis asked "what possible good could be had" out of putting such a turn of phrase in print, reminding him that "you are looking for the right kind of friends as well as the right kind of enemies."[117] Louis subsequently reported back to his son on a follow-up conversation Louis had had with Sarnoff, to whom Lincoln had evidently sent a copy of *Blast*. According to Louis, Sarnoff was "a thoroughly good sport" about the criticisms leveled at him in the book and presumably also his anonymous cameo as the indifferent executive.[118]

In the face of such conflicts and lack of interest from the corporate powers that be, Kirstein and the Caravan carried on, hoping they could slowly build up enough of a reputation to earn a place in the fraught system. Writing to his parents, Kirstein doubled down that he "had no doubt of the excellence of my attraction on an artistic level," and now that more audiences had seen them, NBC and CBS could no longer convince locals that the Caravan wasn't worth their time and money.[119] But he also admitted that his efforts would be slow in producing results. "In spite of all our marvelous reviews and swell reception," he wrote in another lengthy letter, "next year's fight for bookings will only be a little easier," even though "a lot of people at least have seen us and do want us back."[120] It remained to be seen whether such fans enjoyed the Caravan enough "to risk incurring the wrath of the monopolies."[121] "This is the most beastly cut throat business you can imagine," he confided to Muriel Draper, and "the monopoly is not imaginary but real."[122] Even in the face of these setbacks, the Caravan continued to win more friends than enemies and was in a strong enough position to reconvene for a third and final round of touring in the coming year.

CHAPTER 10 | 1939–1940

IN 1939, BALANCHINE'S and Kirstein's projects continued to push forward confidently if independently, while 1940 saw them moving in directions that represented a radical reconfiguration if not a complete abandonment of their earlier goals and priorities. The confusing trajectories of the two men's activities over these two years did not result entirely from their own actions and decisions and should be understood in part as responses to an increasingly daunting set of institutional and even geopolitical challenges. The 1939 invasion of Poland by Germany brought the reality of war to Western Europe, sending many new émigré artists west across the Atlantic for refuge and also fueling internal political debates about the role the United States should play in the growing conflict. In this unlikely moment, Balanchine and Kirstein's ballet enterprise suddenly found their efforts eclipsed by the successful launch of Ballet Theatre, a new American company that billed itself as a response to the dominance of Russian ballet troupes.

On the one hand, Balanchine's and Kirstein's professional projects represented a continuation of the creative careers they had carved out for themselves a year and a half earlier after the collapse of the American Ballet. But on the other hand, they would soon find themselves back where they had started in New York, working in at once familiar and unexpected institutional conditions in order to continue their creative work. Traveling between the coasts in 1939 and early 1940, Balanchine and Zorina completed two additional Hollywood projects—*On Your Toes* and *I Was an Adventuress*—and further established themselves as a formidable creative team. Meanwhile, Kirstein and the newly renamed "American Ballet Caravan" continued their efforts to breach the entertainment monopolies, making a well-received Broadway debut in New York as well as undertaking a second transcontinental tour with two new ballets, *City Portrait* and *Charade*.

By the end of 1940, Balanchine and Kirstein found themselves engaged in projects that seemed to augur the end of the performing arm of their enterprise, with the American Ballet Caravan having run its course and with Balanchine set up for a career grounded primarily in the entertainment industry. Recently naturalized as an American citizen, in May 1940 Balanchine premiered dances for two new Broadway projects, *Louisiana Purchase* (starring Zorina) and *Keep Off the Grass*, and several months later he would make his debut as a Broadway director and producer, collaborating with Vernon Duke and Katherine Dunham on *Cabin in the Sky*. Concurrent with these projects, Kirstein arranged an unlikely final gig for the American Ballet Caravan as part of a revue at the World's Fair Pavilion of the Ford Motor Company, in the midst of which he also assumed a new leadership role at the School of American Ballet. And while Kirstein and others worked up possible schemes by which the American Ballet/Ballet Caravan might be reorganized or even aligned with the newly launched Ballet Theatre, Balanchine was instead recruited to join the Ballet Russe de Monte Carlo. For the erstwhile rival of their enterprise, Balanchine mounted two of the three ballets that were danced for the 1937 Stravinsky Festival—*Le Baiser de la Fée* and *The Poker Game* (the new title of *The Card Party*)—as well as his "first ballet in America," *Serenade*. Thus by the end of 1940, the ballet enterprise of Balanchine and Kirstein had by no means reached an end—most notably through the continued existence of its school—but the organization and its principals had evolved and changed in ways that neither could have envisioned seven years earlier.

———————

Ballet Caravan had concluded its first transcontinental journey across the country with performances in December 1938 at the Eastman Theatre in Rochester, the Kirstein family's home prior to their relocation to Boston.[1] The family's connection to the city did not evidently help sell tickets, and the troupe attracted a "cordial" if "not large" audience that was nevertheless unafraid to "single out for applause technical achievements of various performers."[2] Although the company had already logged thousands of miles on the road, they were not entirely finished with their travels. After a three-week holiday break they reconvened in January for a brief series of performances in the Southeast and New York City. These engagements included the revival of *Pocahontas*, not performed by the company since their first summer of touring in 1936 and programmed in part to provide a featured role for a new member of the troupe, Leda Anchutina.[3] Anchutina had opted to remain with the American Ballet for the duration of its existence (including work on *The Goldwyn Follies*) but found herself looking for new opportunities following the abrupt close of *Great Lady*, in which she had been cast as a lead dancer.

This brief junket took the troupe to Virginia, Georgia, and Florida, concluding with a homecoming performance in New York, and its itinerary replicated the company's previous appearances in heterogeneous cultural spheres. In the Norfolk, Virginia, area they offered two performances on succeeding evenings, perhaps in an effort to reach diverse audiences in the segregated south. They first appeared at the Hampton Institute (known today as Hampton University), a significant institution in the history of African American concert dance and home of the Hampton Creative Dance Group led by choreographer Charles Williams.[4] At the Institute's Ogden Hall they gave a brief matinee show as well as a more substantial performance in the evening, of which many attendees saw only the final numbers owing to a meeting of the "Interracial Council" that overlapped with the performance.[5] The following evening they appeared at Norfolk's Blair Junior High School, where *Pocahontas*, despite being performed close to the locale in which it takes place, was met with "extreme disappointment" owing to the "symphony of discord" created by its costumes and an overall lack of entertainment value.[6] *Air and Variations* was rated a "thoroughly delightful bit of imaginative grace," in which Lew Christensen "led an ensemble of beautiful women and well-knit men through ingenious patterns with consummate skill" while *Billy the Kid* offered "harmonious and ingenious dance forms" and a "more successful approach to a native pantomime" than *Pocahontas*.[7] In Atlanta they were received warmly at the Erlanger Theater, in particular for *Billy*, which "revealed more clearly the style and technique" of the Caravan's contemporary take on ballet.[8] The company's next two stops, in Palm Beach and Augusta, were evidently planned to coincide with the influx of winter vacationers to the region, announced in society column comings-and-goings and in one case preceded by a festive dinner gathering.[9] Upon their return to New York the Caravan offered a final performance at Washington Irving High School.[10] Their program of *Promenade, Air and Variations*, and *Filling Station* (the latter two presented for the first time in New York) received a positive review in *Dance Observer*, which noted that the company "showed much greater technical proficiency and precision" than previously and rated Lew Christensen and Marjorie Moore as standout performers.[11]

The Caravan did not take the stage again until their May appearances as part of a larger project produced under the auspices of the League of Composers, the short-lived "American Lyric Theater." Created in early 1939, in part with support from the WPA's Federal Theater Project, the project's mission was to present new works of musical theater, broadly construed as "operas, operettas, musical plays and other forms of lyric drama."[12] Contemporary American composers would be given a special emphasis, and two new works were planned for its inaugural season: *The Devil and Daniel Webster*, adapted from a short story by Stephen Vincent Benet, and *Susanna*, a "musical romance" inspired by Stephen Foster songs.[13] The organization's mission was aligned with the Caravan's mission in obvious ways, especially given the roster of young composers affiliated with the troupe, and illustrations of costume designs for the Caravan's ballets were subsequently published in *Modern Music*, the League's official publication.[14] Initially scheduled for two weeks of performances, the season closed early after only nine days.[15] But the venture gave the Caravan multiple opportunities to showcase their work and to perform with the benefit of orchestral accompaniment. For performances of *The Devil and Daniel Webster* they presented *Filling Station* as a curtain raiser, in addition to offering a separate all-ballet program of *Pocahontas, Air and Variations* (orchestrated for the occasion by Nicholas Nabokov), and *Billy the Kid* in its New York premiere.[16] Dollar's choreography in *Air and Variations* was praised for its unique combinations, while Nabokov was commended for having had the "good taste to employ instrumentation which is stylistically veracious."[17] John Martin rated both *Air and Variations* and *Pocahontas* as "fair to middling at best" while heaping honors upon *Billy*, which he found not just "perfectly delightful" but a work that "must be called significant."[18] Eugene Loring had proved himself "a young creative talent of genuine importance" having choreographed a ballet "with blood in its veins, a keen imagination, and a fine sense of the theatre."

The company again took the summer off before regrouping in the fall for a second transcontinental tour, for which it was rebranded as the "American Ballet Caravan," the name under which it would operate in its final year. While the motivations for this change are not certain, the new name reflected both past and present realities of the performing arm of Balanchine and Kirstein's endeavors. The Caravan had been closely affiliated with the American Ballet from its inception in 1936, and in late 1939 it stood as the only remaining performing unit of the wider enterprise, a reality that had already been noted by outside observers before the troupe was officially renamed. A review of their May performances in New York characterized the company as "an outgrowth of the now defunct American Ballet."[19] An even earlier report from February 1939 explained that in the wake of the American Ballet's collapse "small remnants of the gallant band which started out so bravely to blaze new trails still dance as the Ballet Caravan."[20]

The second tour featured fewer dates but just as many miles of travel as their previous journey. From their first stop in Lancaster, Pennsylvania, on October 17 they went south via Charlotte as far as Mobile, Alabama.[21] From there they returned north for performances in Chicago and several cities in Wisconsin before crossing into Canada for engagements in Edmonton and Calgary.[22] A journey down the West Coast followed during November, with performances in Vancouver and Portland followed by appearances at major venues in San Francisco, Los Angeles, and San Diego interspersed with more modest engagements in Carmel and Stockton.[23] The company returned home via the Midwest in mid-December, including stops in Topeka and Kansas City before arriving in New York just before the Christmas holiday.[24]

The Caravan's second tour offered a more focused repertoire than any of its previous seasons, retaining only *Air and Variations*, *Filling Station*, and *Billy the Kid* from their existing works and premiering two sharply contrasting new ballets, *City Portrait* and *Charade, or The Debutante*. Eugene Loring's *City Portrait*, with music by Henry Brant and costumes by Forrest Thayr Jr. (termed a "ballet-document" like *Filling Station*) offered a critical take on urban life among workers and tenement dwellers and represented the Caravan's most explicit contribution to left-wing political art of the era. Its characters included bums and drunks and a "Tough Girl" and a "Nice Girl," all of whom dance their way through various city locales to a score that recreated the sounds of the streets, "with incidental parodies and plagiarisms of a dozen different things, from Beethoven . . . to 'La Paloma.' "[25] In a sharply contrasting idiom, Lew Christensen's "ballet romance" *Charade* was an exercise in whimsy and nostalgia, set around the turn of the twentieth century and telling the story of a debutante who is upstaged by the antics of her younger sister. Alvin Colt designed its colorful costumes, and Trude Rittman arranged the score, an assemblage of popular music by Stephen Foster, Louis Moreau Gottschalk, and tunes such as "Good Night, Ladies."[26] The Caravan offered three ballets on any given program, with *Air and Variations* used almost exclusively as an opener and *Charade* most often programmed as a finale.

FIGURE 10.1 Cover of promotional brochure for 1939–40 tour of American Ballet Caravan. Erick Hawkins Collection, Library of Congress.

Reviews of these two new works were mixed, with *Charade* rated a well-executed if inconsequential crowd pleaser and *City Portrait* deemed an uneven essay in political commentary. Loring's choreography "sought to depict barren and hysterical life in the city," oscillating between "stylized symbolic movement" and more "naturalistic, pantomimic" dance.[27] Most critics and audiences found the work too heavy-handed, "burdened with solemnity," and its "somber theme" and score were "not . . . pleasant to the ear."[28] This dark mood was precisely the point of the ballet, as a San Diego critic noted, praising its "color" and "urge" and rating it "significant of the times."[29] The earnestness of *City Portrait* was balanced by the equally determined lack of any pretension in *Charade*, "a fluffy romantic comedy" that was "fetching both in its vivacity and in its humor" and "called forth rounds of applause" and multiple curtain calls at many performances.[30] One astute critic noted of Colt's costumes that no typical 1900 debutante "ever wore skirts so short, nor hung ermine tails on knee-high pantaloons!" but averred that the festive look of the ballet, including "fanciful wigs and headdresses," was nevertheless a clear "knock out."[31] Several critics compared it favorably with the current offerings of the Ballet Russe, describing it as "an absurd combination of *Aurora's Wedding* without the grand entrée, and *Gaite Parisienne* with more than a touch of the toy-shop [*Boutique Fantasque*]".[32]

Following their tour, the American Ballet Caravan had the opportunity to perform the repertoire they had developed over the previous four years as part of a special engagement organized by Frances Hawkins at the St. James Theatre on Broadway. The "Holiday Dance Festival," set to run during the week between Christmas and New Year's, featured the company as one of its anchor ensembles, alongside specialists in Spanish and Korean dance as well as the Martha Graham company, which included not just Caravan alumnus Erick Hawkins but another male dancer newly recruited to the troupe, Mercier Cunningham, not yet billed with his stage name "Merce."[33] The Caravan offered four performances as part of the festival with four ballets presented at each show. In addition to *Billy the Kid, Filling Station*, and *Air and Variations*, these programs included a revival of *Promenade* and the first (and last) New York performances of *City Portrait* and *Charade*.[34] The overwhelmingly positive notices the company received from critics including John Martin, Margaret Lloyd, and Walter Terry would make the engagement all the more poignant in retrospect. Their festival appearance would represent the last time that the core group of dancers would perform together and the last time that many of its ballets would ever be performed.

I Married An Angel closed at the end of February 1939 after a run of over three hundred performances, leaving both Zorina and Balanchine available for new projects, with *The Boys from Syracuse* continuing its Broadway run before closing in early June.[35] Capitalizing on their successful collaboration on *Angel*, Balanchine and Zorina spent most of the year working on two new movie projects in which she would star and he would oversee the dances: a film adaptation of *On Your Toes* (released in fall 1939) and the romantic melodrama *I Was an Adventuress* (released in spring 1940). Even as *On Your Toes* drastically altered the plot and structure of the original musical, it included new versions of the *Princess Zenobia* ballet and *Slaughter on Tenth Avenue*, the latter reconceived for the screen using techniques that Balanchine had developed for *The Goldwyn Follies*. The romantic melodrama *Adventuress* not only saw Balanchine's American screen debut in a brief acting cameo but also included a creatively adapted version of *Swan Lake* in which Zorina was partnered by Lew Christensen. The couple did not have their professional fate entirely in their own hands, since Zorina was still under contract to Goldwyn for the forseeable future. As was common practice at the time, however, she was "lent out" to other studios for these two movies, and she was officially signed with Warner Brothers for *On Your Toes* in early March, shortly after the close of *Angel*.[36] The couple went west in May to begin filming, and Ballet Caravan dancers Christensen and Gisella Caccialanza followed in mid-June (with the company on break prior to their fall tour).[37]

Preview coverage of the film while it was still in production outlined several intriguing concepts for Balanchine's planned adaptation of the dances from the original musical. *Slaughter on Tenth Avenue* was to be reconceived from the "impressionist ballet" in the stage version into a more slapstick comedic number using what we would today call a live-action animation aesthetic.[38] With potentially dizzying layers of parody, the ballet was described as "Balanchine's idea of what the old Imperial Theatre ballet would do with an American gangster story," including a triple murder, striptease number, and "a bunch of jitterbugs in a honky-tonk bar-room dance hall on the west side."[39] Quotes attributed to Balanchine explained that viewers "who expect to see traditional ballet are going to be surprised, and we hope, amused" by this new concept for *Slaughter*, which he likened to a "Mickey Mouse cartoon with human characters."[40] When the police enter the bar in the second half of the ballet, for example, they were to be "dressed like cats and sneak across the floor on their hands and knees as though they were out to catch a rat."[41] In July it was even reported that according to certain sources Balanchine himself would be dancing in the film, a development that did not ultimately materialize.[42]

Ultimately both *Zenobia* and *Slaughter* appeared in the film without any radical reinvention, and despite the movie's substantial changes to the musical's characters and plot, each dance functioned mostly in the same

FIGURE 10.2 Balanchine rehearsing Vera Zorina and Eddie Albert in film version of *On Your Toes*, photographer and exact date unknown. Collection of Robert Greskovic. Choreography by George Balanchine © The George Balanchine Trust.

way as it had in the original musical. Despite their differences from the original versions, the movie's ballets remain the earliest complete versions of any of Balanchine's Broadway choreography to survive today as well as serving as additional evidence of his innovations in dance cinematography. Recollections of several dancers who appeared in *On Your Toes* suggest that even though Balanchine was not working with his own company that he endeavored to provide for the dancers as well as he could. Dancers Ray Weamer and Joan Bayley recall that Balanchine arranged for cots and special partitions to be set up so that dancers would have a place to rest between takes and also saw that buckets of ice were provided so they could relieve their feet, accommodations that were not the norm in Hollywood.[43] Both remember that Balanchine spoke softly and cultivated a reserved and aloof personality; he would typically withdraw to a private space when not at work.[44]

FIGURE 10.3 Balanchine rehearsing with Vera Zorina and Eddie Albert in film version of *On Your Toes*, photographer and exact date unknown. Collection of Robert Greskovic. Choreography by George Balanchine © The George Balanchine Trust. BALANCHINE is a Trademark of The George Balanchine Trust.

As had been the case with *The Goldwyn Follies*, for many viewers the dances of *On Your Toes* were the only redeeming feature of the movie in which they appeared. The film turned out to be more of a comedy than a musical, and even so "the laughs have not always been timed as well as they might have been," as *Variety* explained.[45] The film did not remain long in theaters, and even critics who had eagerly anticipated it were disappointed in the results, despite their admiration for the individual ballets themselves. "I had expected so much of this film," John Newnham of the *Dancing Times* wrote, having enthusiastically plugged the film in two previous columns.[46] But on seeing it he had to "confess to a sense of disappointment," admitting that its disappearance from London cinemas after only a week was more than justified.[47] A New York critic declared the ballets the "chief ornaments" as well as the "sole virtues" of the "ragged

FIGURE 10.4 Balanchine rehearsing Vera Zorina in film version of *On Your Toes*, photographer and exact date unknown. Collection of Robert Greskovic. Choreography by George Balanchine © The George Balanchine Trust. BALANCHINE is a Trademark of The George Balanchine Trust.

and dull" film.[48] Among other problems, for some viewers the satire of the *Zenobia* ballet was once again not obvious enough, and it was only at the end of the sequence that one could be sure "whether it is funny, or just bad dancing."[49] Zorina was praised widely for her charismatic screen presence, and the movie's "faltering script and direction" in no way diminished her star power.[50] "I would have hated to have missed seeing her," as this same critic elaborated, "but she alone is not enough to make the show really good entertainment."[51]

The mixed reception of *On Your Toes* did not dampen Balanchine and Zorina's prospects and they were soon at work on a third film—*I Was an Adventuress*, directed by Darryl Zanuck and produced by Twentieth Century Fox. The couple had opted for the film project in lieu of another Rodgers and Hart show produced by Dwight Deere Wiman, an ultimately unrealized show called *Nice Work*, suggesting that they were in high enough demand to have a certain degree of self-determination.[52] But over the next six months as they set to work on this movie their lives would be impacted by forces greater than mediocre reviews or long-term film contracts. The couple had returned to New York at the end of August, after production wrapped for *On Your Toes*, and they were set to depart for a European vacation. Although Zorina had been to Europe on several occasions in previous years—including a visit in which she was intensely recruited by the pro-Nazi German film industry—this trip would have been Balanchine's first return journey since emigrating six years earlier. Ultimately their trip was postponed indefinitely as the political situation across the Atlantic deteriorated, and Zorina and Balanchine instead remained in New York before returning to the West Coast in November to begin filming *Adventuress*.[53]

I Was an Adventuress featured Zorina at the heart of a story that blended romance and international intrigue, telling the story of a gang of jewel thieves who use their glamorous accomplice, Tanya Vronsky, to entrap potential targets. In the course of one such plot Tanya develops genuine feelings for their mark, and she turns on her former conspirators to marry the rich nobleman. Her partners later return and threaten to expose her sordid past, but her husband eventually finds out about it and forgives her, and through several subsequent plot twists one particularly valuable set of jewels ends up in the bottom of the sea. Before her life of crime, Tanya had been an aspiring ballet dancer, and this character background provided the occasion for Balanchine's short cameo in the movie as the conductor of a ballet performance by the newly wed countess, as well as the final dance sequence featured at the end of the film, a creatively adapted and condensed version of *Swan Lake* loosely occasioned by the plot.

Yet again *Adventuress* seemed to prove that while Zorina and Balanchine were capable of making meaningful contributions to the movies, they were decidedly unlucky in the cinematic vehicles they secured for their talents. *Adventuress* was praised for being "suave" and possessing a "class" that was lacking in other cinematic offerings, and Zorina had "never appeared prettier," but overall the movie was met with only moderate enthusiasm.[54] "Winsome jewel thieves in swanky hostelries are nothing new to our movies," as one critic noted, but even in the context of the shopworn plot Zorina delivered "a very creditable performance" and her dancing gave the movie "a certain 'touch.'"[55] Despite its relatively lavish production values and above average camera work, the film lacked big marquee names and did not have considerable box office staying power.[56] Much like *Angel*, however, the film proved that Zorina could sustain a dramatic role, in part thanks to her "delicate, elusive charm," with her dancing abilities providing a unique dimension to her screen presence, with her husband a key asset in cultivating this hybrid profile.[57]

After completing their work on *Adventuress*, Balanchine and Zorina went back to New York in early March 1940.[58] On his return to the East Coast, Balanchine took a new step toward settling into his new home by officially becoming a citizen of the United States. Dated March 18, 1940, his certificate of naturalization names his former country of citizenship as Russia and lists his home address on 77th Street just east of Central Park.[59] What motivated Balanchine's action at this precise moment is unclear, but given the changing political climate, such a move was practical and reasonable; and it meant that he would be eligible for a US passport in place of the troublesome "Nansen" passport he had previously held, a document that was issued to stateless individuals by the League of Nations. The changing character of his professional career was perhaps another factor, since Balanchine was working almost entirely outside of the ballet enterprise by which he had first secured permission to enter and work in the United States. In any case, regardless of debates about when and how Balanchine became an American in artistic terms, it is notable that he literally became an American citizen between the release of his second and third film projects while married to Zorina, his creative partner in both endeavors.

On the heels of his work on *Adventuress*, Balanchine's career took another new turn: a renewed association with the Ballet Russe de Monte Carlo through a widely praised revival of *Le Baiser de la Fée*, first performed as part of the American Ballet's Stravinsky Festival several years earlier. This project was characterized as a late addition to the company's repertoire—announced only weeks after Balanchine and Zorina had returned to New York—and was scheduled for the last week of the company's three-week March engagement at the Metropolitan Opera.[60] The ballet was even better received than it had been on its first presentation in 1937, when it had been the popular and critical hit of the Stravinsky Festival. "Beauty of scene, dramatic force, and unusually well wrought choreography" characterized the piece, which Walter Terry said deserved "a lasting place in the company's repertory."[61] John Martin reminded readers that when the ballet had its premiere it was "far and away the best ballet" Balanchine had yet created in America, and added that the new production "makes it necessary to repeat that estimate."[62] Even though the Stravinsky score was "beyond the company's present orchestral equipment," as Margaret Lloyd observed, the ballet's striking costumes by Alice Halicka and Balanchine's "unusual" choreography gave the ballet the exact

FIGURE 10.5 George Balanchine's certificate of United States citizenship, 1940. George Balanchine Archive, MS Thr 411 (2806), Houghton Library, Harvard University. BALANCHINE is a Trademark of The George Balanchine Trust.

mix of ingredients "that only rarely blend into a fused performance."[63] Although it was difficult to say precisely what changes had been made to the ballet, Martin noted one improvement, as he did not recall that "the ensembles were so consistently brilliant" in the earlier version.[64] Terry noted similar qualities in these sections, noting that the "corps de ballet demonstrated that it knew something of a group effect" and surmising that perhaps "Balanchine's Broadway experience enabled him to direct the company in the ways of united effort."[65] Thus what critics hailed as "one of the most interesting items" to have emerged from the original repertory of the now defunct American Ballet—a work that evinced an "admirable mingling of fantasy, romance, and fairy tale simplicity"—was given new life, albeit as a new calling card for one of the very organizations that the Balanchine-Kirstein enterprise had been created to supplant.[66]

———

Although the December 1939 Holiday Dance Festival proved in retrospect to be an auspicious final bow for the American Ballet Caravan's core personnel and repertoire, the company had one final chance to perform for the public in late 1940 in an unexpected venue: as the resident dance troupe at the 1940 World's Fair Pavilion of the Ford Motor Company.[67] For almost six months beginning in May the Caravan appeared twelve times a day in a ballet called *A Thousand Times Neigh*, which recounted the history of the automobile from the perspective of its protagonist Dobbin the horse, portrayed by two male dancers in a single costume. The ballet was the centerpiece of a triple bill of free performances that occurred every hour on the hour at the specially built "Ford Theater." Preceding the ballet was a full color stop-action animated film called *Symphony in F*—with "F" not denoting a musical key signature—that tracked the construction of a Ford automobile from start to finish. It was followed by a combination style show and automobile commercial that paired women's fashions from Lord and Taylor with several of Ford's latest cars. Most accounts of this project characterize it as a curious coda in the company's life or a deus ex machina occurrence that gave them one final lease on life—and like the Fair in general it was an obstinate exercise in American optimism in the face of the impending collapse of the world order. However trivial it might appear today, *A Thousand Times Neigh* was hailed as an notable dance event, touted as the first ballet to be sponsored by a corporate patron and the first ballet danced to recorded music. Critical reception of the ballet was exceptionally positive, and a wide range of observers regarded it as a significant contribution to the wider project of American ballet in a popular context. The ballet thus represented an unexpected fulfillment of the goals that had been set for Balanchine and Kirstein's enterprise from the start.

The concept for the ballet originated with industrial designer Walter Dorwin Teague, who was responsible for the larger design and programming of the Ford Pavilion. Teague approached Kirstein about involving the Caravan, and William Dollar was tapped to create the choreography. An associate of Teague's, Edward Mabley, wrote the libretto and song texts, and Tom Bennett, a staff composer and arranger for NBC, was responsible the score. The show was double cast so that dancers performed in no more than six shows each day, and there was a generous reserve of substitutes so that every dancer had one full day off each week, with additional dancers recruited from the School of American Ballet, the newly created Ballet Theatre, and Broadway shows. The dancers seem to have been generally pleased with the engagement, especially since it provided steady employment during the otherwise fallow summer months in a well-appointed and air-conditioned theater.

Comparable in length to the Caravan's previous works, *A Thousand Times Neigh* consisted of three scenes—1903, the year the first Ford

FIGURE 10.6 Entrance Lobby of the Ford Theater, World's Fair Pavilion, 1940, photographer unknown. *A Thousand Times Neigh* Scrapbook, The Benson Ford Research Center.

factory opened; 1920, over a decade after the launch of the Model T; and finally in the present-day 1940 with an eye toward the future; it employed a rotating stage so that sets could shift immediately from one to the next. The ballet opened with the so-called horseless carriage making its debut, with its driver explaining, "It's fast transportation, / A cause for elation / By all in the nation but you—know—who!" whereupon Dobbin "glares" and "bares his teeth" at his new mechanical rival.[68] The next scene, set in 1920 on an American farm, sees the dancers dressed in rustic attire performing a square dance, during which the assembled chorus entreats Dobbin to take them to all the places they need to go, whether to a "husking bee" or the "big cit-ee!" A Model T suddenly intrudes into the Arcadian idyll driven by Dobbin's owner, who purchased not just a car but a Ford tractor and truck as well, explaining that he wants to see "just how it feels / to put this doggoned farm on wheels." Following Dobbin's heartfelt lament at his sudden obsolescence, the scene shifts suddenly to a Ford dealership in "a modern city," which would have brought the audience very much into the present moment, as the auditorium in which they sat was ringed with the newest Ford cars and the backdrop depicted the "highway of the future" that fairground guests could ride along in real life. And of course, a happy solution for the horse's condition quickly emerges, one that in fact ennobles the hardworking animal. "Time was, before the motor car / 'Twas *he* took people places," but now instead the public will "come to *him*, for he's the star / Of the Saratoga races." Thus Dobbin happily makes the transition from hardworking beast of burden to mascot of the leisure class, leaving the work of transportation to the good people of Ford.

Both mainstream observers and more specialized critics offered the ballet unqualified praise. *Billboard* vouched for the dancers as "uniformly good" and the soloists as "more than competent," while *Variety* called it an "ace attraction" that "fully lives up to advance ballyhoo."[69] The *New Yorker* called the ballet "grand stuff" and praised the quality of the recorded music, noting that composer Bennett had produced a "vivacious, amusing, and unpretentious score that develops smoothly with the fresh choreography of William Dollar." According to this same report, the show was also very well attended, and it advised patrons to arrive early

From the Collections of The Henry Ford (64.167.232.1777/THF134315)

FIGURE 10.7 Posed photograph of dancers in *A Thousand Times Neigh*, 1940, photographer unknown. *A Thousand Times Neigh* Scrapbook, The Benson Ford Research Center.

to secure a seat. Other critics welcomed *A Thousand Times Neigh* as a reinvention of ballet in a more popular, American, and even masculine idiom, changes credited in part to the ballet's corporate patronage. The *New York Sun* praised Ford and Dobbin the horse as "doing more to take [ballet] out of the pink tights, white chiffon, too-too-Degas stage than any other two people you can think of," a finding with which cultural critic Gilbert Seldes concurred. The ballet would remind audiences that "ballet isn't something Aunt Susie's pansy friend from Italy thought up," Seldes explained in an annual ballet roundup. Less explicitly homophobic, Seldes and others also voiced their approval for the popular ethos of the show and expressed their wish that ballet in general were produced with "less social oomph and a little more Billyrose." This angle was also noted by John Martin, who fully vouched for the authenticity of the work, which featured all of the women on pointe and a demanding pas de deux at the end. Most important, the ballet struck just the right balance between classical authenticity and popular appeal, and Martin described Dollar's work as "choreography that clings to the academic ballet tradition without being in the least highbrow."

Martin did take issue, however, with a statement made at the opening by Edsel Ford, who had made a "functional" case for ballet and had posited *A Thousand Times Neigh* as a model for future patronage of the art form. Ford explained that in order to flourish "ballet must be functional—useful and used—like music, architecture or any other art."[70] Martin reminded him that at a previous World's Fair, Ford had sponsored a symphony orchestra that had not been required to play music of an automotive theme, and questioned why Ford had not contracted the Caravan to offer some of their own work, such as *Billy the Kid* or even *Filling Station* (which features cars in a supporting rather than starring role). "The function of the dance," Martin explained, "cannot possibly be twisted under such a definition to mean that it must advertise something that somebody manufactures."[71] Nevertheless, Martin did not advise against refusing such corporate largesse on principle, noting drily that "the youngsters in the company can manage to eat over a dull period" thanks to the project, "and that is definitely functional."[72]

The close of the World's Fair at the end of October 1940 marked the dissolution of the American Ballet Caravan, even though it had already become increasingly clear in the course of their engagement that Kirstein's experiment was nearing an end. And even as critics had continued to follow the troupe's efforts, their observations augured an imminent demise of the eternally protean organization. In May, Walter Terry praised the troupe for its work developing American choreographers and "stripping the ballet of preciosity" while at once "fostering robust and vital American themes and turning out many splendid dancers."[73] He surmised that the modest scale of the company's work had made it difficult to gain attention and hoped that eventually enthusiasm for the "blinding glitter of great ballet companies" would be tempered so that "our eyes will be able to discern the fineness of small groups."[74] By September it had been reported that the troupe would not embark on another tour that fall and winter, and whether as cause or effect of the company's uncertain future, many of the Caravan's leading talents had aligned themselves with other enterprises: Erick Hawkins with Martha Graham, Eugene Loring with the newly founded Ballet Theatre, and Lew Christensen pursuing work in the movies.[75] Margaret Lloyd nevertheless optimistically maintained in September that the "small company of 20 members and its original repertoire" still had a "distinctive place to fill in American ballet."[76]

From spring 1939 to the end of 1940 possible plans for reviving the American Ballet and Ballet Caravan—including a possible alignment with Ballet Theatre—were pondered but ultimately came to naught. The various schemes had foundered in part due to an apparent lack of commitment or interest from Balanchine. A year earlier in spring 1939 it had been reported that the "renaissance of the American Ballet" was being plotted by Dwight Deere Wiman, the producer and de facto patron of Balanchine's work for Rodgers and Hart. Wiman had planned to bring back the troupe with Balanchine as its leader and William Dollar and Leda Anchutina as leading dancers, as well as possible guest artists including Zorina, for performances at the Metropolitan Opera.[77]

Concurrent with the Caravan's engagement at the Ford Pavilion, Balanchine returned to Broadway with another trio of overlapping projects that approached his level of activity in 1938. Differing markedly in their overall character and Balanchine's level of personal commitment, this body of new work allowed him at once to branch out in new directions and consolidate his network of previous collaborators. Balanchine premiered dances for two shows almost simultaneously in May, for the short-lived and by most accounts uninspiring revue *Keep Off the Grass* and the musical *Louisiana Purchase*, Irving Berlin's triumphant return to Broadway, which featured Zorina in a starring role and ran for over a year. These two shows gave Balanchine the chance to collaborate again with many of the performers with whom he had worked in previous years, including American Ballet dancers Charles Laskey and Daphne Vane, Ray Bolger (from *On Your Toes*), Betty Bruce (from *The Boys from Syracuse*), as well as forge new working relationships with artists including modern dancer José Limón.

By most accounts, *Keep Off the Grass* was not a project that was especially dear to the heart of anyone associated with it, and Balanchine undertook the work as much as a personal favor to some of its performers as for the modest payday it provided him. Comprising twenty-seven individual scenes, the revue was built around the star power of comedian Jimmy Durante, who anchored the show alongside Ray Bolger, who since appearing as Junior Dolan in *On Your Toes* had made a splash on screen as the Scarecrow in *The Wizard of Oz*. Bolger was credited as "co-carrier" of the show, and it was noted that he was "on for a song and dance about every twenty minutes," either in solo numbers or partnered by dancers Bruce and Vane.[78] Bolger's dances gave audiences plenty of his renowned "rubber-legs hoofing"—"rhumba, standard eccentric, pseudo-ballet and cake walk strut."[79] According to Bolger's recollections, the only "real" ballet created by Balanchine for the revue was a number called *Raffles*, which featured music by Vernon Duke and Bolger as its eponymous protagonist.[80] The "pantomimic" ballet told of the exploits of the "very famous, very elegant" thief Raffles, who breaks into an apartment to steal a pearl necklace from around a woman's neck.[81]

While the show provided other opportunities for lighthearted fun both onstage and off, the revue's comedy mostly wore thin for both performers and audiences, and it eventually closed after only two months. For Limón the presence of the vivacious Bruce "more than compensated for the overall dreariness" of his experience on the show, and he recalled how she "made a pandemonium of rehearsals, mocking, teasing, and insulting, with saucy good humor, everyone in sight," including Balanchine, Bolger, Limón himself, and the rest of the chorus boys, among them Jerome Robbins.[82] But overall the project did not bring out the best in any of its participants, with Limón and Bruce working hard on "completely unrewarding numbers," and at one point Balanchine simply instructed him to scrap what they had been working on to "go in center and do Modern Dance."[83] Limón surmises that the revue flopped because of its out-of-touch triviality, with Nazi Germany beginning its terrifying incursion into Western Europe around the time the show opened.[84] Although he and his fellow performers "went through the motions of performing," they found the proceedings "curiously empty and meaningless," and he credits audiences for seeing through the "cheap vulgarity" of the show in light of the weighty events transpiring elsewhere the world. Reviewers nevertheless praised some of Balanchine's contributions, rating his work on "Old Jitterbug" and "Cops and Robbers" numbers his "best routines" in the show, which was otherwise overlong and "overboard on ballet."[85] Other reviewers concurred with Limón's recollections, noting that the dancer had been "required to go through meaningless posturings and gesturings" that gave him "no opportunity to display his abilities," a condition that equally affected the work of his partner Daphne Vane.[86]

Louisiana Purchase, by contrast, represented a more auspicious return to the stage for both Balanchine and Zorina, who was "no longer an angel," having traded "downy wings for feathered black tights to lead the chorus in a sizzling Conga concocted by her Russian husband."[87] Set in present-day New Orleans, *Louisiana Purchase* "was so thoroughly of its time," in the words of Irving Berlin scholar Jeffrey Magee, as to be virtually "un-revivable in its original form," infused with insider political jokes and other contemporary references.[88] The qualities that make the show unintelligible to modern-day audiences helped make it a hit in its day, and it ran for over 400 performances—the longest of any of Berlin's musicals to that point—before touring the country with its original cast. Any personal investment on Balanchine's part in the political angle of the play was called into question by a gossip item reported in the *Washington Post*. Balanchine recalled that during the show's DC previews Attorney General Frank Murphy had been in attendance at a party thrown for the cast, upon which Zorina corrected him to note that Murphy was in fact an associate justice on the Supreme Court.[89] Balanchine was insistent that he had correctly identified the attorney general in his recent citizenship examination, to which Zorina reminded him that in Washington a lot could change in a few months.

In the context of Balanchine and Zorina's partnership, *Louisiana Purchase* was significant in providing another role that maximized her artistic persona and her husband's choreographic gifts, confirming that theater (more than the movies) was a more successful context for the couple's unique mélange of talents. In the show Zorina portrayed émigré Marina van Linden, who is seeking money to help her mother escape to America from Nazi-controlled Austria. She secures these funds by helping a team of lawyers entrap a senator who is investigating their firm for corruption, the central plot of the musical. Although she was still bound to her film contract and was billed as appearing "by courtesy of Sam Goldwyn," reviews noted that Zorina "virtually makes *Purchase* her show," in part thanks to Balanchine having given her "ample terp opportunities."[90] Zorina was "heavenly to look at and entrancing to watch," in both her ballet turns and dramatic scenes.[91] She was rated "especially impressive" in her ballet numbers partnered by Charles Laskey, but no less entertaining in other scenes, including one in which she "pirouettes and talks to herself about whether children are worth having since they may get the measles."[92] "Whether Miss Zorina is dancing or merely existing," another critic vouched, "she is when visible the everlasting focus of the proceedings."[93]

While *Louisiana Purchase* was under way, Balanchine began work on the first Broadway project in which he would have a greater degree of artistic autonomy as both choreographer and director, the musical *Cabin in the Sky*. By any measure, the musical was a singular event in Broadway history in its content and the makeup of its creative team. Adapted from a book by Lynn Root, a white author from Minnesota, the show featured an all-black cast headlined by Ethel Waters along with dancer and choreographer Katherine Dunham and members of her dance company. It recounted the lives of African Americans living in the South, focused on the efforts of Petunia (Waters) to get her gambling, ne'er-do-well husband Joe into heaven, while Joe is in part tempted by the seductive Georgia Brown (Dunham). The remaining members of the musical's creative team were a trio of émigrés: composer Vernon Duke, set designer Boris Aronson, and Balanchine. Duke's memoirs maintain that discussions about the show began in early 1940 while Balanchine was in Hollywood filming *Adventuress* and Root's script happened to come to their attention.[94] Dunham and her dancers were subsequently recruited to join the project after Balanchine saw them perform in Chicago in their revue *Tropic and Le Jazz "Hot."* Preview coverage eagerly played up a clash-of-cultures backstory, conjuring vivid images of "a threesome of turbulent Russians" clashing with "a tempestuous cast of Negro players from Harlem."[95] "At least a half a dozen times at each rehearsal of *Cabin in the Sky*," the report elaborated, the cast was forced to pause "in puzzlement while the argumentative trio" of Balanchine, Duke, and Aronson "disputed a difference of opinion in their native tongue" with "Russian vowels and consonants flying as thick as borscht."[96]

Balanchine received sole credit for the choreography of *Cabin in the Sky*, even though it is clear that the show's dances were created collaboratively with Dunham and her dancers. Indeed, the show as a whole is a particularly rich site of debate over questions of cultural appropriation, race and aesthetics, and creative ownership in the wider history of Broadway as well as Balanchine's own work with black dance and dancers.[97] For the most part, however, Balanchine and Dunham's collaborative relationship on the show was characterized by mutual respect and shared goals. Dunham regarded the show as a strategic opportunity to gain wider exposure on Broadway and provide a better living for herself her dancers in the process, and Balanchine's involvement in the show gave her confidence that the project would not merely reproduce the stereotyped cultural idioms that her own work sought to challenge.[98] In the course of their work, Balanchine spent time observing Dunham and her dancers in their own classes and rehearsals to get a sense of their movement vocabularies, which he subsequently incorporated into the dances he set on them. And for many of the dances, he granted considerable choreographic autonomy to Dunham, taking responsibility for only entrances and exits and the wider theatrical context, as he had done with dancers in his previous Broadway projects. "I would make a suggestion and he would keep it," as Dunham described their interactions, "or else he'd make a suggestion and I'd say fine."[99] Notably, Dunham also suggests that Balanchine's experimental sensibilities helped cement their creative relationship, for he understood implicitly the "strangeness" of her choreographic approach, which itself was often viewed as "a little bit avant-garde at the time."[100]

Cabin in the Sky stands as a significant moment in the history of African American contributions to the performing arts, and despite its less than realistic depiction of black life, it met with approval from a range of observers, from the black press corps to Eleanor Roosevelt. While Ethel Waters was widely praised for her work in the lead role, Dunham and the show's dances proved to be a decisive factor in its success as well. While crediting only Balanchine, reviews praised the dances as a distinct highlight, in particular the "Egyptian" number, in which the dancing was "properly wild, sometimes a trifle orgiastic."[101] "Musical shows seldom acquire dancing such as he has directed here," observed Brooks Atkinson, who paternalistically suggested in an unfortunate metaphor that if union rules allowed, the show's dancers would return some of their pay to Balanchine "for the privilege of appearing under his direction, for he has released them from the bondage of hack dancing and ugliness."[102] The show had proved that Dunham could do more than just dance, displaying her "natural acting ability, a small but pleasant voice, and a personality that is devastating."[103] Others noted her leadership role in the dancing department, calling her a "striking leader of an excellent chorus."[104]

In addition to standing as a notable work of African American cultural production, *Cabin in the Sky* also represented if not a culmination of Balanchine's previous Broadway work then at the very least a confluence of significant themes and practices he had developed since his arrival in

America. On a formal level, "Egyptian" dances had been a touchstone in various contexts, from his work at the Metropolitan Opera to the homespun *Aida* parody of *Babes in Arms*. And from *On Your Toes* to *Louisiana Purchase*, Balanchine had gained considerable experience with various uses of dance in a Broadway context that allowed him to integrate the dance into the musical in a range of ways. Even more striking is the similarity between the artistic profiles of Dunham and Zorina and Balanchine's interest and ability to create a theatrical context to display their talents. Like Zorina's many roles on stage and screen, Dunham's portrayal of Georgia Brown was successful owing to the way it capitalized on her unique profile, a combination of prodigious choreographic skill, previously untapped acting and singing ability, and charismatic physical beauty. In other words, Dunham's talents and personality lent themselves well to recreating the successful formula that Balanchine had helped develop for Zorina on both stage and screen.

During his work on *Cabin in the Sky*, Balanchine found time for another project, restaging two additional works from the repertoire of the American Ballet for the Ballet Russe de Monte Carlo in mid-October: *The Poker Game* and *Serenade*. *The Poker Game* was offered on the company's opening night at the Metropolitan Opera and was "by all odds the bright spot" of the evening, according to John Martin, and what it lacked in substance it more than made up in "savor and sparkle."[105] Compared to its previous performances by the American Ballet, the work had improved "immeasurably" because of the "greater experience and individuality" of its cast—including Alicia Markova and Alexandra Danilova as two of the Queens, and Frederic Franklin as the Joker—and the result was "not only a rather cute bit of whimsy but a witty and frequently brilliant piece of composition."[106] Several days later *Serenade* was presented on a program that included a more historic revival, a "restoration" of Petipa's choreography for *The Nutcracker*, which had not yet acquired its status as a Christmastime staple. For this version it is maintained that Balanchine added the previously omitted "Tema Russo" movement to the ballet, although new choreography is not described in surviving reviews. Martin predicted that *The Nutcracker* would have more staying power in the company's repertory, despite finding much to admire in *Serenade*. "As a composition it is fresh, impeccably neat and chic, with an admirable musicianship," and he thought its ensemble-forward choreography would improve with further performances. "For those who have the inclination to go with the choreographer along his rather rarefied way," he added, the ballet offered an experience "eminently worth the effort"—a "'musical visualization' with only a hint of classroom 'center practice.' "[107] He also noted that the contributions to the ballet by Marie-Jeanne, identified as a "guest artist" from the American Ballet Caravan, earned her "more flowers than you could shake a stick at."[108]

The premiere of *Cabin in the Sky* and simultaneous revivals of *The Card Party* and *Serenade* portended a stable if eclectic professional horizon for Balanchine moving forward, captured in an overview of the chore-ographer published in *Collier's* around the time of the musical's debut.[109] Since his arrival seven years earlier Balanchine, through his work with the American Ballet as well as on Broadway and in Hollywood, has "done right well" by American dancers, who now "twirl on stages where only Russians have twirled before." The choreographer is quoted—with his accent lightly transliterated—as saying that he accepted the "nize [*sic*] invitation" to come to America mostly with dancers in mind, because he had "plans for those so lovely, pliable bodies of American girrls [*sic*]," hastening to clarify that these were "professional plans, please onderstand [*sic*]." In general, Balanchine seemed to be living the American dream, and equipped with "an elaborate Long Island home and sleek New York apartment" as well as his "brand new American citizenship papers," he declared that he had "no intention of ever leaving behind the land of opportunity." Of course, any possibility of returning to Europe would be unthinkable in the coming years, but nevertheless Balanchine seemed well provided for from a professional perspective. He was in a position to pur-sue "serious work in the Ballet Russe de Monte Carlo" while his work on Broadway "keeps him busy and happy," and most important, "his income tax is large enough to make him feel he's a respectable, paying member of the community." Balanchine's main quarrel was a lingering stereotype he continued to encounter, the misconception that "any Russian artist is automatically a genius," precisely the kind of stereotype that his enterprise with Kirstein had been conceived of to dispel but upon which it had in part been premised.

While such reports left Kirstein out of the picture entirely, other news suggested that their collaborative endeavors had not reached a complete end, and in fact both were putting renewed focus on the last remaining component of their original enterprise, the School of American Ballet. Several weeks before the opening of *Cabin*, the School auditioned over one hundred students for three new scholarship positions, a competition for which both Kirstein and Balanchine served as judges.[110] A promotional brochure touted Balanchine's long-awaited return to the instructional staff for the 1940–41 academic year, an implicit admission of his sporadic involvement in preceding years. "Mr. Balanchine, while intimately connected with The School of American Ballet since its inception," the brochure explained in carefully chosen words, "has, on account of his professional engagements, taught comparatively little in recent years." But in the coming year he would be "resuming his duties as an instructor in the School with added interest."[111]

In less than a decade, George Balanchine and Lincoln Kirstein had faced challenges and opportunities that neither likely envisioned when they first met in the summer of 1933 in London. Their collective enterprise had weathered much: summertime thunderstorms in Westchester county, byzantine politics at the Metropolitan Opera, mediocre reviews and lukewarm audiences, recalcitrant corporate monopolies, and the continued dominance of Russian ballet in the public imagination. They had also notched several notable successes, both in collaboration and on their own. Balanchine had created dances for nine Broadway shows and three feature films. Kirstein and Ballet Caravan had logged tens of thousands of miles of touring from Vancouver to Havana. And the American Ballet had been responsible for creating and recreating works that would forever alter the cultural landscape of the United States if not the world: *Serenade* and *Apollon Musagète* (not to mention the "Bach ballet" inspired by *On Your Toes*). True to Kirstein's original intentions and with or without Balanchine's enthusiastic involvement, the School of American Ballet had functioned as the linchpin of these disparate endeavors and now stood as an indispensable institution of ballet pedagogy. As the United States moved from economic recovery to a more active role on the geopolitical stage in the coming years, Balanchine and Kirstein's collective and individual work would continue to change and evolve.

"It's unfortunate that things are so economically unsettled now," Kirstein had noted at the end of his second letter to Chick Austin in the summer of 1933. He had nevertheless been resolute that it was the time to provide America a new platform for "living art" and "the chance for perfect creation." Seven years later the enterprise and its key players were left with the same stubborn and naïve optimism with which it had begun, and with which Kirstein had concluded this same letter: "May our dream come true."

LIST OF ABBREVIATIONS USED IN NOTES

BG   *Boston Globe*

BS   *Baltimore Sun*

CCP   Lew Christensen–Gisella Caccialanza Papers, Museum of Performance and Design, San Francisco

CSM   *Christian Science Monitor*

CT   *Chicago Tribune*

DO   *Dance Observer*

DT   *Dancing Times*

EHS   Erick Hawkins Scrapbooks, Erick Hawkins Collection, Music Division, Library of Congress (LOC)

DCS   Douglas Coudy Scrapbook, Jerome Robbins Dance Division, New York Public Library for the Performing Arts (JRDD)

GBA   George Balanchine Archive, Harvard Theatre Collection, Houghton Library, Harvard University

HC   *Hartford Courant*

JRDD   Jerome Robbins Dance Division, New York Public Library for the Performing Arts

LAT   *Los Angeles Times*

LEK   Louis Edward Kirstein Business Records, Baker Library, Harvard Business School

LKD   Lincoln Kirstein Diaries, Lincoln Kirstein Papers, JRDD

LOC   Library of Congress

MA   *Musical America*

MDP   Muriel Draper Papers, Yale Collection of American Literature, Beinecke Rare Book and Manuscript Library

MM   *Modern Music*

MPH   *Motion Picture Herald*

NYHT *New York Herald-Tribune*

NYT   *New York Times*

PBC   Popular Balanchine Collection, JRDD

PDP   Yvonne Patterson and William Dollar Papers, JRDD

RRS   Richard Rodgers Scrapbooks, Music Division, New York Public Library for the Performing Arts

VDC   Vernon Duke Collection, Music Division, LOC

WP   *Washington Post*

WSJ   *Wall Street Journal*

NOTES

Introduction

1. Ronald Reagan, "Remarks at the Presentation Ceremony for the Presidential Medal of Freedom, February 23, 1983, http://www.presidency.ucsb.edu/ws/index.php?pid=40963, accessed October 15, 2017.

2. Ronald Reagan to Lincoln Kirstein, May 5, 1983, GBA.

3. Jennifer Homans, *Apollo's Angels: A History of Ballet* (New York: Random House, 2010), 504.

4. Ronald Reagan, "Remarks at the Presentation Ceremony."

5. I am indebted to Lynn Garafola for creating this capacious term to describe Balanchine and Kirstein's collaborative efforts.

6. See, for example, Daniel Albright, *Untwisting the Serpent: Modernism in Music, Literature, and the Visual Arts* (Chicago: University of Chicago Press, 2000); Michelle Clayton, "Touring History: Tórtola Valencia between Europe and the Americas," *Dance Research Journal* 44, no. 1 (Summer 2012): 28–49; Mary Simonson, *Body Knowledge: Performance, Intermediality, and American Entertainment at the Turn of the Twentieth Century* (New York: Oxford University Press, 2013); and Susan Jones, *Literature, Modernism, and Dance* (New York: Oxford University Press, 2013).

7. See Andreas Huyssen, *After the Great Divide: Modernism, Mass Culture, Postmodernism* (Bloomington: University of Indiana Press, 1986); Miriam Bratu Hansen, "The Mass Consumption of the Senses: Classical Cinema as Vernacular Modernism," *Modernism/Modernity* 6, no. 2 (1999): 59–77.

8. David Savran, *Highbrow/Lowdown: Theater, Jazz, and the Making of a New Middle Class* (Ann Arbor: University of Michigan Press, 2009); Laura Tunbridge, ed., "Modernism and Its Others," *Journal of the Royal Musical Association* 139, no. 1 (2014): 177–204, especially Christopher Chowrimootoo, "Reviving the Middlebrow, or: Deconstructing Modernism from the Inside," 187–93.

9. See, among others, Richard Taruskin, *Stravinsky and the Russian Traditions: A Biography of the Works through "Mavra"* (Berkeley: University of California Press, 1996); Sabine Feisst, *Schoenberg's New World: The American Years* (New York: Oxford University Press, 2011); Simon Morrison, *The People's Artist: Prokofiev's Soviet*

Years (New York: Oxford University Press, 2009); Brigid Cohen, *Stefan Wolpe and the Avant-Garde Diaspora* (Cambridge: Cambridge University Press, 2012); Olga Haldey, *Mamontov's Private Opera: The Search for Modernism in Russian Theater* (Bloomington: Indiana University Press, 2012); Carol Oja, *Making Music Modern: New York in the 1920s* (New York: Oxford University Press, 2000).

10. Mark Franko, *Martha Graham in Love and War* (New York: Oxford University Press, 2012); Roger Copeland, *Merce Cunningham: The Modernizing of Modern Dance* (New York: Routledge, 2004); Lynn Garafola, *Diaghilev's Ballets Russes* (New York: Oxford University Press, 1989) and a monograph on Bronislava Nijinska currently in progress.

11. Constance Valis Hill, *Brotherhood in Rhythm: The Jazz Tap Dancing of the Nicholas Brothers* (New York: Oxford University Press, 2000) and *Tap Dancing America* (New York: Oxford University Press, 2010); Susan Manning, *Modern Dance/Negro Dance: Race in Motion* (Minneapolis: University of Minnesota Press, 2004); Janet Mansfield Soares, *Louis Horst: Musician in a Dancer's World* (Durham, NC: Duke University Press, 1992).

12. Though more diffuse in its authorship, this received history of the Balanchine-Kirstein enterprise is akin to the "vast autobiographical and memoiristic legacy" generated by Igor Stravinsky, which as Richard Taruskin has argued can no longer be reliably or responsibly used for scholarly purposes except as primary source material. Taruskin, *Stravinsky and the Russian Traditions*, 12.

13. One exception is perhaps the earliest published account of the enterprise, journalist Ruth Eleanor Howard's *The Story of the American Ballet*, a brochure-length item generously illustrated with photographs and geared toward an audience of dance enthusiasts. Ruth Eleanor Howard, *The Story of the American Ballet* (New York: IHRA Publishing, 1936).

14. Lincoln Kirstein, *Blast at Ballet: A Corrective for the American Audience* (New York: Marstin Press, 1938). Though this book will cite from the first edition, a facsimile reprint of *Blast at Ballet* is included in Lincoln Kirstein, *Ballet: Bias & Belief—Three Pamphlets Collected and Other Dance Writings of Lincoln Kirstein* (New York: Dance Horizons, 1983), 157–284. *Pavel Tchelitchev, Dance Index* 3, nos. 1–2 (January–February 1944); *Stravinsky in the Theatre*, ed. Minna Lederman, *Dance Index* 6, nos. 10–12 (October–November–December 1947).

15. Anatole Chujoy, *The New York City Ballet* (New York: Knopf, 1953).

16. Lincoln Kirstein's *The New York City Ballet* (New York: Knopf, 1973) was originally published as an illustrated large-format book. In honor of the thirtieth anniversary of NYCB Kirstein published a text-only version revised and expanded to encompass the years 1973–78, titled *Thirty Years: Lincoln Kirstein's The New York City Ballet* (New York: Knopf, 1978). Except where noted, this book cites the more widely available 1978 edition, abbreviated as *Thirty Years*.

17. Bernard Taper, *Balanchine, a Biography* (Berkeley: University of California Press, 1996). This fourth and final edition of Taper's biography is referenced in this book.

18. Richard Buckle with John Taras, *George Balanchine, Ballet Master* (New York: Random House, 1988).

19. Robert Gottlieb, *George Balanchine: The Ballet Maker* (New York: Atlas Books/HarperCollins, 2004); Terry Teachout, *All in the Dances: A Brief Life of George Balanchine* (New York: Harcourt, 2004).

20. Martin Duberman, *The Worlds of Lincoln Kirstein* (Evanston, IL: Northwestern University Press, 2008).

21. *Choreography by George Balanchine: A Catalogue of Works* (New York: Viking, 1984), hereafter *Balanchine Catalogue*.

22. Nancy Reynolds, *Repertory in Review: 40 Years of the New York City Ballet* (New York: Dial Press, 1977).

23. Elizabeth Kendall, *Balanchine and the Lost Muse: Revolution and the Making of a Choreographer* (New York: Oxford University Press, 2013).

24. Garafola, *Diaghilev's Ballets Russes*; Susan Jones, *Literature, Modernism, and Dance* (Oxford: Oxford University Press, 2013); Tim Scholl, *From Petipa to Balanchine: Classical Revival and the Modernization of Ballet* (London: Routledge, 1994).

25. Kathrine Sorley Walker, *De Basil's Ballets Russes* (New York: Atheneum, 1983); Vicente García-Márquez, *The Ballets Russes: Colonel de Basil's Ballets Russes de Monte Carlo, 1932–1952* (New York: Knopf, 1990); and Judith Chazin-Bennahum, *René Blum and the Ballets Russes: In Search of a Lost Life* (Oxford: Oxford University Press, 2011).

26. Lynn Garafola, ed., with Eric Foner, *Dance for a City: Fifty Years of the New York City Ballet* (New York: Columbia University Press, 1999).

27. Lynn Garafola, "George Antheil and the Dance," in *Legacies of Twentieth-Century Dance* (Middletown, CT: Wesleyan University Press, 2005), 256–76; "Making an American Dance: *Billy the Kid, Rodeo, and Appalachian Spring*," in *Aaron Copland and His World*, ed. Carol Oja and Judith Tick (Princeton, NJ: Princeton University Press, 2005), 121–47; "Dollars for Dance: Lincoln Kirstein, City Center, and the Rockefeller Foundation," in *Legacies of Twentieth-Century Dance*, 305–16.

28. Debra Hickenlooper Sowell, *The Christensen Brothers: An American Dance Epic* (Amsterdam: Harwood Academic, 1998).

29. Mark Franko, *The Work of Dance: Labor, Movement and Identity in the 1930s* (Middletown, CT: Wesleyan University Press, 2002); Gay Morris, *A Game for Dancers: Performing Modernism in the Postwar Years, 1945–1960* (Middletown, CT: Wesleyan University Press, 2006).

30. Andrea Harris, *Making Ballet American: Modernism before and beyond Balanchine* (New York: Oxford University Press, 2017).

31. Charles Joseph, *Stravinsky and Balanchine: A Journey of Invention* (New Haven, CT: Yale University Press, 2002).

32. Charles Joseph, *Stravinsky's Ballets* (New Haven, CT: Yale University Press, 2012).

33. Stephanie Jordan, *Moving Music: Dialogues with Music in Twentieth-Century Ballet* (London: Dance Books, 2000); *Stravinsky Dances: Re-Visions across a Century* (London: Dance Books, 2007).

34. Elizabeth Bergman Crist, *Music for the Common Man: Aaron Copland in the Depression and War* (New York: Oxford University Press, 2008).

35. Adrienne McLean, *Dying Swans and Madmen: Ballet, the Body, and Narrative Cinema* (New Brunswick, NJ: Rutgers University Press, 2008); Beth Genné, "Glorifying the American Woman: George Balanchine and Josephine Baker," *Discourses in Dance* 3, no. 1 (2005).

36. Constance Valis Hill, *Brotherhood in Rhythm: The Jazz Tap Dancing of the Nicholas Brothers* (New York: Cooper Square Press, 2002); Sally Banes, "Balanchine

and Black Dance," in *Writing Dancing in the Age of Postmodernism* (Hanover, NH: Wesleyan University Press, 1994), 53–69; Brenda Dixon Gottschild, *Digging the Africanist Presence in American Performance: Dance and Other Contexts* (Westport, CT: Greenwood Press, 1996).

Chapter 1

1. On Kirstein and his family's background, see Martin Duberman, *The Worlds of Lincoln Kirstein* (Evanston, IL: Northwestern University Press, 2008), 1–71.

2. Among his publications during this time period were "The Diaghilev Period," *Hound & Horn* 3, no. 4 (1930): 468–501 and "Dance Chronicle: Kreutzberg; Wigman; *Pas d'Acier*; The Future," *Hound & Horn* 4, no. 4 (1931): 573–80.

3. Louis Kirstein's 1938 annual salary from Filene's was reported as $80,000, far above average weekly industry wages of $17.86. "Salaries and Wages," *New Republic*, December 27, 1939, 280–81.

4. Louis Kirstein to Henry Kirstein, September 18, 1934, LEK.

5. "Mina Curtiss, Author and Editor, Dies at 89," *NYT*, November 5, 1985.

6. "Publisher George Kirstein," *CT*, April 5, 1986; "George Kirstein; Publisher of Liberal Weekly," *LAT*, April 5, 1986.

7. The most definitive account of Balanchine's upbringing and early career, from which the following information has been summarized, is Kendall, *Balanchine and the Lost Muse*.

8. On Balanchine's work for Diaghilev, see Garafola, *Diaghilev's Ballets Russes*, 134–41.

9. On the Diaghilev diaspora of the early 1930s, see Kathrine Sorley Walker, *De Basil's Ballets Russes* (New York: Atheneum, 1983); Vicente García-Márquez, *The Ballets Russes: Colonel de Basil's Ballets Russes de Monte Carlo, 1932–1952* (New York: Knopf, 1990); and Judith Chazin-Bennahum, *René Blum and the Ballets Russes: In Search of a Lost Life* (Oxford: Oxford University Press, 2011).

10. For a concise overview of the history of *Hound & Horn*, see Michael Faherty, "*Hound and Horn* (1937–34)" in *The Oxford Critical and Cultural History of Modernist Magazines*, eds. Peter Brooker and Andrew Thacker, vol. 2 (North America, 1894–1960), 420–36.

11. On the organization and activities of the Harvard Society for Contemporary Art and its relationship to the nascent Museum of Modern Art, see Nicholas Fox Weber, *Patron Saints: Five Rebels Who Opened America to a New Art, 1928–1943* (New York: Knopf, 1992), 1–123.

12. Lincoln Kirstein to Rose Kirstein, October 11, 1933, LEK.

13. Lincoln Kirstein, "Ballet," *Vogue*, November 1, 1933.

14. Taper, *Balanchine, a Biography*, 151. Robert Gottlieb's more recent biography similarly maintains that starting a school was one of the non-negotiable conditions laid down by Balanchine before agreeing to come to the United States in 1933. Gottlieb, *George Balanchine: The Ballet Maker*, 70.

15. LKD, June 15, 1933.

16. On Blum, de Basil, and the organization of the Ballets Russes de Monte Carlo, see Sorley Walker, *De Basil's Ballets Russes*, 3–9; García-Márquez, *The Ballets Russes*, 5–6; Chazin-Bennahum, *René Blum and the Ballets Russes*, 99–105 and 115–17.

17. Sorley Walker, *De Basil's Ballets Russes*, 7–9 and 20–21; García-Marquez, *The Ballets Russes*, 6–9; Chazin-Bennahum, *René Blum and the Ballets Russes*, 119–27.

18. On *Cotillon*, see García-Marquez, *The Ballets Russes*, 10–21; Chazin-Bennahum, *René Blum and the Ballets Russes*, 119–21; *Balanchine Catalogue*, 109–10. On *La Concurrence*, see García-Marquez, *The Ballets Russes*, 21–27; Chazin-Bennahum, *René Blum and the Ballets Russes*, 121–24; *Balanchine Catalogue*, 110.

19. On Les Ballets 1933, see Sorley Walker, *De Basil's Ballets Russes*, 21, and García-Márquez, *The Ballets Russes*, 46. On Dimitriev's background, see Kendall, *Balanchine and the Lost Muse*, 213–14.

20. Walker, *De Basil's Ballets Russes*, 1–2; Chazin-Bennahum, *René Blum and the Ballets Russes*, 139–40.

21. Ibid.

22. References to this longer history of Warburg and Kirstein's interest in ballet appear in later press accounts of the American Ballet's early performances. "Ballet Will Make Debut December 6," *HC*, November 23, 1934; "American Ballet School Gets Test This Week," *BS*, December 2, 1934.

23. Edward M. M. Warburg, *As I Recall, Some Memoirs* (privately published, 1978), 32.

24. Garafola, *Diaghilev's Ballets Russes*, 188–200 and 262–69.

25. Romola Nijinsky's *Nijinsky* was published in 1934, and Kirstein received no official credit for his work on the volume. Kirstein's manuscript is held by JRDD–NYPL.

26. On Virgil Thomson's career during this period, see Alexandra Gail Sundman, "The Making of an American Expatriate Composer in Paris: A Contextual Study of the Music and Critical Writings of Virgil Thomson, 1921–1940" (PhD diss., Yale University, 1999), 365–433.

27. Thomson's memoirs report of "daily morning visits from Lincoln Kirstein, deeply excited by the ballets and looking for a way to work with them." Virgil Thomson, *Virgil Thomson* (New York: Knopf 1966, reprinted 1967), 224.

28. LKD, June 3, 1933.

29. LKD, June 7, 1933.

30. Ibid.

31. While the ballet's German title is *Die sieben Todsünden*, and the work is today best known by the English title *The Seven Deadly Sins*, Kirstein's diary refers to it as *The Seven Capital Sins*, a more literal translation of the ballet's original French title, as it was billed upon its premiere on June 7, 1933, *Les Sept Péchés capitaux: Spectacle sur des poèmes de Bert Brecht*. On the ballet's genesis and background and for a discussion and analysis of its scenario and score, see Stephen Hinton, *Weill's Musical Theater: Stages of Reform* (Berkeley: University of California Press, 2012), 199–213.

32. LKD, June 7, 1933.

33. Ibid.

34. Ibid.

35. Ibid.

36. LKD, June 16, 1933.

37. Ibid.

38. LKD, June 23, 1933.

39. LKD, June 14, 1933.

40. Ibid.

41. LKD, July 8, 1933.

42. Ibid.

43. Ibid.

44. LKD, July 11, 1933.

45. Ibid.

46. Ibid.

47. Ibid.

48. Ibid.

49. Ibid.

50. Kirstein, *Thirty Years*, 30.

51. LKD, July 13, 16, 1933.

52. LKD July 16, 1933.

53. Ibid.

54. Kirstein, *Blast at Ballet*, 28.

55. The original letter, dated July 16, 1933, is located in the archives of the Wadsworth Atheneum in Hartford, Connecticut, and a facsimile reproduction is included in (S) *MGZRS-Res.+ 82-4201, Producing Company of the School of American Ballet Scrapbook, NYPL. A published version of the letter, cited here, is found in Francis Mason, ed., *I Remember Balanchine: Recollections of the Ballet Master by Those Who Knew Him* (New York: Doubleday, 1991), 113–19.

56. On Chick Austin's life and career, see Eugene R. Gaddis, *Magician of the Modern: Chick Austin and the Transformation of the Arts in America* (New York: Knopf, 2000), and also Weber, *Patron Saints*.

57. See Gaddis, *Magician of the Modern*, 198–271.

58. LKD, July 21, 1933.

59. Kirstein, *Thirty Years*, 31.

60. Kirstein to Austin, July 16, 1933, in Mason, *I Remember Balanchine*, 116.

61. Ibid.

62. Ibid., 117.

63. Ibid.

64. Ibid., 115–16.

65. Ibid., 117, emphasis in original.

66. Ibid.

67. Ibid., 116.

68. Despite the liberal politics of the dance establishment, black dancers faced significant challenges to full involvement in training and performance activities in both ballet and modern dance, due to segregation imposed by studio landlords and theater managers or the reluctance of many white students to take classes alongside African Americans. See Julia Foulkes, *Modern Bodies: Dance and American Modernism from Martha Graham to Alvin Ailey* (Chapel Hill: University of North Carolina Press, 2002), 54–56, and Brenda Dixon Gottschild, *Joan Meyers Brown and the Audacious Hope of the Black Ballerina* (New York: Palgrave, 2012).

69. LKD, July 19, 1933.

70. Ibid.

71. Ibid.

72. Austin to Whom It May Concern, August 9, 1933, Producing Company of the School of American Ballet Scrapbook.

73. Ibid.

74. LKD, August 7, 1933.

75. Lincoln Kirstein to Chick Austin, August 11, 1933. Original letter in archives of Wadsworth Atheneum, Hartford, Connecticut with facsimile reproduction located in Producing Company of the School of American Ballet Scrapbook.

76. Ibid.

77. Vladimir Pavlovich Dimitriev was an opera singer turned impresario who was responsible for organizing the tour of Germany that allowed Balanchine, Tamara Geva, and Alexandra Danilova to emigrate west. Dancer Lidia Ivanova was also to have traveled with the group but was killed in a mysterious boating accident two weeks prior to their departure. See Kendall, *Balanchine and the Lost Muse*, 213–14 and 219–29.

78. Lincoln Kirstein to Chick Austin, August 11, 1933. Omitted text illegible.

79. Ibid.

80. LK Diaries, July 19, 1933.

81. Ibid.

82. Ibid.

83. Ibid.

84. Ibid.

85. Lincoln Kirstein to Chick Austin, August 12, 1933, Producing Company of the School of American Ballet Scrapbook.

86. On the courtship and marriage of Felix Warburg and Frieda Schiff, see Ron Chernow, *The Warburgs: The Twentieth-Century Odyssey of a Remarkable Jewish Family* (New York: Random House, 1993), 45–54.

87. Warburg, *As I Recall*, 53.

88. LKD, October 17, 1933.

89. "Ocean Travelers," *NYT*, October 17, 1933.

90. LKD, October 17, 1933.

91. Ibid.

92. Ibid.

93. "Project Free School for Ballet Here," *HC*, October 18, 1933.

94. "Ballet in Hartford," *HC*, October 18, 1933.

95. Ibid.

96. "Two Arrive Here Today to Set Up School of Ballet," *HC*, October 19, 1933.

97. Marc Blitzstein, "Forecast and Review: Talk–Music–Dance; New York, 1933," *MM*, November–December 1933, 35.

98. Ibid., 36.

99. John Martin, "The Dance: The American Ballet," *NYT*, October 22, 1933.

100. Ibid.

101. Ibid.

102. LKD, October 4, 1933.

103. The remark about apartments is found in the unpublished memoirs of James T. Soby: "It was rather difficult to explain to [Balanchine] in French that people in Hartford did not build or live in apartments in the eighteenth century." Quoted in Gaddis, *Magician of the Modern*, 217.

104. Kirstein, *Thirty Years*, 33.

105. Ibid., 32–33.

106. "Dance Teachers Object to Free School of Ballet," *HC*, October 19, 1933.

107. "Says Ballet School Won't Harm Teachers," *HC*, October 22, 1933.

108. LKD, October 19, 1933.

109. Ibid.

110. Ibid.

111. Gaddis, *Magician of the Modern*, 177.

112. LKD, October 17, 18, 1933.

113. Kirstein, "The Ballet in Hartford," 66.

114. Ibid., 67.

115. Ibid.

116. Ibid.

117. LKD, October 20, 1933.

118. Ibid.

119. Ibid.

120. "Plans Abandoned Here for American Ballet," *HC*, October 30, 1933.

121. *Hartford Times*, October 28, 1933, quoted in Gaddis, *Magician of the Modern*, 219–20.

122. Philip Johnson to Chick Austin, September 28, 1933, facsimile located in Producing Company of the School of American Ballet Scrapbook.

123. Philip Johnson to Chick Austin, October 26, 1933, facsimile located in Producing Company of the School of American Ballet Scrapbook.

124. Ibid.

125. Advertisement, *NYT*, November 26, 1933; Advertisement, *NYHT*, December 3, 1933.

126. "School of American Ballet Opens Dec. 11," *NYHT*, December 3, 1933.

127. John Martin, "The Dance: Massine Again," *NYT*, December 17, 1933.

128. LKD, December 27, 28, 1933.

129. LKD, December 29, 1933.

130. School of American Ballet website, http://www.sab.org/school/history/1934.php, accessed October 28, 2013.

131. "School of American Ballet Opens Dec. 11," *NYHT*, December 3, 1933.

132. John Martin, "The Dance: Massine Again," *NYT*, December 17, 1933.

133. Ibid.

134. John Martin, "Lifar Makes Debut; Diaghileff Protégé," *NYT*, November 6, 1933; "Serge Lifar Makes American Debut," *MA*, November 10, 1933, 29.

135. "Coming of Monte Carlo Ballet a Thrill for New York Public," *MA*, December 25, 1933, 11; W. P. T., "The Monte Carlo Ballet Russe," *CSM*, December 30, 1933.

Chapter 2

1. LKD, January 22, 1934. On the role of the Littlefield sisters and other Philadelphia dancers in the early history of the American Ballet and its School, see Sharon Skeel, "First Steps: Balanchine's Early Ties to Philadelphia," paper presented at the Dance Critics Association, Philadelphia, June 2014.

2. LKD, January 22, 1934.

3. Ibid.

4. LKD, January 6, 1934.

5. LKD, January 18, 22, 23, 25, 1934.

6. LKD, February 21, 1934.

7. Quoted in Reynolds, *Repertory in Review*, 44.

8. Ibid.

9. Ibid.

10. *Les Songes* is not discussed in Milhaud's autobiography *Notes without Music*, and the only mention of Balanchine is in relation to a ballet for which Milhaud did not write the music, a passing reference the 1925 *Barabau*, the choreographer's first original project for Diaghilev's Ballets Russes, with a score by Vittorio Rieti and decor by Maurice Utrillo. Darius Milhaud, *Notes without Music* (New York: Knopf, 1952), 145–46.

11. Quoted in Reynolds, *Repertory in Review*, 42. Per the *Balanchine Catalogue*, Milhaud's score for *Les Songes* "could not be obtained for performance in America."

12. Publication date per the catalogue of works in Paul Collaer, *Darius Milhaud*, translated and edited by Jane Hohfeld Galante (San Francisco: San Francisco Press, 1988), 322. On Milhaud's business correspondence and general attitudes regarding the relationship between art and finance, see Louis K. Epstein, "Toward a Theory of Patronage: Funding for Music Composition in France, 1918–1939" (PhD diss., Harvard University, 2013), 260–85.

13. Lynn Garafola, "George Antheil and the Dance," in *Legacies of Twentieth-Century Dance* (Middletown, CT: Wesleyan University Press, 2005), 256–76, 261.

14. Ibid., 261–65.

15. Ibid., 262, 264.

16. George Antheil, *Bad Boy of Music* (Garden City, NY: Doubleday, Doran, 1945), 276.

17. For a comprehensive survey of the origins of *Serenade* and the significant changes made to the ballet subsequently, see Alastair Macaulay, "Serenade: Evolutionary Stages," *Ballet Review* 44, no. 4 (Winter 2016–17), 70–119.

18. Ruthanna Boris, "Serenade," in Robert Gottlieb, ed., *Reading Dance: A Gathering of Memoirs, Reportage, Criticism, Profiles, Interviews, and Some Uncategorizable Extras* (New York: Pantheon Books, 2008), 1063, 1066. Boris recalls that the ballet was begun "in late 1933," which is inconsistent with evidence cited in the previous chapter that the school held its first classes on December 29, 1933.

19. Annabelle Lyon Interview, 1979, conducted by Elizabeth Kendall, MGZMT 3-1861 (transcript), JRDD–NYPL, 68, hereafter "Annabelle Lyon Interview."

20. Ibid.

21. LKD, March 14, 1934.

22. Boris, "Serenade," 1064.

23. LKD, March 14, 1934.

24. Boris, "Serenade," 1064.

25. Annabelle Lyon Interview, 59.

26. LKD, March 15, 21, 1934.

27. LKD, March 21, 1934.

28. LKD, March 15, 1934.

29. Ibid.

30. The de Basil company had begun their 1933–34 US tour with performances at the St. James Theatre on Broadway, opening December 22, 1933, giving dancers such as Lyon the opportunity to see *Cotillon* and *La Concurrence* at precisely the time when the American Ballet school was being organized. See Sorley Walker, *De Basil's Ballets Russes*, 31–34.

31. Annabelle Lyon Interview, 47, 48, 50.

32. LKD, January 26, February 2, 13, April 17, 26, 1934.

33. LKD, March 29, 1934.

34. LKD, April 24, 1934.

35. Arnold Haskell, "Dancing in the United States," *DT*, April 1934, 12.

36. Advertisement, *DO*, February 1934, 10.

37. "Persistence for the Ballet," *DO*, March 1934, 14.

38. "American Ballet?" *DO*, May 1934, 38.

39. Edward M. M. Warburg in Mason, *I Remember Balanchine*, 125.

40. *Serenade* is identified as such in literally innumerable sources. Three such examples are these: "The ballet was the first created by Balanchine when he came to the United States," Peter Brisson and Clement Crisp, *The International Book of Ballet* (New York: Stein and Day, 1971), 225; "Balanchine's first ballet in America . . ." Nancy Reynolds and Malcolm McCormick, *No Fixed Points: Dance in the Twentieth Century* (New Haven, CT: Yale University Press, 2003), 268; "*Serenade*, to music by Tchaikovsky, was Balanchine's first American ballet," Jennifer Homans, *Apollo's Angels: A History of Ballet* (New York: Random House, 2010), 515.

41. LKD, May 20, 1934.

42. Ibid.

43. LKD, May 31, June 5, 6, 8, 1934.

44. John Martin, "The Dance: CWA Project," *NYT*, June 10, 1934.

45. Chernow, *The Warburgs*, 95.

46. Ibid., 95–96.

47. Ibid., 92–94.

48. Invitation enclosed in letter from George Antheil to Mary Louise Curtis Bok, June 5, 1934, George Antheil Collection, LOC.

49. Helen Warden, "Junior Ballet to Dance for Warburg Guests," *New York World-Telegram*, undated clipping, PDP.

50. Ibid.

51. LKD, June 8, 1934. All details in this paragraph from this diary entry.

52. LKD, June 9, 1934. All details in this paragraph from this diary entry.

53. "Rain Defers Recital of Ballet School, *NYT*, June 10, 1934.

54. American Ballet Programs, *MGZB (Programs), JRDD-NYPL.

55. "Ballet School Gives 2 World Premieres," *NYT*, June 11, 1934.

56. Lucius Beebe, "This New York," *NYHT*, June 16, 1934.

57. Ibid.

58. Ibid.

59. Ibid.

60. American Ballet Programs, *MGZB (Programs), JRDD-NYPL.

61. Edward Warburg to Jo Mielziner, June 28, 1934, MGZM Res War E Warburg, JRDD–NYPL.

62. Ibid.

63. LKD, July 12, 1934.

64. Ibid.

65. Ibid.

66. LKD, July 13, 1934.

67. LKD, July 14, 1934.

68. LKD, July 19, 1934.

69. Ibid.

70. Ibid.

71. "Dance and Studio Notes," *DO*, June–July 1934, 59.

72. Ibid.

73. LKD, August 27, 1934.

74. LKD, August 27, 28, 29, 30, 1934.

75. LKD, September 6, 1934.

76. LKD, September 12, 1934.

77. LKD, September 18, 19, 1934.

78. LKD, June 9, 1934.

79. LKD, October 16, 1934. In addition to being listed in numerous press notices, this schedule of all four performances was printed in the "gala premiere" Thursday night program, facsimile located in Producing Company of the School of American Ballet Scrapbook; a program for the Saturday matinee performance (in which the order was *Mozartiana, Alma Mater, Transcendence*) is located in Yvonne Patterson and William Dollar Papers, (S) *MGZMD 259, Scrapbook 1934–36, Box 18, JRDD–NYPL, hereafter PDP.

80. LKD, September 26, 1934.

81. LKD, September 28, 1934.

82. LKD, February 11, 1933.

83. Ibid.

84. LKD, February 14, 1933.

85. Ibid.

86. Ibid.

87. LKD, April 14, 1934.

88. Ibid.

89. Ibid.

90. LKD, May 5, 22, 1934.

91. LKD, May 23, 1934.

92. LKD, June 11, 1934.

93. Ibid.

94. On the commission of *Alma Mater*, the Kay Swift–Gershwin affair, and Swift's subsequent divorce from James Warburg, see Vicky Ohl, *Fine and Dandy: The Life and Work of Kay Swift* (New Haven, CT: Yale University Press, 2004), 88–89.

95. LKD, June 21, 1934.

96. The score for *Alma Mater* remains unpublished, but drafts and final versions of the score as well as complete sets of orchestral parts are located in the Kay Swift Papers, Irving S. Gilmore Music Library, Yale University.

97. Weber, *Patron Saints*, 258.

98. Reynolds, *Repertory in Review*, 39.

99. Quoted in Reynolds, *Repertory in Review*, 39.

100. Ibid.

101. LKD, September 28, 1934.

102. LKD, September 27, 1934.

103. LKD, April 14, 1934.

104. On the method and philosophy of "period modernism" first developed by Diaghilev around 1915, see Garafola, *Diaghilev's Ballets Russes*, 90–97.

105. LKD, September 28, 29, October 1, 4, 1934.

106. LKD, October 1, 1934.

107. Marya Mannes, "Vogue's Spotlight," *Vogue*, February 15, 1935, 52.

108. *Balanchine Catalogue*, 121–22.

109. LKD, October 15, 1934.

110. LKD, October 18, 19, 1934.

111. LKD, October 19, 1934.

112. Collaer, *Darius Milhaud*, 322.

113. Chazin-Bennahum, *René Blum and the Ballets Russes*, 43–46.

114. LKD, October 9, 25, 1934; Program for Saturday December 8 matinee performance, PDP.

115. Edward Warburg, "Can Ballet Go Native?" *Dance*, January 1937, 12.

116. Kirstein, *Thirty Years*, 41.

117. Press release, Producing Company of the School of American Ballet Scrapbook.

118. Advertisement, *NYT*, November 18, 1934; Advertisement, *NYHT*, November 25, 1934; Advertisement, *NYT*, December 2, 1934; Advertisement, *HC*, December 6, 1934; "Camera Panorama," *WP*, November 18, 1934; "Ballet Artists in Rehearsal," *LAT*, November 25, 1934.

119. "Hartford to See First Production of U. S. Ballet," *NYHT*, November 16, 1934.

120. "American Ballet," *BS*, November 18, 1934; "Hartford to See First Production of U. S. Ballet," *NYHT*, November 16, 1934.

121. "Hartford to See First Production of U. S. Ballet," *NYHT*, November 16, 1934.

122. Ralph Renaud, "Utopia in All Its Glory Beckons to New York," *WP*, November 24, 1934; "Hartford to See First Production of U. S. Ballet," *NYHT*, November 16, 1934.

123. Press release, Producing Company of the School of American Ballet Scrapbook; Ralph Renaud, "Utopia in All Its Glory Beckons to New York," *WP*, November 24, 1934

124. "Ballet Will Make Debut December 6," *HC*, November 23, 1934; "American Ballet School Gets Test This Week," *BS*, December 2, 1934. Subsequent quotes in this paragraph are from these two articles.

125. In interviews conducted by McNeil Lowry, Balanchine toward the end of his life maintained that he "couldn't even speak English" when he arrived in the United States and that around 1935 "I really couldn't read; I couldn't understand what I read." McNeil Lowry, "Our Local Correspondences: Conversations with Balanchine," *New Yorker*, September 12, 1983, 57.

126. "*Alma Mater* Given at American Ballet Opening in Hartford," *CSM*, December 7, 1934.

127. "Hartford Sees Premiere of Ballet School," *NYHT*, December 7, 1934.

128. "Ballet Appears in a Burlesque of Our Foibles," *WP*, December 7, 1934.

129. T. H. P[arker], "Ballet Wins Ovation in Avery Debut," *HC*, December 7, 1934.

130. Ibid.

131. Ibid.

132. "American Ballet," *BS*, November 18, 1934; "American Ballet," *WP*, December 2, 1934.

133. "*Alma Mater* Given at American Ballet Opening in Hartford," *CSM*, December 7, 1934; "Ballet Wins Ovation in Avery Debut," *HC*, December 7, 1934.

134. Weber, *Patron Saints*, 257; Ohl, *Fine and Dandy*, 93.

135. Lucius Beebe, "An Evening Dedicated to the Arts," *NYHT*, December 9, 1934.

136. Ibid.

137. Ibid.

138. Ibid.

139. John Martin, "The Dance: New Company," *NYT*, December 16, 1934.

140. Ibid.

141. LKD, December 16, 1934.

142. LKD, December 17, 1934.

143. Louis Kirstein to Lincoln Kirstein, December 17, 1934, LEK.

144. LKD, December 8, 1934.

145. LKD, December 6, 1934.

146. T. H. Parker, "New Ballet School Is Busy Scene," *HC*, November 30, 1934.

147. LKD, December 6, 1934. I am grateful to Robert Greskovic for advising of the location of the drawing of William Okie's design at Museum of Modern Art (MoMA).

148. LKD, December 7, 1934.

149. LKD, December 8, 1934.

150. Ibid.

Chapter 3

1. Kirstein, *Blast at Ballet*, 28. On John Martin's life, career, and views on modernism and modern dance, see Gay Morris, "Modernism's Role in the Theory of John Martin and Edwin Denby," *Dance Research* 22, no. 2 (Winter 2004): 168–84.

2. Taper, *Balanchine: A Biography*, 161–62; Gottlieb, *George Balanchine: The Ballet Maker*, 81; Teachout, *All In the Dances: A Brief Life of George Balanchine*, 66. Balanchine's biographers situate Martin's conversion in 1948, in the wake of Ballet Society's premiere of *Orpheus*: Taper, *Balanchine: A Biography*, 225, 236; Gottlieb, *George Balanchine: The Ballet Maker*, 113; Teachout, *All In the Dances: A Brief Life of George Balanchine*, 92.

3. David Nice, *Prokofiev: From Russia to the West, 1891–1935* (New Haven, CT: Yale University Press, 2003); Elizabeth Bergman Crist, *Music for the Common Man*; Deborah Jowitt, *Time and the Dancing Image* (Berkeley: University of California Press, 1988), 151–233; Foulkes, *Modern Bodies*, 27–50; Michael Denning, *The Cultural Front: The Laboring of American Culture in the Twentieth Century* (London: Verso, 1997/2010); Ellen Graff, *Stepping Left: Dance and Politics in New York City, 1928–1942* (Durham, NC: Duke University Press, 1997); Mark Franko, *Dancing Modernism/Performing Politics* (Bloomington: Indiana University Press, 1995).

4. "Serge Lifar Makes American Debut," *MA*, November 10, 1933.

5. W. P. T., "The Monte Carlo Ballet Russe," *CSM*, December 30, 1933.

6. John Martin, "New Ballet Russe Warmly Greeted," *NYT*, December 23, 1933.

7. John Martin, "Spirited Program by Russian Ballet," *NYT*, March 17, 1934.

8. John Martin, "*Thamar* Revived by Ballet Russe," *NYT*, October 12, 1935.

9. Henry Prunieres, "The Ballet in Paris," *NYT*, August 20, 1933.

10. L. Franc Scheuer, "Ballets Russes de Monte Carlo and Ballets 1933," *DT*, July 1933.

11. For a more detailed discussion of Massine's symphonic ballets, especially *Choreartium*, see Stephanie Jordan, *Moving Music: Dialogues with Music in Twentieth-Century Ballet* (London: Dance Books, 2000), 50–56.

12. Ibid.

13. Anatole Chujoy, "The Case against Massine," *Dance*, December 1936, 28–29.

14. Anatole Chujoy, *The Symphonic Ballet* (New York: Kamin, 1937), 42.

15. LKD, December 10, 1934.

16. Martin Duberman writes that this "discord among the four principals" was somewhat old hat, and that the "arguments and accusations among them had by this point become repetitive." Duberman, *The Worlds of Lincoln Kirstein*, 272.

17. LKD, October 23, 1934. All subsequent quotes in this paragraph from this entry.

18. LKD, December 19, 1934.

19. Ibid.

20. Annabelle Lyon Interview, 64.

21. LKD, October 19, 1934.

22. LKD, January 23, 1935.

23. Ibid.

24. LKD, June 18, 1934.

25. Warburg, *As I Recall*, 54.

26. LKD, October 11, 1934.

27. LKD, January 2, 1935.

28. LKD, December 12, 1934.

29. LKD, December 27, 1934.

30. LKD, January 4, 1935.

31. LKD, January 5, 1935.

32. LKD, January 18, 1935.

33. LKD, February 11, 1935; John Martin, "The Dance: Ballet Debut," *NYT*, February 24, 1935.

34. "Dance Notes," *NYHT*, February 10, 1935; "American Ballet Opens Here March 1 at Adelphi Theater," *NYHT*, February 17, 1935; "American Ballet Broadens Season," *NYT*, February 22, 1935.

35. LKD, June 14, 22, 1934.

36. LKD, September 19, 1934.

37. LKD, January 27, 1935.

38. LKD, January 28, 1935.

39. LKD, February 12, 13, 1935.

40. LKD, February 14, 1935.

41. LKD, July 4, 1934.

42. LKD, November 13, 1934.

43. Ibid.

44. Ibid.

45. LKD, December 29, 1934.

46. Ibid.

47. LKD, January 12, 1935.

48. LKD, January 28, 1935.

49. "Dance Notes," *NYHT*, February 10, 1935; "American Ballet Opens Here March 1 at Adelphi Theater," *NYHT*, February 17, 1935.

50. Advertisement, *NYHT*, February 3, 1935.

51. Advertisement, *NYHT*, February 3, 1935; "American Ballet: New Dance Group Under Balanchine in Program at Bryn Mawr College," unidentified clipping, PDP; "Notes of Social Activities in New York and Elsewhere," *NYT*, February 1, 1935.

52. LKD, February 7, 1935.

53. Program, PDP.

54. LKD, February 7, 1935.

55. Ibid.

56. Ibid.

57. LKD, February 8, 1935.

58. Ibid.

59. "American Ballet: New Dance Group under Balanchine in Program at Bryn Mawr College," unidentified clipping, PDP.

60. "Artistic Offering by American Ballet," unidentified clipping, PDP.

61. "Artistic Offering by American Ballet," "American Ballet: New Dance Group under Balanchine," PDP.

62. "American Ballet: New Dance Group under Balanchine," PDP.

63. "Artistic Offering by American Ballet," unidentified clipping, PDP.

64. "American Ballet: New Dance Group under Balanchine," PDP.

65. Ibid.

66. Ruth Page to Marian Heinly Page, February 11, 1935, Ruth Page Collection, (S) *MGZMD 16, Correspondence, Folder 35C1, JRDD–NYPL.

67. John Martin, *Ruth Page, An Intimate Biography* (New York: Marcel Dekker, 1977), 74–75.

68. Ruth Page to Marian Heinly Page, February 11, 1935, Ruth Page Collection, JRDD.

69. Ibid.

70. Ibid.

71. LKD, February 15, 1935.

72. LKD, February 17, 1935.

73. LKD, February 18, 1935.

74. Ibid.

75. LKD, March 1, 3, 1935. At least one photo survives of Haakon with the hoop in discussion with Balanchine. George Balanchine Clippings File, JRDD–NYPL, Folder 1 "1926–64," uncredited photo from *Delineator*, September 1935.

76. LKD, February 12, 1935.

77. LKD, February 12–13, 1935.

78. LKD, February 14, 1935.

79. LKD, February 20, 1935.

80. Ibid.

81. LKD, February 20.

82. Kirstein records that his first lesson with Hawkins took place on January 24, 1935, and that they continued on a regular basis through as late as June. On Stuart, see Jennifer Dunning, "Muriel Stuart, 90, Dancer for Pavolva and Teacher," *NYT*, January 30, 1991.

83. "American Ballet Gets Ready for Premiere Here," *NYHT*, February 25, 1935.

84. Ibid.

85. On this period in Balanchine's youth see Kendall, *Balanchine and the Lost Muse*, 113–71.

86. LKD, February 19, 1935.

87. Ibid.

88. Ken Bloom, *The Routledge Guide to Broadway* (New York: Routledge, 2007), 82–83.

89. Advertisement, *The Billboard Theatrical Index, 1933–34*, 19.

90. Ibid.; "Theatres with Plays Presented (With Seating Capacities)," *The Billboard Theatrical Index, 1934–35*, 51.

91. LKD, February 4, 1935.

92. "American Ballet Opens Here March 1 at Adelphi Theater," *NYHT*, February 17, 1935.

93. "American Ballet Broadens Season," *NYT*, February 22, 1935.

94. LKD, February 4, 1935.

95. John Martin, "The Dance: Ballet Debut," *NYT*, February 24, 1935.

96. Ibid.

97. "American Ballet Gets Ready for Premiere Here," *NYHT*, February 25, 1935.

98. LKD, February 25, 1935.

99. LKD, February 27, 1935.

100. LKD, February 27, 1935. Antheil's orchestration of *Serenade* is widely considered not to be extant and is listed as such in Linda Whitesitt, *The Life and Music of George Antheil* (Ann Arbor, MI: UMI Research Press, 1983), 140, 249. Although Antheil discusses his work with Balanchine in his memoirs, he does not mention *Serenade* by name, discussing only *Dreams*. Antheil, *Bad Boy of Music*, 270–71, 276–77. Per Laurel Fay of G. Schirmer, Inc., the score could be located among uncatalogued Antheil holdings at the Curtis Institute or the New York Public Library for the Performing Arts. When the Antheil estate was acquired by Schirmer in 1995, the *Serenade* orchestration was not among the items received, though documentation at the time alluded to other Balanchine-related materials which "may be rotting somewhere in an ABT warehouse." The Antheil orchestration of *Serenade* and these other unidentified materials still await discovery. Personal correspondence with Laurel Fay, February 20, 2013.

101. Lincoln Kirstein to Muriel Draper, February 28 [1935], Box 5, Folder 167, MDP. Notably, Antheil continued to tout his work on *Serenade* as an accomplishment in correspondence with his patron Mary Louise Curtis Bok, mentioning the ballet in a letter of September 29, 1935, George Antheil Collection, LOC.

102. LKD, February 28, 1935.

103. American Ballet Adelphi Flier, PDP.

104. Ibid.

105. Ibid.

106. American Ballet Program 1935, PDP.

107. Lincoln Kirstein, "The Diaghilev Period," *Hound & Horn*, July–September 1930, 469–70.

108. Lincoln Kirstein, "In Defense of the Ballet," *MM*, May–June 1934, 190.

109. LKD, February 12–13, 1935.

110. LKD, February 17, 19, 1935.

111. LKD, February 19, 1935.

112. LKD, March 1, 1935.

113. "American Ballet Opens at Adelphi with Four Dances," *New York American*, undated clipping, PDP.

114. LKD, March 1, 1935.

115. LKD, March 2, 5 1935.

116. LKD, March 1, 1935. All subsequent quotes in this paragraph from this entry.

117. LKD, March 4, 1935/.

118. Ibid.

119. LKD, March 8, 1935.

120. Ibid.

121. LKD, March 12, 1935.

122. Ibid.

123. LKD, March 10, 1935.

124. Ibid.

125. Stephen Walsh, *Stravinsky: The Second Exile, France and America, 1934–1971* (New York: Knopf, 2006), 12.

126. LKD, March 10, 1935.

127. LKD, March 17, 1935, for this and all details in this paragraph.

128. R. M. S., "American Ballet Opens at Adelphi with Four Dances," *New York American*, undated clipping, PDP.

129. Samuel Chotzinoff, "Words and Music: The American Ballet" *New York Post*, PDP.

130. Ibid.

131. Uncredited photo of Tamara Geva, William Dollar, and Charles Laskey, PDP.

132. "Dance: American Ballet," *CSM*, March 2, 1935.

133. Ibid.

134. Samuel Chotzinoff, "Words and Music: The American Ballet" *New York Post*, PDP.

135. LKD, March 3, 1935.

136. Lehmann Engel, "Les Ballets Américains," *MM*, March–April, 1935, 138–41.

137. Ibid., 139.

138. Ibid.

139. Ibid., 140, 141.

140. "The American Ballet, Adelphi Theatre, from March 1 to March 17," April 1935, *American Dancer*, PDP.

141. Ibid.

142. H[enry] G[ilfond], "American Ballet, Adelphi Theatre, Wednesday Eve., March 14, 1935," *DO*, April 1935, 42.

143. Ibid.

144. Ibid.

145. John Martin, "American Ballet Makes Its Debut," *NYT*, March 2, 1935.

146. Ibid.

147. John Martin, "American Ballet Opens Second Bill," *NYT*, March 6, 1935.

148. John Martin, "The Dance: The Ballet," *NYT*, March 10, 1935.

149. Engel, "Les Ballets Américains," 139.

150. P. S., "Premiere Here Given by American Ballet," *New York World-Telegram*, March 2, 1935, PDP.

151. John Martin, "The Dance: The Ballet," *NYT*, March 10, 1935.

152. LKD, March 2, 1935.

153. LKD, March 6, 1935.

154. LKD, March 16, 1935.

155. Kirstein, *Blast at Ballet*, 28.

156. Jack Beall, "Satirical Ballet Wins Plaudits for Americans," *NYHT*, March 2, 1935.

157. Ibid.

158. P. S., "Premiere Here Given by American Ballet," *New York World-Telegram*, March 2, 1935, PDP.

159. Several such accounts of *Serenade*, all of which attend mostly to the ballet's first presentation in 1934 at Woodlands, are found in Taper, *Balanchine: A Biography*, 155–60; Gottlieb, *George Balanchine: The Ballet Maker*, 77–80; Teachout, *All In the Dances*, 62–6; and Homans, *Apollo's Angels*, 515–19.

Chapter 4

1. Chujoy, *The New York City Ballet*, 52; Buckle with Taras, *George Balanchine, Ballet Master*, 94; Gottlieb, *George Balanchine: The Ballet Maker*, 82; Teachout, *All In the Dances: A Brief Life of George Balanchine*, 68.

2. Kirstein, *Blast at Ballet*, 29.

3. For general accounts of the Metropolitan Opera's history discussed in this chapter, see Irving Kolodin, *The Metropolitan Opera, 1883–1966, a Candid History* (New York: Knopf, 1966), 368–90; *The Golden Horseshoe: The Life and Times of the Metropolitan Opera House* (New York: Viking Press, 1965), 159–95; Martin Mayer, *The Met: One Hundred Years of Grand Opera* (New York: Simon and Schuster, 1983), 202–8; and Joanna Fiedler, *Molto Agitato: The Mayhem behind the Music at the Metropolitan Opera* (New York: Doubleday/Nan A. Talese, 2001), 27–35.

4. Lillian Moore, "The Metropolitan Opera Ballet Story," *Dance Magazine*, January 1951, 20–29, 39–48; George Dorris, "The Metropolitan Opera Ballet, Fresh Starts: Rosina Galli and the Ballets Russes, 1912–1917, *Dance Chronicle* 35, no. 2 (2012), 173–207; Tullia Limarzi, "Metropolitan Opera Ballet," *International Encyclopedia of Dance*, Ed. Selma Jeanne Cohen, New York and London: Oxford University Press, 2005.

5. Ibid.

6. On Augustus Juilliard and the creation of the Juilliard Music Foundation, see Andrea Olmstead, *Juilliard: A History* (Urbana: University of Illinois Press, 1999), 59–65.

7. On the mismanagement of the Juilliard funds by Juilliard heir Frederick Juilliard and trustee Eugene Noble, and the ill-conceived and short-lived Juilliard Graduate School, see Olmstead, *Juilliard: A History*, 62–80.

8. Ibid., 126–27.

9. Ibid.

10. Ibid., 127.

11. On John Erskine's background, interest in opera, and initiatives to promote opera at Juilliard, see Olmstead, *Juilliard: A History*, 101–8, 125–31.

12. "Juilliard Foundation Agrees to Cover Metropolitan Deficit," *BS*, March 4, 1935; "Juilliard Foundation Takes Leading Role at Metropolitan," *CSM*, March 7, 1935; "Juilliard Plan to Aid Opera Is Accepted by Metropolitan," *NYHT*, March 7, 1935; "Opera Accepts Juilliard Terms; Witherspoon to Succeed Gatti," *NYT*, March 7, 1935.

13. Ibid.

14. Ibid.

15. "The New Order at the Metropolitan," *NYHT*, March 9, 1935; Edward Moore, "Metropolitan Opera to Go 'Democratic,'" *CT*, March 24, 1935.

16. Olin Downes, "The Opera's Future," *NYT*, March 10, 1935.

17. Mayer, *The Met*, 205; *The Golden Horseshoe*, 195.

18. Ibid.

19. "Witherspoon Dies of Heart Seizure at Metropolitan," *NYHT*, May 11, 1935; "Opera Head Drops Dead," *LAT*, May 11, 1935; "Witherspoon, Opera Leader, Dies in Office," *CT*, May 11, 1935;

20. "Vacancy Stirs Speculation at Metropolitan," *NYHT*, May 12, 1935; "Metropolitan May Act Today on New Chief," *NYHT*, May 13, 1935; "Johnson Takes Manager's Post at Metropolitan," *CSM*, May 16, 1935; "Johnson Made Opera Head," *NYT*, May 16, 1935.

21. Lincoln Kirstein's history of NYCB mentions this prior relationship but otherwise does not attribute the Metropolitan offer to Warburg connections: "Warburg's father was from olden times an associate of Otto H. Kahn, who with Puccini, Caruso, and Gatti-Casazza before the First World War had led the Met to surpass La Scala as the prime opera house of the world." Kirstein, *Thirty Years*, 52.

22. On Frank Damrosch, James Loeb, and the founding of the Institute of Musical Art, see Olmstead, *Juilliard: A History*, 7–29; on the creation of the Juilliard Music Foundation and the merger of the Institute with the Foundation, 58–95.

23. Olmstead, *Juilliard: A History*, 83.

24. "Juilliard Group of 4 Named to Opera's Board," *NYHT*, May 9, 1935.

25. LKD, January 10, 1935; February 1, 1935.

26. LKD, January 10, 1935.

27. Mayer, *The Met*, 202.

28. On Page's career, see John Martin's monograph (cited below) and Joellen Meglin's forthcoming monograph.

29. Ruth Page to Marian Heinly Page, undated letter, postmarked February 11, 1935, Ruth Page Collection, NYPL–JRDD, Correspondence, Folder 35C1.

30. Ruth Page to Marian Heinly Page, undated letter, postmarked April 2, 1935, Ruth Page Collection, NYPL–JRDD, Correspondence, Folder 35C2.

31. John Martin, *Ruth Page, an Intimate Biography* (New York: Marcel Dekker, 1977), 86.

32. LKD, March 5, 1935.

33. John Martin, "The Dance: At the Opera," *NYT*, March 17, 1935.

34. Ibid.

35. LKD, April 11, 1935.

36. LKD, May 20, 1935.

37. LKD, May 22, 1935.

38. Ibid.

39. LKD, May 24, 1935.

40. Ibid.

41. Ibid.

42. LKD, July 24, 1935.

43. LKD, August 6, 1935.

44. Ibid.

45. "New Ballet Corps Engaged for the Metropolitan," *NYT*, August 8, 1935.

46. Russell Rhodes, "The Coming American Season," *DT*, September 1935, 615.

47. "Editorials: A New Home," *DO*, October 1935, 74.

48. Ibid.

49. Ibid.

50. John Martin, "The Dance: At the Opera," *NYT*, August 18, 1935.

51. "John Martin took a dim view of the new appointment and spared neither vitriol nor space to make his view public"; and "What an ogre John Martin seemed to the ballet world that summer!" Anatole Chujoy, *The New York City Ballet*, 52, 55; "The first voice to be raised in opposition was John Martin's." Richard Buckle with John Taras, *George Balanchine, Ballet Master*, 95.

52. John Martin, "The Dance: On the Road," *NYT*, June 9, 1935.

53. John Martin, "The Dance: At the Opera," *NYT*, August 18, 1935.

54. Ibid.

55. Ibid.

56. Ibid.

57. Ibid.

58. Lincoln Kirstein, "The Dance: A Letter," *NYT*, August 25, 1935.

59. LKD, August 19, 1935.

60. Lincoln Kirstein, "The Dance: A Letter," *NYT*, August 25, 1935.

61. Ibid.

62. On the Wigman debate in American dance circles, see Susan Manning, *Ecstasy and the Demon: Feminism and Nationalism in the Dances of Mary Wigman* (Berkeley: University of California Press, 1993), 275–79, and Ellen Graff, *Stepping Left*, 114–16. For a more recent assessment of Hanya Holm's American career, see Tresa Randall, "Hanya Holm and an American *Tanzgemeinschaft*," in *New German Dance Studies*, ed. Susan Manning and Julia Ruprecht (Urbana: University of Illinois Press, 2012), 79–98.

63. "Opera Signs American Ballet," *NYHT*, August 8, 1935.

64. Russell Rhodes, "The Coming American Season," *DT*, September 1935, 615.

65. "Opera Signs American Ballet," *NYHT*, August 8, 1935.

66. Ibid.

67. Lynn Garafola has summarized the underlying impulse of Fokine's realism as follows, tenets that find a striking echo in Balanchine's statements in defense of his opera choreography decades later: "From the start of [Fokine's] choreographic career, an acute historical sense informed his work. He believed that theme, period, and style in ballet

must conform to the time and place of the scenic action; that empirical observation and research must accompany the act of creation; that expressiveness stemmed directly from the fidelity of a representation to nature. Under the aegis of history, Fokine mounted his attack on ballet convention." Lynn Garafola, *Diaghilev's Ballets Russes*, 10.

68. Edward Moore, "New Heights Predicted for U.S. Dance," CT, August 25, 1935.

69. "Ballet Director Sees U.S. as Fertile Field," BS, August 18, 1935.

70. Edward Moore, "New Heights Predicted for U.S. Dance," CT, August 25, 1935; Claudia Cassidy, "On the Aisle," *Chicago Journal of Commerce*, August 17, 1935, copy in George Balanchine Clippings, Box 1, Folder "1926–35," JRDD.

71. "Ballet Director Sees U.S. as Fertile Field," BS, August 18, 1935.

72. Ibid.; Claudia Cassidy, "On the Aisle."

73. "Ballet Director Sees U.S. as Fertile Field," BS, August 18, 1935; Claudia Cassidy, "On the Aisle."

74. "Music Notes," NYT, August 23, 1935; "Metropolitan Seeks Dancers," NYHT, August 23, 1935.

75. "Metropolitan's Ballet Director Tries Out Fifty," NYHT, August 25, 1935.

76. Michel Mok, "Russia's Ancient Ballet Art Goes Yankee," *New York Post*, September 7, 1935, PDP.

77. John Martin, "The Dance: In a Busy Season," NYT, July 7, 1935.

78. Anatole Chujoy mentions both the Lewisohn and Robin Hood Dell performances in his *The New York City Ballet*, 51–52. He states that the Lewisohn engagement had originally been scheduled for August 5 and was rained out, but neither press reports nor Kirstein's diaries corroborate this.

79. On the history of Lewisohn Stadium with a particular focus on classical music performances at the venue, see Jonathan Stern, "Music for the (American) People: The Lewisohn Stadium Concerts, 1922–1964" (PhD diss., City University of New York, 2009).

80. "Ricci to Make Stadium Debut on August 11," NYHT, July 25, 1935; "Stadium Plans," NYHT, July 28, 1935.

81. John Martin, "The Dance: In a Busy Season," NYT, July 7, 1935; "Ricci to Make Stadium Debut on August 11," NYHT, July 25, 1935; "Stadium Plans," NYHT, July 28, 1935.

82. "Stadium Crowd Sees American Ballet Program," and Henriette Weber, "Ballet Scores at Stadium," unidentified clippings, PDP.

83. John Martin, "5,000 Witness Dances by American Ballet," NYT, August 13, 1935.

84. Henriette Weber, "Ballet Scores at Stadium," unidentified clipping, PDP.

85. Henriette Weber, "Ballet Scores at Stadium," and Danton Walker, "American Ballet Wins Plaudits at Stadium," unidentified clippings, PDP.

86. Ibid.

87. Russell Rhodes, "The Coming American Season," DT, September 1935, 612.

88. Ibid.

89. "Stadium Plans," NYHT, August 4, 1935; "2 *Carmen* Presentations to Close Stadium Operas; Shower Prevents Reappearance of American Ballet," NYHT, August 15, 1935; "*Carmen* for Stadium," NYT, August 15, 1935; LKD, August 13, 14, 1935.

90. "American Ballet in Final Program," NYT, August 20, 1935.

91. Henriette Weber, "Ballet Scores at Stadium," unidentified clipping, PDP.

92. "Ballet Is Seen at the Stadium," unidentified clipping, PDP.

93. "Stadium Crowd Sees American Ballet Program," unidentified clipping, PDP.

94. Henriette Weber, "Ballet Scores at Stadium," unidentified clipping, PDP.

95. Danton Walker, "American Ballet Wins Plaudits at Stadium," unidentified clipping, PDP.

96. Russell Rhodes, "The Coming American Season," *DT*, September 1935, 615.

97. Julian Seaman, "Music," *Daily Mirror*" and "Ballet Is Seen at the Stadium," PDP.

98. "Stadium Crowd Sees American Ballet Program," and Henriette Weber, "Ballet Scores at Stadium," PDP.

99. Ibid.

100. LKD, August 12, 1935.

101. Ibid.

102. Ibid.

103. Ibid.

104. LKD, August 6, 1935.

105. Ibid.

106. "American Ballet Listed at Dell Next Thursday," PDP.

107. Anatole Chujoy claims that both the Thursday and Friday night shows were rained out and that the troupe performed on Saturday and Sunday nights. See Chujoy, *The New York City Ballet*, 51. One clipping mentions a rain delay, though it does not specify the specific day: "The performance scheduled for last night was rained out," "Limbering Up for the Dell," *Philadelphia Record*, undated clipping, PDP. Philip Klein's review in the *Daily News* references two performances by the company but does not state which days they occurred on.

108. Philip Klein, "Dell Patrons Welcome American Ballet Company," *Daily News*, undated clipping, PDP.

109. Ibid.

110. Ibid.

111. Ibid.

112. Ibid.

113. LKD, August 19, 1935.

114. "Ballet in Westchester to Aid Girl Scout Camp," *NYHT*, August 11, 1935; "Ballet Opens Tomorrow," *NYT*, September 27, 1935.

115. Program, PDP, Box 1, Folder 2.

116. Ibid.

117. "Ballet Opens Tomorrow," *NYT*, September 27, 1935.

118. Ibid.

119. LKD, September 28, 1935.

120. Ibid.

121. Ibid.

122. Ibid.

123. LKD, September 30, 1935.

124. Michel Mok, "Russia's Ancient Ballet Art Goes Yankee," *New York Post*, September 7, 1935, PDP.

125. Kathrine Sorley Walker, *De Basil's Ballets Russes* (New York: Atheneum, 1983), 33–36.

126. Uncredited photos, apparently taken from a small personal camera, PDP.

127. "Tour Started by American Ballet Troupe," *NYHT*, October 16, 1935.

128. LKD, October 15, 1935.

129. "Tour Started by American Ballet Troupe," *NYHT*, October 16, 1935.

130. Ibid.

131. Ibid.

132. Ibid.

133. Program, DCS; "American Ballet Starts Bus Tour," *NYT*, October 16, 1935; "Tour Started by American Ballet Troupe," *NYHT*, October 16, 1935. Anatole Chujoy gives October 14 as the start of the tour, a date that is contradicted by Kirstein's diary, news reports, and a surviving program from Greenwich; see Chujoy, *The New York City Ballet*, 58. Richard Buckle and John Taras's biography of Balanchine also lists October 14 as the first day and says that two performances were given in Greenwich; see Buckle, with Taras, *George Balanchine, Ballet Master*, 95.

134. Program, William Dollar, MGZB Programs, Vertical File, JRDD; "American Ballet Starts Bus Tour," *NYT*, October 16, 1935; "Tour Started by American Ballet Troupe," *NYHT*, October 16, 1935.

135. Program, DCS; "American Ballet Starts Bus Tour," *NYT*, October 16, 1935; "Tour Started by American Ballet Troupe," *NYHT*, October 16, 1935.

136. "Ballet Pleases in Repertoire," *New Haven Courier*, undated clipping, PDP.

137. LKD, October 18, 1935.

138. Program, DCS; "Ballet to Carry Out Metropolitan Plans," *NYT*, October 27, 1935.

139. "American Ballet Acclaimed Here as Tour Begins," *Allentown Morning Call*, unidentified clipping, PDP.

140. Ibid.

141. Program, DCS; Programs, William Dollar, Joseph Levinoff, MGZB Programs, Vertical File, JRDD; "Ballet to Carry Out Metropolitan Plans," *NYT*, October 27, 1935.

142. LKD, October 23, 1935.

143. Ibid.

144. Program, William Dollar, MGZB Programs, Vertical File, JRDD.

145. "American Ballet Well Received," *Harrisburg Patriot*, undated clipping, PDP.

146. Ibid.

147. Ibid.

148. Ibid.

149. Kirstein, *Thirty Years*, 51.

150. LKD, October 17, 1935.

151. LKD, October 19–21, 1935.

152. LKD, October 22, 1935.

153. Ibid.

154. LKD, October 23, 1935.

155. Ibid.

156. Ibid.

157. Ibid.

158. "Ballet to Carry Out Metropolitan Plans," *NYT*, October 27, 1935.

159. Ibid.

160. Ruth Phillips, "Money Trouble Ends American Ballet Tour," *Daily Mirror*, undated clipping, PDP.

161. "Distracted by the sudden and supposedly to him, mysterious turn of events, Mr. Merovitch strode up and down his office at 30 Rockefeller Plaza in his shirt sleeves, berating those whom he felt had let him down and pleading with his lawyer, B. Meredith Langstaff, to make everything all right. The whole trouble, it seemed, lay with George Birse, road manager for Mr. Merovitch, who is reported to have returned from Scranton on Wednesday and then to have departed for an unidentified sanatorium, suffering from a nervous breakdown." "Executive Stubs Toe and Ballet Tour Collapses," unidentified clipping, PDP.

162. Ibid.

163. Anatole Chujoy's account of the collapse of the tour, written three decades before the first of Balanchine's biographies, alludes to a sense of shock and trauma among the dancers: "A sad and disillusioned group of dancers returned to New York that evening. . . . They knew the cancellation of the tour was not their fault, nor the fault of the direction of the American Ballet, yet they felt a certain guilt for it. Also, they were a little ashamed." Chujoy, *The New York City Ballet*, 59.

164. LKD, October 23, 1935; "Tour Started by American Ballet Troupe," *NYHT*, October 16, 1935.

165. Flier for American Ballet Chicago performances, GBA.

166. "Tour Started by American Ballet Troupe," *NYHT*, October 16, 1935.

167. Ibid.

168. Additional cities mentioned in press coverage of the tour are, in alphabetical order, Akron, Austin, Detroit, El Paso, Fort Wayne, Grand Rapids, Lansing, Lincoln, Milwaukee, Oshkosh, Pasadena, Phoenix, St. Joseph, St. Paul, San Antonio, Santa Barbara, Spokane, Stillwater, Syracuse, and Waco. "American Ballet Seeks New Works," *NYT*, September 27, 1935; "Tour Started by American Ballet Troupe," *NYHT*, October 16, 1935; "Ballet to Carry Out Metropolitan Plans," *NYT*, October 27, 1935; Ruth Phillips, "Money Trouble Ends American Ballet Tour," *Daily Mirror*, undated clipping, PDP; Russell Rhodes, "The Coming American Season," *DT*, September, 1935, 612.

169. Russell Rhodes, "The Coming American Season," *DT*, September 1935, 612.

170. LKD, October 22, 1935.

171. Lincoln Kirstein to Louis Kirstein, October 30, 1935, LEK.

172. Ibid.

Chapter 5

1. "4,200 Jam Metropolitan, Hail American Regime," *NYHT*, December 17, 1935.

2. Olin Downes, "Traviata Hailed for Its Artistry," *NYT* December 17, 1935.

3. "3 Make Debuts in Faust at Metropolitan," *NYHT*, December 20, 1935.

4. LKD, October 29, 1935; November 18, 1935.

5. LKD, November 20, 1935.

6. LKD, November 18, 1935.

7. "New Subscriptions Set Opera Record" *NYT*, December 8, 1935.

8. John Martin, "The Dance," *NYT*, December 15, 1935.

9. American Ballet Program Files, JRDD; LKD, February 10, 1936.

10. American Ballet Program Files, JRDD; "Metropolitan Opera," *NYHT*, March 8, 1936.

11. "The Opera," *NYT*, December 24, 1935.

12. Ibid.

13. "Hotcha Wiggling," *Billboard*, January 25, 1936.

14. Ibid.

15. "Ponselle as Carmen," *Variety*, January 8, 1936.

16. "Pop Ballets for Broadway," *Variety*, November 27, 1935; "Ballet Dancers for *Follies*," *NYHT*, November 21, 1935.

17. John Martin, "The Dance," *NYT*, November 24, 1935.

18. "Ziegfeld Follies," *Variety*, February 5, 1936.

19. "Ziegfeld Follies," *Billboard*, February 8, 1936.

20. Stirling Brown, "The New Follies," *WSJ*, February 3, 1936; Gilbert Gabriel, "The Follies, 1936," undated clipping, VDC.

21. John Anderson, "Ziegfeld Follies," *New York Evening Journal*, January 31, 1936, VDC; Burns Mantle, "New Follies at Winter Garden," undated clipping, VDC.

22. Program, VDC; Arthur Pollack, "The Theater," undated clipping, VDC.

23. Vincente Minnelli Portfolio, *Theatre Arts Monthly*, January 1936, 42.

24. Edith Isaacs, "Plays for Puritans and Others—Broadway in Review," *Theatre Arts Monthly*, March 1936, 175–84, 184.

25. "Play Reviews," undated clipping, VDC; John Anderson, "Ziegfeld Follies," *New York Evening Journal*, January 31, 1936, VDC.

26. Interview with Fayard Nicholas by Constance Valis Hill, *Babes in Arms* Dossier, PBC.

27. Wolfe Kaufman, "Hartford Arty Festival Flivs," *Variety*, February 19, 1936.

28. John Martin, "The Dance," *NYT*, March 8, 1936; "Final Opera Concert," *NYHT*, March 23, 1936.

29. Edwin Denby, "With the Dancers," *MM*, March–April 1937, 173–75, 173.

30. Ibid.

31. Ibid.

32. Gervaise N. Butler, "American Ballet," *DO*, June–July 1937, 67.

33. "They decided it was not enough just to be good at the job; they had to be constantly different also. The one possible formula was: *Don't have a formula*; the one rule for success: *Don't follow it up*" [emphasis in original]. "The Boys from Columbia," *Time*, September 26, 1938, 35–39, reprinted in *The Richard Rodgers Reader*, ed. Geoffrey Block (New York: Oxford University Press, 2002), 47–53, 48. For an overview of this period of Rodgers and Hart's collaboration see also Geoffrey Block, *Richard Rodgers* (New Haven, CT: Yale University Press, 2003), 75–93.

34. "The Boys from Columbia," 35–39.

35. Burns Mantle, "*On Your Toes* Pretty Exciting," *New York Daily News*, April 13, 1936. On the competition to control the legacy of the Ballets Russes following the death of Diaghilev in 1929, see Kathrine Sorley Walker, *De Basil's Ballets Russes* (New York: Atheneum, 1983); Vicente García-Márquez, *The Ballets Russes: Colonel de Basil's Ballets Russes de Monte Carlo, 1932–1952* (New York: Knopf, 1990); and Judith Chazin-Bennahum, *René Blum and the Ballets Russes: In Search of a Lost Life* (New York: Oxford University Press, 2011). At the time of the premiere of *On Your Toes*,

the Ballet Russe de Monte Carlo had yet to split into competing troupes, as would happen in 1938, and was still under the direction of the enterprising Colonel de Basil.

36. Richard Rodgers, *Musical Stages: an Autobiography*, New York: Random House, 1975, 174; William Hyland, *Richard Rodgers* (New Haven, CT: Yale University Press, 1998), 105.

37. Percy Hammond, *New York Herald*, April 13, 1936, and Arthur Pollock, "On Your Toes at the Imperial Theater," *Brooklyn Daily Eagle*, April 13, 1936, RRS.

38. Notice in *Theatre Arts Monthly*, October 1936, *MGZR Clippings *On Your Toes*, Music Division–New York Public Library.

39. Although songs from *On Your Toes* are available in numerous recorded versions as well as in published piano/vocal score and song anthologies, the full book, lyrics, and score remain unpublished. This and all subsequent references to and quotations from the book and lyrics are based on a 1936 script held by the Music Division of the New York Public Library for the Performing Arts: Richard Rodgers, *On Your Toes*, RM 262 (scripts). The cover page of this script includes the note: "As played at the Imperial Theatre, N.Y.C., Opening April 11, 1936."

40. Interview with Tamara Geva, 1976, conducted by Nancy Reynolds, *MGZMT 5-654 (transcript), JRDD–NYPL, hereafter "Tamara Geva Interview," 47.

41. Herbert Drake, "The Stage: On Your Toes," *Cue*, April 18, 1936; John Mason Brown, *New York Post*, April 13, 1936, RRS.

42. Interview with Tamara Geva, "Rethinking the Balanchine Legacy," conducted by Constance Valis Hill, *MGZIC 9-3945, cassette two, JRDD–NYPL.

43. Tamara Geva Interview, 48.

44. Ray Bolger in *I Remember Balanchine: Recollections of the Ballet Master by Those Who Knew Him*, ed. Francis Mason (New York: Doubleday, 1991), 156.

45. For an analysis and discussion of *Slaughter* more focused on other real-life attempts to create such hybrid works, see Daniel Blim, "Patchwork Nation: Collage, Music, and American Identity" (PhD diss., University of Michigan, 2013), 149–65.

46. Rowland Field, "On Your Toes, a Gay New Musical Comedy," *Brooklyn Times-Union*, April 13, 1936, RRS.

47. "*On Your Toes* Smash Tuner: Cinch Material for Films," *Hollywood Reporter*, April 13, 1936, RRS.

48. "New Play in Manhattan," *Time*, April 20, 1936, RRS.

49. Arthur Pollock, "On Your Toes at the Imperial Theater," *Brooklyn Daily Eagle*, April 13, 1936, RRS.

50. Robert Garland, "Ray Bolger, a Dancer Who Looks Like Jack Donahue's Inheritor, Has Leading Role," *New York World-Telegram*, April 13, 1936, RRS.

51. Russell Rhodes, "Burlesquing the 'Ballets Russes," *DT*, June 1936, 282.

52. Ruth Woodbury Sedgwick, *Stage*, May 1936 (*MGZR Clippings *On Your Toes* and RR Scrapbook).

53. Garland, "Ray Bolger, a Dancer Who Looks Like Jack Donahue's Inheritor."

54. Interview with Tamara Geva, 46–47.

55. Ibid., 47.

56. Helen Eager, *Boston Traveler*, March 23, 1936, RRS.

57. Russell Rhodes, "Burlesquing the 'Ballets Russes,'" *DT*, June 1936, 282.

58. For a more detailed discussion of this aspect of the number, see James Steichen, "Balanchine's Bach Ballet and the Dances of *On Your Toes*," *Journal of Musicology*, 35, no. 2 (Spring 2018), 267–93.

59. Helen Eager, *Boston Traveler*, March 23, 1936, RRS.

60. Russell Rhodes, "Burlesquing the 'Ballets Russes,'" *DT*, June 1936, 282.

61. *On Your Toes* playbill from Imperial Theater, dated August 17, 1936, *MGZB Programs, *On Your Toes*, MD–NYPL.

62. Ibid.

63. Fred Danieli Interview, *On Your Toes* Dossier, PBC.

64. Grace Houston Case Interview, *On Your Toes* Dossier, PBC.

65. Ibid.

66. Ibid.

67. LKD, November 7, 1933.

68. Arnold Haskell, *Balletomania, Then and Now* (New York: Knopf, 1977), 98.

69. *Choreography by George Balanchine: A Catalogue of Works* (New York: Viking, 1984).

70. The opera will be hereafter referred by the abbreviated title *Orpheus*, although the particular spelling in sources quoted will be preserved, e.g., *Orfeo, Orfeo ed Euridice*, or *Orphée*.

71. From the start of his tenure as mayor in 1934, La Guardia pushed hard to make the city more livable through the expansion of public housing and social service agencies, a vastly enlarged park system, and other opportunities for physical and cultural recreation, all of which were paid for in large part by generous financing from the Roosevelt administration and New Deal agencies, with whom he formed strong working relationships. See Mason Williams, *City of Ambition: FDR, La Guardia, and the Making of Modern New York* (New York: Norton, 2013), 175–211.

72. F. D. P., "Donizetti Opera on Double Bill at Metropolitan," *NYHT*, May 21, 1936.

73. Pitts Sanborn, "*Lucia* and New Ballet at the Met, "*New York World-Telegram*, May 21, 1936.

74. American Ballet South America Tour Brochure, June–December 1941, American Ballet Programs, JRDD-NYPL. Translation from Spanish mine.

75. Pitts Sanborn, "*Lucia* and New Ballet at the Met," *New York World-Telegram*, May 21, 1936.

76. "*Orpheus* on Bill for Opera May 22," *NYT*, May 14, 1936; F. D. P., "Donizetti Opera on Double Bill at Metropolitan," *NYHT*, May 21, 1936.

77. "Metropolitan Gives *Aida* and *La Traviata*," *NYHT*, May 31, 1936; "Spring Operas," *NYHT*, May 31, 1936; Francis D. Perkins, "The Spring Season," *NYHT*, June 7, 1936.

78. "Spring Season Given Lively Start at Metropolitan," *MA*, May 25, 1936; Francis D. Perkins, "The Spring Season," *NYHT*, June 7, 1936.

79. "Spring Season Given Lively Start at Metropolitan," *MA*, May 25, 1936.

80. Ibid.

81. Ibid.

82. Ibid.

83. Kirstein, *Blast at Ballet*, 32.

84. LKD, March 6, 1936.

85. Donald Windham, "The Stage and Ballet Designs of Pavel Tchelitchew," *Dance Index* 3, nos. 1–2 (January–February 1944): 4–32, 18.

86. Parker Tyler, *The Divine Comedy of Pavel Tchelitchev* (New York: Fleet Publishing, 1967), 386.

87. Windham, "The Stage and Ballet Designs of Pavel Tchelitchew," 18.

88. Kirstein, *Blast at Ballet*, 33.

89. Elliott Carter in Mason, *I Remember Balanchine*, 163–69, 165.

90. Ibid.

91. Ibid.

92. A generous amount of visual evidence from the production survives, in the form of Tchelitchev's sketches for the sets and costumes, held by NYPL: *MGZA Tch P Orp 1 and 2; scene design for Elysian Fields, *MGZB Tch P Orp 1; scene design for act IV "Milky Way" *MGZB Tch P Orp 2. A series of posed studio photographs by George Platt Lynes and live performance photos of the opera offer a collective sense of how the work was realized on the stage, especially when put in dialogue with the observations of reviewers and the recollections of dancers. A mixture of the Platt Lynes studio photographs and live performance photos are held by NYPL in *MGZEA *Orpheus and Eurydice* (Balanchine) photographs and *MGZEB New York (City) Museum of Modern Art Photographs: Ballet c. 1900–50, Vol. 28.

93. Lincoln Kirstein, introductory essay to *Pavel Tchelitchev: An Exhibition in the Gallery of Modern Art, 20 March through 19 April 1964* (New York: Foundation for Modern Art, 1964), 37.

94. Annabelle Lyon Interview, 84.

95. Ibid.

96. Windham, "The Stage and Ballet Designs of Pavel Tchelitchew," 18.

97. Ibid.

98. Tyler, *The Divine Comedy of Pavel Tchelitchev*, 386; Windham, "The Stage and Ballet Designs of Pavel Tchelitchew," 18.

99. Quoted in Debra Hickenlooper Sowell, *The Christensen Brothers: An American Dance Epic* (Amsterdam: Harwood Academic, 1998), 115.

100. Ibid.

101. Sowell, *The Christensen Brothers*, 115.

102. Annabelle Lyon Interview, 84–85.

103. Ibid.

104. Quoted in Reynolds, *Repertory in Review*, 46.

105. Tyler, *The Divine Comedy of Pavel Tchelitchev*, 386.

106. Ibid.

107. On this central debate over *Regieoper* with a focus on the case of Verdi, see James Hepokoski, "Operatic Stagings: Positions and Pardoxes: A Reply to David J. Levin," in *Atti del convegno internazionale, Parma, New York, New Haven, 24 gennaio-1 febbraio 2001* [Proceedings of the international conference, Parma, New York, New Haven, 24 January–1 February 2001], ed. Fabrizio Della Seta, Roberta Montemorra Marvin, and Marco Marica (Florence: L.S. Olschki, 2003), vol. 2, 477–83.

108. On the history and discourse surrounding unconventional operatic production, see David J. Levin, *Unsettling Opera: Staging Mozart, Verdi, Wagner, and Zemlinsky* (Chicago: University of Chicago Press, 2007).

109. "Travesty on Gluck," *Time*, June 1, 1936.

110. John Alan Haughton, "Manhattan Musical Events," *BS*, May 31, 1936.

111. Jerome Bohm, "*Orpheus and Eurydice* at Metropolitan," *NYHT*, May 23, 1936.

112. "Travesty on Gluck," *Time*, June 1, 1936.

113. Jerome Bohm, "*Orpheus and Eurydice* at Metropolitan," *NYHT*, May 23, 1936.

114. John Alan Haughton, "Manhattan Musical Events," *BS*, May 31, 1936.

115. Jerome Bohm, "*Orpheus and Eurydice* at Metropolitan," *NYHT*, May 23, 1936.

116. Ibid.

117. "Travesty on Gluck," *Time*, June 1, 1936.

118. Russell Rhodes, "New York Letter," *DT*, July 1936, 380–82.

119. "Travesty on Gluck," *Time*, June 1, 1936.

120. John Alan Haughton, "Manhattan Musical Events," *BS*, May 31, 1936; Russell Rhodes, "New York Letter," *DT*, July 1936, 380–92.

121. LKD, May 24, 1936.

122. Ibid.

123. For the second *Orpheus* performance on May 29, the second half of the bill was not *Cavalleria* but rather the other part of the "Cav-Pag" pairing, *Pagliacci*. "*Pagliacci* Is Sung at Metropolitan," *New York Times*, May 30, 1936.

124. Handwritten meeting minutes titled "Meeting of Board of Directors of the Metropolitan Popular Season." Although undated, the text begins by stating that "The new season which opened May 11 has now run 2 weeks." Metropolitan Opera Archives.

125. LKD, May 24, 1936.

126. Ibid.

127. Glenway Wescott, "Pleasure from *Orpheus*," *Time*, June 15, 1936.

128. LKD, May 24, 1936.

129. Ibid.

130. T. H. Parker, "The Lively Arts," *HC*, May 8, 1936.

131. "Tap Dancer at Met Opera," *Variety*, May 6, 1936.

132. Kirstein mentions *On Your Toes* in several diary entries prior to his attendance at the show itself in Boston and New York. See LKD, February 7, 25, March 3, 6, 10, 1936.

133. LKD, February 25, 1936.

134. For an overview of Paul Draper's background and career highlights, see Valis Hill, *Tap Dancing America*, 190–92. See also Paul Draper, "Tapping into the Classics," in Rusty Frank, *Tap! The Greatest Tap Dance Stars and Their Stories, 1900–1955* (New York: William Morrow, 1990), 231–40, 236–37.

135. LKD, April 16, 28, 1936.

136. LKD, April 20, 21, 1936.

137. LKD, April 29, 1936.

138. Ibid.

139. Ibid.

140. LKD, May 31, 1936. The prospectus and budget for the "Collaborative Evenings" series was included as an enclosure in a May 20, 1937, letter from Lincoln Kirstein to Anna Bogue, secretary of the William C. Whitney Trust, LEK.

141. Lincoln Kirstein to Anna Bogue, May 20, 1937, LEK.

142. "Ballet," *Dance*, May 1937, clipping located in EHS.

143. Since Bach's D minor concerto BWV 1043 (composed ca. 1730–31) is his only such extant work for two violins, we can assume that this was the music specified by Kirstein in 1937 and was in all likelihood the music for the ballet as conceived of a year earlier in 1936.

144. Sally Banes, "Balanchine and Black Dance," in *Writing Dancing in the Age of Postmodernism* (Hanover: Wesleyan University Press/University Press of New England, 1994), 53–69; Brenda Dixon Gottschild, "Stripping the Emperor: George Balanchine and the Americanization of Ballet," in *Digging the Africanist Presence in American Performance: Dance and Other Contexts* (Westport, CT: Greenwood Press, 1996), 59–79.

145. For a more complete account of this project and its relationship to the dances of *On Your Toes*, see James Steichen, "Balanchine's 'Bach Ballet' and the Dances of *On Your Toes*," *Journal of Musicology* 35, no. 2 (Spring 2018): 267–93.

Chapter 6

1. This chapter is a condensed version of James Steichen, "The American Ballet's Caravan," *Dance Research Journal* 47, no. 1 (April 2015): 69–94. I am grateful to the editors of the journal for permission to reprint the material here.

2. See, for example, Reynolds, *Repertory in Review*, 34, and Lynn Garafola, "Dance for a City," in *Dance for a City: Fifty Years of the New York City Ballet*, ed. Lynn Garafola with Eric Foner (New York: Columbia University Press, 1999), 4.

3. Kirstein, *Blast at Ballet*, 41–48.

4. Kirstein, *Thirty Years*, 78.

5. Ibid.

6. On these and other similar ballets in the Caravan's later repertoire, see Mark Franko, *The Work of Dance: Labor, Movement and Identity in the 1930s* (Middletown, CT: Wesleyan University Press, 2002), 119–23; Lynn Garafola, "Making an American Dance: *Billy the Kid, Rodeo*, and *Appalachian Spring*," in *Aaron Copland and His World*, ed. Carol Oja and Judith Tick (Princeton, NJ: Princeton University Press, 2005); Elizabeth Bergman, *Music for the Common Man: Aaron Copland during the Depression and War* (New York: Oxford University Press, 2005), 111–32; Jennifer L. Campbell, "Shaping Solidarity: Music, Diplomacy, and Inter-American Relations, 1936–1946" (PhD diss., University of Connecticut, 2010), 123–224; and Beth Levy, *Frontier Figures: American Music and the Mythology of the American West* (Berkeley: University of California Press, 2012), 318–50.

7. On the influence of Popular Front and left-leaning political movements on American culture, see Michael Denning, *The Cultural Front: The Laboring of American Culture in the Twentieth Century* (New York: Verso, 1997/2010); on regionalism in American art, see Erika Doss, *Benton, Pollock, and the Politics of Modernism: From Regionalism to Abstract Expressionism* (Chicago: University of Chicago Press, 1995); on dance and politics in the 1930s, see Mark Franko, *Dancing Modernism/Performing Politics* (Bloomington: Indiana University Press, 1995), and Graff, *Stepping Left*. On Kirstein's political leanings and their influence on the activities of Ballet Caravan, see Andrea Harris, *Making Ballet American: Modernism Before and Beyond Balanchine* (New York: Oxford University Press, 2017).

8. Chujoy, *The New York City Ballet*, 75–78; Debra Hickenlooper Sowell, *The Christensen Brothers*, 122–24; Martin Duberman, *The Worlds of Lincoln Kirstein*, 315–18.

9. Ballet Caravan Brochure, DCS.

10. John Martin, "The Dance: A New Troupe," *NYT*, June 28, 1936. In subsequent reports on the group, Martin identifies the Caravan as "the cooperative group from the American Ballet" and "the summer company recruited from the ranks of the American Ballet." See "The Dance: Importations," *NYT*, July 5, 1936, and "The Dance: New Literacy," *NYT*, August 2, 1936.

11. "Summer Theatres," *BG*, August 23, 1936; "Summer Theatres," *BG*, August 30, 1936.

12. Sali Ann Kriegsman, *Modern Dance in America: The Bennington Years* (Boston: G. K. Hall, 1981), 57; Russell Rhodes, "New York Letter," *DT*, September 1936, 596.

13. Kirstein's diaries indicate that he and Coudy had begun spending time together outside of the studio in March 1936 and by the time of the summer tour were lovers, sharing rooms for many of the troupe's stops. LKD, March 6, May 26, June 9, 16, 24, July 24, August 29, 1936.

14. John Martin, "Odyssey of the Dance," *NYT*, September 13, 1936.

15. Dollar's ballet *Promenade* is discussed below. On his appearance in Lincoln Kirstein's 1936 lectures, see Kriegsman, *Modern Dance in America*, 54.

16. Margaret Lloyd, "Ballet Caravan—Farewell, Hail," *CSM*, November 10, 1936.

17. Annabelle Lyon Interview, 91.

18. Lincoln Kirstein, *Thirty Years*, 68.

19. Lynn Garafola, "Lincoln Kirstein, Modern Dance, and the Left," *Dance Research* 23, no. 1 (Summer 2005), 18–35.

20. Kirstein, *Thirty Years*, 69. On Kirstein's earlier and more critical views of modern dance, directed with particular vehemence against Mary Wigman, see Susan Manning, *Ecstasy and the Demon: Feminism and Nationalism in the Dances of Mary Wigman* (Berkeley: University of California Press, 1993), 259–65. Sally Banes characterizes the Caravan's organizational model as "more like the small American modern dance company than the traditional ballet troupe" and speculates that Kirstein's embrace of modern dance was a cunning strategic decision. Sally Banes, "Sibling Rivalry," in *Dance for a City: Fifty Years of the New York City Ballet*, ed. Lynn Garafola with Eric Foner (New York: Columbia University Press, 1999), 83. As Banes explains, "In attempting to create an alternative to the émigré Russian companies that he had come to despise," most notably Colonel de Basil's Ballet Russe de Monte Carlo, "despite his classical taste he looked for allies in the modern dance world." This common-enemy theory is entirely plausible, since as Mark Franko and Gay Morris have observed, ballet and modern dance in America for much of the mid-twentieth century developed and defined themselves in a subtle if sometimes unacknowledged dialogue with one another as well as through a shared antagonism toward existing popular and commercial dance cultures. Mark Franko, *The Work of Dance*, 107–23; Gay Morris, *A Game for Dancers: Performing Modernism in the Postwar Years* (Middletown, CT: Wesleyan University Press, 2006), 38–63.

21. Janet Mansfield Soares, *Martha Hill and the Making of American Dance* (Middletown, CT: Wesleyan University Press, 2009), 83–85.

22. John Martin's June 28 column announcing the formation of the Caravan makes no mention of the Bennington performances, which were subsequently announced in his column of July 5, barely two weeks in advance. Kirstein for his part mentioned the

Bennington dates in a July 9 letter to his parents, then vacationing in France, and first referenced the engagement in his diary on July 15.

23. Soares, *Martha Hill*, 84.

24. In Sali Ann Kriegsman's chronologies of the festival, the Caravan's performances of 1936 (and 1937) are classified among "Lectures, Special Events, Recitals, and Student Demonstrations," distinct from the official "Bennington Festival Series." Kriegsman, *Modern Dance in America,* 53–62 (1936 season) and 63–73 (1937 season).

25. "The present season is marked by a doubling of these activities and the addition of a pair of performances outside the regular festival series of the newly formed Ballet Caravan, which made its début here in the little college theatre," Martin, "The Dance," *NYT*, August 9, 1936; "In addition, the newly formed Ballet Caravan staged an unscheduled appearance," Wallace Parks, "A New Center of the Dance," *BS*, September 13, 1936; "This last season [the festival] unexpectedly presented two programs by the Ballet caravan, a summer offshoot of the American Ballet," Margaret Lloyd, "On with the Dance," *CSM*, November 10, 1936.

26. On the ways in which Kirstein self-consciously embraced the aesthetics, politics, and larger ethos and institutional infrastructure of modern dance through the Caravan, see Garafola, "Lincoln Kirstein, Modern Dance, and the Left" and Banes, "Sibling Rivalry," 82–86.

27. Soares, *Martha Hill*, 88.

28. LKD, July 24, 1936.

29. On Kirstein and Graham's correspondence and relationship around this time, see Lynn Garafola, "Lincoln Kirstein, Modern Dance, and the Left," 22–24 and Soares, *Martha Hill*, 85–86.

30. LKD, July 24, 1936.

31. On the touring activities of Denishawn and Martha Graham, see Janet Mansfield Soares, *Louis Horst: Musician in a Dancer's World* (Durham, NC: Duke University Press, 1992).

32. Kriegsman, *Modern Dance in America*, 15.

33. Kirstein, *Thirty Years*, 68–69.

34. LKD, July 24, 1936.

35. LKD, August 7, 1934.

36. LKD, June 11, 1936.

37. Russell Rhodes, "New York Letter," *DT*, August 1936, 499; "Summer Theatres: Ogunquit Playhouse," *BG*, September 1, 1936; John Martin, "Odyssey of the Dance," *NYT*, September 13, 1936; Margaret Lloyd, "Ballet Caravan—Farewell, Hail," *CSM*, November 10, 1936.

38. Russell Rhodes, "New York Letter," *DT*, August 1936, 499; "Summer Theatres: Ogunquit Playhouse," *BG*, September 1, 1936; John Martin, "Odyssey of the Dance," *NYT*, September 13, 1936; Margaret Lloyd, "Ballet Caravan—Farewell, Hail," *CSM*, November 10, 1936.

39. Russell Rhodes, "New York Letter," *DT*, August 1936, 499; John Martin, "Odyssey of the Dance," *NYT*, September 13, 1936; Margaret Lloyd, "Ballet Caravan—Farewell, Hail," *CSM*, November 10, 1936.

40. "Summer Theatres: Ogunquit Playhouse," *BG*, September 1, 1936.

41. Kirstein, *Blast at Ballet*, 42.

42. LKD, June 9, July 4, 1936.

43. LKD, July 2, 9, 1936.

44. LKD, June 5, 11, 1936.

45. Russell Rhodes, "New York Letter," *DT*, August 1936, 499.

46. Ballet Caravan Brochure, DCS.

47. *Mazurka* (Glinka), *Morning Greeting* (Schubert), *Pas de deux* (Liebling), *Gitana* (Torré), *Can-Can* ([Johann?] Strauss), *Pas Classique* (Benjamin Godard), *Rhapsody* (Liszt), *Valse* (Ravel), and *March* (Prokofiev). Kriegsman, *Modern Dance in America*, 57.

48. LKD, July 2, 1936.

49. On the ideology of Kirstein's drive to distinguish ballet from popular dance performance and similar efforts on the part of John Martin in relation to modern dance, see Mark Franko, *The Work of Dance*, 107–23.

50. Marjorie Church, *DO* 3, no. 7 (August–September 1936): 78.

51. Two pianists, David Steimer and Edmund Horn, are credited in the Caravan's 1936 performances. See programs in DCS.

52. "Dance Notes," *NYHT*, July 12, 1936; LK Diaries, July 24, 1936.

53. LKD, July 24, 1936. This evidence contradicts the performance chronology of Kriegsman, which lists seven divertissements for each of the Caravan's performances. This could be because she was working from the printed programs, which would not have reflected this last-minute decision. Kriegsman, *Modern Dance in America*, 57.

54. John Martin, "Odyssey of the Dance," *NYT*, September 13, 1936; Margaret Lloyd, "Ballet Caravan—Farewell, Hail," *CSM*, November 10, 1936.

55. Margaret Lloyd, "Ballet Caravan—Farewell, Hail," *CSM*, November 10, 1936.

56. Edwin Denby, "With the Dancers," *MM*, November–December 1936, 49–53, 52.

57. LKD, July 15 and August 13, 1936.

58. Sowell, *The Christensen Brothers*, 123–24.

59. LKD, August 29, 1936.

60. John Martin, "The Dance: A New Troupe," *NYT*, June 28, 1936; "Ballet Caravan Forms to Give Performances," *NYHT*, July 5, 1936; Russell Rhodes, "New York Letter," *DT*, August 1936, 499. Martin Duberman recounts the story of *Rondo* but does not include the ballet's name and misidentifies the composer of its music as Anton Webern. *The Worlds of Lincoln Kirstein*, 317–19.

61. LKD, June 5, 9, 11, 16, 24, 25 and July 2, 4, 1936.

62. LKD, June 16, 24, 1936.

63. LKD, May 28, July 2, 1936.

64. John Martin, "The Dance: A New Troupe," *NYT*, June 28, 1936; "Ballet Caravan Forms to Give Performances," *NYHT*, July 5, 1936; Russell Rhodes, "New York Letter," *DT*, August 1936, 499.

65. Ballet Caravan Brochure 1936a, DCS.

66. On Martha Graham and Erick Hawkins's partnership, see Mark Franko, *Martha Graham in Love and War* (London: Oxford University Press, 2012), esp. 28–30 on their initial meeting in 1936.

67. Lincoln Kirstein to Rose and Louis Kirstein, July 9, 1936, LEK; LKD, July 24, 1936.

68. LKD, July 24, 1936.

69. LKD, August 29, 1936; "Ballet Closes Tour," *NYHT*, August 30, 1936.

70. John Martin, "Odyssey of the Dance," *NYT*, September 13, 1936.

71. LKD, August 29, 1936.

72. Program, DCS.

73. "Manchester Plans Ballet Caravan for Summer Visitors," *NYHT*, August 9, 1936. It is not clear whether this performance by the Caravan actually took place, however, since no program survives nor is it mentioned in any other report or in Kirstein's diaries. If the troupe did perform, it would have amounted to a doubleheader of an evening, since several sources verify that the troupe performed in Dorset on that same evening, seven miles away from Manchester. LKD, August 29, 1936; "Ballet Closes Tour," *NYHT*, August 30, 1936; Program, DCS.

74. "Maureen V. Smith Is Guest at Dinner," *NYT*, August 1, 1936; "Nancy Van Vleck Honored at Party," *NYT*, July 28, 1936; "Brothers to Honor Maureen V. Smith at Dance Friday," *NYHT*, July 30, 1936.

75. "Notes of Social Activities in New York and Elsewhere," *NYT*, August 7, 1936.

76. LKD, August 13, 1936.

77. "Political Satire Irks Blooded Gentry," *Variety*, August 25, 1936, CCP.

78. Lincoln Kirstein to Rose and Louis Kirstein, July 9, 1936, LEK; "Ballet Numbers at Westport," *NYHT*, August 2, 1936; John Martin, "The Dance: New Literacy," *NYT*, August 2, 1936; "American Ballet at Westport," *MA*, August 1936, 31; Russell Rhodes, "New York Letter: The Autumn Season," *DT*, September 1936, 595–6.

79. John Martin, "The Dance: New Literacy," *NYT*, August 2, 1936; Russell Rhodes, "New York Letter: The Autumn Season," *DT*, September 1936, 595–96.

80. LKD, August 7, 1936.

81. "Summer Theatres," *BG*, August 23, 1936; John Martin, "The Dance: A Pantomime," *NYT*, August 30, 1936; "American Ballet Group Completes New England Tour," *MA*, September 1936.

82. Program, DCS.

83. "Ballet Closes Tour, Will Fill Week's Engagement in Ogunquit, Me.," *NYHT*, August 30, 1936.

84. "Summer Theatres: Ogunquit Playhouse," *BG*, September 1, 1936.

85. Ibid.

86. LKD, September 25, 1936.

87. LKD, August 29, 1936.

88. John Martin, "The Dance: Miscellany," *NYT*, September 6, 1936; Program, *MGZB Programs (vertical file), "Douglas Coudy," JRDD–NYPL.

89. John Martin, "The Dance: Jooss Ballet Appearance," *NYT*, October 11, 1936; "Music Notes," *NYHT*, October 13, 1936.

90. "Current Happenings on College Campuses," 1936; Lincoln Kirstein to Louis Kirstein, October 6, 1936, LEK; Programs, DCS.

91. Program, DCS.

92. Lincoln Kirstein to Louis Kirstein, November 4, 1936, LEK; "Ballets Are Brilliantly Performed," *Hartford Courant*, December 2, 1936, DCS; "Ballet: Caravan," *Dance*, December 1936, 26.

93. John Martin, "The Dance: A New Troupe," *NYT*, June 28, 1936.

94. John Martin, "Odyssey of the Dance," *NYT*, September 13, 1936.

95. "Twenty-One New Singers Are Announced by Metropolitan," *NYHT*, November 16, 1936.

96. LKD, October 12, 1936.

97. Undated Ballet Caravan Brochure, DCS.

98. "Ballet Makes Debut," *MA*, November 10, 1936, 30.

99. Edwin Denby, "With the Dancers," *MM*, November–December 1936, 49–53, 52.

100. Kirstein, *Blast at Ballet*, 41.

101. Ibid., 42.

102. LKD, May 25, 27, 1936.

103. LKD, May 27, 1936.

104. LKD, May 25, 1936.

105. LKD, May 28, 1936.

106. LKD, June 11, 1936.

107. LKD, June 24, 1936.

108. LKD, August 1, 1936.

109. LKD, June 4, 1936.

110. LKD, June 5, 1936.

111. LKD, June 6, 1936.

112. LKD, June 17, 1936.

113. LKD, June 25, 1936.

114. Ibid.

115. LKD, July 28, 1936.

116. LKD, August 1, 1936.

117. LKD, August 7, 1936.

118. Ibid.

119. LKD, June 11, 1936.

120. "Ballets Are Brilliantly Performed," *HC*, December 2, 1936, DCS.

121. Ibid.

122. Ibid.

123. Ruthanna Boris, "The Ballet Caravan," *Dance Herald* 1, no. 1 (October 1937): 1.

124. Edwin Denby, "With the Dancers," *MM*, November–December 1936, 49–53, 52.

125. Nancy Reynolds, "In His Image," in Lynn Garafola and Nancy Van Norman Baer, eds., *The Ballets Russes and Its World* (New Haven, CT: Yale University Press, 1999).

126. Margaret Lloyd, "Ballet Caravan—Farewell, Hail," *CSM*, November 10, 1936.

127. Ibid.

128. Edwin Denby, "With the Dancers," *MM*, November–December 1936, 49–53, 52.

129. Kirstein, *Blast at Ballet*, 42.

130. John Martin, "Odyssey of the Dance," *NYT*, September 13, 1936.

131. LKD, August 29, 1936.

132. Ibid.

133. In LEK correspondence, the last letter from Lincoln to Louis on School of American Ballet letterhead is dated October 6, 1936, and a letter of November 4, 1936, is the first to use Ballet Caravan letterhead.

Chapter 7

1. John Martin, "The Dance: Among the Educators," *NYT*, March 7, 1937.

2. John Martin, *NYT*, May 23, 1937.

3. Wilella Waldorf, "Musical Comedy," *New York Post*, September 13, 1937, RRS.

4. Olin Downes, "*Caponsacchi* Has Premiere Here," *NYT*, February 5, 1937.

5. "*Gioconda* Revival," *NYT*, February 19, 1937.

6. "*Aida* Presented," *NYT*, January 1, 1937.

7. Ibid.

8. "*Aida* Is Presented," *NYT*, January 21, 1937.

9. "Balanchine on *Babes*," *Variety*, October 14, 1936; "Rialto Gossip," *NYT*, December 20, 1936.

10. James Agate, "For Us Alone," *Tatler*, September 1, 1937, RRS.

11. Andrea Most, *Making Americans: Jews and the Broadway Musical* (Cambridge, MA: Harvard University Press, 2004), 66–100.

12. John Mason Brown, April 17, 1937, RRS.

13. Ibid.

14. Edith J. R. Isaacs, "In the Spring—Broadway in Review," *Theatre Arts Monthly*, 420–29, 424.

15. Constance Valis Hill, "Notes on the Major Dance Numbers," *Babes in Arms* Dossier, PBC.

16. Ibid.

17. Anthea Kraut, *Choreographing Copyright: Race, Gender, and Intellectual Property Rights in American Dance* (New York: Oxford University Press, 2015).

18. Leo Gaffney, "Snappy Pace to Babes in Arms," *Boston Evening American*, March 26, 1937, RRS.

19. M. B., "About Rodgers and Hart," *American*, March 14, 1937, RRS.

20. Ibid.

21. Elinor Hughes, "Babes in Arms," *Boston Herald*, March 26, 1937, RRS.

22. "Shubert Theatre: Babes in Arms," *BG*, March 26, 1937, RRS; Edith J. R. Isaacs, "In the Spring—Broadway in Review," *Theatre Arts Monthly* 21, no. 6 (June 1937), 420–29.

23. Douglas Gilbert, "Fine Entertainment," *World Telegram*, April 15, 1937, RRS.

24. Constance Valis Hill, "Notes on the Major Dance Numbers," *Babes in Arms* Dossier, PBC.

25. These videos were screened as part of the *Rethinking the Balanchine Legacy* conference held at the New York Public Library and are included in the videorecording of Constance Valis Hill's interview with Fayard Nicholas.

26. Constance Valis Hill interview with Fayard Nicholas, *Babes in Arms* Dossier, PBC.

27. John Mason Brown, "What Babes in Arms Can Claim," *New York Post*, April 17, 1937; Robert Benchley, "The Theatre," *New Yorker*, April 24, 1937, both RRS.

28. On the Nicholas family's history including an account of their work on *Babes in Arms*, to which the present account is deeply indebted, see Constance Valis Hill, *Brotherhood in Rhythm: The Jazz Tap Dancing of the Nicholas Brothers* (New York: Cooper Square Press, 2002).

29. Constance Valis Hill interview with Fayard Nicholas, *Babes in Arms* Dossier, PBC.

30. Brooks Atkinson, "Babes in Arms," *NYT*, April 15, 1937.

31. Mourdaunt Hall, "Babes in Arms," *Boston Evening Transcript*, March 26, 1937, RRS.

32. Ibid.

33. Ibid.

34. "Plays Out of Town," *Variety*, March 31, 1937.

35. John Anderson, "Babes in Arms," *Evening Journal,* April 15, 1937.

36. Douglas Gilbert, "Fine Entertainment," *World Telegram*, April 15, 1937; Rob Wagner, "Script," September 18, 1937, both RRS.

37. "Stage: Stork Wiman," *News Weekly*, April 24, 1937, RRS.

38. Constance Valis Hill interview with Marjorie Jane, *Babes in Arms* Dossier, PBC.

39. LKD, February 28, April 9, 1937.

40. LKD, April 9, 1937.

41. Lucius Beebe, *NYHT*, April 18, 1937, RRS. All further references in this paragraph to this article.

42. Stephanie Jordan, *Moving Music: Dialogues with Music in Twentieth-Century Ballet* (London: Dance Books, 2000) and *Stravinsky Dances: Re-Visions across a Century* (London: Dance Books, 2007). Charles Joseph, *Stravinsky and Balanchine: A Journey of Invention* (New Haven, CT: Yale University Press, 2002) and *Stravinsky's Ballets* (New Haven, CT: Yale University Press, 2012).

43. Untitled review, *American Dancer*, June 1937, EHS.

44. Gervaise Butler, "American Ballet," *DO*, June–July 1937, 67.

45. Charles Joseph, *Stravinsky and Balanchine*, 139–40.

46. LKD, August 1, 1936.

47. Kirstein, *Blast at Ballet*, 39; Duberman, *Worlds of Lincoln Kirstein*, 331.

48. In addition to previously cited work by Lynn Garfola, Stephanie Jordan, and Charles Joseph, see discussions of *Apollo* in Hope Randel, "Un-Voicing Orpheus: The Powers of Music in Stravinsky and Balanchine's 'Greek' Ballets," *Opera Quarterly* 23, no. 2 (Spring 2013): 101–45 and Susan Jones, *Literature, Modernism, and Dance* (Oxford: Oxford University Press, 2013).

49. A recording of the earlier version of *Apollon* is included in the video compilation *Jacques D'Amboise: Portrait of a Great American Dancer*, Pleasantville, NY: Vai, 2006.

50. Gervaise N. Butler, "American Ballet," *DO*, June–July 1937, 67.

51. Oscar Thompson, "New Stravinsky Ballet Achieves World Premiere," *MA*, May 10, 1937.

52. Jerome Bohm, "Three Ballets of Stravinsky Are Presented," *NYHT*, [no date given], EHS.

53. Winthrop Sargeant, "Stravinsky's Card Party Joyous Ballet Spectacle," *New York American*, April 28, 1937, EHS.

54. Danton Walker, "Stravinsky Ballets Cheered at the Met," unidentified, EHS.

55. Untitled review, *American Dancer*, June 1937, EHS.

56. Oscar Thompson, "New Stravinsky Ballet Achieves World Premiere," *MA*, May 10, 1937.

57. Elliott Carter, "With the Dancers," *MM*, May–June 1937, 237–39, 239.

58. Ibid.

59. LKD, April 22, 24, 27, 1937.

60. Program, *MGZB Programs (vertical file), "Kathryn Mullowny," JRDD–NYPL.

61. Gervaise N. Butler, "American Ballet," *DO*, June–July 1937, 67.

62. Elliott Carter, "With the Dancers," *MM*, May–June 1937, 237–39, 239.

63. Oscar Thompson, "New Stravinsky Ballet Achieves World Premiere," *MA*, May 10, 1937.

64. Ibid.

65. John Martin, "The Dance: New Ballets," *NYT*, May 2, 1937.

66. Elliott Carter, "With the Dancers," *MM*, May–June 1937, 237–39, 239.

67. Oscar Thompson, "New Stravinsky Ballet Achieves World Premiere," *MA*, May 10, 1937.

68. Untitled review, *American Dancer*, June 1937, EHS.

69. Danton Walker, "Stravinsky Ballets Cheered at the Met," unidentified, EHS.

70. Gervaise N. Butler, "American Ballet," *DO*, June–July 1937.

71. Untitled review, *American Dancer*, June 1937, EHS.

72. Elliott Carter, "With the Dancers," *MM*, May–June 1937, 237–39, 238.

73. Oscar Thompson, "New Stravinsky Ballet Achieves World Premiere," *MA*, May 10, 1937.

74. Ibid.

75. John Martin, "The Dance: New Ballets," *NYT*, May 2, 1937.

76. Ibid.

77. LKD, April 26, 1937.

78. Ibid.

79. LKD, April 27, 1937.

80. LKD, April 28, 1937.

81. Ibid.

82. Lincoln Kirstein to Louis Kirstein, June 10, 1937, LEK.

83. Kirstein, *Blast at Ballet*, 41.

84. Ibid.

85. Lincoln Kirstein, untitled essay, *New Theatre*, September 1936.

86. John Selby, "How Lincoln Kirstein Runs Ballet Caravan," BG, June 12, 1938.

87. Ibid.

88. LKD, December 18, 1936; January 17, 1937.

89. Kirstein first mentions this concept in his diaries on February 6, 14, and 26, 1937.

90. LEK Collection, correspondence from May 12 to June 8, 1937. This project is discussed in Duberman, *Worlds of Lincoln Kirstein*, 334–37 and Chujoy, *The New York City Ballet*, 91–92.

91. Prospectus included in letter from Lincoln Kirstein to Anna Bogue, May 20, 1937, LEK.

92. "Ballet," *Dance*, May 1937, EHS.

93. John Martin, "The Dance," *NYT*, May 23, 1937.

94. Lincoln Kirstein to Louis Kirstein, May 26, 1938, LEK.

95. John Martin, *NYT*, May 23, 1937

96. Debra Sowell, *The Christensen Brothers*, 140–41.

97. "The Ballet in U.S.A.," *Manchester Guardian*, July 6, 1937.

98. Ibid.

Chapter 8

1. "Along the Rialto," *Film Daily*, February 25, 1937, 4.

2. Ibid.

3. Catherine Jurca, "What the Public Wanted: Hollywood, 1937–1942," *Cinema Journal* 47, no. 2 (Winter 2008): 3–25.

4. *The Goldwyn Follies* is commercially available. A draft copy of the screenplay is located in the Vera Zorina Papers, Houghton Library, Harvard University. On the production history of *The Goldwyn Follies*, see A. Scott Berg, *Goldwyn: A Biography* (New York: Knopf, 1989), 298–305.

5. "Million Dollar Pix to Soar to New High," *Film Daily*, July 6, 1937, 3.

6. Ralph Wilk, "A Little from Hollywood Lots," *Film Daily*, March 5, 1937, 19; Vera Zorina, *Zorina* (New York: FSG, 1986).

7. On the Gershwin brothers' involvement in *The Goldwyn Follies*, see Howard Pollack, *George Gershwin: His Life and Work* (Berkeley: University of California Press, 2006), 684–90.

8. Manuscript copies of Duke's scores for the film are located in the George Balanchine Archive, Houghton Library, Harvard University. For an overview of the Gershwins' involvement in the *Goldwyn Follies*, including Ira Gershwin's work with Vernon Duke after George's death, see Howard Pollack, *George Gershwin: His Life and Work* (Berkeley: University of California Press, 2006), 684–90.

9. Gershwin is mentioned as being of interest to Balanchine and Warburg in Kirstein's diaries on November 8, 1935; April 18, 1936; July 28, 1936.

10. Ralph Wilk, "A Little from Hollywood Lots," *Film Daily*, February 27, 1937, 7; Pollack, *George Gershwin: His Life and Work*, 685.

11. Typescript of ballet scenario located in Box 10, Folder 10, George and Ira Gershwin Collection, LOC.

12. These events are recounted in Berg, *Goldwyn* and Pollack, *George Gershwin*.

13. "News of the Screen," *NYT*, July 16, 1937.

14. Johanna Lawrence, "Balanchine in Hollywood," *DT*, October 1937, 24.

15. Paul Harrison, "Hollywood News and Gossip," dated August 23, 1937, published in *The China Press*, December 13, 1937.

16. Ibid.

17. "Hollywood Men Fail to Charm Ballet Sirens," *WP*, August 9, 1937.

18. George Balanchine, "The Ballet and the Film: The Making of the *Goldwyn Follies*," *Dance Herald* 1, no. 6 (April 1938): 1, 7–8.

19. Ibid.

20. "Hollywood to Get New Type of Glamour," *LAT*, July 28, 1937.

21. Ibid.

22. George Balanchine, "Ballet in Films," *Dance News*, December 1944, 8 (reprint of 1937 article, located in *The Goldwyn Follies* Dossier, PBC).

23. Ibid.

24. Ibid.

25. "Goldwyn Follies Sets Mark," *Film Daily*, February 9, 1938, 2; "Goldwyn Follies First to Go Third at Oriental," *Film Daily*, March 8, 1938, 7.

26. "The Goldwyn Follies," *Film Daily*, January 27, 1938, 5.

27. "Sam Goldwyn's Big Parade," *Hollywood Spectator*, February 5, 1938, 7.

28. John K. Newnham, "Dance Film Notes: Balanchine's Perfect Screen Technique," *DT*, April 1938, 33.

29. Ibid.

30. "Goldwyn Follies Disappoints; Draggy, Overlong Musical," *Film Bulletin*, February 12, 1938, 11.

31. Ibid.

32. Jack Hazlett, Exhibitor report on *Goldwyn Follies, MPH*, April 30, 1938, 58.

33. A. E. Eliasen, Exhibitor report on *Goldwyn Follies, MPH*, May 28, 1938, 86.

34. Ibid.

35. Seymour Stocker, Exhibitor report on *Goldwyn Follies MPH*, September 24, 1938, 59.

36. W. E. McPhee, Exhibitor report on *Goldwyn Follies, MPH*, May 21, 1938, 52.

37. Bill Simon, Exhibitor report on *Goldwyn Follies, MPH*, July 16, 1938, 80.

38. Ibid.

39. Oaty Elmore and Robert Crickmore, Exhibitor report on *Goldwyn Follies, MPH*, September 3, 1938, 51.

40. L. A. Irwin, Exhibitor report on *Goldwyn Follies, MPH*, May 28, 1938, 86.

41. "News of the Screen," *NYHT*, November 3, 1937; "Coming and Going," *Film Daily*, December 23, 1937, 2.

42. Herbert Drake, "The Playbill," *NYHT*, November 21, 1937; "News of the Stage," *NYT*, November 27, 1937.

43. "Studio and Screen," *Manchester Guardian*, November 11, 1937.

44. Francis Perkins, "Carlo Tagliabue," *NYHT*, December 3, 1937.

45. Olin Downes, "Samson et Dalila," *NYT*, December 9, 1937.

46. "*Romeo* Is Heard at Metropolitan," *NYT*, December 17, 1937.

47. John Martin, "The Dance," *NYT*, February 6, 1938.

48. Olin Downes, "*Salome* Is Heard," *NYT*, February 8, 1938.

49. "Superb *Salome*," *WSJ*, February 8, 1938.

50. "Balanchine Quits Metropolitan Opera," *MA*, April 25, 1938, 8.

51. "Metropolitan Opera to Offer Its Own Ballet," *NYHT*, April 14, 1938.

52. Ibid.

53. Ibid.

54. John Martin, "The Dance: Opera Ballet," *NYT*, April 17, 1938.

55. Ibid.

56. "Balanchine at the Diamond Horseshoe," *DO*, May 1938,

57. "The End of an Unhappy Ballet Experiment at the Opera," *MA*, April 25, 1938.

58. Ibid.

59. Lincoln Kirstein to Louis Kirstein, November 13, 1937, LEK.

60. Chujoy, *The New York City Ballet*, 102–6.

61. "Native Scenes Pictured by Dance Group," unidentified clipping, CCP.

62. "By Eleanor Roosevelt," *World-Telegram*, June 15, 1938, RRS.

63. Grace Davidson, "Agree on Music for First Dance," *Boston Post*, June 13, 1938; [Title not included with clipping], *NYT*, June 19, 1938, RRS.

64. "I Married an Angel," *Variety*, April 16, 1938, RRS.

65. Ibid.

66. A short excerpt of these dances is included in Ann Barzel's dance films held at JRDD–NYPL.

67. [Title not included with clipping], *Variety*, May 18, 1938, RRS.

68. Excerpts from playscript pertaining to dance numbers are reproduced in the *I Married an Angel* Dossier, PBC. All quotes from scenario from this source.

69. Brooks Atkinson, "I Married an Angel," *NYT*, May 12, 1938.

70. "I Married an Angel," *Variety*, April 16, 1938, RRS.

71. Helen Eager, "Dwight Wiman Presents Rodgers and Hart Musical," *Boston Traveler*, April 20, 1938, RRS.

72. Ibid.

73. Johua Logan, *My Up and Down, In and Out Life*, (New York: Delacorte, 1976).

74. Walter Winchell, *Daily Mirror*, November 24, 1938, *The Boys from Syracuse* Dossier, PBC.

75. [Title not included with clipping], *Billboard*, December 3, 1938, *The Boys from Syracuse* Dossier, PBC.

76. John Anderson, "Jimmy Savo," *New York Journal-American*, November 25, 1938; *Boston Traveler*, November 8, 1938. *The Boys from Syracuse* Dossier, PBC.

77. Peggy Doyle, [title not included with clipping], *Boston Evening American*, November 8, 1938, *The Boys from Syracuse* Dossier, PBC.

78. [Title not included with clipping], *Variety*, November 9, 1938, *The Boys from Syracuse* Dossier, PBC.

79. Brooks Atkinson, *"The Boys from Syracuse," NYT*, November 24, 1938.

80. Burns Mantle, "The Boys from Syracuse," *NY Daily News*, November 24, 1938, *The Boys from Syracuse* Dossier, PBC.

81. Harold M. Bee, [title not included with clipping], *Variety*, undated, *The Boys from Syracuse* Dossier, PBC.

82. Brooks Atkinson, *"The Boys from Syracuse," NYT*, November 24, 1938.

83. Walter Winchell, *Daily Mirror*, November 24, 1938, *The Boys from Syracuse* Dossier, PBC.

84. Walter Winchell, *Daily Mirror*, November 24, 1938; *NY World Telegram*, November 25, 1938, *The Boys from Syracuse* Dossier, PBC.

85. Arthur Pollock, *Brooklyn Daily Eagle*, November 25, 1938; Harold M. Bee, *Variety*, undated, *The Boys from Syracuse* Dossier, PBC.

86. *New Haven Journal-Courier*, November 4, 1938; *Variety*, November 9, 1938, *The Boys from Syracuse* Dossier, PBC.

87. George Church, *Dancing Amongst the Stars*, unpublished memoir, JRDD–NYPL, 98.

88. [Title not included with clipping], *New Haven Journal Courier*, November 4, 1938, *The Boys from Syracuse* Dossier, PBC.

89. Peggy Doyle, [title not included with clipping], *Boston Evening American*, November 8, 1938, *The Boys from Syracuse* Dossier, PBC.

90. "The Stage," *BG*, November 23, 1938.

91. Russell Rhodes, "New York Letter," *DT*, January 1939, 509.

92. Interview with Annabelle Lyon by Barbara Palfy, *Great Lady* Dossier, PBC.

93. Ibid.

94. L. A. Sloper, *"Great Lady* at the Schubert," *CSM*, November 23, 1938.

95. Russell Rhodes, "New York Letter," *DT*, January 1939, 509–10.

96. Ibid.

97. "The Stage," *BG*, November 23, 1938.

98. L. A. Sloper, *"Great Lady* at the Schubert," *CSM*, November 23, 1938.

99. Annabelle Lyon Interview by Barbara Palfy, *Great Lady* Dossier, PBC.

100. Alicia Alonso Interview by Barbara Palfy and Camille Hardy, *Great Lady* Dossier, PBC.

101. [Uncredited clipping,] *NY World Telegram*, December 17, 1938, *Boys from Syracuse* Dossier, PBC.

102. "The Theatre," *WSJ*, December 3, 1938.

Chapter 9

1. Lincoln Kirstein, *Thirty Years*, 71.

2. "The Ballet Comes to Old Saybrook," EHS.

3. Ibid.

4. "Women Compete in Green Mountain Golf Tournament," *NYHT*, July 25, 1937.

5. "Bar Harbor Season Nears Peak; Concerts and Recitals Featured," *NYHT*, August 8, 1937

6. John Martin, "The Dance," *NYT*, June 6, 1937.

7. Ballet Caravan brochure, DCS.

8. "Mrs. E. K. Peeples Receives at Party," *WP*, October 12, 1937; Margaret Lloyd, "Back to the Ballet," *CSM*, November 24, 1937.

9. John Selby, "How Lincoln Kirstein Runs Ballet Caravan," *BG*, June 12, 1938.

10. Kirstein, *Blast at Ballet*, 43.

11. Cecil Smith, "Ballet Caravan Makes Bow to Chicago Today," *CT*, October 16, 1938.

12. Ballet Caravan brochure 1937, DCS.

13. Ibid.

14. Ibid.

15. "Ballet Caravan," Robin Hood Dell, July 19–20, 1937, EHS.

16. Ballet Caravan brochure 1937, DCS.

17. L. B., "Ballet Caravan Opens Festival," *New York World-Telegram*, February 19, 1938, EHS.

18. "Classic Mode Modern Dance: Ballet Caravan Feature at Armory; Is Not in College Course," *Bennington Bulletin*, July 26, 1937, EHS.

19. Marian Murray, "Filling Station Wins Acclaim Here in Presentation by Ballet Caravan," *Hartford Times*, January 6, 1938, EHS.

20. Ibid.

21. Irving Kolodin, "American Ballets Dance," *New York Sun*, December 13, 1937, EHS.

22. Ibid.

23. Elliott Carter, "With the Dancers," *MM*, January–February 1938, 119.

24. Ibid.

25. Mildred Wile, "Ballet Caravan," *DO*, August–September, 1937, 81.

26. Albertina Vitak, "The Ballet Caravan," *American Dancer*, February 1938 [Brooklyn Academy of Music, November 29 performance], EHS.

27. Elliott Carter, "With the Dancers," *MM*, January–February 1938, 119–20.

28. Albertina Vitak, "The Ballet Caravan," *American Dancer*, February 1938 [Brooklyn Academy of Music, November 29 performance], EHS.

29. Ibid.

30. Ibid.

31. Mildred Wile, "Ballet Caravan," *DO*, August–September, 1937, 81.

32. "Classic Mode Modern Dance: Ballet Caravan Feature at Armory; Is Not in College Course," *Bennington Bulletin*, July 26, 1937, EHS.

33. Ibid.

34. "Ballet Dancers Show Ability in Opening Civic Performance," *Syracuse Post-Standard*, November 19, 1937, EHS.

35. Ibid.

36. Mildred Wile, "Ballet Caravan," *DO*, August–September, 1937, 81.

37. John Martin, "The Dance: On Awards," *NYT*, May 15, 1938.

38. Elliott Carter, "With the Dancers," *MM*, January–February, 1938, 122.

39. "Ballet Dancers Show Ability in Opening Civic Performance," *Syracuse Post-Standard*, November 19, 1937, EHS.

40. Grace Deschamps, "Ballet Caravan Scores at Clark," November 12, 1937, EHS.

41. "Ballet Caravan Delights Capacity Audience Here," *Lowell Courier*, November 8, 1937, EHS.

42. "Ballet Caravan," Robin Hood Dell, July 19–20 [1937], EHS.

43. Ibid.

44. "Dance Recitals," *Brooklyn Eagle*, November 30, 1937, EHS.

45. Ibid.

46. Mildred Wile, "Ballet Caravan," *DO*, August–September, 1937, 81.

47. Brochure, DCS and EHS.

48. Lincoln Kirstein, "Dance International 1900–1937," *DO*, January 1938, 7.

49. Marian Murray, "Filling Station Wins Acclaim Here in Presentation by Ballet Caravan," *Hartford Times*, January 6, 1938, EHS.

50. Ibid.

51. Ballet Caravan brochure 1937, DCS.

52. Ibid.

53. "Ballet Group Finds Drama in Gas Station," *Newsweek*, January 17, 1938, 25–26.

54. Ibid.

55. Elliott Carter, "With the Dancers," *MM*, January–February, 1938, 122.

56. T. H. Parker, "Ballet's Premiere Given in Hartford," *MA*, February 10, 1938, 202.

57. "Lincoln Kirstein Lectures on Dance," *BG*, January 21, 1938.

58. John Martin, "Caravan Dancers in Three Ballets," *NYT*, February 19, 1938.

59. Margaret Lloyd, "Ballet Americana," *CSM*, January 24, 1938.

60. Ibid.

61. Ibid.

62. John Martin, "Caravan Dancers in Three Ballets," *NYT*, February 19, 1938.

63. Nancy Reynolds, *Repertory in Review*, 60.

64. Jerome Bohm, "Ballet Caravan," American Ballet Caravan clippings, JRDD.

65. Ibid.

66. John Chapman, "Pocahontas, Billy the Kid in Dance Form," *New York News*, May 25, 1939, EHS.

67. Pitts Sanborn, "Brilliant Program," American Ballet Caravan clippings, JRDD.

68. Joseph Bobbitt Jr., "Ballet Caravan Leaves a Critic a Bit Confused," [publication not given], Norfolk, January 19, 1939, EHS.

69. "Ballet Dances Again Tonight," *Charleston Post*, April 30, 1938, EHS.

70. Ibid.

71. Ibid.

72. Ibid.

73. Lincoln Kirstein to Muriel Draper, [April 1938] written from Charleston, South Carolina, MDP, Box 5, Folder 159.

74. Ibid.

75. Programs located in DCS and EHS.

76. Alicia Alonso interview by Barbara Palfy and Camille Hardy, November 13, 2001, *Great Lady* Dossier, PBC.

77. Juan Bonich, "El Ballet Caravan en Pro-Arte," *El Mundo*, May 7, 1938, EHS (translations by author).

78. "Pro-Arte: El Ballet 'Caravan,'" *Diario de la Marina*, May 6, 1938, EHS (translations by author) .

79. Ibid.

80. The Caravan's fall tour schedule is documented in an itinerary and programs and clippings in the Erick Hawkins Scrapbook, Kirstein's correspondence with Muriel Draper and his parents, and other press accounts.

81. Lincoln Kirstein, *Blast at Ballet*, 46.

82. Lincoln Kirstein, "About *Billy the Kid*," *DO*, October, 1938, 116.

83. Ibid.

84. Otis Ferguson, "Billy the Kid," *New Republic*, June 14, 1939.

85. Lincoln Kirstein to Muriel Draper, October 28, 1938, MDP, Box 5, Folder 159.

86. Lincoln Kirstein to Muriel Draper, [1938?] written in Kansas City, MDP, Box 5, Folder 159.

87. Lincoln Kirstein to Muriel Draper, December 3, 1938, MDP, Box 5, Folder 159.

88. Ibid.

89. Ibid.

90. Lincoln Kirstein to Muriel Draper, [November 24, 1938], El Paso, MDP, Box 5, Folder 159.

91. John Selby, "How Lincoln Kirstein Runs Ballet Caravan," *BG*, June 12, 1938.

92. Lincoln Kirstein to Muriel Draper, [April 1938] from Charleston, South Carolina, MDP, Box 5, Folder 171.

93. Lincoln Kirstein to Muriel Draper, [1938?] Hotel Clark, Los Angeles letterhead, MDP, Box 5, Folder 159.

94. Lincoln Kirstein to Muriel Draper, October 26, 1938, MDP, Box 5, Folder 159.

95. Lincoln Kirstein to Muriel Draper, 1938?] Jacksonville, Florida, letterhead, MDP, Box 5, Folder 159.

96. Lincoln Kirstein to Muriel Draper, October 26, 1938, MDP, Box 5, Folder 159.

97. Lincoln Kirstein to Muriel Draper, [1938?] written in Kansas City, MDP, Box 5, Folder 159.

98. Lincoln Kirstein to Muriel Draper, [1938?] Hotel Clark, Los Angeles letterhead, MDP, Box 5, Folder 159.

99. Lincoln Kirstein to Muriel Draper, [April 1938] written in Charleston, South Carolina MDP, Box 5, Folder 171.

100. Ibid.

101. Lincoln Kirstein, *Blast at Ballet*, 53.

102. Ibid.

103. Ibid., 56.

104. Ibid., 50.

105. Ibid., 50–51.

106. Ibid., 51.

107. Louis Kirstein to Lincoln Kirstein, December 6, 1937, LEK.

108. Lincoln Kirstein to Louis Kirstein, December 16, 1937, LEK.

109. Louis Kirstein to Lincoln Kirstein, December 17, 1937, LEK.

110. Lincoln Kirstein to Louis Kirstein, December 21, 1937, LEK.

111. Lincoln Kirstein to Louis Kirstein, January 4, 1938, LEK.

112. Lincoln Kirstein to Louis Kirstein, January 3, 1938, LEK.

113. Lincoln Kirstein to Louis Kirstein, July 13, 1938, LEK.

114. Lincoln Kirstein to Muriel Draper, [1938?] Hotel Clark, Los Angeles letterhead, MDP, Box 5, Folder 159.

115. For a discussion of Louis Kirstein's role in Lincoln Kirstein's development as a dance impresario, as well as the advisory role played by Louis's secretary E. R. "Effie" Beverley, see James Steichen, "The Education of Lincoln Kirstein: 'One Can't Refuse What One Knows Will Go So Far,'" *Dance Chronicle* 38, no. 3 (2015): 336–59.

116. Lincoln Kirstein, *Blast at Ballet*, 49.

117. Louis Kirstein to Lincoln Kirstein, October 24, 1938, LEK.

118. Louis Kirstein to Lincoln Kirstein, December 3, 1938, LEK.

119. Lincoln Kirstein to Rose and Louis Kirstein, [November 1938?], written from Los Angeles, LEK.

120. Lincoln Kirstein to Rose and Louis Kirstein, November 20, 1938, El Presidio Hotel, Tucson, Arizona, letterhead, LEK.

121. Lincoln Kirstein to Louis Kirstein, November 20, 1938, LEK.

122. Lincoln Kirstein to Muriel Draper, [1938 from Los Angeles?], MDP, Box 5, Folder 159.

Chapter 10

1. Program, EHS; Louis Kirstein to Lincoln Kirstein, December 3, 1938, LEK.

2. Stewart Sabin, "Ballet Caravan Makes First Visit Here," [unidentified clipping], CCP.

3. John Martin, "The Dance," *NYT*, January 8, 1939.

4. "Ballet Caravan Headed for Hampton Institute," *Chicago Defender*, January 14, 1939. On Williams and the Hampton Creative Dance Group, see John O. Perpener III, *African-American Concert Dance* (Urbana: University of Illinois Press, 2001), 78–100.

5. Norvleate Downing, *New Journal and Guide* [Norfolk, Va.], February 4, 1939.

6. Joseph Bobbit Jr., "Ballet Caravan Leaves a Critic a Bit Confused," [publication not given], Norfolk, January 19, 1939, EHS.

7. Ibid.

8. Mozelle Horton Young, "Ballet Caravan Thrills Atlantans," *Atlanta Constitution*, January 22, 1939.

9. "At Colonies in Mid-South," *NYT*, January 22, 1939; "Dinners Precede Palm Beach Show," *NYT*, January 26, 1939.

10. Program, PDP.

11. E[lizabeth] S[herbon], "Washington Irving, Ballet Caravan, January 28, 1939," *DO*, March 1939, 187.

12. "Group Formed to Present U.S. Operatic Works," *NYHT*, January 11, 1939.

13. Ibid.

14. Sketches of *Pocahontas* and *Billy the Kid, MM*, May–June, 1939.

15. "American Lyric Theater to End Season Saturday," *NYHT*, May 25, 1939.

16. Pitts Sanborn, "The American Lyric Theater," *CSM*, May 27, 1939; Programs, May 24, 25, and 26, 1939, EHS; Flier, Clipping File for American Ballet Caravan, JRDD.

17. Jerome Bohm, "Ballet Caravan," *NYHT*, May 25, 1939.

18. John Martin, "Ballet Caravan in Seasonal Debut," *NYT*, May 25, 1939.

19. Russell Rhodes, "New York Letter," *DT*, July 1939, 412.

20. Russell Rhodes, "New York Letter," *DT*, February 1939, 618.

21. "Ballet Caravan Plans Transcontinental Tour," *CSM*, October 10, 1939; "Dance Notes," *NYHT*, October 15, 1939; "Will Appear with Famous Dance Group," undated clipping [Charlotte], CCP.

22. "Ballet Caravan Plans Transcontinental Tour," *CSM*, October 10, 1939; Cecil Smith, "Two New Ballets Given," *CT*, October 30, 1939.

23. Stanley Bligh, "Unique Dance Group Scores Distinct Hit," *Vancouver Sun*, November 14, 1939, CCP; Stanley Bligh, "Dancers Score a Second Hit," *Vancouver Sun*, November 15, 1939, CCP; "Program Given by Ballet Caravan," *Salinas Post*, November 1939, CCP; Alfred Frankenstein, "Bach Ballet Performance Is Persuasively Executed," *San Francisco Chronicle*, November 27, 1939, CCP; Program [Stockton, Ca.], William Dollar Program Files, JRDD; "American Ballet Caravan Program Is Announced," *Stockton Record*, November 24, 1939, CCP; W. E. Oliver, "American Ballet Is Presented," *Los Angeles Evening Herald*, December 2, 1939, CCP; Sally Brown Moody, "American Ballet Caravan Captivates S. D. Crowd," *SD Cal. Union*, December 4, 1939, CCP.

24. Program [marked "Wichita"], William Dollar Program File, JRDD.

25. Reynolds, *Repertory in Review*, 62.

26. Ibid., 61–62.

27. W. E. Oliver, "American Ballet Is Presented," December 2, 1939, CCP; Alfred Frankenstein, "Bach Ballet Performance," November 27, 1939, CCP. For this and the following footnotes 28–32 no publication is noted in the clippings from the scrapbook.

28. Alexander Fried, "Ballet Caravan Praised," November 27, 1939, CCP.

29. Sally Brown Moody, "American Ballet Caravan," December 4, 1939, CCP.

30. Alexander Fried, "Ballet Caravan Praised," November 27, 1939, CCP; Stanley Bligh, "Dancers Score a Second Hit," November 15, 1939, CCP.

31. Marjory Fisher, "Ballet Caravan Opens Stetson," November 27, 1939, CCP.

32. Isabel Morse Jones, "Ballet Caravan Wins High Favor," undated 1939, CCP.

33. "Holiday Dance Festival," *NYT*, December 10, 1939; John Martin, "Martha Graham," *NYT*, December 28, 1939.

34. Program (December 26), EHS; Walter Terry, "Bach Variations," *NYHT*, December 29, 1939; Margaret Lloyd, "American Ballet Caravan," *CSM*, December 22, 1939.

35. Geoffrey Block, *Richard Rodgers*, 113–15.

36. Ralph Wilk, "A Little from Hollywood Lots," *Film Daily*, March 6, 1939.

37. "Coming and Going," *Film Daily*, May 9, 1939; May 29, 1939; and June 23, 1939.

38. John K. Newnham, "Dance Film Notes," *DT*, December 1939, 138.

39. Ibid.

40. John K. Newnham, "Dance Film Notes," *DT*, December 1939, 139.

41. Ibid.

42. John K. Newnham, "Dance Film Notes," *DT*, July 1939, 411.

43. Interview with Ray Weamer and Joan Bayley by Beth Genné, Hollywood Films Dossier, PBC.

44. Ibid.

45. *"On Your Toes,"* *Variety*, October 25, 1939.

46. John Newham, "Dance Film Notes," *DT*, April 1940.

47. Ibid.

48. Howard Barnes, "On the Screen," *NYHT*, October 21, 1939.

49. *"On Your Toes* Screened," *CSM*, November 3, 1939.

50. Howard Barnes, "On the Screen," *NYHT*, October 21, 1939.

51. Ibid.

52. "Vera Zorina Quits Wiman's Musical," *NYT*, November 4, 1939.

53. "Coming and Going," *Film Daily*, August 22, 1939.

54. "On the Screen," *NYT*, May 20, 1940.

55. John Scott, "Zorina Wins Favor," *LAT*, May 9, 1940.

56. *"I Was an Adventuress,"* *Variety*, May 1, 1940.

57. "Zorina Makes Picture," *CT*, June 17, 1940.

58. "Coming and Going," *Film Daily*, March 4 and March 6, 1940.

59. Citizenship certificate located in GBA.

60. "Ballet Russe Opens," *NYT,* March 26, 1940; "Dance Notes," *NYHT*, April 7, 1940.

61. Walter Terry, "Balachine's *Baiser,"* *NYHT*, April 11, 1940.

62. John Martin, "Novelties Given by Ballet Russe," *NYT*, April 11, 1940.

63. Margaret Lloyd, *"Le Baiser de la Fée* Is Hit," *CSM*, April 22, 1940.

64. John Martin, "Novelties Given by Ballet Russe," *NYT*, April 11, 1940.

65. Walter Terry, "To Better Ballet," *NYHT*, April 21, 1940.

66. Russell Rhodes, "New York Letter," *DT*, June 1940, 539.

67. Details in this section regarding *A Thousand Times Neigh* have been drawn from two archival sources: MGZR Thousand Times Neigh Dance Clipping File, JRDD–NYPL and the *A Thousand Times Neigh* Scrapbook, Benson Ford Research Center, The Henry Ford.

68. Script located in *A Thousand Times Neigh* Scrapbook, The Henry Ford.

69. Unless otherwise noted, these and all other press quotes regarding this ballet are taken from clippings located in *A Thousand Times Neigh* Dance Clipping File, JRDD.

70. Quoted in John Martin, "The Dance: Dobbin et al.," *NYT*, June 30, 1940.

71. John Martin, "The Dance: Dobbin et al.," *NYT*, June 30, 1940.

72. Ibid.

73. Walter Terry, "A Ballet Club," *NYHT*, May 19, 1940.

74. Ibid.

75. Margaret Lloyd, "Ballet Carries On," *CSM*, September 5, 1940.

76. Ibid.

77. Russell Rhodes, "New York Letter," *DT*, April 1939, 31–32; Russell Rhodes, "New York Letter," *DT*, May 1939, 154.

78. "Plays Out of Town," *Variety*, May 8, 1940.

79. Ibid.

80. Ray Bolger in *I Remember Balanchine: Recollections of the Ballet Master by Those Who Knew Him*, ed. Francis Mason (New York: Doubleday, 1991), 156.

81. Ibid.

82. José Limón, *An Unfinished Memoir*, Ed. Lynn Garafola (Hanover, NH: University Press of New England, 1998), 92–93.

83. Ibid., 93.

84. Ibid., 94.

85. "Plays Out of Town," *Variety*, May 8, 1940.

86. L. A. Sloper, "Premiere of *Keep Off the Grass*," *CSM*, May 1, 1940.

87. "Zorina," *Harper's Bazaar*, August 1940, 65.

88. These and other details regarding *Louisiana Purchase* from Jeffrey Magee, *Irving Berlin's American Musical Theatre* (New York: Oxford University Press, 2012), 195–98.

89. Leonard Lyons, "The New Yorker," *WP*, June 2, 1940.

90. "Plays on Broadway," *Variety*, June 5, 1940.

91. Unidentified clippings, *Louisiana Purchase* Scrapbook, Irving Berlin Collection, LOC.

92. Ibid.

93. Ibid.

94. Vernon Duke, *Passport to Paris* (Boston: Little, Brown, 1955). 382–83.

95. George Ross, "Russian Harangue Jars Rehearsals," [unidentified clipping], *Cabin in the Sky* Scrapbook (1940), VDC.

96. Ibid.

97. For a recent new account of Dunham's life and career, see Joanna Dee Das, *Katherine Dunham: Dance and the African Diaspora* (New York: Oxford University Press, 2017). Balanchine and Dunham's collaboration on *Cabin in the Sky* is also discussed in Carol Oja, *Bernstein Meets Broadway: Collaborative Art in a Time of War* (New York: Oxford University Press, 2014).

98. Interview of Katherine Dunham by Constance Valis Hill, *Cabin in the Sky* Dossier, PBC.

99. Katherine Dunham in *I Remember Balanchine: Recollections of the Ballet Master by Those Who Knew Him*, ed. Francis Mason (New York: Doubleday, 1991), 190.

100. Ibid.

101. Burns Mantle, "Ethel Waters, *Cabin in the Sky*," *Cabin in the Sky* Scrapbook (1940), VDC.

102. Brooks Atkinson, "The Play," *NYT*, October 26, 1940.

103. George Freedley, "The Stage Today," [unidentified clipping], *Cabin in the Sky* Scrapbook (1940), VDC.

104. "New Plays," *Cue*, November 2, 1940, *Cabin in the Sky* Scrapbook (1940), VDC.

105. John Martin, "Season Is Opened by Ballet Russe," *NYT*, October 15, 1940.

106. Ibid.

107. John Martin, "The Ballet Russe in Two Premieres," *NYT*, October 18, 1940.

108. Ibid.

109. Luther Davis and John Cleveland, "Russian Genius," *Collier's*, [undated clipping], Cabin in the Sky Scrapbook (1940), VDC.

110. "School of Ballet Trials," *NYT*, October 5, 1940.

111. School of American Ballet Brochure, 1940, GBA.

BIBLIOGRAPHY

Archival and Unpublished Sources

BAKER LIBRARY, HARVARD BUSINESS SCHOOL

Louis Edward Kirstein Business Records

BEINECKE RARE BOOK AND MANUSCRIPT LIBRARY

Muriel Draper Papers, Yale Collection of American Literature

BENSON FORD RESEARCH CENTER, THE HENRY FORD

A Thousand Times Neigh Scrapbook

THE FRICK ART REFERENCE LIBRARY, THE FRICK COLLECTION

Edward Warburg, *As I Recall: Some Memoirs*

IRVING S. GILMORE MUSIC LIBRARY, YALE UNIVERSITY

Kay Swift Papers

HARVARD THEATRE COLLECTION, HOUGHTON LIBRARY, HARVARD UNIVERSITY

George Balanchine Archive
Vera Zorina Archive

MUSIC DIVISION, LIBRARY OF CONGRESS

George Antheil Collection
Irving Berlin Collection
Vernon Duke Collection
George and Ira Gershwin Collection
Erick Hawkins Collection

MUSEUM OF PERFORMANCE AND DESIGN, SAN FRANCISCO

Lew Christensen–Gisella Caccialanza Papers

JEROME ROBBINS DANCE DIVISION AND MUSIC DIVISION, NEW YORK PUBLIC LIBRARY
FOR THE PERFORMING ARTS

Ann Barzel Collection

George Church Memoir
Douglas Coudy Scrapbook
Dance Films by Ann Barzel
Tamara Geva Interview
Lincoln Kirstein Papers
Annabelle Lyon Interview
Museum of Modern Art Photographs Collection
On Your Toes Script
Orpheus and Eurydice Photographs Collection
Ruth Page Collection
Yvonne Patterson and William Dollar Papers
Popular Balanchine Collection
Producing Company of the School of American Ballet Scrapbook
Rethinking the Balanchine Legacy Collection
Richard Rodgers Scrapbooks
Pavel Tchelitchev *Orpheus and Eurydice* Set and Costume Designs
Clippings and Program Files
    American Ballet Caravan
    Anchutina, Leda
    Babes in Arms
    Balanchine, George
    Caccialanza, Gisella
    Dollar, William
    Hasburgh, Rabana
    Laskey, Charles
    Levinoff, Joseph
    Lyon, Annabelle
    Mullowny, Kathryn
    On Your Toes
    A Thousand Times Neigh

UNIVERSITY OF ILLINOIS ARCHIVES

W. McNeil Lowry Papers

Newspapers and Magazines

    Baltimore Sun
    Billboard Theatrical Index
    Boston Globe
    Chicago Defender
    Chicago Tribune
    Christian Science Monitor
    Dance
    Dance Magazine
    Dance Observer
    Dancing Times
    Film Daily

Film Herald
Hartford Courant
Hound & Horn
Jewish Advocate
Los Angeles Times
Modern Music
Motion Picture Herald
Musical America
New Republic
New York Herald-Tribune
New York Times
Newsweek
Theatre Arts Monthly
Time
Variety
Vogue
Wall Street Journal
Washington Post

Selected Books, Articles, and Dissertations

Albright, Daniel. *Untwisting the Serpent: Modernism in Music, Literature, and the Visual Arts*. Chicago: University of Chicago Press, 2000.

Antheil, George. *Bad Boy of Music*. Garden City, NY: Doubleday, Doran, 1945.

Badger, Anthony. *The New Deal: The Depression Years, 1933–1940*. New York: Hill and Wang, 1989.

Balanchine, George, and Francis Mason. *101 Stories of the Great Ballets*. New York: 1954; reprinted by Anchor Books, 1989.

Banes, Sally. "Balanchine and Black Dance." In *Writing Dancing in the Age of Postmodernism*, 53–69. Hanover, NH: Wesleyan University Press/University Press of New England, 1994.

Banes, Sally. "Sibling Rivalry." In *Dance for a City: Fifty Years of the New York City Ballet*, ed. Lynn Garafola with Eric Foner. New York: Columbia University Press, 1999, 73–98.

Bernstein, Leonard. *The Joy of Music*. New York: Simon and Schuster, 1959.

Block, Geoffrey. *Enchanted Evenings: The Broadway Musical from Showboat to Sondheim and Lloyd Webber*. New York: Oxford University Press, 2004.

Block, Geoffrey. *Richard Rodgers*. New Haven, CT: Yale University Press, 2003.

Block, Geoffrey, Ed. *The Richard Rodgers Reader*. New York: Oxford University Press, 2002.

Boris, Ruthanna. "Serenade." In Robert Gottlieb, ed., *Reading Dance: A Gathering of Memoirs, Reportage, Criticism, Profiles, Interviews, and Some Uncategorizable Extras* (New York: Pantheon Books, 2008), 1063–66.

Brisson, Peter and Clement Crisp. *The International Book of Ballet*. New York: Stein and Day, 1971.

Buckle, Richard, with John Taras, *George Balanchine, Ballet Master*. New York: Random House, 1988.

Chazin-Bennahum, Judith. *René Blum and the Ballets Russes: In Search of a Lost Life.* Oxford: Oxford University Press, 2011.

Chernow, Ron. *The Warburgs: The Twentieth-Century Odyssey of a Remarkable Jewish Family.* New York: Random House, 1993.

Choreography by George Balanchine: A Catalogue of Works. New York: Viking, 1984.

Chujoy, Anatole. *The New York City Ballet.* New York: Knopf, 1953.

Chujoy, Anatole. *The Symphonic Ballet.* New York: Kamin, 1937.

Collaer, Paul. *Darius Milhaud.* Translated and edited by Jane Hohfeld Galante. San Francisco: San Francisco Press, 1988.

Crist, Elizabeth Bergman. *Music for the Common Man: Aaron Copland in the Depression and War.* New York: Oxford University Press, 2008.

Das, Joanna Dee. *Katherine Dunham: Dance and the African Diaspora.* New York: Oxford University Press, 2017.

Denning, Michael. *The Cultural Front: The Laboring of American Culture in the Twentieth Century.* London: Verso, 1997/2010.

Dorris, George. "The Metropolitan Opera Ballet, Fresh Starts: Rosina Galli and the Ballets Russes, 1912–1917." *Dance Chronicle* 35, no. 2 (2012): 173–207.

Dorris, George. "The Metropolitan Opera Ballet, Fresh Starts: The Influence of the Ballets Russes, 1917–1919." *Dance Chronicle* 35, no. 3 (2012): 281–314.

Draper, Paul. "Music and Dancing." In *Making Music for Modern Dance*, ed. Katherine Teck. New York: Oxford University Press, 2011, 284–86.

Draper, Paul. "Tapping into the Classics." In Rusty Frank, *Tap! The Greatest Tap Dance Stars and Their Stories, 1900–1955*, 231–40. New York: William Morrow, 1990.

Duberman, Martin. *The Worlds of Lincoln Kirstein.* Evanston, IL: Northwestern University Press, 2008.

Duke, Vernon. *Passport to Paris.* Boston: Little, Brown, 1955.

Dunning, Jennifer. *"But First a School," The First Fifty Years of the School of American Ballet.* New York: Viking, 1985.

Epstein, Louis K. "Toward a Theory of Patronage: Funding for Music Composition in France, 1918–1939." PhD diss., Harvard University, 2013.

Faherty, Michael. *"Hound and Horn* (1937–34)." In *The Oxford Critical and Cultural History of Modernist Magazines*, ed. Peter Brooker and Andrew Thacker, vol. 2 (North America, 1894–1960), 420–36.

Fiedler, Joanna. *Molto Agitato: The Mayhem behind the Music at the Metropolitan Opera.* New York: Doubleday/Nan A. Talese, 2001.

Foulkes, Julia. *Modern Bodies: Dance and American Modernism from Martha Graham to Alvin Ailey.* Chapel Hill: University of North Carolina Press, 2002.

Franko, Mark. *Dancing Modernism/Performing Politics.* Bloomington: Indiana University Press, 1995.

Franko, Mark. *Martha Graham in Love and War.* London: Oxford University Press, 2012.

Franko, Mark. *The Work of Dance: Labor, Movement and Identity in the 1930s.* Middletown, CT: Wesleyan University Press, 2002.

Gaddis, Eugene. *Magician of the Modern: Chick Austin and the Transformation of the Arts in America.* New York: Knopf, 2000.

Garafola, Lynn. *Diaghilev's Ballets Russes.* Oxford: Oxford University Press, 1989.

Garafola, Lynn. "George Antheil and the Dance." In *Legacies of Twentieth-Century Dance*, 256–76. Middletown, CT: Wesleyan University Press, 2005.

Garafola, Lynn. "Lincoln Kirstein, Modern Dance, and the Left." *Dance Research* 23, no. 1 (Summer 2005), 18–35.

Garafola, Lynn. "Making an American Dance: *Billy the Kid, Rodeo*, and *Appalachian Spring*." In *Aaron Copland and His World*, ed. Carol Oja and Judith Tick. Princeton, NJ: Princeton University Press, 2005, 121–47.

Garafola, Lynn, ed., with Eric Foner. *Dance for a City: Fifty Years of the New York City Ballet*. New York: Columbia University Press, 1999.

García-Márquez, Vicente. *The Ballets Russes: Colonel de Basil's Ballets Russes de Monte Carlo, 1932–1952*. New York: Knopf, 1990.

The Golden Horseshoe: The Life and Times of the Metropolitan Opera House. New York: Viking Press, 1965.

Gottlieb, Robert. *George Balanchine: The Ballet Maker*. New York: Atlas Books/ HarperCollins, 2004.

Gottlieb, Robert, ed. *Reading Dance: A Gathering of Memoirs, Reportage, Criticism, Profiles, Interviews, and Some Uncategorizable Extras*. New York: Pantheon Books, 2008.

Gottschild, Brenda Dixon. *Digging the Africanist Presence in American Performance: Dance and Other Contexts*, Westport, CT: Greenwood Press, 1996.

Gottschild, Brenda Dixon. *Joan Meyers Brown and the Audacious Hope of the Black Ballerina*. New York: Palgrave, 2012.

Graff, Ellen. *Stepping Left: Dance and Politics in New York City, 1928–1942*. Durham, NC: Duke University Press, 1997.

Harris, Andrea. *Making Ballet American: Modernism before and beyond Balanchine*. New York: Oxford University Press, 2017.

Haskell, Arnold. *Balletomania, Then and Now*. New York: Knopf, 1977.

Hill, Constance Valis. *Brotherhood in Rhythm: The Jazz Tap Dancing of the Nicholas Brothers*. New York: Cooper Square Press, 2002.

Hill, Constance Valis. *Tap Dancing America*. New York: Oxford University Press, 2010.

Homans, Jennifer. *Apollo's Angels: A History of Ballet*. New York: Random House, 2010.

Howard, Ruth Eleanor. *The Story of the American Ballet*. New York: IHRA, 1936.

Hyland, William. *Richard Rodgers*. New Haven, CT: Yale University Press, 1998.

Jenkins, Nicholas, ed. *By, With, To & From: A Lincoln Kirstein Reader*. New York: Farrar, Straus & Giroux, 1991.

Jones, Susan. *Literature, Modernism, and Dance*. Oxford: Oxford University Press, 2013.

Jordan, Stephanie. *Moving Music: Dialogues with Music in Twentieth-Century Ballet*. London: Dance Books, 2000.

Jordan, Stephanie. *Stravinsky Dances: Re-Visions across a Century*. London: Dance Books, 2007.

Joseph, Charles. *Stravinsky and Balanchine: A Journey of Invention*. New Haven, CT: Yale University Press, 2002.

Joseph, Charles. *Stravinsky's Ballets*. New Haven, CT: Yale University Press, 2012.

Jowitt, Deborah. *Time and the Dancing Image*. Berkeley: University of California Press, 1988.

Kendall, Elizabeth. *Balanchine and the Lost Muse: Revolution & the Making of a Choreographer*. London: Oxford University Press, 2013.

Kirstein, Lincoln. *Ballet: Bias & Belief—Three Pamphlets Collected and Other Dance Writings of Lincoln Kirstein*. Introduction and Comments by Nancy Reynolds. New York: Dance Horizons, 1983.

Kirstein, Lincoln. "The Ballet in Hartford." In *A. Everett Austin, Jr., A Director's Taste and Achievement*. Hartford, CT: Wadsworth Atheneum, 1958, 63–74.

Kirstein, Lincoln. *Blast at Ballet: A Corrective for the American Audience*. New York: Marstin Press, 1938.

Kirstein, Lincoln. *Dance: A Short History of Classic Theatrical Dancing*. New York: Dance Horizons, 1935; reprinted 1977.

Kirstein, Lincoln. "Dance Chronicle: Kreutzberg; Wigman; *Pas d'Acier*; The Future." *Hound & Horn* 4, no. 4 (1931): 573–580.

Kirstein, Lincoln. "The Diaghilev Period." *Hound & Horn* 3, no. 4 (1930): 468–501.

Kirstein, Lincoln. Introductory essay to *Pavel Tchelitchev: An Exhibition in the Gallery of Modern Art, 20 March through 19 April 1964*. New York: Foundation for Modern Art, 1964.

Kirstein, Lincoln. *The New York City Ballet*. New York: Knopf, 1973.

Kirstein, Lincoln. *Tchelitchev*. Santa Fe: Twelvetrees Press, 1994.

Kirstein, Lincoln. *Thirty Years: Lincoln Kirstein's The New York City Ballet*. New York: Knopf, 1978.

Kolodin, Irving. *The Metropolitan Opera, 1883–1966, a Candid History*. New York: Knopf, 1966.

Kriegsman, Sali Ann. *Modern Dance in America: The Bennington Years*. Boston: G. K. Hall, 1981.

Levin, David, J. *Unsettling Opera: Staging Mozart, Verdi, Wagner, and Zemlinsky*. Chicago: University of Chicago Press, 2007.

Levine, Lawrence. *Highbrow/Lowbrow: The Emergence of Cultural Hierarchy in America*. Cambridge, MA: Harvard University Press, 1988.

Limarzi, Tullia. "Metropolitan Opera Ballet" in *International Encyclopedia of Dance*, Ed. Selma Jeanne Cohen, New York and London: Oxford University Press, 2005.

Limón, José. *An Unfinished Memoir*. Ed. Lynn Garafola with an introduction by Deborah Jowitt. Hanover, NH: University Press of New England, 1998.

Macaulay, Alastair. "Serenade: Evolutionary Stages." *Ballet Review* 44, no. 4 (Winter 2016–2017).

Manning, Susan. *Ecstasy and the Demon: Feminism and Nationalism in the Dances of Mary Wigman*. Berkeley: University of California Press, 1993.

Manning, Susan. *Modern Dance, Negro Dance: Race in Motion*. Minneapolis: University of Minnesota Press, 2004.

Martin, John. *Ruth Page, an Intimate Biography*. New York: Marcel Dekker, 1977.

Mason, Francis, ed. *I Remember Balanchine: Recollections of the Ballet Master by Those Who Knew Him*. New York: Doubleday, 1991.

Mayer, Martin. *The Met: One Hundred Years of Grand Opera*. New York: Simon and Schuster, 1983.

Mayor, A. Hyatt. "Comment." *Dance Index* 3, nos. 1–2 (January–February 1944): 3.

McLean, Adrienne. *Dying Swans and Madmen: Ballet, the Body, and Narrative Cinema.* New Brunswick, NJ: Rutgers University Press, 2008.

McMillin, Scott. *The Musical as Drama.* Princeton, NJ: Princeton University Press, 2006.

Milhaud, Darius. *Notes without Music.* New York: Knopf, 1952.

Mordden, Ethan. *Sing for Your Supper: The Broadway Musical in the 1930s.* New York: Palgrave Macmillan, 2005.

Morris, Gay. *A Game for Dancers: Performing Modernism in the Postwar Years, 1945–1960.* Middletown, CT: Wesleyan University Press, 2006.

Morris, Gay. "Modernism's Role in the Theory of John Martin and Edwin Denby." *Dance Research* 22, no. 2 (Winter 2004): 168–84.

Nice, David. *Prokofiev: From Russia to the West, 1891–1935.* New Haven, CT: Yale University Press, 2003.

Ohl, Vicky. *Fine and Dandy: The Life and Work of Kay Swift.* New Haven, CT: Yale University Press, 2004.

O'Leary, James. "*Oklahoma!*, 'Lousy Publicity,' and the Politics of Formal Integration in the American Musical Theater." *Journal of Musicology* 31, no. 1 (Winter 2014): 139–82.

Olmstead, Andrea. *Juilliard: A History.* Urbana: University of Illinois Press, 1999.

Randall, Tresa. "Hanya Holm and an American *Tanzgemeinschaft.*" In *New German Dance Studies*, ed. Susan Manning and Julia Ruprecht. Urbana: University of Illinois Press, 2012, 79–98.

Reynolds, Nancy. "In His Image: Diaghilev and Lincoln Kirstein." In *The Ballets Russes and Its World*, ed. Lynn Garafola and Nancy Van Norman Baer. New Haven, CT: Yale University Press, 1999, 291–311.

Reynolds, Nancy. *Repertory in Review: 40 Years of the New York City Ballet.* New York: Dial Press, 1977.

Reynolds, Nancy, and Malcolm McCormick. *No Fixed Points: Dance in the Twentieth Century.* New Haven, CT: Yale University Press, 2003.

Rodgers, Richard. *Musical Stages: An Autobiography.* New York: Random House, 1975.

Savran, David. *Highbrow/Lowdown: Theater, Jazz, and the Making of the New Middle Class.* Ann Arbor: University of Michigan Press, 2009.

Scheijen, Sjeng. *Diaghilev: A Life.* New York: Oxford University Press, 2009.

Scholl, Tim. *From Petipa to Balanchine: Classical Revival and the Modernization of Ballet.* New York: Routledge, 1994.

Skeel, Sharon. "First Steps: Balanchine's Early Ties to Philadelphia." Paper presented at the Dance Critics Association, Philadelphia, June 2014.

Soares, Janet Mansfield. *Louis Horst: Musician in a Dancer's World.* Durham, NC: Duke University Press, 1992.

Soares, Janet Mansfield. *Martha Hill and the Making of American Dance.* Middletown, CT: Wesleyan University Press, 2009.

Souritz, Elizabeth. *Soviet Choreographers in the 1920s.* Translated by Lynn Visson; edited by Sally Banes. Durham, NC: Duke University Press, 1990.

Sowell, Debra Hickenlooper. *The Christensen Brothers: An American Dance Epic.* Amsterdam: Harwood Academic, 1998.

Steichen, James. "The American Ballet's Caravan." *Dance Research Journal* 47, no. 1 (April 2015): 69–94.

Steichen, James. "Balanchine's 'Bach Ballet' and the Dances of *On Your Toes*." *Journal of Musicology* 35, no. 2 (Spring 2018): 267–93.

Steichen, James. "The Education of Lincoln Kirstein: 'One Can't Refuse What One Knows Will Go So Far.'" *Dance Chronicle* 38, no. 3 (2015): 336–59.

Stern, Jonathan. "Music for the (American) People: The Lewisohn Stadium Concerts, 1922–1964." PhD diss., City University of New York, 2009.

Sundman, Alexandra Gail. "The Making of an American Expatriate Composer in Paris: A Contextual Study of the Music and Critical Writings of Virgil Thomson, 1921–1940." PhD diss., Yale University, 1999.

Taper, Bernard. *Balanchine, a Biography.* New York: Times Books, 1984.

Teachout, Terry. *All in the Dances: A Brief Life of George Balanchine.* New York: Harcourt, 2004.

Tyler, Parker. *The Divine Comedy of Pavel Tchelitchev.* New York: Fleet Publishing, 1967.

Volkov, Solomon. *Balanchine's Tchaikovsky: Interviews with George Balanchine.* Translated by Antonina W. Bouis. New York: Simon and Schuster, 1985.

Walker, Kathrine Sorley. *De Basil's Ballets Russes.* New York: Atheneum, 1983.

Walsh, Stephen. *Stravinsky: The Second Exile: France and America, 1934–1971.* New York: Knopf, 2006.

Weber, Nicholas Fox. *Patron Saints: Five Rebels Who Opened America to a New Art, 1928–1943.* New York: Knopf, 1992.

Whitesitt, Linda. *The Life and Music of George Antheil.* Ann Arbor: UMI Research Press, 1983.

Williams, Mason. *City of Ambition: FDR, La Guardia, and the Making of Modern New York.* New York: Norton, 2013.

Windham, Donald. "The Stage and Ballet Designs of Pavel Tchelitchew." *Dance Index* 3, nos. 1–2 (January–February 1944): 4–32.

Zeller, Jessica. *Shapes of American Ballet: Teachers and Training before Balanchine.* New York: Oxford University Press, 2016.

Zorina, Vera. *Zorina.* New York: Farrar, Straus & Giroux, 1986.

INDEX

A Thousand Times Neigh (Dollar), 225–228
Air and Variations (Dollar), 200, 201, 214
Alma Mater (Balanchine)
    Adelphi Theatre performances of,
        72, 75–77
    American Ballet tour performances of,
        96–98, 102
    Bryn Mawr performances of, 66–67,
    Conception and planning of, 47–49, 62
    Hartford performances of, 51–54
    Lewisohn Stadium performances
        of, 92–93
    Philadelphia performances of, 94
    Westchester performance of, 95
Alonso, Alicia, 187–88, 201
Adelphi Theatre, 68–69, *See also*
    American Ballet
American Ballet
    Adelphi Theatre performances
        (1935), 63–80
    Ballet Caravan and, 127–30,
        138–39, 162–65
    Bryn Mawr performances (1935), 65–67
    The Goldwyn Follies, 172
    Dissolution of, 164–65, 178–79
    Hartford performances (1934), 46–56
    Lewisohn Stadium performances
        (1935), 91–94
    Metropolitan Opera and, 84–87, 149–50
    Philadelphia performances (1935), 94
    Plans for revival of, 229

Stravinsky Festival (1937), 156–62, 212
    Transcontinental tour (1935), 95–102
    Westchester performance (1935), 94–95
    Woodlands performances (1934), 41–45
American Ballet Caravan, *See* Ballet
    Caravan
American Ballet Theatre, *See* Ballet Theatre
Anchutina, Leda, 187, 213, 229
Antheil, George, 9, 38, 48, 52, 71
Apollon Musagète (Balanchine)
    Ballets Russes premiere of, 17
    Early plans to remount in America, 25
    Lifar, Serge and, 19
    Metropolitan Opera performances of, 176
    Stravinsky Festival performances of, 156,
        158–59, 162
Ashton, Frederick, 163
Askew, Constance and Kirk, 22, 54
Asquith, Ruby, 121, 129
Atkinson, Brooks, 154, 181, 185, 233
Austin, A. Everett "Chick,"
    Adelphi Theatre, attendance at, 72
    American Ballet school in Hartford,
        involvement with, 24–28,
        28–30, 31–32
    Filling Station premiere and, 197
    Hartford performances by American
        Ballet, 47
    Hartford gala event arranged by, 108
    Woodlands performance,
        attendance at, 45

Babes in Arms, 147–49, 161
Baker, Josephine, 107–8
Balanchine, George
  African American dancers, viewpoints on,
    25, 116–17
  American dancers, viewpoints on, 22, 53,
    68, 69–70, 89
  American ballet, viewpoints on,
    90–91, 96
  Ballet Caravan, involvement with, 140–42
  Ballet Russe de Monte Carlo, involvement
    with, 223–24, 234–35
  ballets by, *See* respective titles
  certificate of naturalization, 224
  childhood and early career of, 16–17
  dance on screen, viewpoints on, 172–74
  experimental tendencies of, 58–59,
    61–62, 106–7, 158–59
  films with dances by, *See* respective titles
  health problems of, 22, 23, 45–46, 67–68,
    96, 139–41
  musicals with dances by, *See* Musicals
  naturalization as United States
    citizen, 223
  opera ballets by, 105–7, 118–19,
    149–50, 176
  women dancers, viewpoints on, 53, 66,
    68, 172, 235
  Zorina, Vera, relationship with, 188, 234
Balanchivadze, Georges, *See*
  Balanchine, George
Balanchivadze, Georgi, *See*
  Balanchine, George
Balanchivadze, Meliton, 16
Balanchivadze, Maria Vasilieva, 16
Balanchivadze, Tamara, 16
Ballet Caravan
  American Ballet, relationship with,
    127–30, 138–39, 162–65
  American Ballet Caravan, renaming
    as, 214
  Ballet Russe de Monte Carlo and, 234
  ballets performed by, *See* individual titles
  dissolution of, 217, 228–29
  formation of, 127–30
  The Goldwyn Follies and, 218
  World's Fair performances (1940),
    224–228

Touring by,
  East coast (1936), 131–39
  East coast (1937), 191–96
  East coast (1939), 212–13
  Mid-Atlantic, southeast and Cuba
    (1938), 196–201
  Transcontinental (1938), 201–5
  Transcontinental (1939), 214–17
  School of American Ballet and,
    130, 192–93
Ballet Russe de Monte Carlo
  American Ballet merger with, 179
  American tours of, 39–41
  Le Baiser de la Fée, revival of, 223–24
  The Card Party, revival of, 234
  La Concurrence, 18–19, 33, 40, 58
  Cotillon, 18–19, 33, 40, 58
  Massine, Léonide and, 6, 18
  Les Présages, 21, 22, 66
  On Your Toes caricature of, 109–10
  Serenade, revival of, 234–35
  Union Pacific, 41
Ballets Russes (of Serge Diaghilev), 6, 9,
    16–17, 18, 54, 100, 156
Ballet Theatre, 225, 229
The Bartered Bride (Balanchine), 118–19
The Bat (Balanchine), 118, 149
Bennington College, 130–31, 191
Berlin, Irving, 231
Billy the Kid (Loring), 197, 202, 213, 214
Blitzstein, Marc, 29
Blum, René, 18
Bolger, Ray, 111–12, 230
Bombs in the Icebox (Dollar), 192
Boris, Ruthanna
  Alma Mater, 49
  Ballet Caravan, 129, 142
  Mozartiana, 37
  Orpheus and Eurydice, 121
  Serenade, 38–39
  The Solider and the Gypsy, 134
Bouché, Louis, 71–72
Le Bourgeois gentilhomme, See The Would-
  Be Gentleman
Bowles, Paul, 195
The Boys from Syracuse, 137, 183–87, 217
Bruce, Betty, 186, 230
Bryn Mawr College, 65–67

CBS, 190, 205–8
Cabin in the Sky, 232–34
Caccialanza, Gisella
 Le Baiser de la Fée, 161
 Dimitriev, Vladimir opinions on, 43
 Ballet Caravan, 129, 200
 I Was an Adventuress, 218
 Mozartiana, 37
 Westchester American Ballet
  performance, 95
The Card Party (Balanchine), 140,
 156–57, 159–60, 234
Carter, Elliott
 Apollon Musagète, review of, 159
 Le Baiser de la Fée, review of, 161
 Bombs in the Icebox, 192
 The Card Party, review of, 160
 Filling Station, review of, 199
 Hound & Horn and, 17
 Orpheus and Eurydice, recollections
  of, 119–20
 Pocahontas, 132, 133, 143
 Show Piece, review of, 194
 Yankee Clipper, review of, 195
Charade, or The Debutante
 (Christensen), 215–17
La Chatte (Balanchine), 19, 33, 58
Christensen, Harold, 129, 203
Christensen, Lew,
 Apollon Musagète, 158, 159
 Ballet Caravan and, 9, 10, 129, 132, 229
 Charade, or The Debutante, 215–17
 Encounter, 132, 133, 137, 141
 Filling Station, 197, 201
 I Was an Adventuress, 218
 Orpheus and Eurydice, 121, 122
 Performances by, 118, 194, 195, 200, 213
 Pocahontas, 132, 133, 143
 The Would-Be Gentleman, 137
Chujoy, Anatole, 7, 60, 176, 179
Church, George, 186
City Portrait (Loring), 215–17
Concerto (Dollar and Balanchine), 108, 149
Concerto Barocco (Balanchine), 105, 125
La Concurrence (Balanchine), 19, 22,
 33, 40, 58
Copland, Aaron, 9, 57, 71, 164, 202
Cotillon (Balanchine), 19, 33, 40, 58–59

Coudy, Douglas, 129, 133, 134, 141, 193
cultural appropriation, 151–52, 232–33
Cunningham, Merce, 5, 217
Curitss, Mina, 15, 29, 46, 67, 72

Dalí, Salvador, 54, 107, 182–83
Danieli, Fred, 116, 194
de Basil, Wassily "Colonel," 6, 18,
 19, 33, 58
de Mille, Agnes, 66, 67, 72, 85, 86–87
Denby, Edwin, 108, 134, 139, 142, 144
Diaghilev, Serge,
 Antheil, George and, 50
 Ballet Caravan and, 128, 142–43
 Ballets Russes and, 5, 6, 9, 18, 54, 100, 156
 Balanchine, George and, 17, 32, 42, 47,
  61, 62, 76, 87, 92, 98
 Kirstein, Lincoln and, 20, 132, 143
 On Your Toes caricature of, 109, 110
Dimitriev, Vladimir
 Balanchine, George and, 26–27, 36,
  39, 46, 50
 Balanchine, George, criticism of,
  60–63, 77, 78
 Early career of, 19
 Kirstein, Lincoln and, 89, 162
 School of American Ballet and, 28–32,
  40, 46, 51, 89
 Warburg, Edward and, 44, 55, 74
Dollar, William
 A Thousand Times Neigh, 225, 227–28
 Air and Variations, 200, 214
 Alma Mater, 78, 93
 American Ballet and, 9, 64, 96, 139, 229
 Ballet Caravan and, 129, 141
 Bombs in the Icebox, 192
 Concerto, 108
 The Goldwyn Follies, 172
 Great Lady, 187
 On Your Toes, 116
 Orpheus and Eurydice, 121–23
 Performances by, 50, 66, 71, 72, 78,
  160, 161
 Promenade, 132, 133
Downes, Olin, 105, 176
Draper, Muriel
 American Ballet, opinions on, 94, 123
 Draper, Paul and, 45, 124

Draper, Muriel (*cont.*)
    Kirstein, Lincoln, correspondence with,
        26, 71, 202, 204, 209
    Woodlands performance, 45
Draper, Paul
    Babes in Arms opening, 155
    "Bach ballet" featuring, 104,
        123–25, 163
    Draper, Muriel and, 45, 124
    The Goldwyn Follies, 171
    Woodlands performance, 45
Dreams (Balanchine)
    Adelphi Theatre performances of, 47, 63,
        67, 69, 76–78
    Antheil, George and, 38
    Conception and planning of, 28, 36–38
    Kirstein, Lincoln and, 65
    Les Ballets 1933 performances of, 21, 22
    Milhaud, Darius and, 37
    Woodlands performances of, 42–44
Duberman, Martin, 8, 157
Duke, Vernon (Vladimir Dukelsky)
    Cabin in the Sky, 232
    The Goldwyn Follies, 171–72
    Keep Off the Grass, 230
    Words without Music, 104, 107
Duncan, Isadora, 59, 71
Dunham, Katherine, 232–34

Encounter (Christensen), 132, 137,
    141, 193
Errante (Balanchine)
    Adelphi Theatre performances of, 47, 58,
        69, 72, 74–78
    Conception and planning of, 63–64, 68
    Les Ballets 1933 performances of, 21, 22
    Metropolitan Opera performances of, 106
    Orpheus and Eurydice and, 119
    School of American Ballet and, 36
    Serenade and, 39
Erskine, John, 82, 86
Exposition (Balanchine), 171–72

The Fairy's Kiss, see *Le Baiser de la Fée*
Filling Station (Christensen), 196,
    197–99, 201
Film
    Balanchine, George, viewpoints on dance
        in, 172–74

    See Exposition
    See Goldwyn, Samuel
    See The Goldwyn Follies
    Kirstein, Lincoln, viewpoints on dance
        in, 163
    See I Was An Adventuress
    See On Your Toes (1939 film)
Fisher, Tom, 85–86
Fokine, Michel, 39, 59, 60, 92, 93
Folk Dance (Coudy), 193
Ford, Edsel, 228
Ford Motor Company, 225

Galli, Rosina, 82
Gatti-Casazza, Giulio, 82–83
Gershwin, George, 54, 71, 171
Gershwin, Ira, 171
Geva, Tamara, 63–64, 71, 75, 110–11, 114
The Goldwyn Follies, 162, 169–75, 204–5
Goldwyn, Samuel, 162, 170–72, 188,
    204, 231
Graham, Martha, 5, 58, 131, 135, 163,
    217, 229
Great Lady, 186–88

Haakon, Paul, 63, 67, 72, 106
Harlequin for President (Loring), 132, 136,
    137, 141, 143, 193
Harper, Herbert, 115–16
Hart, Lorenz, 108–9, 183, 184
Haskell, Arnold, 40, 117
Hawkins, Erick
    Balanchine, George and, 141
    Ballet Caravan and, 128, 129, 203
    Dimitriev, Vladimir opinions on, 43
    Graham, Martha and, 217, 229
    Kirstein, Lincoln and, 68, 72, 159
    Rondo, 134–35, 141
    School of American Ballet and, 68
    Show Piece, 135, 193–94
    The Would-Be Gentleman, 137
Hawkins, Frances
    Ballet Caravan and, 131–32, 136,
        138, 191
    Kirstein, Lincoln and, 140, 163
    Holiday Dance Festival, 217
Hollywood, *See* Film
Holm, Hanya, 89
Hound & Horn, 17

Howard, Holly
  Balanchine, George and, 36, 65, 68, 98
  The Bat, 118
  Great Lady, 187
  Performances by, 51, 74, 95, 106
Humphrey, Doris, 58, 85, 131, 138
Hurok, Sol, 100, 179, 190

I Married an Angel, 175, 180–83, 217
I Was an Adventuress, 221–23

James, Edward, 19
Jane, Marjorie, 151, 153, 155
Jeu de Cartes, See The Card Party
Johnson, Edward, 83–87, 93, 105, 177
Johnson, Philip, 32
Juilliard Music Foundation, 82–84

Keep Off the Grass, 229–231
Kirstein, George, 15
Kirstein, Lincoln,
  A Thousand Times Neigh and, 225
  Balanchine's Broadway work,
    involvement with, 155
  Ballet Caravan, management of,
    127–45, 191–93
  Billy the Kid, writings on, 202
  Blast at Ballet, 7, 57, 78, 81, 127, 132,
    139, 144, 157, 162, 193, 205–7
  Childhood and education, 15, 17
  Dance Observer, writings in, 196, 202
  Diaghilev, Serge and, 20, 132, 143
  Dimitriev, Vladimir and, 89, 162
  Draper, Paul and, 124–25
  Draper, Muriel and, 26, 71, 94, 202–4, 209
  Film, viewpoints on dance in, 163
  Harvard University and, 17
  Harvard Society for Contemporary Art and, 17
  Hawkins, Erick and, 68, 72, 159
  Hound & Horn and, 17
  Kirstein, Rose and Louis (parents), 15,
    17, 55, 102, 207–8
  Loring, Eugene and, 96
  Martin, John and, 29, 55, 57, 63, 88–89
  Massine, Léonide and, 21
  School of American Ballet, initial
    planning, 22–28
  School of American Ballet, Hartford
    location of, 28–32

School of American Ballet, involvement
    with, 18, 235–36
  Thirty Years, 7, 29, 51, 99, 127, 130,
    189, 203–4
  Warburg, Edward, collaboration with, 20,
    27–28, 55–56, 120, 162
Kirsten, Louis, 15, 17, 55, 102, 207–8
Kirstein, Rose, 15, 17

La Princesse Zenobia (Balanchine), see
    Princess Zenobia ballet (Balanchine)
Laskey, Charles
  Ballet Caravan and, 129
  Dimitriev, Vladimir opinions on, 43
  Keep Off the Grass, 230, 232
  I Married an Angel, 181, 183
  Performances by, 51, 106
  School of American Ballet and, 63
Leitch, Helen, 94
Les Ballets 1933, 19–23, 32, 36, 58, 63, 80
Lewisohn Stadium, 91–93
Le Baiser de la Fée (Balanchine), 161, 223–24
Lifar, Serge, 17, 19, 21–22, 33, 58
Limón, José, 230–31
Littlefield, Catherine, 36
Littlefield, Dorothie, 36, 66
Lloyd, Margaret, 143, 199, 217, 223, 229
Loewe, Frederick, 187
Logan, Joshua, 183
Loring, Eugene
  Balanchine, George and, 141
  Ballet Caravan and, 9, 129, 203
  Ballet Theatre and, 229
  Billy the Kid, 197, 202, 213, 214
  City Portrait, 215–17
  Harlequin for President, 132, 136, 137,
    141, 143, 193
  Kirstein, Lincoln and, 96
  The Would-Be Gentleman, 137
  Yankee Clipper, 195, 201
Louisiana Purchase, 229, 231–32
Lyon, Annabelle
  Ballet Caravan and, 129, 130,
  Dimitriev, Vladimir opinions on, 43
  Great Lady, 187
  Orpheus and Eurydice, 120, 121
  Performances by, 95
  School of American Ballet and, 40, 61, 63
  Serenade, 38, 39

Marie-Jeanne, 37, 201, 203, 235
Martin, John
American Ballet, reporting on, 42, 54–55, 63, 69, 91, 92, 148
American Ballet, reviews of, 2, 77–79, 87–88
Balanchine, George, views on, 58–59, 88, 223–24, 234
Ballet Caravan, reporting on, 135, 138, 164, 199
Ballet Caravan, reviews of, 144, 164, 200, 214, 217, 228
Ballet Russe de Monte Carlo, reviews of, 58–59, 223–24, 234
Film, reporting on, 148
Kirstein, Lincoln, and, 29, 55, 57, 63, 88–89
Loring, Eugene, reviews of, 195, 214
Metropolitan Opera, reporting on, 81, 85, 87–89, 106, 177
Modern dance and, 57, 81, 85
Musicals, reporting on, 107
School of American Ballet, reporting on, 29, 32–33, 63
Stravinsky Festival, reviews of, 157, 160–61
Massine, Léonide
Balanchine, George and, 22, 61, 74–75
Ballets Russes and, 17
Ballet Russe de Monte Carlo and, 6, 18–20, 40, 41, 179
Draper, Muriel and, 94
Kirstein, Lincoln and, 21
On Your Toes caricature of, 110
Les Présages, 21, 22, 59–60, 66, 80
"Symphonic ballet" and, 39, 59–60, 80, 90
Union Pacific, 41
McBride, Robert, 194
McHale, Duke, 108, 151, 154–55
Merovitch, Alexander, 100–101
Metropolitan Opera
American Ballet affiliation with, 84–91, 96, 176–78, 229
American Ballet works performed at, 106, 108, 118, 149, 176
Balanchine, George, and, 148, 176–77
Ballet Caravan and, 129, 138, 164, 192
Ballet instruction at, 82, 186

Ballet Russe de Monte Carlo
performances at, 109, 223, 234
The Goldwyn Follies and, 170, 172
Juilliard Music Foundation and, 82–86
Leadership changes at, 82–84
On Your Toes caricature of, 109, 112
Opera ballets performed at, 105–7, 118–19, 149–50, 176
Orpheus and Eurydice production at, 117–23
Page, Ruth, and, 85–86
Spring season initiative at, 83, 117–19, 123–24
Stravinsky Festival at, 156–62
Warburg, Edward and, 84–87
Milhaud, Darius, 36–37
modernism, 5–6
Molière, 136–37
Moore, Hannah, 129
Moore, Marjorie, 213
Mozartiana (Balanchine)
Adelphi Theatre performances of, 63, 69
American Ballet tour performances of, 97–98,
Conception and planning of, 28, 32
Hartford performances of, 47, 51, 53, 55
Les Ballets 1933 performances of, 21, 22,
Metropolitan Opera performances of, 106, 176
School of American Ballet and, 36–37, 40, 61
Serenade and, 39
Westchester performance of, 95
Woodlands performances of, 42–45
Mullowny, Kathryn, 75, 94, 161
Musicals
See Babes in Arms
See The Boys from Syracuse
See Cabin in the Sky
"Dream ballet" in, 154–55
Formal integration in, 111–14, 183, 185
See Great Lady
See I Married an Angel
See Louisiana Purchase
See On Your Toes

Nabokov, Nicholas, 40, 214
New York City Ballet, 1, 3, 4, 7–8, 9
Nicholas Brothers (Fayard and Harold), 108, 151–52, 153–54

Nijinska, Bronislava, 17, 50, 156
Nijinsky, Romola, 20, 22–23, 25
Nijinsky, Vaslav, 20
NBC, 190, 205–8
The Nutcracker (Petipa), 67, 234

On Your Toes (1936 musical),
    108–17, 123–24
On Your Toes (1939 film), 217–21
Opera
    Balanchine, George, opera
        ballets by, 105–7, 118–19,
        149–50, 176
    See The Bartered Bride
    See Metropolitan Opera
    See Orpheus and Eurydice
Orpheus and Eurydice (Balanchine),
    117–23, 155

Page, Ruth, 67, 85–86
Paley, William, 207
Patterson, Yvonne, 96, 99, 187
Pelus, Marie-Jeanne, *See* Marie-Jeanne
Petipa, Marius, 42, 60, 65, 234
Pierce, Johnny, 151
Pocahontas (Christensen), 132–33,
    143, 212–14
The Poker Game, See The Card Party
Les Présages (Massine), 21, 22,
    59–60, 66, 80
Princess Zenobia ballet (Balanchine),
    112–14, 218–19
The Prodigal Son (Balanchine), 17, 19
Prokofiev, Sergei, 57
Promenade (Dollar), 132, 133, 193

Reagan, Ronald, 1, 3
Reiman, Elise, 50, 68
Reminiscence (Balanchine)
    Adelphi Theatre performances of, 63, 67,
        69, 72, 74–78
    American Ballet tour performances
        of, 96–99
    Conception and planning of, 38,
        58, 64–65
    Lewisohn Stadium performances
        of, 92–93
    Metropolitan Opera performance of, 106
    Philadelphia performances of, 94

School of American Ballet and, 94
    Westchester performance of, 95
Revues
    See Keep Off the Grass
    See Ziegfeld Follies (1936)
Rittman, Trude, 200, 215
Robbins, Jerome, 187, 230
Rockefeller, Nelson, 40, 44, 54, 163, 207
Rodgers, Richard, 3, 108–9, 183–84
Romeo and Juliet ballet
    (Balanchine), 172–73
Rondo (Hawkins), 134–35, 141
Roosevelt, Eleanor, 180, 233
Rubinstein, Ida, 50, 156

Sarnoff, David, 207, 208
School of American Ballet
    Ballet Caravan and, 192–93, 225
    Early planning for, 18, 22–28
    First day of classes at, 33
    Hartford location of, 23–25, 28–32
    Hawkins, Erick and, 68
    Instruction at, 61–63, 68
    New York, relocation to, 31–33
    Performances at, 40
    Producing Company of, 50–51
    Scholarship competition in 1940
        at, 235–36
Seldes, Gilbert, 45, 228
Serenade (Balanchine)
    Adelphi Theatre performances of, 47, 63,
        69, 72, 75–80
    American Ballet tour performances
        of, 96, 98
    Antheil, George orchestration for, 71
    Ballet Russe de Monte Carlo revival
        of, 234–35
    Bryn Mawr performances of, 66–67
    Carter, Elliott viewpoints on, 159
    Conception and planning of, 38–39
    Hartford performances of, 47, 52, 55–56
    Historical accounts of, 2, 35–36
    Kirstein, Lincoln and, 38, 65
    Lewisohn Stadium performances
        of, 92–93
    Metropolitan Opera performances of,
        106, 149
    Philadelphia performances of, 94
    Les Présages and, 59–60

Serenade (Balanchine) (*cont.*)
  School of American Ballet and, 38–40,
    60, 62–63
  "Symphonic ballet" and, 58–60
  Woodlands performances of, 42–44
Show Piece (Hawkins), 135, 193–94
Slaughter on Tenth Avenue (Balanchine),
  110–12, 218–19
The Soldier and the Gypsy (Coudy),
  134, 137
Les Songes (Balanchine), *See Dreams*
Stravinsky Festival (1937) *See*
  American Ballet
Stravinsky, Igor, 2, 3, 10, 47, 71, 74,
  156–162
Stuart, Muriel, 68
Swift, Kay, 48–49, 54, 75
Symphonic ballet, 21, 39, 59–60, 80, 90, 200

Tap dance, 114–17, 151–52
Taper, Bernard, 7, 18
Tchelitchev, Pavel, 75, 117, 119, 121,
Terry, Walter, 217, 223–24, 228–29
Thomson, Virgil, 20, 47, 72, 197, 199, 201
Transcendence (Balanchine)
  Adelphi Theatre performances of, 63, 69,
    74, 76–78
  Antheil, George orchestration for, 50, 52
  Bryn Mawr performances of, 66–67
  Conception and planning of, 49–50
  Hartford performances of, 47, 52, 53, 62
  Kirstein, Lincoln and, 65
  School of American Ballet and, 61

Union Pacific (Massine), 41

Van Vechten, Carl, 93, 123
Vane, Daphne, 122, 162, 231
Vladimirov, Pierre, 44, 46, 61, 67
Vosseler, Heidi, 66, 186

Warburg, Edward
  Adelphi Theatre engagement and,
    60, 73–74
  Alma Mater and, 47–51, 62

American Ballet, involvement with, 62,
  74, 93, 95, 96
American Ballet, separation from, 127,
  129, 140, 141, 179–79
American Ballet tour, management of,
  100–101
Balanchine, George and, 28, 48, 50–51,
  55, 62–64, 74, 157
Bryn Mawr performance and, 65
Errante and, 63–64
Family background of, 27–28
Gershwin, George and, 49, 171
Juilliard Music Foundation and, 84
Kirstein, Lincoln, collaboration with, 20,
  27–28, 55–56, 120, 162
Metropolitan Opera and, 85–87, 105,
School of American Ballet and, 62,
  67–68, 89
Stravinsky Festival and, 156–58
Woodlands performances and, 41–45
Warburg, Felix, 27, 40, 42, 45, 84, 178
Warburg, Frieda, 27, 42
Water Nymph ballet (Balanchine), 172–74
Weill, Kurt, 21, 47
Wigman, Mary, 89
Wiman, Dwight Deere, 109, 151, 184, 229
Witherspoon, Herbert, 83–84, 85–86
The Would-Be Gentleman, 136–37
World's Fair (1940), 225, 228
Words without Music (Balanchine), 104, 107

Yankee Clipper (Loring), 145, 155, 193,
  195, 201

Ziegfeld Follies (1936), 107–8, 151
Zorina, Vera
  Balanchine, George, collaboration with,
    167–71, 175, 234
  Balanchine, George, marriage to, 188
  The Goldwyn Follies, 170–74
  I Married an Angel, 175, 180–83, 217
  I Was an Adventuress, 221–23
  Louisiana Purchase, 229, 231–32
  On Your Toes (1939 film), 217–21
Zukofsky, Louis, 17